D0215396

Library
University of Texas
at San Antonio

WITHDRAWN
UTSA Libraries

Immigration and Welfare

Immigration and Welfare avoids simplistic and unhelpful notions of the 'threat' of immigration to analyse the effects of immigration on national welfare states in an integrating Europe. It explores the challenges posed to various types of national welfare state by international migration, and the dynamics of inclusion and exclusion in these national welfare states. This book pays close attention to new migration challenges such as asylum seeking, as well as examining the impact of free movement within the EU for migration and welfare.

The book's international panel of experts in the field considers pertinent and at times controversial issues such as:

- the increasingly restrictive immigration policies across Europe
- whether immigration erodes the national welfare state
- how asylum seekers are systematically excluded from the welfare system
- whether new immigrants are perceived as undeserving of welfare state benefits
- whether new migration within the EU undermines national welfare states

This timely and original book addresses issues which are central to current social and political debates regarding European immigration policies, welfare state restructuring and European integration. It also looks at the implications of such debates for immigrant and immigrant-origin communities across Europe. It is essential reading for all those interested in the debates surrounding immigration and the welfare state.

Michael Bommes is Senior Researcher and member of the board of the Institution for Migration Research and Intercultural Studies (IMIS) at the University of Osnabrück, Germany. **Andrew Geddes** is Senior Lecturer in the School of Politics and Communication Studies at the University of Liverpool.

Routledge/EUI studies in the political economy of welfare
Series editors: Martin Rhodes and Maurizio Ferrera
The European University Institute, Florence, Italy

This series presents leading edge research on the recasting of European welfare states. The series is interdisciplinary, featuring contributions from experts in economics, political science and social policy. The books provide a comparative analysis of topical issues, including:

* reforms of the major social programmes – pensions, health, social security
* the changing political cleavages in welfare politics
* policy convergence and social policy innovation
* the impact of globalisation

1 Immigration and Welfare
Challenging the borders of the welfare state
Michael Bommes and Andrew Geddes

2 Corporation and the Welfare State
Gerhard Lehmbruch and Frans van Waarden

Immigration and Welfare

Challenging the borders of the
welfare state

Edited by
**Michael Bommes and
Andrew Geddes**

London and New York

First published 2000
by Routledge
2 Park Square, Milton Park, Abingdon, Oxon, OX14 4RN

Simultaneously published in the USA and Canada
by Routledge
270 Madison Ave, New York NY 10016

Routledge is an imprint of the Taylor & Francis Group

Transferred to Digital Printing 2005

This collection © 2000 Michael Bommes and Andrew Geddes;
individual chapters © the contributors

Typeset in Baskerville by Exe Valley Dataset Ltd, Exeter

All rights reserved. No part of this book may be reprinted or
reproduced or utilised in any form or by any electronic,
mechanical, or other means, now known or hereafter invented,
including photocopying and recording, or in any information
storage or retrieval system, without permission in writing from the
publishers.

British Library Cataloguing in Publication Data
A catalogue record for this book is available from the British Library

Library of Congress Cataloging in Publication Data
Immigration and welfare: challenging the borders of the welfare
state/edited by Michael Bommes and Andrew Geddes.
   p.   cm.
Includes bibliographical references and index.
  1. Europe–Emigration and immigration–Government policy.
  2. Europe–Emigration and immigration–Social aspects.
  3. Welfare state. 4. Immigrants–Services for–Europe.
  I. Bommes, Michael. II. Geddes, Andrew, 1965–

JV7590 .I4555 2000
325.4–dc21   00-042468

ISBN 0–415–22372–5

Contents

Tables and figures

Tables

Figures

Contributors

Valérie Amiraux graduated in History and Arabic from the Sorbonne, Paris, and studied for her Ph.D. at the Institut d'Etudes Politiques in Paris. Her Ph.D. thesis was based on a study of Turkish Muslims in Germany and will be published by L'Harmattan in 2000. Since 1998, she has been a Research Fellow at the Robert Schuman Centre at the European University Institute, Florence, Italy, where she co-ordinates the Mediterranean Programme.

Maria Ioannis Baganha is Associate Professor of Sociology in the Faculty of Economics at the University of Coimbra, Portugal, and a Senior Research Fellow of the Centro de Estudos Socials, University of Coimbra. During the academic year 1997–8 she was a Jean Monnet Fellow in the European Forum on International Migration at the European University Institute, Florence, Italy. Her recent publications include, as editor, *Immigration in Southern Europe* (1997).

Roland Bank is a Research Fellow at the Max-Planck-Institute for Comparative Public Law and International Law in Heidelberg, Germany. He studied law in Tübingen and Freiburg. During the academic year 1997–8 he was a Jean Monnet Fellow in the European Forum on International Migration at the European University Institute, Florence, Italy. He has published widely on public international law, in particular, human rights.

Keith G. Banting is Director of the School of Policy Studies at Queen's University, Kingston, Ontario, Canada. He has been a visiting scholar at a number of institutions, including the London School of Economics, the Brookings Institution and, during 1997–8, Harvard University. He is the author of *Poverty, Politics and Policy* (1979) and *The Welfare State and Canadian Federalism* (1982). He has also edited and co-authored another ten books dealing with public policy and constitutional issues in Canada and other countries, the most recent of which is *Degrees of Freedom: Canada and the United States in a Changing World* (1997). He has also contributed a lengthy list of articles to professional journals and other books.

Michael Bommes is Senior Researcher at the Institute for Migration Research and Intercultural Studies, University of Osnabrück. During the academic year 1997–8 he was a Jean Monnet Fellow in the European Forum on International Migration at the European University Institute, Florence, Italy. He is the author of *Migration und nationaler Wohlfahrtsstaat* (1999).

Andrew Geddes is Senior Lecturer in the School of Politics and Communication Studies at the University of Liverpool. During the academic year 1997–8 he was a Jean Monnet Fellow in the European Forum on International Migration at the European University Institute, Florence, Italy. He is the author of *Immigration and European Integration: Towards Fortress Europe?* (2000).

Virginie Guiraudon is chargée de recherches at the National Council for Scientific Research (CNRS) in France. She was a Jean Monnet Fellow in the European Forum on International Migration at the European University Institute, Florence, Italy, during 1997–8 and a visiting Fellow at the Center of International Studies, Princeton University, in 1998–9. She holds a Ph.D. in political science from Harvard University (1997) and is the author of *Les politiques d'immigration en Europe* (2000).

Jost Halfmann is Professor of Sociology at the Technical University of Dresden. He has held visiting fellowships at the European University Institute, Florence, Italy, and in the USA at the University of California at Berkeley, Harvard University and Cornell University. He is the co-editor with Michael Bommes of *Migration in nationalen Wohlfahrtsstaaten* (1998) and author of *Bounded Sovereignty in the World Polity: The Evolution of the German Nation-State* (2001).

James F. Hollifield is Arnold Professor of International Political Economy and Director of International Studies at Southern Methodist University, Dallas, Texas. He is the author of *Immigrants, Markets, and States* (1992), *Controlling Immigration* (1994) with Wayne Cornelius and Philip Martin, *L'immigration et l'Etat-Nation* (1997), *Pathways to Democracy* (2000) with Calvin Jillson, and *Migration Theory: Talking Across Disciplines* (forthcoming) with Caroline Brettell. His most recent work, *The Myth of Globalization*, looks at the rapidly evolving relationship between trade, migration, and the nation state.

Uwe Hunger is Assistant Professor in the Department of Political Science at the University of Muenster, Germany. He studied political science, economics, sociology and philosophy between 1991 and 1997, gained an M.A. in political science in 1997 and was awarded his Ph.D. in 1999. He is currently working on 'Social Capital Formation in Immigrant Networks. Assimilation and Pluralism in Comparative Perspective', a project sponsored by the Volkswagen Foundation.

Magnus Ryner is Lecturer in the Department of Government, Brunel University, London. His publications include, as editor, *Neoliberal Hegemony and the Political Economy of European Restructuring* (special issue of the *International Journal of Political Economy*), and *Capitalist Restructuring, Globalisation and the Third Way: The Case of the Swedish Model*. During the academic year 1997–8 he was a Jean Monnet Fellow in the Department of Social and Political Sciences at the European University Institute, Florence, Italy.

Series editors' preface

As editors we are pleased and proud to present this book as the first in our new series on the Political Economy of Welfare. For not only is this book inter-disciplinary in perspective, but it straddles two traditionally insulated arenas of academic study – immigration and the welfare state – and makes a pioneering attempt to bring them together. The subject itself is of great topicality. At a time of mounting concern about the viability of the traditional welfare state in an increasingly 'globalised' world of open borders, the issue of immigration and population flows has gained increasing salience. However, the reality of that threat – which has been dramatised and exploited for political gain by nationalist forces – is less than clear. As the editors state clearly in their conclusion, 'the perspective "migration is a threat to welfare" is much too abstract and general'.

As in other areas of the globalisation debate, there are pessimistic and optimistic interpretations of the consequences of more porous borders for welfare and social citizenship. Both views are represented in this book. While the loss of the ties that bind the citizen to territory, and the fragmentation of welfare support have both been predicted – alongside a more general erosion of continental welfare states in a deregulated, liberal Anglo-American direction – the contributions to this book taken as a whole reveal a much more nuanced picture. As Banting argues, immigration does not necessarily weaken or fragment support for the welfare state, although this may occur if nationalist parties identify migrant groups as feckless contributors to long-term welfare dependency and burdens. Moreover, most European welfare states have accommodated migrants within their welfare systems without subjecting those systems, or their bases of political support, to undue stress. That said, immigrant control and immigrant inclusion policies always co-exist in a state of tension, and the politics of providing migrants with social citizenship is never unproblematic. Indeed, as Hollifield and others in this book point out, weakening the welfare position of migrants is sometimes used as an indirect means of immigration control – as illustrated most markedly in policies towards asylum seekers. And in countries with less robust systems of social inclusion, migrants frequently become members – alongside national citizens – of a marginalised underclass.

Nevertheless, although differing in their receptiveness to foreigners, and in their capacity to cope with future migration, European welfare states have largely adjusted pragmatically to the immigration challenge, providing social inclusion (if not always full citizenship) to migrant workers and to the families that have followed them. This is not to say, of course, that the welfare systems can always adapt smoothly to increasing rates of immigration or will always be open to migrant flows. All nations have filters, one of the most common being the skills filter which separates out 'desirable' migrants in terms of their labour market potential. This is not just true of most advanced welfare states (although some like Sweden have sought to limit such policies) but of developing countries too. Some types of welfare state are better at providing social inclusion than others – typically those that are better at, and more committed to, providing social and employment rights to their own citizens. As Geddes argues, European integration is complicating this picture still further by producing new forms of closure (towards new migrants) while assisting the social inclusion of the EU's third country nationals, and creating new interdependencies between different types of welfare state. These interdependencies – reinforced by potentially greater cross-border flows following EU enlargement – will continue to feed into national debates about welfare provision and social citizenship.

The great merit of *Immigration and Welfare* lies in its novel, comprehensive and high-quality treatment of these issues via both thematic and single-case study analyses. Having been peripheral to welfare studies in the past, this book makes a timely and persuasive argument that issues of migration should be at the centre of our understanding of the past development and future perspectives of Western welfare states.

Martin Rhodes and
Maurizio Ferrera

Acknowledgements

The contributions to this book developed from papers presented to a conference on Immigration and the Welfare State held at the European University Institute, Florence, Italy, in May 1998. The conference was convened as part of the European Forum on International Migration directed by Professors Christian Joppke and René Leboutte. This project and many of the book's contributors benefited immensely from the stimulating environment for collaborative work provided by the European Forum.

The project could not have developed into this book without the support of Professor Yves Mény, Director of the EUI's Robert Schuman Centre, and Professor Martin Rhodes, also of the EUI. The success of the Florence conference was assured by the organisational expertise and administrative support provided by Kathinka Espana, Monique Cavallari and Catherine Divry in the Robert Schuman Centre. The editors are also indebted to Sigrid Pusch of the Institute for Migration Research (IMIS) at the University of Osnabrück for her invaluable assistance with preparation of the final manuscript.

1 Introduction

Immigration and the welfare state

Michael Bommes and Andrew Geddes

This book's sub-title – *Challenging the Borders of the Welfare State* – reflects a commonly held assumption about relations between immigration and the welfare state. The book's task is to map the challenge, which requires avoiding simplistic and misleading constructions of immigration as a 'threat' or 'danger' and, instead, directing attention towards the ways that international migration in its various forms structurally challenges the organisation and conceptual borders of national welfare states. We seek an enhanced understanding of relations between migration and welfare in diverse national settings, in relation to various types of migration, and in the light of supranational socio-economic developments such as European integration.

First of all, it is important to emphasise that the 'migration problem' in modern society did – and still does even in the era of European integration – refer to migration that crosses state borders. Internal migration within nation states refers to just one form of social mobility among others based on freedom of movement that is both socially expected and supported because it marks the willingness of individuals to improve their chances of social inclusion within the territory. Border crossing international migration refers to the same kinds of efforts to improve chances of social inclusion as a result of geographical mobility; but the crucial difference is that international migration confronts the three basic elements of nation state sovereignty: population, territory and the physical means of violence. It is, of course, very clear that nation states differentiate the population over which they claim sovereignty as citizens from other populations and attempt to control access to the state's territory. The sovereignty of nation states over a given territory and population was and still is based on the exchange of the political provision of welfare in exchange for the *internal loyalty* of their citizens. If loyalty is one side of the coin, then the other side is *external closure* at the borders of nation states. National welfare states have evolved as international 'thresholds of inequality' (Stichweh 1998), which means that international migration can be seen as an effort to overcome these thresholds. Generally speaking these two dimensions – of loyalty and welfare state provision – structure relations between migrants and the state: migrants become viewed as a potential problem as a result of questions about their political loyalty or because of welfare claims (or both). Immigration control and immigrant inclusion policies seek to regulate migration processes and their social consequences in relation to loyalty and welfare state entitlements within a territorially circumscribed national unit.

These relations between migration and welfare occur in a variety of national settings that provide distinct repertoires of political institutions, of modes by which nations and national loyalty are defined, and conceptualisations of welfare and the organisational infrastructure of welfare provisions (Esping-Andersen 1990). Nation states have also been affected by immigration in different ways relating to each state's international political relations such as its colonial traditions, involvement in competitive nation-building processes, as well as historically established concepts of the nation and specific welfare regimes. These conditions define the background against which welfare states operate. National welfare states can be viewed as political filters that mediate efforts by immigrants to realise their chances for social participation. These filters exclude certain forms of unwanted migration, define a variety of legal conditions for immigration and residence, combine them with differentiated welfare entitlements and, consequently, pave the social options for those who enter the country. The ascription of individuals to various categories of migrants such as refugees, asylum seekers, family migrants, labour migrants, illegal/undocumented migrants does not refer to the quality of the individuals falling into these categories, but to the labelling capacity arising from the political differentiation of migrants.

The chances for migrant inclusion within these national welfare states is a key theme of this book. The evolution of nation states as welfare states during the twentieth century put an end to the period of 'minimal state intervention' characteristic of nineteenth-century Europe (Moch 1992: 107). Increased and enhanced welfare provision was combined with political efforts to circumscribe those viewed as members of the community of legitimate welfare receivers. T. H. Marshall's famous essay (1950) described the institutionalisation of citizenship as the successive establishment and expansion of civil, political and social rights, in that order. He interpreted the state's welfare obligations as being tantamount to the realisation of the structural implications of the concept of citizenship. Modern citizenship represented the institutionalisation of the social expectation that the state was to assume responsibility for the inclusion of its citizens into society and into the national community. When viewed from a contemporary perspective, this interpretation is problematic for several reasons but does highlight the self-perception of European welfare states and their underlying conceptual frame – the national community – at a time in the early 1950s just before Europe became a major world region of immigration (Halfmann and Bommes 1998).

The emergence of highly elaborated welfare states did not hinder immigration and the end of 'minimal state intervention' was not the end of migration. Between 1945 and the middle of the 1970s there appeared to be a prevailing assumption among countries of immigration that they possessed the capacity to steer, manage and control migration processes.[1] National welfare states did not hinder the inclusion of non-citizen immigrants into welfare rights (Hammar 1990; Hollifield 1992; Soysal 1994). But, as a result of this inclusion of non-citizens, states have recurrently been confronted with the expectation that this legitimises the inclusion of migrants relative to the claims and entitlements of their own citizens and to the state's capacity to deliver welfare provision. In fact, this could be characterised as representing international migration's challenge posed to national welfare states.

Responses to immigration in national welfare states differed enormously with social inclusion and exclusion mediated by national historical, social and political contexts with a strong emphasis on territoriality and by diverse organisational and decisional infrastructures of different welfare state types. These are a major condition for the specific design of immigration and immigrant policies and have important consequences for the conditions of immigration, the status of migrants, and their social entitlements. The administrative infrastructure of states is also decisive for the way that the social consequences and conflicts arising in response to immigration are handled by the state.

The book's first three chapters deal with welfare state development in comparative perspective, illustrate the strong links between welfare state and territory, and demonstrate the ways in which debates about migration are nested within broader debates concerning welfare state development. Keith Banting discusses the relation between migration and the European welfare state in a broad historical and comparative perspective. He shows that it is simplistic to perceive immigration as fragmenting the political constituencies that support the welfare state and eroding the sense of community on which a vibrant conception of social citizenship depends. In order to show that a more complex approach is necessary Banting looks 'in three directions'. First, he asks if cultural diversity within nation states undermined historically the institutionalisation of strong welfare states. He argues that even if there is a relation between cultural heterogeneity/homogeneity and social spending, this relation is modified to a large extent by the structure of political institutions and their capacity to produce consent. Second, he shows that seen from a broad comparative perspective, a common element of social democratic and corporatist European welfare states is their rather successful incorporation of new immigrant minorities. The main reaction to immigration in these countries has been less exclusion from welfare combined with a rather strong accent on restrictive immigration policies. In this respect they differ from countries with liberal welfare state traditions where immigration has either provoked rather strong anti-immigrant reactions and social exclusion and/or further weakened the commitment to welfare and social citizenship. Banting then argues, that growing sub-state nationalism in countries like Belgium, Spain and Canada has a severe effect on common welfare constituencies and the notion of social citizenship framed by a national state. He concludes that it seems less likely that migration constitutes a major context for reshaping the foundations of the welfare regimes in continental Europe.

Jost Halfmann's analysis centres on the principle of territoriality that underpins the modern national welfare state. Globalisation and European integration have made it apparent that the interventionist capacity of modern nation states is limited by territoriality. By this he means that the sovereignty of states ends at their borders whereas economic, legal, scientific, educational and informational processes transcend these borders. Halfmann argues that territoriality, alongside a people and a central government, is a key constitutive principle of the modern nation state and has been an historical precondition for the evolution of modern politics understood as the institutional capacity to produce collectively binding decisions. According to Halfmann this successful institutionalisation process rested from the outset on the political provision of welfare for a population bound by legal, economic and political investment to the national state territory and thence transformed into national citizens. The other side of the internal social mobilisation enforced by the nation state was the implicit assumption that each individual would be assigned to one nation state. Seen from this angle migration challenges the tight relationship between the state (as welfare state) and the people because, as Halfmann puts it, 'when the territorial clamp between citizens and states loosens up state sovereignty is at bay'. Halfmann agrees with 'pessimists' that see national welfare states as losing their capacity to bind their citizens to the state, losing control over access to their territories, and being unable to maintain a clear distinction between citizens and non-citizens. In this sense some of the historical evolutionary advantage of the nation state and its principle of territoriality have been eroded; but this principle still remains indispensable as a central foundation for the political inclusion of individuals. Halfmann concludes that even if this provides the main reason for the present vulnerability of the national welfare state no political alternative is yet in view.

Magnus Ryner's chapter provides an overview of welfare state development after the Second World War. He describes the post-war era until the 1970s as the institutionalisation of the Keynesian welfare state (KWS) corresponding to the production regime of Fordism. In the context of European integration and market liberalisation he argues that the KWS is being replaced by a neo-liberal welfare regime restructuring welfare in a way that erodes the substantial core of the KWS, i.e. social citizenship understood as the provision of welfare as a universal social right. This is substituted by a type of welfare based on social need and means testing and expectations of individual economic self-reliance. According to Ryner the role of migration in both the KWS and the neo-liberal paradigm differs. The social citizenship of the KWS was never meant to include the labour migrants of the 1960s and 1970s but contrary to political intentions the rule of law and the mode of functioning of national welfare states made exclusion impossible. In the present neo-liberal context, migrants are among the socially most vulnerable groups who form potential allies for the old welfare state constituencies of the KWS. But internal social competition, discrimination and xenophobia drive these groups apart and render the preservation of elements of social citizenship less likely.

The book's focus then moves towards closer specification of these issues in national settings. One clear trend within 'mature' national welfare states (Heisler and Heisler 1990) was that the scope for social citizenship for migrants widened after the Second World War because non-national immigrants and their descendants were included on the basis of the principle of 'denizenship' (Hammar 1990). Welfare states have an internal tendency to produce entitlements and social rights for those legally residing on their territory. The labour migrants of the 1950s, 1960s and 1970s were included in social insurance systems partly because of the expansionist climate of the time concerning welfare and rights during this period and partly because welfare schemes cannot allow for exemptions without eroding their own operative principle. This provided the basis for the extension of rights to legally resident non-nationals – or what was called 'denizenship' for newly arrived immigrants waiting in the 'ante-chamber of national citizenship' (Hammar 1990). It allowed incomplete membership for non-nationals when these non-national migrants deviated from the traditional patterns of welfare state inclusion. Moreover denizenship did not necessitate a rethink of the territorial principle underpinning national welfare states (Brubaker 1989). The emphasis on territoriality could be maintained with the eventual acquisition of nationality as the device to 'repair' incomplete membership. From this perspective, as Freeman (1986) put it, the 'logic' of welfare state closure could be maintained by a judicious combination of restrictive immigration policies and the social inclusion of legally resident migrants on the basis of denizenship with the possibility of naturalisation.

Against this background Virginie Guiraudon asks how and why non-nationals have acquired social rights and welfare benefits since the 1970s given that according to Marshall's assumption social citizenship is supposed to be the final step in the acquirement of full citizenship rights? She takes the reversal of the Marshallian progression of citizenship rights as a puzzle, which she analyses by comparing the evolution of the rights of foreigners in France, Germany and The Netherlands since 1973. After discussing the shortcomings of existing theories about migration and welfare, she describes social rights legislation in the three countries and develops an explanatory model emphasising the role of state bureaucracies and courts for safeguarding and expanding social rights for migrants. She demonstrates that it is the mode of operation of state bureaucracies and the functioning of courts and the law which directs them in favour of equal treatment and social rights for migrants. Assuming that rights are more likely to be granted when they are confined to bureaucratic or judicial venues, Guiraudon then argues that welfare benefits could be granted through regulations after a bureaucratic debate or were the object of court decisions in venues biased in favour of equality before the law. This appears different to the case of political rights, such as the right to vote, that require constitutional reform or at least legislative debate. Spillover into a wider electoral arena makes the granting of these rights less likely.

Welfare bureaucracies and courts define one of the decisive contexts for opening access to welfare for immigrants. Michael Bommes' chapter develops this theme by dealing with the relation between the institutionalisation of the modern life course by national welfare states and the impact of immigration on this arrangement. He develops his argument based on a case study comparing the position of ethnic Germans (the *Aussiedler*) with the position of labour migrants in the German welfare system. The chapter starts from the observation that one central structural form of providing social inclusion has been the institutionalisation of the modern life course. Bommes discusses the reasons why this institutionalisation of the life course and the safeguard within it of individuals with a structured biography have become central for the mode of operation of welfare states. He then shows that international migration highlights some very specific social preconditions of these arrangements for inclusion. If biographies are understood as the result of a sequential process in which chances for social participation supported by welfare states are accumulated, then migrants are likely to be structurally poor because of their specific relation to national welfare states. The chapter then develops these core observations with a case study of the immigration of ethnic Germans and labour migrants in Germany. It shows that migration can be taken as part of a process that erodes the classical arrangement by which welfare states provide an ordered life course for the members of the national community, i.e. for their citizens in exchange for political loyalty.

Jim Hollifield's chapter deals with immigration control and the politics of rights. This topic affects the question of welfare in at least two ways. First, restricting rights means restricting access to welfare. Second, weakening the welfare position of migrants is seen as an indirect means of immigration control (see also Geddes and Bank in this volume). Hollifield focuses on the French case in order to discuss the politics of rights in liberal immigration countries. He assumes that liberal states usually opt for external strategies of immigration control emphasising border controls or control of territory. If external control cannot be efficiently established, then internal control policies come into play, raising questions about how far liberal states can go in imposing controls on individuals and groups in (civil) society, and whether foreigners and immigrants should be considered members of civil society. By outlining the history of French post-war immigration policies and their dynamics, Hollifield advances the argument that ideas, institutions, and culture, as well as certain segments of civil society that may resist encroachments by the state on negative and/or positive freedoms, impose limits on the expansion of internal state control. With respect to internal control, liberal states it seems are constrained institutionally, ideologically, culturally, and ultimately by their civil societies. If the immigration policies of the last twenty years are understood as outcomes of a 'grand bargain' between anti- and pro-immigration forces in liberal democracies, then future development depends on the strength of civil institutions. Consequently, it remains unclear how far a liberal republic can go towards limiting the rights of immigrants and foreigners as a way of controlling immigration without eroding its own fundament.

This issue, identified by Hollifield, has become a very pressing concern since the late 1980s when the international relations of migration changed completely after the end of the Cold War. It became questionable whether states any longer possessed the capacity to control access to their territories (Weiner 1995). The dynamics of modern society – of 'globalisation' and 'world society' (Giddens 1990; Sassen 1996; Luhmann 1997) – confront welfare states with the familiar problems of maintaining their capacity to secure economic, social and cultural participation for their members. In the era of the global economy, capital and multinational companies are in a position to use the option to withdraw, but welfare states are bound by their territorial borders and experience a reduction in their capacity to 'oblige' (Streeck 1998b). The effect has been a shift of political style to a mode of negotiation under conditions of international competition between welfare states trying to combine welfare provision with economic competitiveness (Esping-Andersen 1996).

The result has been that the maintenance and enforcement of politically standardised and generalised 'normal conditions' of employment and social participation have become increasingly difficult. Migrants are drawn into view in this context in two ways. First, as those who often have lower chances of inclusion than the majority of the autochthonous population (Miles and Thränhardt 1995). Second, as those who perceive and take advantage of emerging employment chances in 'deregularised' labour markets (see Vogel 1999 and Maria Baganha's contribution to this volume). On the one hand, immigrants are major welfare state clients that require specific and intense endeavours to secure social inclusion. On the other hand, immigrants can appear within labour markets as competitors who subvert standards established by the welfare state. With this as the background, the obligation of states to provide for the 'social integration' of non-citizens can become controversial. Alongside the inclusion of many immigrants within welfare provisions and the extension of social rights to non-citizens since the Second World War there have also been growing efforts to control access to territory for migrants and to limit social rights. The further inclusion of non-citizens is then politically constructed as a threat to the capacity of the welfare state to care for its own citizens. The result of this is that the maintenance of the threshold of inequality at the borders of the national welfare state retains its relevance as the political reference point for the definition of the community of legitimate receivers of welfare.

This is a point developed in Andrew Geddes' consideration of the recent development of UK immigration and asylum policy. He shows that British immigration policy has consistently since the 1960s shrunk the categories of people entitled to move to the UK in a bid to secure the external frontiers of 'fortress Britain'. The UK was aided in this endeavour by the existence of strong executive authority that empowered the implementing agencies in the face of a largely subservient legislature and weak courts. Yet, despite the pursuit of ever more stringent immigration controls, the UK has during the 1990s been confronted with 'unavoidable' – due to international and domestic legal obligations – increases in migration resulting from asylum seeking. The response has been development of internal controls 'anormalising' the lives of asylum seekers by denying access to cash-paid benefits for asylum seekers and introducing a national dispersal system. The UK has pursued the opposite of welfare state policies: asylum seekers are denied chances for social inclusion in order to attempt to ensure that the migration process is reversible.

These points are then developed in a broader European perspective in Roland Bank's chapter. He demonstrates that a key aspect of the politicisation of the asylum issue is the assumption that many asylum-seekers are 'bogus' and seeking to circumvent strict immigration controls. Bank demonstrates that asylum has acquired a European resonance and elicited a European level response, albeit focused on the co-ordination of national responses rather than harmonisation in the form of a common policy (although the enactment of the Amsterdam Treaty may change this). Policies for the reception of asylum seekers can be characterised as the opposite of welfare state policies in that they seek to prevent access to the territory of the country in which the claim for asylum is being made as a way of preventing access to welfare entitlements. It seems that international standards underpinning the asylum system offer only the barest guarantees in the face of political discretion in the design and operation of asylum systems in EU member states. The 'anormalisation' of social life for asylum seekers constitutes a form of immigration control that guards the frontiers of the national welfare state.

European integration clearly constitutes a major aspect of the challenge to the national welfare state. In the modern era international migration became a problem because it transgressed nation state borders. The integration of Europe redefines the meaning of borders. The institutionalisation of free movement for EU citizens also creates a distinction between

'Europeans' and 'non-Europeans'. The capacity to define categories of migrants based on diversified legal status still resides to a large extent with nation states, but the distinction between Europeans and non-Europeans starts to over-determine national efforts to redefine different categories of migrants. European integration also challenges national welfare states which evolved in the course of nation state building in Europe. Scholars differ when considering the question of how far-reaching the effects of European integration on national welfare states and their capacities of provision have been (Leibfried and Pierson 1995b; Offe 1998; Albert 1998). It seems fair to say that the European challenge to welfare states is partly articulated and partly reinforced by migration processes. On the one hand, the EU is a frame for new migration opportunities such as free movement for people and services which have redefined in different ways the relation between welfare states, citizens and migrants (Eichenhofer 1997; Hunger 1998). On the other hand, immigration by third-country nationals (TCNs) after the Second World War, that was originally initiated and structured by the migration regimes of single nation states, has gained a new meaning in the evolving EU framework with feedback effects into national welfare systems (Bommes 1999).

The EU's single market has left national welfare states formally untouched and welfare remains part of the member states' sovereignty, but single market integration has been accompanied by a commitment to some form of 'social dimension'. The solution to this was provision backed by EU law for transferability of social entitlements for EU citizens exercising free-movement rights. This was to be based on a regime of legal regulations co-ordinating the different welfare systems and repairing problematic cases resulting from collisions between different welfare rules (Eichenhofer 1997, 1998). The right to transferable social entitlements is, however, restricted to nationals of member states and thus formally excludes around 11 million legally resident third-country nationals. However, the institutionalisation of the single market has various 'silent effects' on national welfare regimes and the capability to preserve them (Leibfried and Pierson 1995b). Free movement for people and services opens migratory options with direct effects on national welfare systems. Is the continued closure of national welfare states still possible in a Europe configured by international migration and within which borders between member states are being removed?

A telling case in this respect is Maria Baganha's chapter on immigration in Portugal and the position of immigrants on the Portuguese labour market, which provides a link with the chapters on the relation between immigration, welfare and European integration. The example of Portugal provides an extremely valuable indication of linkages between migration and welfare in countries with weak welfare traditions. Baganha argues that in Portugal, where welfare traditions are not deeply entrenched and where considerable sections of the population have not fully internalised their own citizenship rights, there is likely to be less pressure on the state to extend to immigrants social rights that pass from formal laws to everyday reality. Baganha observes that since the 1980s southern European countries became, for the first time, powerful magnets for growing numbers of immigrants and that it was the informal economy that was the primary space of insertion for new arrivals during the 1990s. In formal terms, foreign residents have the same rights as Portuguese citizens. But a large number of immigrants, especially those from Portuguese-speaking African countries, do not have legal residence status and work in informal or illegal economic sectors. Baganha analyses the positions of different immigrant groups on formal and informal labour markets and argues that there are two main reasons for the relative ease, compared to other European countries, of living as an illegal migrant in Portugal, especially in the urban area of Lisbon. First, social networks among immigrants open access to the informal labour market. Second, is the state's relative incapacity to efficiently regulate and control the labour market. Baganha demonstrates that especially male immigrants from Portuguese-speaking African countries replace a large portion of the Portuguese labour force in the construction and building industries because of the redeployment of Portuguese workers to other EU states such as Belgium, France and Germany arising from the EU's provisions for freedom of services. In this way she identifies important European interdependencies. Baganha concludes that immigrants' access to full social citizenship is, on the one hand, an effect of the immigrant's own behaviour, short-term interests and residential status and, on the other, that the weak Portuguese welfare tradition forms the background for rather limited exclusionary efforts of the state. Baganha concludes by suggesting that Portuguese citizens do not expect to be efficiently protected by the state and that this may be a reason why they do not press the state to extend social rights to immigrants. It can also be added that this could be taken as the background for why they don't expect the state to act in a more exclusionary manner either.

Uwe Hunger's chapter follows Maria Baganha's contribution and re-inforces the point about European interdependencies. Hunger demonstrates how the right of free establishment for businesses in the EU has created 'posted workers' moving from low-wage to high-wage EU member states. The German construction industry is a particularly interesting example because during the post-reunification construction boom, cheaper foreign labour has been imported with lowering effects on levels of pay, workplace organisation and safety. Hunger views European integration as a vehicle for the importation into Germany of an Anglo-American liberal welfare regime with corrosive effects on the institutional architecture of German consensus capitalism. He looks at the internal political debate created by posted workers and at the developments of arguments that these forms of intra-EU migration need to be more closely regulated at national and European level to ensure that they do not erode welfare provision. He also outlines the stances of the institutional actors such as trade unions and employers' organisations with a stake in the existing organisational form of welfare provision.

The process of Europeanisation of migration and welfare is examined by Andrew Geddes who seeks the meaning of 'migrant social inclusion' in relation to the specific sources of legal, political and social power associated with European integration. This involves assessing arguments for inclusion and how these arguments connect with the EU's core market-making activities and forms of 'economic citizenship' centred on the civil right to enter into contract. The evolution of the EU's social dimension is explored, as too is its seeming irrelevance for third-country nationals (TCNs) for whom that national welfare state retains its inclusionary pre-eminence. That said, pressure developed during the 1990s for action at EU level to accompany restrictive immigration policies (Europeanised external closure) with inclusionary measures regarding the social rights of TCNs. Geddes' chapter pays particular attention to the actions, motivations and alliance-building strategies of key EU level actors (the member states, NGOs, EU institutions) in order to locate the development of Europeanised migrant inclusion that so far provides us with only a 'thin' version of social rights.

A key implication of the emergence and development of new patterns of governance associated with European integration and, more generally, with 'globalisation' is that vocabularies of social and political analysis that take national welfare states as their point of reference are challenged. States may well remain key actors but they are no longer the only actors. Developments beyond the nation state also suggest that the universalising project of welfare states bound by the nation state now possess a dimension configured by supra-, trans- and post-national developments. Valérie Amiraux's chapter explores transnational developments and the associated forms of ethnic and migrant organisation that have emerged as a side-effect of the increased interdependency and porousness of nations. In this sense, transnationalism can be understood as being composed of forms of action or mobilisation that are enabled outside of the existing opportunity structures of national welfare state politics. Amiraux demonstrates that these transnational developments have a strong spatial dimension and can be understood as involving the translation of goods, ideas, discourses and votes and the new transnational configurations that arise as a result of this non-state-centred social and political action. The key point is that the creation of transnational social spaces creates the potential for development of alternative forms of welfare provision for transnational communities. Amiraux analyses transnational communities and social spaces created by Muslim communities in France and Germany to demonstrate that they can only fully be understood in the context of the ideas about welfare and the organisational dynamics of the French and German welfare states, but that there also emerges scope for complementary forms of welfare organisation, for example, in the area of educational provision.

The contributions to this book provide an overview of the ways in which migration challenges the border of national welfare states. Our central concern is to show how the definition of the community of legitimate receivers of welfare has been defined and redefined in relation to various forms of immigration, in diverse national settings, and in relation to developments beyond the nation state such as European integration. We demonstrate the importance of the relation between immigration and the welfare state, while also illustrating that debates about welfare and immigration are nested within broader debates about welfare state development. In this book, we seek to bring migration to the forefront of analysis and to illustrate its centrality to analysis of the dynamics of inclusion and exclusion in modern welfare states.

Note

1 It is necessary to distinguish between the belief in control and the actual organisation of control. It could be argued that welfare states have expanded the organisation of control to include internal measures precisely because they no longer believe in realisation of strict external control (Cornelius, Martin and Hollifield 1994).

2 Looking in three directions

Migration and the European welfare state in comparative perspective

Keith G. Banting

Introduction

International migration is reshaping the politics of virtually every western democracy, and contributing to vigorous debates about the nature of identity, community and citizenship in the contemporary era. The politics of social policy seem to be particularly sensitive to this transition. From their inception, social programmes have been influenced by prevailing interpretations of the nature of inequality. Changing images of the groups that are most disadvantaged and vulnerable in a society can have powerful consequences for the definition of social problems, the discourse within which they are debated, and the political alliances that form around them. In addition, the history of social programmes has been powerfully influenced by conceptions of community and the boundaries of inclusion and exclusion, which define both those who are full members of existing networks of reciprocity and deserve support, and those who are 'strangers' or 'others' to whom little is owed. In the contemporary period, migration is unsettling traditional definitions of inequality and community, and introducing new tensions into the politics of social policy. This new landscape has led some analysts of European experience to fear that immigration is fragmenting the political constituencies that support the welfare state and eroding the sense of a common community on which a vibrant conception of social citizenship depends. For example, in his study of the rise of radical right parties, Kitschelt worries that a multicultural welfare state may not be politically viable, and asks: 'will the multiculturalisation of still by and large homogeneous or ethnically stable Western Europe lead to a decline of the welfare state?' (Kitschelt 1995: 258–9, 270). A decade earlier, Freeman was even more definitive. Immigration, he asserted, 'has been little short of a disaster', and 'has led to the Americanisation of European welfare politics' (Freeman 1986: 61).[1]

Such analysts can legitimately highlight many points of tension between multiculturalism and social citizenship in contemporary Europe. Nevertheless, a more broadly comparative perspective provides less stark assessments and more nuanced conclusions about the scope for a stable accommodation between multiculturalism and the welfare state. In particular, our understanding is enhanced by looking in three directions.

First, looking back in time is important to an analysis of the relationship between ethno-linguistic diversity and social policy. Anxiety about the implications of migration is often premised, implicitly if not explicitly, on the assumption that ethnic pluralism is invariably corrosive of the social role of the state. An historical view of the development of the welfare state in the post-war period provides a more complex view, and helps to understand the contexts in which ethnic diversity has and has not played a significant part in shaping the social role of the state.

Second, looking beyond the borders of Europe, and comparing European experience with that of western democracies more generally produces a different image. The impact of migration on social citizenship has varied considerably from country to country, and the European pattern appears less problematic when viewed through a wider lens. This wider perspective also helps to identify factors that mediate potential tensions between migration and social citizenship. At first glance, one might assume that countries with long experience of multiculturalism, such as the 'settler societies' of North America and Australia, would have less difficulty incorporating new immigrant communities into their social policy regimes. As we shall see, however, this has not been the case. Instead, the nature of the welfare state that different countries created in the post-war years seems to have been much more important to the ease with which immigrant minorities have been extended the same social rights as are enjoyed by citizens.

Third, looking beyond migration to a more multifaceted view of multiculturalism also provides a more balanced view. The modern politics of ethno-linguistic diversity in western countries reflects not only changing patterns of international migration but also a resurgence of substate nationalism. In defiance of integration theory, ancient cultures have taken on fresh political importance in recent decades, and powerful nationalist and separatist movements have emerged in a number of countries: the Catalans and Basques in Spain, the Flemish and Wallonian communities in Belgium, the Québécois in Canada, the Scots and Welsh in the United Kingdom. The challenge to social citizenship posed by the politics of international migration seems less compelling when compared with the politics of contending nationalisms, where the conception of the political community within which redistribution should take place is contested much more directly and powerfully.

To develop this analysis, the paper proceeds through several stages. The first section sets out the issues and briefly examines theoretical debates about them. The second section then asks whether there is a general tension between ethno-linguistic diversity and social policy by examining the factors that shaped the development of the welfare state in the post-war era. The third section shifts attention to the contemporary period, and surveys the social policy response to international migration across western democracies, focusing in particular on the experience in different clusters of welfare states. The fourth section contrasts the impact of migration on social citizenship with the challenge generated by the mobilisation of substate nationalist movements. A final section then draws together the main threads of the argument, and reflects on the role of social policy in a multicultural age.

Social citizenship and multiculturalism

The dominant post-war view of the welfare state was rooted in a conception of social citizenship. In his celebrated study of welfare capitalism, Esping-Andersen starts from the premise that 'social citizenship constitutes the core idea of a welfare state' (1990: 21); and Taylor-Gooby agrees, arguing that 'the history of the welfare state is the story of the development and defence of citizenship welfare rights' (1994: 190). The earliest exponent of this tradition, T. H. Marshall (1950), argued that over the centuries citizenship has been invested with a formidable array of civil, political and social rights. He saw this evolution, especially the addition of social rights in the twentieth century, as part of a powerful process of social integration, which steadily incorporated emerging economic classes into a national community. Although social rights might mitigate the gap between rich and poor, they did not eliminate the economic realities of class. Rather, a common citizenship generated a new equality of status, a symbolic moral ordering that would mute the divisiveness of unconstrained class inequality. This equality of status was deeply related to the emergence of a shared sense of community: in the first instance, citizenship reflected the emergence of a national community, which Marshall saw as developing well before the extension of social rights; but the extension of social benefits to all citizens also reinforced the sense of a common community. Citizenship, he argued, requires 'a sense of direct community membership based on loyalty to a civilisation that is a common possession' (ibid.: 24–5).

　Why would multiculturalism challenge this conception of the welfare state? The essential fear is that such cultural diversity fragments the sense of a common community, and weakens political support for social citizenship. In principle, this erosion could come from both cultural minorities and cultural majorities. Minorities may feel that social rights are defined by the dominant culture, and are insensitive to the diversity of needs and beliefs that exist today. At the extreme, they might reject universal public services as instruments of assimilation and homogenisation rather than cultural pluralism, and seek communal or private provision for important services. More critical, however, is the possible retreat of cultural majorities from a commitment to social citizenship. Minority challenges to mainstream culture – in the form of demands for affirmative action, group rights or greater autonomy for the expression of cultural difference – may generate a backlash amongst traditional supporters of the welfare state, dividing pro-welfare coalitions. Alternatively, majorities may simply withdraw support from programmes that channel resources to communities they do not recognise as their own, by denying benefits to newcomers, reducing programmes that disproportionately serve minorities, or restricting social programmes in general. This danger is presumably heightened when income inequality and cultural difference are highly correlated, when the poor are mostly minorities and the minorities are mostly poor. In these circumstances, dominant groups may abandon the idea of a set of wider obligations and quietly disengage, psychologically and perhaps even physically, from the wider society, shifting their allegiance to more conservative political philosophies and parties.

Echoes of these concerns reverberate in theoretical debates over the meaning of citizenship in the contemporary world. For example, Kymlicka argues that

> Marshall's theory of integration does not necessarily work for culturally distinct immigrants, or for various other groups which have historically been excluded from full participation in the national culture – such as blacks, women, religious minorities, gays and lesbians. Some members of these groups still feel excluded from the 'common culture' despite possessing the common rights of citizenship.
>
> (Kymlicka 1995: 180; see also Barbalet 1988)

As a result, a more diversified conception of citizenship, premised on the legitimacy of some group rights, is essential (Taylor 1991, 1992). Other theorists, however, worry about the reaction of cultural majorities and the centrality of a sense of common community to the redistributive state. For example, when Young celebrates group differences and argues that 'the ideal state is composed of a plurality of nations or cultural groups' (1990: 179–80), Miller replies that achieving social justice requires trust and solidarity 'not merely within groups but also across them', and that such solidarity depends on a common sense of community (1995: 140). Wolfe and Klausen agree, and argue that 'the threat to the welfare state which exists from supranational pressures towards globalisation meets threats to the welfare state from subnational group power and recognition' (1997: 241). Similarly, Taylor-Gooby (1994) fears that post-modern thought and practice represent a 'great leap backwards', which diverts the attention of the political left from the agenda of the welfare state and the fight against class inequality.[2]

Are these fears justified? More particularly, is there evidence for the view that enthno-linguistic diversity constrains the redistributive role of the state? And are international migration and the politics of multiculturalism eroding the commitment to social citizenship in western democracies? The next sections examine the evidence more directly.

Social citizenship, ethno-linguistic diversity and the post-war welfare state

There is remarkably little research on the impact of ethno-linguistic diversity on the social role of the state. Over a decade ago, Gould and Palmer argued that 'more heterogeneous populations seem to experience more income inequality', and 'encounter great difficulty in reaching consensus on public policies to address problems caused by income inequality'. However, they went on to concede that 'to argue this point conclusively and empirically, we would like to have a wealth of comparable data not available ... as far as we know, anywhere' (1988: 426–7). Although the available evidence has expanded since then, it is still not fully conclusive.

It is possible to gain some perspective on the issue by examining the expansion of the welfare state during the post-war decades. Public expenditure on social programmes rose steadily across OECD countries during those years, increasing from an average of 10 per cent of GDP in 1960 to approximately 20 per cent by 1980 (OECD 1994). Despite a common expansionist trajectory, however, the social role of the state differed significantly from one country to another, in terms of the scope of public expenditures of social programmes, the structure of core welfare programmes, and their impact on both labour markets and the larger social structure. The most celebrated typology identifies three types of welfare states (Esping-Andersen 1990). Social democratic welfare states, which emerged most definitively in Scandinavia, were built on the basis of expansive and powerfully redistributive programmes reflecting the principles of social citizenship, universalism, and the decommodification of labour. Corporatist welfare states, which developed in countries such as Austria, France, Germany and Italy, also generated expansive social spending; but their social programmes were designed to preserve traditional status differentials among economic classes and occupations, and their redistributive impact was more limited. Finally, liberal or residualist welfare states, which developed in Australia, Canada, Switzerland, the United Kingdom and the United States, preserved a major role for private insurance systems, involved lower levels of public spending, relied heavily on means-tested benefits, and reflected a less complete commitment to the ethos of social rights.[3]

The leading theoretical approach to the development of the welfare state attributes such variations in social provision to the distribution of power resources among economic classes in different countries. In particular, the political strength of the working class was critical: large redistributive welfare states were most likely to emerge in countries in which large proportions of the labour force were unionised, unions were incorporated into strong federations, and organised labour enjoyed close relations with powerful social democratic political parties (Korpi 1983,

1989). Another version of this approach places more weight on the pattern of coalitions among different classes during the transition from a rural economy to an urban, post-industrial economy. Different historical relationships among workers, farmers and the emerging middle classes pushed the welfare state in different directions in different western democracies. In Esping-Andersen's words, 'the history of political class coalitions is the most decisive cause of welfare-state variations' (1990: 1).

In comparison, the literature on the post-war welfare state pays much less attention to the role of ethno-linguistic diversity. However, the implication of class-based analysis would seem to be that cultural pluralism has the potential to weaken the class coalitions associated with the most expansive welfare states by dividing organised labour along ethnic and linguistic lines and making it more difficult to focus politics on an agenda of economic equality as opposed to inter-communal relations and tensions. Support for this inference comes from one major study of the post-war era that did tackle the issue directly. In keeping with many other studies, Stephens (1979) found that the expansion of the welfare state in western nations was closely correlated with the strength of organised labour. But he also found that ethnic and linguistic diversity was strongly and negatively correlated with the level of labour organisation, and therefore represented an indirect constraint on the expansion of a powerful social citizenship regime.

Few, if any, other studies have systematically examined the question among OECD countries since then. Development economists, however, have analysed the impact of ethnic diversity on the role of government in a much wider range of countries, including both rich and poor nations. Their findings suggest that the relationship between ethnic diversity and the overall size of government is weak (Mueller and Murrell 1986), but studies that focus on more specific features of the public sector have found more powerful relationships. For example, spending on income-transfer programmes tends to be lower in countries with high levels of ethnic and cultural diversity (McCarty 1993); and spending on private as opposed to public education tends to be higher in such countries (James 1987, 1993). More broadly, a study by the World Bank concludes that ethnic fragmentation tends to be associated with rent-seeking behaviour, reduced support for public goods, lower schooling, and higher government deficits (Easterly and Levine 1997). Because the evidence in these studies relates to a much wider range of countries, the conclusions cannot be applied directly to western democracies. Nevertheless, in combination with the Stephens study, they do provide at least partial support for the proposition that there is an underlying tension between ethno-linguistic diversity and social redistribution.

This tension is complex, however, and clearly mediated by a variety of other factors. Most importantly, the influence of ethno-linguistic diversity in the post-war period was conditioned by the structure of political institutions through which different countries developed their welfare policy regimes. The combination of social homogeneity and centralised political institutions did facilitate the expansion of the welfare state in a number of countries, including the social democratic welfare states of Sweden, Norway and Denmark. These societies were remarkably homogeneous in terms of ethnicity, religion and language; their cultural solidarity facilitated political mobilisation around class divisions and the agenda of the welfare state; and although programmes were often delivered locally, basic policy decisions were made nationally in highly concentrated political processes. It was these countries that gave the fullest expression to the concept of social citizenship.

A second group of countries demonstrates that social heterogeneity is not necessarily fatal to an expansive conception of social citizenship. The consociational democracies of Europe, such as Belgium, Austria and The Netherlands, were able to build comprehensive welfare states despite deep cleavages rooted in religion, language and other cultural divisions. These countries operated through centralised state structures, but the elements of the consociational model of governance – consensus decision-making, collaboration among political elites representing distinct sub-cultures, and proportionality in the distribution of public resources – provided a formula for managing inter-communal tensions (Lijphart 1968, 1977, 1995). Although the cultural divisions in The Netherlands and Austria were not rooted primarily in ethnicity or language, the large welfare state constructed in post-war Belgium demonstrates the extent to which consociational practices could manage the interface between redistributive politics and a culturally plural society.

A third group of countries does highlight a tension between social heterogeneity and the post-war welfare state. Countries such as the United States, Canada and Switzerland managed ethno-linguistic diversity without the advantages of consociational institutions and practices. The nature of the tension varies among these countries, in some cases being relatively direct and in others more indirect. The quintessential case of overt tension is the United States, where the politics of race have shaped social policy throughout the country's history, and constrained the capacity of welfare advocates to build stable political coalitions. Passage of the Social Security Act of 1935 was secured in part by largely excluding blacks from the new benefits: agricultural and domestic labourers were ineligible for the social insurance components of Social Security, denying coverage to three-fifths of black workers; and southern congressmen led a successful campaign in the name of 'states' rights' against national standards in public assistance, leaving southern blacks at the mercy of local authorities (Orloff 1988; Quadagno 1988). In the decades that followed, the New Deal coalition of southern whites and northern liberals, union members, white ethnic groups and black voters 'could endure only so long as the issue of race was submerged' (Williams 1998: 420). In the 1950s and 1960s, however, the politics of civil rights forced race to the forefront of the American political agenda. Minorities increasingly gained access to social benefits, and black and Hispanic groups became significantly over-represented among the beneficiaries of key programmes such as Aid to Families With Dependent Children. In the end, the politics of race drove a wedge through the heart of the New Deal coalition, and steadily corroded support for the War on Poverty of the 1960s and the Family Assistance Plan in the early 1970s (Quadagno 1990, 1994).

The politics of race continues to shape social policy in the United States. Racial attitudes remain the most important source of opposition to welfare among the white population (Gilens 1995, 1996), and Republican electoral campaigns in the 1980s capitalised on the unpopularity of programmes associated with poor blacks. The party reaped major electoral gains among white union members, urban ethnic voters and southerners, creating the political room for significant cuts to social programmes, especially those with disproportionately minority clienteles (Skocpol 1991). In the 1990s, the Democratic Party sought to insulate itself by embracing hard-edged welfare reform itself, promising to 'end welfare as we know it'. The reform package that emerged from the struggle between the Republican Congress and President Clinton replaced Aid to Families with Dependent Children (AFDC) with Temporary Assistance to Needy Families (TANF), a block grant to state governments which eliminates the entitlement to welfare and adopts firm time limits on benefits for recipients. These racial tensions have played themselves out, not only at the national level, but in local politics as well. A study of the provision of public goods in municipalities found that high levels of ethnic diversity are associated with reduced provision of roads, schools, libraries and trash collection (Alesina, Baqir and Easterly 1997).

In other countries in this third cluster, such as multilingual Canada and Switzerland, the tension between cultural pluralism and the welfare state has been more indirect. The politics of social policy in these countries have only occasionally pitted major language groups directly against each other.[4] Rather, territorially concentrated linguistic communities led to the establishment of fragmented, decentralised political institutions, with important consequences for the development of the welfare state. Cross-national studies of the determinants of social spending have found that federalism, decentralisation and other forms of institutional fragmentation are associated with lower levels of spending (Crepaz 1998; Huber, Ragin and Stephens 1993; Hicks and Swank 1992; Hicks and Misra 1993; Cameron 1978). Obviously, federal institutions alone were not a decisive brake on the welfare state in countries such as Germany and Austria, two federal countries which are relatively homogeneous in ethno-linguistic terms, and in which policy-making is relatively consolidated at the national level even if programmes are delivered at the regional level. In Canada and Switzerland, however, the building of the welfare state was conditioned by complex, decentralised institutions that fragmented power in important ways: Canada proceeded through a decentralised federation; Switzerland did likewise, but with the addition of a vigorous plebiscitary tradition. In both cases, institutional fragmentation constrained the redistributive role of the state (Banting 1987, 1998; Immergut 1992).

Thus, the post-war experience does help to clarify the relationship between social heterogeneity and social citizenship. There is prima facie evidence of a general, underlying tension between ethno-linguistic diversity and social redistribution, and certainly the politics of ethnic diversity have constrained the expansion of the welfare state in a number of specific countries. Nevertheless, the relationship is highly contingent, and was strongly mediated by the structure of political institutions. The tension was most marked in countries that managed the political tensions inherent in cultural pluralism through fragmented political institutions, and even here the tension was often indirect rather than direct. The consociational democracies of Europe, operating through centralised institutions and consensual traditions, were able to accommodate cultural diversity and powerful welfare states. Thus, although there may well be a general tension between ethno-linguistic diversity and social citizenship, there is clearly no inevitability.

Multiculturalism and social citizenship in the contemporary era

As in the post-war era, contemporary tensions between multiculturalism and social citizenship play out in diverse ways, reflecting important contrasts in the institutional structures and policy legacies of different countries. To appreciate the factors at work, however, requires looking beyond contemporary Europe and incorporating the experience of western democracies generally. It is also critical to examine the response across different types of welfare states. As we shall see, variations in the shape of the welfare state itself increasingly define the political landscape on which tensions between diversity and social policy are managed by governments.

The politics of international migration suggests that the real challenge to social citizenship comes from majorities rather than minorities. In contrast to nationalist minorities discussed below, immigrant minorities tend to seek incorporation into the mainstream of society. To be sure, they normally strive to preserve their traditions, and often live in transnational communities, with psychological attachments to both their country of origin and their new home. Migrants also press the social institutions of their new country to be more tolerant of cultural differences, and normally support political agendas focused on equity across ethno-cultural boundaries. Nevertheless, the dominant political impulse is to be accepted as full members of the wider society, and this emphasis on inclusion seems to shape their overall orientation to social programmes. Members of minority communities often encounter problems with public services, and education in particular can become a battleground over the recognition of difference.

But there is little evidence of migrant communities themselves mounting political challenges to the basic idea of a common social citizenship.

The deeper tension between migration and the welfare state is rooted in the reaction of majorities. This is hardly surprising, since majorities normally carry more weight than minorities in democratic politics. Three types of majority response to ethnic and racial diversity are possible. First, new immigrant populations might be incorporated into the existing social regime with little challenge to the underlying societal consensus on social policy. Second, vulnerable sections of the dominant culture – such as young, less educated, blue-collar workers – might be driven by a 'welfare chauvinism' that supports the welfare state but rejects open immigration policies and the ready access of foreigners to social benefits (Andersen and Bjørklund 1990; Andersen 1992; Kitschelt 1995). Third, a political backlash against immigration and multiculturalism might help fuel a more comprehensive neo-liberal attack on the welfare state, contributing to the emergence of new radical right parties and/or the retreat of established parties from social redistribution.

All three of these reactions are occurring in western democracies, but the balance among them varies considerably from country to country. As noted earlier, one might expect that previously homogeneous countries would face the most difficulty incorporating new minorities into social citizenship regimes, and that countries with traditions as immigrant societies or long experience with ethno-linguistic diversity would have the least trouble. This is not the case. A critical variable seems to be the nature of the welfare state established in the post-war period. In countries that established expansive welfare states, whether of social democratic or corporatist inspiration, the balance tilts towards social incorporation. In countries that established more liberal welfare states, welfare chauvinism seems to be leaving a heavier imprint.

In the expansive welfare states of Europe, immigrants enjoy formal social rights that differ only at the margin from those of citizens (Soysal 1994; Brubaker 1992). Full benefits are denied to asylum seekers while their claims are being processed (Bank 1998), but once residency is confirmed, inclusion in the full regime of benefits is the norm. Analysts vary in their explanation for this pattern. Soysal (1994) argues that social benefits have slowly become detached from national definitions of citizenship, and that the incorporation of immigrants reflects an increasingly transnational conception of human rights. Although the underlying normative discourse may well reflect this transition, it cannot explain variations in the extent of incorporation across different countries and different types of welfare states.[5] The 'ethos of equality' inherent in expansive welfare states may well be important (Heisler and Heisler 1990), but more structural forces are also probably at work. Organised labour does not want to see competition between their members and immigrants 'who would have to accept any payment and any working conditions' (Radtke

1997: 251); and within the European Union, the mobility provisions for EU nationals make formal discrimination against non-EU migrants more obvious and more difficult.

Incorporation is not uncontested, and European countries also reveal signs of welfare chauvinism. Welfare chauvinism can take two forms: restrictive benefit policy, designed to deny resident foreigners access to social benefits; and restrictive immigration policy, designed to prevent foreigners coming into the country and having access to comprehensive social programmes. Although both forms have figured in political discourse in European nations, the bigger impact in policy terms has been on immigration policy. Successive waves of restrictive legislation have sharply reduced immigration, especially economic immigration, and regulations in the 1990s reduced the flow of refugees seeking asylum. In comparison, denial of social benefits to resident foreigners has been very limited. Pressures to turn social policy into an instrument of immigration control have also been turned back. In 1993, for example, plans for a more draconian immigration policy being developed within the French government initially included serious restrictions on the access of foreigners to social security, especially health care; but opposition within the government from the social affairs minister blocked the proposals (Hollifield 1998). The formal denial of social benefits to resident immigrants has been largely limited to occasional actions at the local level.[6] The employment-related basis of social insurance systems that predominate in these countries does implicitly disadvantage immigrants with weak ties to the labour market, especially in the case of pension credits which build slowly over time – a distinction that takes on greater significance when we examine the response of liberal welfare states below. Nevertheless, welfare chauvinism has had more impact on immigration policy than social policy in expansive welfare states.

Political reaction to a multicultural reality has also contributed to a neo-liberal strain in these countries, but the impact on the politics of social policy has not been decisive. Across Europe, radical right parties have combined elements of ethnocentrism with strains of authoritarianism and neo-liberalism or anti-state populism, with France representing the proto-typical case (Kitschelt 1995; Betz 1994). However, these parties have not broken through to the centre of politics. Although they have had a significant impact on immigration policy, they do not appear to have seriously challenged the underlying consensus on social policy. There is no evidence that welfare states in general, or major social programmes in particular, are losing support over time in European countries. There are ups and downs in popular support, reflecting shifts in partisan debates, electoral campaigns and other factors; but there is no evidence of a long-term, steady decline in support for the social role of the state (Borre and Scarborough 1995).

In contrast, the social-policy response to new minorities has been less inclusive in countries with more limited, or 'liberal' welfare states, such as

Australia, the United Kingdom and the United States. These countries start with weaker social commitments. Several of them are immigrant societies with relatively open processes of naturalisation, and closing the borders has been less of an option (Brubaker 1989b). Moreover, in contrast to European social-insurance systems in which pension and other credits accumulate slowly through employment, liberal welfare states rely more heavily on means-tested benefits, for which newly arrived, unemployed or poor migrants might qualify immediately on arrival. For example, under the family reunification provisions of the immigration policies of most of these countries, young migrants can sponsor their parents for admission, and many of these elderly people would potentially qualify for means-tested pensions from the outset. In this context, welfare chauvinism and neo-liberalism have figured more prominently.[7] In Australia, immigrants must be resident for ten years before they can receive the age pension, or five years before they are eligible for a sole-parent pension or disability pension; and the resident waiting period for a wide range of other allowances such as unemployment and sickness benefits has recently been extended from six months to two years.[8] In the United Kingdom, immigrants are precluded from a number of benefits, such as Income Support, Housing Benefit and Council Tax Benefit; and this list was extended in 1996 to include Attendance Allowance, Disability Living Allowance, Disability Working Allowance, Family Credit, Invalid Care Allowance and Severe Disablement Allowance.

The United States illustrates the most potent cocktail of welfare chauvinism and neo-liberalism. Ending welfare 'as we know it' involved not only the politics of race but also the politics of welfare chauvinism. Indeed, the largest savings from welfare reform came not from the restructuring of AFDC but from restrictions on immigrants' benefits (Weaver 1998). Immigrants were denied access to Food Stamps and Supplementary Security Income, which provides means-tested pensions for the elderly, until they become citizens. Other means-tested programmes, such as Medicaid and social assistance, were denied to new immigrants for a period of five years.[9] Backlash against immigrants was especially potent in California, where referendums challenged the access of immigrants' children – including those born in the United States – to education and health care. Subsequent political battles eased some of the cuts to immigrant benefits at the national level. Yet the multiracial and multicultural nature of American society has clearly helped to fragment support for the welfare state, and the political left faces a formidable task in rebuilding a multi-ethnic, multiracial coalition dedicated to redistributive policies (Wilson 1996).

Canada stands as something of an exception in this group of liberal welfare states. There is a residency period for Old Age Security, a non-contributory component of the public pension system. Otherwise, legal immigrants and refugees have the same benefit entitlements as citizens. There are muted strains of welfare chauvinism in Canada. A government review of social policy in the mid-1990s found considerable public concern about the reliance of new immigrants on social assistance and publicly-financed language training, and recommended changes in admission criteria to enhance the selection of immigrants less likely to need such support (Canada 1994). Moreover, backlash against multiculturalism helped to launch the new Reform Party, a populist, neo-conservative party that advocates an overall reduction in the social role of the state.[10] In the 1997 federal election, the Reform Party emerged as the second largest party and the official opposition in Parliament. As the party has become a more established part of the system, it has struggled to mute the strains of ethnocentrism in its ranks, and its parliamentary caucus now includes people of colour. Nevertheless, Reform remains committed to a deeply individualist approach to social issues, and uses its prominent position in the House of Commons to advance its agenda in national political discourse.

Clearly, the European experience of international migration and social citizenship appears less problematic when viewed from the broader perspective of the experience of western democracies generally. Moreover, the type of welfare states developed on the continent during the post-war decades has been important to that response. Countries that established a strong social regime, whether of social-democratic or corporatist complexion, have been more successful in incorporating new immigrants without eroding mass support for the welfare state. If there has been a price to be paid, it has been more restrictive immigration policies and limits on the full set of political rights implicit in citizenship. It is in countries where the welfare state has a weaker base and relies more heavily on means-tested benefits and where immigration is a strongly entrenched tradition, that new forms of cultural diversity have tended to weaken support for redistribution generally or for inclusive definitions of social programmes. Freeman (1986) seems unduly concerned when he warns, as we saw earlier, that immigration has led to the 'Americanisation of European welfare politics'. It has, however, accentuated the American nature of US welfare politics.

Substate nationalism and social citizenship

The implications of international migration in contemporary Europe are also placed in perspective by comparison with the challenge to social citizenship rooted in substate nationalism. Countries such as Belgium, Canada, Spain and the United Kingdom face a second dimension of cultural pluralism: a multi-nation society and the mobilisation of substate nationalist movements rooted in distinctive linguistic and cultural traditions. The strength of nationalist movements varies considerably across these countries, but their agendas tend to reflect common themes. In contrast to immigrant minorities that normally seek incorporation into the larger society, nationalist movements seek to enhance a distinctive political identity and to expand the political autonomy enjoyed by their communities, either within the context of the existing state or through the formation of a separate state altogether. In several of these multi-nation countries, conflicts rooted in competing political identities pose a significant challenge to a common conception of social citizenship. Unlike the case of immigrant minorities, however, the pressure can come from minorities as well as majority communities, and the resulting political dynamics are more complex.

Although the welfare state established in the post-war years was often smaller in multi-nation federations, it none the less represented a form of social citizenship. Multi-nation states generally established a common framework for major income-security and health-care programmes, and provided comparable levels of benefits to citizens across the country as a whole. A variety of mechanisms were used to sustain a country-wide framework. In the case of income security programmes, such as pensions, unemployment benefits and family allowances, responsibility was usually left with the central government; in other areas such as health care, framework or organic legislation applied across the country but allowed considerable scope for regional or communal variation in design and implementation. Such frameworks gave life to the idea of social citizenship in these plural societies, and presumably provided an indirect measure of an underlying sense of community.

In recent decades, substate nationalism has placed intense pressure on this social framework in a number of countries. Conflicts in these countries often centre on control over social programmes, and to some extent the welfare state itself helped to create this new challenger. As governments have become more intimately involved in people's lives, national minorities increasingly wish for a state that speaks their own language and reflects their cultural traditions. The result has been extensive redesigning of state structures. In Canada, a separatist movement has established a powerful position in the province of Quebec, and responsibility for a number of social programmes has been decentralised in a series of incremental steps over the last twenty years. In other countries such as Belgium, Spain and the United Kingdom, previously centralised and unitary state structures have given way to more decentralised systems, in the form of federal, quasi-federal, or regional institutions. In addition, the financial transfers between rich and poor regions, which underpin a country-wide framework of social benefits, have become politically controversial in several of these countries. Decentralisation and reduced inter-communal redistribution represent a potent combination that can dissolve a common definition of social citizenship.

These dynamics play out in different ways, depending on the strength of nationalist mobilisation, the level of centralisation in existing political institutions, and whether substate nationalism represents a rebellion of the rich or the poor. Belgium, Canada and Spain display three distinct patterns. In Belgium, the mobilisation of Flemish nationalism and the gradual transition to a federal system have unleashed powerful new political pressures on the comprehensive welfare state built up in the post-war era. Social security, including income transfers and health care, remains the last major function still lodged with the central government, and social programmes involve a significant implicit transfer of income from Flanders, the Flemish-speaking, affluent region in the north of the country, to Wallonia, the French-speaking, poorer region in the south. Indeed, studies completed in the early 1990s pointed to an 'income paradox': although primary or earned income was higher in Flanders, the actual disposable income available to citizens after the effects of taxes and social security benefits was actually higher in Wallonia, suggesting that the redistributive mechanisms were over-compensating for inter-communal inequalities (Alen *et al.* 1990: 141–51). Flemish politicians increasingly attacked the transfer system, with more radical spokesmen asserting that, in effect, Flemish taxes had bought each Wallonian family a new car in recent years.

Flemish nationalists have demanded a significant decentralisation of social security in order to reduce the inter-communal subsidies and to increase their capacity to shape their own social future. The Flemish government has carefully laid the groundwork for an assault on the centralised system: in 1992, it commissioned a substantial research programme to document more fully the size of the transfers from Flanders to Wallonia, and to propose a new regime; in 1994 the research group issued a report which recommended the decentralisation of health care and family benefits; in 1996 the government gave its endorsement to the proposal; and in 1997 the State Reform Commission of the Flemish parliament adopted the same position virtually unanimously.[11] More recently, the Flemish government has also raised the issue of greater fiscal autonomy for community and regional governments, which currently depend heavily on transfers from the central government, raising less than 10 per cent of their budgets from own-source revenues. A government discussion paper recommends a significant increase in own-source revenues, and suggests the decentralisation of personal income taxes, which would have a powerful inter-communal impact.

Separately and in combination, these proposals would transform the Belgian welfare state. Unless accompanied by a common policy framework, which is not anticipated in the Flemish proposals, they would end a common social citizenship in health and family benefits; and unless accompanied by substantial inter-regional transfers, they would result in weaker social programmes in Wallonia. The issue of inter-regional transfers remains highly controversial. On this dimension, the consensus within *Flanders is not yet complete. The dominant view is that any transfers should be explicit, transparent, reversible and less comprehensive than the subsidies to Wallonia embedded in the current system.* However, the Flemish Socialist Party is concerned about the dangers implicit in opening up the finances of social programmes completely, fearing that they might end up with a less generous system even in the north, and they tend to favour retaining the current funding mechanisms. Nevertheless, the Socialists are members of the government and support the general decentralisation initiative.[12]

Under the Belgian constitution, constitutional changes require a two-thirds vote in the Belgian parliament. The Flemish government hopes that another round of constitutional reform will begin after elections in 1999, with the major issues being resolved during negotiations over the formation of a new government. However, the decentralisation of social security is rejected completely in Wallonia, which insists on the importance of social solidarity across communal lines. Because the Wallonian community does not have its own agenda for constitutional reform in this round of negotiations, the prospects for a compromise package of reforms are considerably reduced and change may well be blocked. Such an outcome would severely strain inter-community relations. In the words of one observer, 'failure to reach an acceptable compromise on this issue would be regarded by some in Flanders as a signal that no more could be achieved through inter-community dialogue. At that point, some would seek to put separatism on the agenda' (Fitzmaurice 1998). As a result, some incremental change is likely following the elections.

Canada reveals another version of the same dynamic. There are, of course, important differences from the specifics of the Belgian case. Québécois nationalism represents a challenge from a less affluent, minority community. Although there has been considerable convergence in the standard of living of English- and French-speaking Canadians over the last generation, the population of Quebec is still a net beneficiary of the transfers embedded in the Canadian welfare state. In addition, Canada is already a relatively decentralised federation. The federal government has considerable responsibility for pensions and unemployment insurance and still sets general parameters of public health insurance, but the provincial governments have the exclusive or predominant role in education, health care, social assistance and social services. Despite these differences, the underlying patterns are not unlike Belgium. In the post-war period, a set of federal social programmes and conditional grants to provincial governments established a country-wide framework for the Canadian welfare state, and a pan-Canadian definition of social citizenship. Since the 1960s, however, the federal role in social policy has been a source of continuing conflict. The province of Quebec, supported at times by other provinces, has struggled for control over social programmes, arguing that social policy is an instrument of cultural definition, essential to the preservation of a French-speaking nation that is surrounded by an overwhelming English-speaking majority on the North American continent.

The pressure for decentralisation does not go uncontested. Pan-Canadian social programmes are often seen as part of the social glue holding together an otherwise divided country (Banting 1987, 1995). Major social programmes, such as Medicare, represent spheres of shared experience, which all Canadians share, irrespective of the region in which they live and the language they speak. Support for national social programmes is most marked in English-speaking Canada. There are, of course, recurring frictions between the federal and provincial governments in the English-speaking parts of the country over financial issues and questions of programme design, tensions that were particularly acute during a period of retrenchment of the mid-1990s. Nevertheless, English-speaking Canadians take considerable pride in having developed a more expansive welfare state than exists to the south in the United States, and regard programmes such as Medicare as one of the defining characteristics of their national identity. Such sentiments are weaker among Quebecers. Although they are supportive of redistributive programmes, their political identity is rooted much more in language and culture, and some commentators insist that social programmes cannot link Quebec more firmly to Canada (Kymlicka 1995; Taylor 1991). However, federal politicians argue that the integrative potential of pan-Canadian social policy is also relevant in Quebec. They resist nationalist demands for complete decentralisation of social policy on the grounds that the central government's social role gives it a relevance in the daily lives of ordinary Quebecers and contributes to their sense of attachment to Canada, making many voters in the province more ambivalent about the separatist project than they would otherwise be.[13]

The role of social citizenship as an instrument of social cohesion, even on the rocky terrain of Canada–Quebec relations, is no guarantee that common social programmes will remain vibrant. The fiscal weakness of the federal government in recent years substantially reduced its leverage in the system, and nationalist political forces in Quebec continue to press their historic agenda. An asymmetrical status for Quebec is not acceptable to the rest of the country, and a general decentralisation to all provinces is often advocated as a means of accommodating Quebec's jurisdictional aspirations while preserving formal equality across the provinces. Decentralist steps have recently been taken in labour-market training and social assistance programmes, and there are similar demands in the case of the universal Medicare programme. As its fiscal position improved in the late 1990s, the federal government began to reassert itself in social policy and in 1999 it agreed to a new set of rules for the co-management of social programmes with the provinces. However, Quebec rejected the compromise, and nationalist forces continue to press for greater decentralisation and a regionally varied conception of the social role of the state.

In addition, opposition to inter-regional transfers, although not as marked as in Belgium, is growing in the rest of the country. Once again, this sentiment is strongest in the Reform Party, whose support among voters is also strongly correlated with anti-Quebec feelings. During the 1997 federal election campaign, Reform proposed a revision in the equalisation grants programme, which supports poorer provinces. If adopted, the proposal would have the effect of removing Quebec from the list of recipient provinces (Reform Party 1997a, 1997b). A continuing decentralisation of responsibility for social programmes, unaccompanied by some mechanism for sustaining a pan-Canadian approach to social policy and a substantially enhanced inter-regional equalisation, would clearly erode the post-war experiment in a common social citizenship.

Spain represents a third configuration of the nationalist dynamic. As in Canada, the Catalan and Basque nationalists represent minority communities; but as in Belgium, they come from relatively affluent regions that are net contributors to inter-regional fiscal flows. Spain is at a different phase of the developmental cycle, however, and is still defining its version of the welfare state and its version of federalism. In theory, the emerging distribution of power in the quasi-federal system resembles the post-war pattern of most multi-nation federations: major income security programmes are designed and delivered directly by the central government; the basic parameters of health insurance are set centrally through an organic law; but the design and delivery of health and education services themselves are decentralised (Agranoff 1996; Guillén 1997; Rico 1997). In practice, however, the balance between the central government and the regional governments is still highly asymmetrical. Only 7 of the 18 Autonomous Communities have assumed full responsibility for major programmes such as education and health. Moreover, Spain has still not come to grips psychologically with the regional diversity implicit in a federal state. When the Basque regional government established a *salario social*, a minimum income for the poor designed to combat social exclusion, the central government reacted strongly against the initiative, on the grounds that the benefit 'might violate the constitutional right to equality of treatment for all Spanish citizens' (Laparra and Hendrickson 1997: 528; also Linz 1989).[14] In the contemporary context, the commitment to social citizenship tends to constrain nationalist impulses.

However, Spain is also still finding its equilibrium in intergovernmental fiscal relations, which are critical to reconciling decentralisation and social citizenship. The Autonomous Communities have recently been ceded greater capacity to raise their own revenues, and 45 per cent of the 1998 budget of the autonomous region of Catalonia came from own-source revenues. However, grants from the central government still constitute the most important revenue source, and inter-regional redistribution embedded in the system of central transfers means that the Catalan government has less total revenue per person than do poorer regions (Solé-Vilanova 1998). This pattern is unlikely to be stable. Given the relative balance between the contributor and beneficiary regions, it would hardly be surprising if inter-regional fiscal solidarity becomes politicised in the years to come.

Clearly, the political challenge to common social rights inherent in substate nationalism is more formidable than the dynamics generated by immigrant minorities. National minorities as well as majorities can disengage from a common social citizenship, generating much more complex political patterns. Moreover, nationalist movements often mobilise substantial portions of the population, generating political forces that can challenge the very concept of a common social citizenship and a shared political identity and community on which it rests. These are powerful political forces. The politics of international migration have seldom, if ever, focused this sort of power on the social citizenship regimes of contemporary Europe.

Conclusions and reflections

Broadening the focus generates important insights into the social-policy issues posed by international migration in contemporary Europe. First, looking back in time to the development of the post-war welfare state provides important qualifications to the assumption that cultural heterogeneity inevitably undermines the social role of the state. There is evidence of an underlying tension between ethno-linguistic diversity and social spending, and heterogeneity undoubtedly constrained the welfare state in a number of countries. However, the relationship was conditioned by other factors, especially the structure of political institutions through which different countries gave shape to their social citizenship regimes. European countries with consociational patterns of governance were able to manage any tensions between inter-communal relations and an expansive welfare state. It was countries that managed ethnic diversity through less consensual processes and fragmented political institutions that tended to build less expansive welfare states. Although consociational patterns of governance may not be as vibrant as in the past, consensual politics is still a tradition in many European countries, and the pattern of the post-war era suggests that this may represent an important advantage.

Second, looking beyond the borders of Europe to western democracies generally provides a broader basis for evaluating European experience. The expansive welfare states of continental Europe, whether of social-democratic or corporatist inspiration, appear to have been more successful in incorporating new immigrant minorities into their social-citizenship regimes. If there has been a price to be paid in response to political resistance from majority populations, it has taken the form of more restrictive immigration policies and, in some countries, barriers to the acquisition of formal citizenship, rather than the denial of social rights to newcomers or the erosion of mass support for the welfare state. In comparison, in a number of other countries where the welfare state has a weaker base and immigration is a strongly entrenched tradition, new forms of cultural diversity have weakened the commitment to social citizenship. Social programmes have been defined in less inclusive terms, or a reaction against diversity has contributed to a weakening of support for the welfare state more generally.

In part, the importance of expansive welfare states to the incorporation of new forms of diversity reflects the simple reality that social programmes, once created, become embedded in institutional relationships and public expectations, giving them a durability that may outlast the political coalitions that created them in the first place. In addition, the different design choices made in the post-war period set in motion distinctive policy logics that help shape the response to changing economic and social pressures. In particular, the predominance of social insurance as opposed to means-tested benefits, especially in the case of pensions for the elderly, generates very different political dynamics around the inclusion of immigrants in social benefit regimes. In effect, choices in earlier eras created a form of path dependency in the historical development of the welfare state, creating distinctive logics that shape responses to the changing demographic profile of western societies.[15]

Finally, looking at different dimensions of contemporary ethno-linguistic diversity also provides a more nuanced assessment of the implications of immigration for the welfare state. The resurgence of substate nationalism in a number of countries represents a much more formidable challenge to a common conception of social rights. Whereas immigrant communities normally seek incorporation within the mainstream of society, nationalist movements seek a wider sphere of political autonomy in order to develop their own institutions and their own conception of the social contract. As a result, they contest much more fundamentally the Marshallian notion of a shared social citizenship. Moreover, in the case of international migration, defection from a common conception of social citizenship is most likely to come from the majority rather than minority communities. In the case of contending nationalisms, both minorities and majorities may choose, for different reasons, to withdraw for a common social space. Finally, the politics of contending nationalisms can be a very potent politics, capable of fragmenting not only a common definition of social citizenship, but also the basic structures of the state itself. The politics of international migration seems less likely to reshape the very foundations of social-citizenship regimes.

None of this is to minimise the issues facing contemporary Europe, as it seeks to forge a more multicultural conception of society and the welfare state; nor is it to minimise the discrimination faced by immigrants in labour markets and housing, or the barriers to the formal acquisition of citizenship itself in some countries. Nevertheless, broader perspectives do highlight the extent to which European countries have been able to incorporate new forms of social diversity in a common conception of social citizenship in the last years of the twentieth century.

Notes

1 This paper has benefited from the research assistance of Peter Ciganik and Frieda Fuchs, and the comments of participants at the conference on

Migration and the Welfare State in Contemporary Europe at the European University Institute in May 1998. The author also wishes to acknowledge research funding from the Major Collaborative Research Initiative programme of the Social Sciences and Humanities Research Council of Canada. The paper builds on Banting (1998).
2 For more optimistic views, see Penna and O'Brien (1996); also Plant (1991, 1994).
3 Esping-Andersen's typology stimulated debates about whether additional categories should be added to capture distinctive elements in countries such as Australia (Castles and Mitchell 1993) or the southern Mediterranean countries (Ferrera 1996).
4 Tension between English- and French-speaking Canadians was a subtheme in debates over the introduction of Family Allowances in 1994; and recent referendums in Switzerland over the restructuring of social programmes have received different levels of support in German- and French-speaking cantons. Nevertheless, these tend to be exceptions in the overall politics of social policy in both countries.
5 Nor does an emphasis on a transnational commitment to human rights explain the continued exclusion of immigrants from full political rights in many of the countries that provide the fullest social benefits. For discussions of this difference, see Brubaker (1989, 1992) and Guiraudon (1998).
6 In the French town of Vitrolles, for example, the National Front introduced a special 'birth allowance' for families with new babies, but denied the benefit to immigrant families. National authorities asked the administrative courts to strike down the measure as unconstitutionally discriminatory (Whitney 1998).
7 This paragraph relies heavily on information from OECD (forthcoming).
8 These residency requirements can be waived if disability or lone parenthood takes place after immigration, or if adverse economic circumstances result from factors beyond the individual's control, such as the death of a financial sponsor.
9 State jurisdictions do have the flexibility to provide Medicaid and TANF to new immigrants within the five-year period from their own funds, but it is unclear how many states are doing so.
10 The 1993 Canadian Election Study found that opposition to immigration and multicultural policy was especially concentrated in the support base of the Reform Party. As is seen below, the party's electoral support is also correlated strongly with anti-Quebec feelings.
11 The research group issued a lengthy list of reports on the social security system. However, their proposals for the future are set out in Pieters (1994) and Bertels *et al.* (1997).
12 Based on interviews with officials of the Flemish parliament, May 1998.
13 During two referendums on separation held by the Quebec government in 1980 and 1995, the question of whether social programmes are more effectively protected inside or outside of Canada was an important one, especially for less nationalist Quebec voters.
14 Other regions have since established salario social programmes, but there remains significant regional variation: 'some regions have established important programs that reach most of the severely poor population, while in other cases the programs barely exist' (Laparra and Hendrickson 1997: 528).
15 On the role of path dependency in the evolution of the welfare state, see Pierson (1997) and Tuohy (1999).

3 Welfare state and territory

Jost Halfmann

Introduction

In modern society, territorial borders are constitutive only for the political system. This means that geographical extension (a bordered state territory, *Staatsgebiet*, Vitzthum 1987) is an indispensable precondition of modern stateness. The other preconditions are – if one wishes to follow the German legal tradition of defining stateness – a people (*Staatsvolk*, Grawert 1987) and a central government (*Staatsgewalt*, Randelzhofer 1987). In one respect, states have 'bodies' in a sense similar to human beings. Just as the human consciousness would not operate well or at all without a bodily base, states without territories would not be states;[1] they would not be able to do what they do – make collectively binding decisions for those subjected to government within the realm.

If one agrees that states are organisations (or networks of organisations) designed to use power for the effective processing of binding decisions it seems puzzling that states need territories for this purpose and that states must be immobile. Other organisations in society with different purposes are not in the least as dependent on 'fixed bodies'. Business enterprises as organisations of the economic system are certainly coupled to physical extensions such as production and administration facilities; but economic organisations – just like human beings – can move their bodies and are not forced to occupy the same space all the time in order to maintain their organisational identity. The corporeal 'lightness' of business enterprises is, however, constrained to a certain degree by the companies' dependence on functioning legal and political institutions, which again depend on the existence of stable territorial nation states. In other words, transaction costs weigh down on business firms. Similarly, universities or research institutes as the typical organisations of the scientific system also have physical substrates – laboratories, lecture halls, administration buildings; but not only can these facilities be demolished and rebuilt elsewhere without necessarily stopping scientific work, the scientific activities can even be done while these 'bodies' are moving. This is evidently possible because the

function of the scientific system – the production of new and true knowledge – is less tightly coupled to its physical base. States, however, have
names and derive their identity from a people and a territory; states can
extend their territories and lose some of them, but their recognition
depends on spatial demarcation. The territorial fixation of the state must
be due to a specificity of the modern mode of inclusion in the political
system, i.e. the mode of identifying and maintaining the collectivity for
which political decisions become binding.

The theory of functional differentiation allows us to relate the question
about state territoriality to political rule in a particular way. This theory
distinguishes conceptually between function systems and organisation
systems. Function systems denote realms of exclusive preoccupation with
societal problems such as truth, power, possession or justice which, once
they are established as distinguishable contexts of communication, provide
communicative contexts for organised forms of problem solutions such as
the creation of new and true knowledge (science), the production and
allocation of goods (economy), the stabilisation of normative expectations
about social behaviour (law) (Luhmann 1982b).[2] The differentiation of a
political system within society implies the (permanently challenged)
attempt at tying the use of power exclusively to political instances and at
separating power from other activities in society, such as transactions of
goods and services on markets or information processing and distribution
in the media. It also means that in principle all social affairs can be viewed
and treated as political problems. The operative units that actually process
decisions are organisations. The references made by these decision
practices to societal 'problems' identifies the belonging of organisations to
function systems.[3] Organisations regulate the inclusion or exclusion of
individuals on the basis of rules. Organisations also engage in exchanges
with other organisations. For instance, states extract taxes from business
enterprises and generate political decisions, which provide the legal
background for economic transactions. Both types of organisation provide
environments for each other whose performance can increase or decrease
the decisional capacities of organisations, states and/or enterprises. 'Round
tables' with participation from the business community, labour associations
and government are examples of attempts at reducing frictions between
politics and the economy and at creating positive synergies from the
inevitable tight coupling between those two systems.

Within this theoretical frame, states are organisational units of the
political system of world society. States are the organisational forms by
which political power – the transaction medium of the political system – is
actually processed; at the current phase of societal evolution, states are the
organisational nuclei of the political system (Luhmann 1990a).[4] This role of
the state as the 'identity form' of the political system is, however,
permanently endangered. The distinction between the political system and
the state, therefore, also has empirical relevance; it responds to the fact that

in modernity a variety of other political organisations in domestic (social movements, NGOs, Mafia-type organisations) and supranational politics[5] compete with nation states for the exercise of political rule. In other words, more than ever the state faces challengers to its status of representing the unity of the political system (Luhmann 1990a).[6]

Why then the importance of bordered territory for states? Territory is both a competitive advantage and a liability for states in exercising and defending sovereignty. I wish to develop this claim in two steps. First, I will briefly restate how the territory-based form of centralised rule has succeeded in crowding-out other forms of rule during the evolution of the political system in early modernity. Second, I will discuss the function of territory for the expectation that political decisions should be binding. This will lead to the chapter's third section, which explores the role of the welfare state in binding people effectively to the state. I conclude by assessing the disadvantage of territory for the future success of states as welfare states in defending their claim to the exclusive use of political power.

The view taken in this chapter is state-centric – not in a politically conservative, but in a theory-strategic sense. Modern nation states are taken as 'fragile' forms of social organisation. In terms of social evolution, territorial states (and their more recent successors: nation states) are transitory forms of concentrating political power which emerged, very generally speaking, when functional differentiation created historically new political problems such as the emergence of an international system of states and the inclusion of the masses in the political system. In very different ways and for very different reasons, citizens, other states and supranational organisations are taken not only as necessary conditions of modern nation stateness, but also as irritating environments which threaten the state's capacity for maintaining its unity and borders. From the evolutionary perspective of sociological systems theory, states – just like all other social systems – appear as improbable forms of order whose elements are events (communications) which – because of their time-boundedness – disappear as soon as they have appeared. Sociological systems theory conceives of society as a network of such communications. Under these conditions of imminent decay, social systems can uphold their structure only by permanently reproducing it through communications. Their reference to prior communicative sequences provides communications with the necessary memory, which allows social systems to reflect and identify themselves as continuous in time (Luhmann 1995a). Since states are organisation systems, their types of communication are decisions; the identity of states, thus, depends on their capacity to make these decisions collectively binding and to preserve the capacity for this capacity *vis-à-vis* turbulent environments.

The argument presented in this chapter rests on the following reasoning. In order to uphold their identity, nation states are oriented towards clear criteria for distinguishing between citizens and aliens. Nation states are also interested in tying their citizens to their institutions. Especially within the European state tradition, welfare state programmes were geared at fostering these special relationships between citizens and the state. Migration disturbs these territorially defined relationships and prompts attempts at controlling it. In pursuing this goal, states try to engage their citizens, other states or supranational organisations in supporting their interest in preserving their nation state identity – a critical endeavour with considerable impact on the future evolutionary success of the nation state.

The modern state and territory

Societal associations have always possessed a spatial component, even in their early nomadic modes (Giddens 1981: 45). Political rule, however, is not necessarily territorial or territorially fixed – particularly not when it is organised around kinship structures (Ruggie 1993: 149). This holds particularly true for early forms of rule in tribal societies. 'Clans, tribes, and kinship groups ... are not bound by territorial rule. Clan leaders and tribal leaders exercise authority over individuals as members of that collectivity' (Spruyt 1994: 35). The cities of the Greek antiquity and especially the Roman Republic did, however, exert a territorial form of rule. 'Within the territory they governed directly, the Romans were practical administrators who sought clear and comprehensive systems of rules – uncontrolled or unassigned territory was anathema to them' (Anderson 1996: 14). Although some terms of Roman Law such as dominium (property) and imperium (authority) inspired the legal reasoning of the Catholic church and medieval rulers, the concept of clearly circumscribed territories lost its precise meaning over a period of almost a millennium.

> Feudalism, the church and the Holy Roman empire lacked territorial fixity and exclusivity. Rule was not premised on territorial delimitation .... So, although one might say that feudal rule occupied a given space, inclusion in the feudal structure was not defined by physical location. That is, territory was not determinative of identity and loyalty.
>
> (Spruyt 1994: 35)

Although feudalism was based on control over circumscribed portions of land and of population living on this land it did not yet distinguish between political rule over a territory and private property of land.[7] Only with the advent of the modern nation state[8] and with the possibility of buying and selling land freely – an institutional development which indicates the emerging differentiation between an economic and a political function system – did territorial borders become relevant indicators of the extension and limits of political rule.

Territoriality acquires a crucial importance only in its modern form of political rule. 'The chief characteristic of the modern system of territorial rule is the consolidation of all parcelised and personalised authority into one public realm' (Ruggie 1993: 151). In terms of the formation of the modern state as a nation state territoriality created two problems to be solved by any modern system of political rule. First, territoriality required a centralised instance of political rule, which could effectively control the realm. 'At the level of territorial state formations, the key parametric condition to be fixed was precisely where in society (i.e. around which power aggregation) the right to rule would crystallise' (Ruggie 1993: 161). The second challenge concerned the creation of a territorially defined collectivity over which to rule. This problem lies at the basis of the creation of a criterion by which to decide the territorial belonging of people: the modern solution is citizenship (Halfmann 1998).

The establishment of territorial rule demands clear-cut borders which replace the older demarcation between realms by way of frontiers (Giddens 1985). Territorial states are 'disjoint, fixed and mutually exclusive' (Ruggie 1993: 168): the drawing of borders along spatial dimensions makes states not only immobile and circumscribes the extension of one centre of political rule among others, but also implies that there are other states beyond the borders with their own autonomous instances of political rule. Territoriality as a condition for exerting political power is a rather recent outcome of the evolution of the political system.[9] Territoriality became important in the course of state development with the emergence of an international system of states (Tilly 1992; Spruyt 1994[10]). The treaty of the Pyrenees of 1659 between France and Spain may well have been the first attempt at agreeing about mutual borders (Kratochwil 1986: 33). State claims on territorial sovereignty imply the acknowledgement (or even acceptance) of neighbouring states' sovereignty over their territories. Sovereign states and the international system of states co-evolved and mutually reinforced each other. Territorial borders signify the segmentary differentiation of the political system of world society into states (Luhmann 1990b). The postulate of mutual recognition of territorial sovereignty distinguishes modern states from empires which had always claimed (but rarely achieved) exclusive authority over the whole space known to them. The integrity of state sovereignty is such a strong issue in international law and politics that violations of territorial sovereignty almost always involve the 'community of states' (Meyer 1980).[11] The political relations between states imply accepting the fact that politics also takes place beyond the borders of the own nation state and that states have certain political interests in common, which may even warrant lasting supranational organisational arrangements.

Territory and centralised political authority were the most important advantages of the modern state[12] during the period of struggle for evolutionary primacy among the competing forms of political rule in the sixteenth and seventeenth centuries (Spruyt 1994: 154). Whatever the concrete historical causes – the reduction of economic transaction costs (Spruyt 1994) or the need of warlords for effective administration of newly conquered territories (Tilly 1992) – those forms of rule turned out to be most stable over time which could establish central control within clear-cut borders. Borders indicate the authority limits of one state and the existence of the authority of another state beyond the borders. Borders condense the relationships between states because the transgression of borders at one particular point invokes the authority of the state as a whole (Luhmann 1982c).[13] From the point of view of the system of states, territorial borders are opportunities for exchange and conflict between states.[14] The exertion of state control at the borders is a permanent test of the degree of sovereignty which a state can muster.[15] Because of the political and material costs of providing sufficient state authority over the whole extension of state borders modern states tend to rule over coherent territorial spaces; territorial fragmentation and enclaves (such as Spain's Mellila and Ceuta in Morocco) become the exception in the modern shape of nation states. Stable states became reliable partners in diplomatic exchanges, and international agreements strengthened the standing of governments in domestic power games. Sovereign territorial states emerged as the dominant form of political rule outcompeting other territorial (city states) and non-territorial (city-leagues, the church, feudalism) forms of rule.

There is yet another reason for the evolutionary success of the territorial nation state – the creation of a clear-cut collectivity of people over which to rule by means of territorial circumscription. In replacing the older forms of overlapping and multiple obligations the principle of territoriality was an historical innovation in the sense that it promised to provide an exact criterion for the identification of those individuals who belong to a state. 'The modern state defines the human collectivity in a completely novel way. It defines individuals by spatial markers, regardless of kin, tribal affiliation or religious belief' (Spruyt 1994: 34–5). Historically, the process of identifying those individuals who were supposed to be subject to a state's jurisdiction was in many cases nothing less than the creation of that collectivity by separating wanted from unwanted individuals and by driving the unwanted across the borders to the neighbouring territorial state. The creation of the territorially defined collectivity of citizens was sanctified in the permanence postulate of the citizen–state relationship, which promises that the bond between the state and the citizens cannot be dissolved unilaterally by the state. This postulate originated in the feudal tenure order where it referred to the prerogative of the lord to untie the allegiance of his vassals. When transferred into the context of modern stateness it meant that state membership was maintained independently of the geographic location of a citizen (Grawert 1973: 232–5).[16]

Sovereignty has international and domestic ramifications. In international relations, sovereignty means independence of states from the domination of other states and legal equality among all states. In domestic politics sovereignty means the exclusion of private powers from political rule and the (always contestable) installation of the state as the highest legitimate political authority (Randelzhofer 1987). Territorial borders limit the spatial extension of political authority. Territorial borders provide a spatial reference for identifying individuals who belong to the realm over which state authority is exerted. The identification of those who are subject to state authority was a major logistic and policy problem for the emerging territorial states. Territorial states were founded in a world and placed in a context that knew much migration and had little interest in spatial demarcations. States had to make legal, financial and political 'investments' in their populations to transform them into citizens. It is in this climate that the welfare state and the nation state provided solutions to the problem of identifying and binding individuals to the territorial state.

The welfare state and territorial inclusion

The modern nation state had two ambitions: to determine and control those people who belonged to its territory and to impose legally embedded decisions on those organisations of the emerging function systems (such as the economy) which operated on its territory. The first innovation of modern nation states, which was supposed to bind populations to a territorial state, was the institution of citizenship. Citizenship is a particular form of inclusion in the political system under conditions of generalised exclusion of individuals in a functionally differentiated society. Different from premodernity, individuals are no longer included in society via inherited status. Instead, they are included in a variety of social systems such as the economic or legal system only via specific role expectations. As persons, individuals remain excluded from society and in this respect, they are free (Halfmann 1998). Citizenship is expressed as a particular legal relation of individuals to the state. Citizenship is permanent, a right which cannot be revoked by a state once it is attributed to an individual by birth; it is exclusive, because as a rule one cannot be a citizen of several states; and it is immediate, that is, in the political system no other allegiances are allowed to interfere in the citizen–state relationship (Grawert 1987).

The French Revolution may be taken as the most dramatic event in replacing the older forms of personal dependence by this new form of direct, but impersonal relationship between the citizen and the state (Bendix 1964). To foster this relationship states needed to know who their citizens were and how to make them acting citizens whose loyalty could be counted on. The migrant poor were the first targets of state policies seeking to transform subjects into citizens. This is the origin of the welfare state. The welfare state started as an agent of policing the poor. 'The eighteenth century workhouses were aimed at converting the poor into citizens through the discipline of work' (de Swaan 1988: 44). The disciplining of the poor in the workhouses was definitely geared towards prevention of the poor from continuing to migrate and, by restricting their mobility, turning them into reliable members of the state. The idea behind this policy was not only the attempt at restoring the old order 'which had been destabilised by urbanisation, monetarisation of the economy and religious conflicts' (Axtmann 1993: 41), but also at changing the lives of the people according to certain standards of order.

This was the beginning of 'one of the major tasks of government: the ruling authorities claimed a general competence in the combating of all social disorders for which existing law and custom did not provide a remedy' (Axtmann 1993: 41). As a welfare state, the modern nation developed into an organisation with interventionist ambitions into the emerging social systems of the economy, the education, arts and science. The nation state therefore had not only a keen interest in their citizens for purposes of military conscription and tax extraction (Giddens 1985), but also for reasons of controlling its territorial segment of the whole array of function systems. Over time, the emerging modern state expanded its interventionist role from this early practice of 'policing' people to becoming a moderator between the inclusionary universalism of function systems and the exclusionary practice of organisations. The inclusionary universalism of function systems offers chances, but not guarantees for inclusion; it is organisations which factually include people, but only those people fitting the organisational membership rules. Organisations regulate membership according to ascribed or acquired role attributes such as entitlements or qualifications; individuals who do not meet these criteria can be excluded from membership. Continuous education programmes, social security insurance systems or labour market policies are the means by which the welfare state furthers the chances of individuals for effective inclusion.

From the individual's point of view the major effect of welfare state policies is partial protection from and modification of, market-mediated rules of inclusion in the economic system. This is the standard 'progressive' interpretation of the societal function of the welfare state (Leibfried and Pierson 1995b: 43; Offe 1999). What is more important in this context is the relation between the welfare state and the nation: the concepts of equality and solidarity associated with the modern welfare state cannot be understood without the original restriction of welfare state policies to the members of the nation. This was also the premise of T. H. Marshall's theory of social citizenship (Marshall 1950). From the point of view of the state, welfare policies are meant to impose a territorial criterion on the politics of inclusion in the political system and even of the moderation of inclusion in other function systems. This includes the attempts of the nation state to restrict the welfare state benefits to its citizens or to demand the consumption of the benefits on the state territory (Leibfried and Pierson 1995b: 50).

The price which states and people had to pay for their territorial coexistence was, therefore, the nationalisation of the state–people relationship.

> Internally, states undertook to impose national languages, national education systems, national military service, and much more. Externally, they began to control movement across frontiers, to use tariffs and customs as instruments of economic policy, and to treat foreigners as distinctive kinds of people deserving limited rights and close surveillance. As states invested not only in war and public services but also in economic infrastructure, their economies came to have distinctive characteristics, which once again differentiated the experiences of living in adjacent states.
>
> (Tilly 1992: 115–16)

For this reason, citizenship has acquired a territorial component whether it is based on *ius sanguinis* or *ius soli*. It is, therefore, not surprising that there is a close connection between territory and national identity, as Anthony Smith noticed (Smith 1991: viii).

As a fully fledged apparatus of the regulation of work conditions, of a social security system, of the legal framing of industrial relations and – even in some cases – of governmental employment policies (Offe 1999), the welfare state can be seen as an enormous effort at forging populations into communities of citizens. Strong welfare states raised the costs of emigration and attempted to shut out unwanted immigrants. This exclusionary effect of welfare state politics was a latent premise for the processes of democratisation of nation states. Niklas Luhmann makes a similar point when he argues that territorial borders are 'a prerequisite for a good deal of political regionalisation and this, again in turn, (is) a condition for a sufficient degree of consensus-formation, which makes democracy possible' (Luhmann 1982c: 240). T. H. Marshall's vision of the nation state as a democratic community of citizens is built on the premise that all members of a national society are citizens (Marshall 1950). This vision precludes migration by non-citizens and is ill-prepared for the question of how to include aliens in the community of citizens (Halfmann and Bommes 1998). Migration – even when it is initiated by the welfare state (e.g. 'guest worker' migration) – destroys the tight relationship between the state (as welfare state) and the people. When the territorial clamp between citizens and states loosens up state sovereignty is at bay.

Migration: the dilemma of territoriality

With the emergence of the sovereign territorial state political rule changed from a personal to an impersonal mode. Political rule became immobile and fixed to a territory. The ambition of the territorial state, especially of the modern nation state to tie its citizens to the territory was doomed to fail from the beginning. During its first decades the German Reich of 1871, for instance, did little to save Germans who lived outside of the territory from losing their citizenship (Mommsen 1996: 129; Halfmann 1997). The reason for the nation state's failure to prevent migration is functional differentiation. The nationalist rhetoric raised the expectation that society can be a community of solidarity and that individuals might belong fully to their nation state. But the organisations in modern society include individuals only with respect to particular roles. As persons (that is, as selves with biographical identities) individuals typically remain outside of function systems.[17] And because of their territorial indexation states have problems in exerting political rule of social realms (function systems) whose modes of inclusion are not based on territorial criteria.

The nation state seemed to be the exception from the rule that individuals are not fully included in social systems. The nationalist semantics suggested full inclusion of individuals as persons in the political system (Gellner 1983). But the attempt of states at forging strong loyalties by associating citizenship with membership in a community of fellow nationals was not a long-term success. It has worked and works only in the process of nation state building when citizens can expect additional material or social gains from a powerful nation state. These gains may be citizenship empowerment through democratic government or increased welfare from a nation state's exercise of (military and diplomatic) power over other states. Nationalism is the institutionalised expectation of citizens that their state can do something for them that they cannot achieve individually.[18] But, when nation states lose the ability to promise their citizens comparatively more gains than citizens of other states, then nationalism loses its attraction.[19] Nationalism also loses its attraction when cross-border mobility of people has become a normal affair.[20] This is the case when the agenda of organisations of important function systems (particularly, the economy) is no longer dominated by nation states. This implies that organisations of 'de-nationalised' function systems define membership rules irrespective of national reference. This is, for instance, the case when university certificates of one state are universally accepted or particular qualification profiles for jobs in business enterprises are the same all over the world.

The nation state could not prevent migration (see Bommes 1999: 175–223). On the contrary, welfare differences between nation states were an important reason for workers to migrate. The major cause for migration is, however, that political demarcations of territory are less than ever the 'natural' limits for commercial activities. In other words, nation states have not only not succeeded in keeping their citizens inside their territory, they are also increasingly losing control over 'their' spatial segment of the function systems. Their 'country of origin' less and less binds organisations of the economic system; as a future development, new legal forms of transnational corporations without any direct nation state base may emerge. At the same time, territorial belonging loses some of its former existential importance for individuals; individuals are more inclined to follow organisations or to seek inclusion in organisations in other countries.

Migration poses a problem for the welfare state because it undermines its evolutionary rationale of tying citizens to their state. In many liberal countries, legal alien residents share with citizens of a state the same rights in the procurements of the welfare state. The constitutional principles of liberal states demand that all legal residents of a territory, irrespective of their country of origin, should be treated equal with respect to social security entitlements and work conditions. Over time court decisions have led to the enforcement of equal treatment of foreigners and citizens in many legal and social issues – despite the interests of the state in privileging citizens and in preserving the prerogative of treating foreigners according to principles of 'reason of state'. In the terms of sociological systems theory, it is the universalism of a functionally autonomous legal system that produces legal decisions that may be counter to the 'national interest' as determined by the government of a state.[21] In this sense, the modern nation state loses some of its sovereignty to independent national legal organisations.

In addition, particularly the growing interdependency of the states of the European Union has taken away some of the sovereignty of nation states even with respect to social policy.

> The European Union now intervenes directly in the social policies of member states in two ways: by enacting some significant social policy initiatives of its own and by striking down features of national systems that are deemed incompatible with the development of the single market.
>
> (Leibfried and Pierson 1995b: 70)

Although the assessment of the degree of supranational competencies in welfare state politics is still debated controversially,[22] it seems obvious that in the medium term, national states will lose more of their control over social policies than they will win.

> EU social policy interventions have grown out of the market-building process itself. These interventions ... have created a structure in which national welfare regimes are now part of a larger, multi-tiered system of social policy. This arrangement ... (is) clearly one whereby the governance of social policy occurs at multiple levels. Member states profoundly influence this structure, but they no longer control it.
>
> (Leibfried and Pierson 1995b: 77)

One need not assume that the shaping of national welfare policies by decisions at the European Union level will lead to a European social policy (see also Kaufmann 1997: 132–3) when one acknowledges that the territory-bound exclusivity of state–citizen relations will suffer from European integration.

Thus, territorial belonging will lose some of its primary importance for the life-chances of individuals. For the welfare state, the decreasing importance of territorial borders as criteria for inclusion poses a new problem of control because the internationalisation of access to the welfare state is currently not sufficiently complemented by transnational rules, which regulate the distribution of the financial burdens. As a consequence and counter to growing interstate mobility of people and goods, states try to enforce the rules of access to their territories.

Conclusion

Territorial nation states had evolutionary advantages over other forms of political rule during their formative period. This advantage resulted from the capacity of nation states to bind populations to that particular form of centralised political authority. Strong nation states must try to keep their populations within the realm and to regulate migration rigorously. The main means by which states won the loyalty of their populations was not only nationalism (Gellner 1983), but more importantly the welfare state. The welfare state gave the idea of the nation substance by granting entitlements only to citizens. Nation states like the US with much migratory mobility and small welfare states cannot derive their concept of the nation from the privileges involved in the immediacy of citizen–state relationships; they must rely instead on substitutes and supporting ideologies – a civil religion, the belief in certain uniquely American virtues – for creating and maintaining a nation.[23] Nation state sovereignty is challenged from several sides: supranational organisations such as NATO and the EU, from international financial and trade organisations and from the citizens of nation states (Halfmann 1998).

The evolutionary advantage of modern states and particularly of nation states consisted of their capacity to include populations in the political system and to mediate their inclusion in other function systems. This was made possible by tying populations to a territory and by making individual claims to inclusion contingent on territorial belonging. Hence the importance of citizenship legislation for nation states. Migration has turned this asset into a liability. The legal tradition has made homogenisation and integration of the population a primary goal of the social policy of modern nation states. As a consequence, migrants are turned into real or quasi-real nationals while states, at the same time, increase their efforts in trying (with limited success) to control and reduce immigration. This complementarity between the inclusion of past migrants with residence rights and strict control of further immigration needs to be stressed to understand the seeming contradictions of the current politics of inclusion and exclusion in many nation states.

Their dependence on the loyalty of citizens makes states subject to pressures from their populations. States are either confronted with calls for the enhancement and enlargement of citizenship (left-liberal, 'communitarian' strand of popular protest, Cohen and Arato 1992) or with demands for stricter exclusion of foreigners from the privileges which welfare states used to grant their citizens (neo-nationalist strand of popular protest, Halfmann 1995). Both forms of protest create the impression that states are trapped in their territories and can become captive to their residents' loyalty. Citizens' protests against the devaluation or for a revaluation of citizenship and states' policies at shoring up their borders appear to reaffirm the importance of territory for nation states. On the other hand, territory has also lost some of its earlier importance for states and their competitive relations among each other since the 'wealth of nations' has shifted from the exploitation and processing of minerals and fossil energy resources to the creation and commercialisation of information and services. Herz has argued that air war and nuclear weapons have undermined the military importance of territory because they have rendered the hard shell of states permeable (Herz 1956/7: 488).

In this chapter I have argued that territory is constitutive for the political system of world society because of its segmentation into nation states and because of the territorial indexation of the mode of political inclusion. Territory plays an important role for nation states in their attempt to constitute, identify and maintain a collective for which political decisions can be made binding; this problem remains pressing until today because of the effects of migration on the identity of nation states. This finding needs to be stressed, especially with regard to recent 'post-modernist' debates on the role of territory in society. Within this discursive context, some authors have postulated that space loses its social importance in relation to time, due to globalisation, particularly to the revolution in information and communication technologies (Harvey 1989).[24] There are two arguments involved in this position, which need to be reflected upon separately. One argument refers to the overcoming of nation-state boundaries in the international exchange of goods, services or information; the other refers to the more basic observation of a decoupling of time and space in the process of social signification. The 'globalisation' argument does not really mean that space loses its importance, but only that decisions made at one spatial point may have effects at other very distant geographic locations due to 'space-contracting' technologies. The 'disjunction' of time and space dates back to the invention of instruments for abstract time measurement, such as clocks which allow departure from the early practice of determining time sequences (such as daily or seasonal changes) by spatial positions. The 'liberation' of time from space is also a liberation of the future from the past. A 'detraditionalised' society perceives decisions made in the present as having consequences in the future which can be treated as chances or risks (Giddens 1990).

The social predominance of time over space is certainly an important feature of modern society, and the decoupling of future orientations from traditional restrictions on possible options have obviously extended the opportunities for risk taking, particularly in economic and also in scientific systems. But the political system is much more bound by spatial considerations because of the mode of including people. Apart from the fact that 'hard shells' and fossil energy and minerals still make territory a valuable asset in international relations,[25] territory remains an indispensable attribute of stateness for reasons of political inclusion. Currently, states cannot do without territorial markers when they want to maintain their established practices of including citizens into the political system.[26] Territory remains essential for nation states and that makes them vulnerable to organisations and people with resources to evade the authority claims of the territorial state.

From this perspective, territory might be viewed as a disadvantage for modern nation states in preserving their sovereignty *vis-à-vis* strong competition from organisations without territorial basis and challenges from mobile segments of their populations. But nation states have no functional equivalent for territory. Therefore, states will have to deal with the threats to their sovereignty either by finding new ways of binding mobile populations other than through the welfare state and 'civil religions' or by pooling their territories in supranational organisations (such as the EU) to accommodate the increased mobility of their citizens. None of these strategies can be ultimately successful. This speaks to the fact 'that states, as we know them, will not last forever, and may soon lose their incredible hegemony' (Tilly 1992: 4)[27] and that 'there is a tendency toward erosion of the exclusivity associated with the traditional notion of territoriality' (Kratochwil 1986: 27). And it may very well be, that the former advantage of sovereign nation states – territorial control and attraction of populations via nationalism and welfare state – will turn into a major stumbling stone for their future evolutionary success. But against all 'post-modernist' anticipations of the end of the territorial nation state,[28] it is worth noting that evolutionary alternatives to the territorial nation and welfare state and its accompanying 'political-territorial ideal' (Murphy 1996) are not yet in sight.

Notes

1 This was particularly emphasised during the age of 'geopolitics' around the turn of the century. 'Whatever we may think of the meaning of the state, we cannot imagine it lacking territory. The space which it covers and controls may change; its borders can be pushed forward or backward. But its essence cannot be removed without the state transforming into something else ...' (Sieger 1919: 3–4; translation by author); hence the reference to the corporeal character of border fortifications as the 'hard shell' of modern states (Herz 1956/7: 474).

2 Luhmann's version of sociological systems theory does not assume that functions can be derived from structural exigencies of maintaining societal equilibria. Luhmann choses an empirical approach by studying the evolution of society with respect to the factual emergence of realms of exclusive preoccupation with problems for which all societal forms have developed solutions; but only modern society addresses these problems by way of functional differentiation. This allows departure from Parsons' 'analytic' AGIL schematism and its ensuing architectural rigidities. There are more than four function systems: apart from economics, politics and law there are the education, art, science or mass media systems; there is, however, no cultural system which would provide the overarching integration of society. And not all 'candidates' such as sports have (yet?) developed into functions systems. Finally, as there is no function system in modern society which would treat problems of society as a whole there is no form of inclusion of individuals into society as such. This explains, as will be argued later on, why the basic relation of individuals to society is that of exclusion and why inclusion is organised social system specific – and is structurally precarious because it needs to be *organised* (Luhmann 1997).

3 Organisations often belong to several function systems such as universities which address problems of the scientific as well as the education system.

4 The distinction between state and political system departs from the conventional difference between state and society which is still prevalent in much of political science. This conventional notion of the state carries too many connotations of older reflections on the state as the ethical and civilisational pinnacle of society. This centre position of the state was expressed in the term 'sovereignty' (Koselleck *et al.* 1990). Not only 'globalisation', but already the 'democratic revolution' in the aftermath of the French Revolution have eroded this aura of 'elevatedness' of the state.

5 For example, NATO, which can change the behaviour of non-member states by military means or the EC which can bind its member states by legal means.

6 Charles Tilly argued with reference to the economic integration of the European community 'that states as we know them will not last forever, and may soon lose their incredible hegemony' (Tilly 1992: 4).

7 A distinction which was of great importance for the Roman Republic (Bleicken 1978) but which got lost during the following centuries.

8 'The linear and exclusive state frontier, in the sense currently understood, scarcely existed before the French Revolution' (Anderson 1996: 1). Anderson shows that the prerequisites for fixed borders – exact maps, frontier markers – existed long before the revolution (Anderson 1996: 20–1). The difference to earlier forms of demarcated frontiers results from the capacity of a centralised state to exert control over the whole territory including the borders.

9 For the notion of the evolution of the political system, see Wimmer 1996.

10 For an overview of the debate in historical sociology, see Axtmann 1993.

11 The importance of the legal principle of non-intervention (UN Charter, Article 2 (4) and 2 (7)) in international relations became visible in the reluctance of the international community of states to become involved in what they considered at first a civil war in the collapsing Yugoslav state of the 1990s. Only after having recognised the separatist entities as states did military intervention appear justifiable. On the other hand, the dissolution of Yugoslavia is also an example for the erosion of the principle of non-intervention as peacekeeping operations of the UN also led to involvement in the civil war in Bosnia (Berman 1994). The Kosovo conflict shows that states are no longer free to act as they wish within their realm. The

'community of states' implicitly or explicitly defines a code of behaviour which states are supposed to follow even with respect to domestic politics. That this code is difficult to enforce and that double standards prevail (as the much laxer attitude toward African states such as Rwanda shows) goes without saying.

12 I will follow Tilly's definition of states as 'coercion-wielding organizations that are distinct from households and kinship groups and exercise clear priority in some respects over all other organizations within substantial territories' (Tilly 1992: 1).

13 This distinguishes borders from frontiers which indicated zones of diminished influence of an empire (for the distinction between borders and frontiers, see Giddens 1985: 120). A frontier such as the Roman Limes was not much more than a 'temporary stopping place where the potentially unlimited expansion of the Pax Romana had come to a halt' (Kratochwil 1986: 35–6).

14 Kratochwil (1986) also describes the diverse forms by which the clear-cut character of territorial borders has been modified in the past (neutral zones, suzerainties, protectorates, buffer states) and present (spheres of responsibility, spheres of abstention, functional regimes).

15 It is for this reason that supranational political organisations such as the EC at the same time pose and solve a problem for nation states. They pose a problem because they challenge the identity of states (in the sense of devalidating in one or the other respect the territorial demarcations of the collectivity over which single states have claimed to exercise authority in the past). They solve a problem as states can quasi-extend their territories to deal with transnational problems such as migration. The current process of European integration leaves the member states uncertain about whether the union is a political zero-sum or positive-sum game for them as the diverse acts of reaffirmation of state sovereignty show (see, e.g., the German constitutional court ruling of October 1993 on the Maastricht treaty that the German state must remain master of the treaties (Weiler 1995); note also that the German court spoke of the EU as a '*Staatenverbund*', a confederation of (independent) states and prohibited the development of the EU into a state in its own right (see Kahl 1994; Hommelhoff and Kirchhof 1994). Even though the integration process may have acquired an irreversible momentum toward single statehood, the member states still sway between the impulse to reaffirm established territorial definitions of statehood and to embrace the idea of pooling state authority in a supranational organisation.

16 Until states had clarified the continued validity of state membership beyond their borders by international agreements, the permanence postulate seemed to be quite similar to feudal allegiance. For almost one hundred years (from approximately 1790 to 1870), England did not recognise their citizens' wish to become US Americans and deported British emigrants from American ships whose territorial belonging to the US England denied uncompromisingly (Grawert 1973: 233).

17 This makes individuals who fully 'identify' with their organisation and do not submit to the expected role distance prone to becoming ridiculed despite occasional 'corporate culture'-type propaganda to the contrary.

18 Only then can states expect citizens to do something for them (e.g. fight wars).

19 What remains is neo-nationalism. Neo-nationalism only works for those groups of citizens who consider the mobility of (foreign) people the major threat to their life-chances.

20 But nationalism can be revived temporarily by groups of citizens who perceive migration as a threat to the achieved level of welfare provisions in 'their'

nation state. This shows that the main effect of welfare statism is the creation of interstate inequalities in standards of living.

21 This has been shown for the discrepancy between court decisions and state policy goals in the case of 'guest-workers' in Germany by Bommes (1997).

22 See, for instance, Lange (1992); Streeck (1995a); Rhodes and van Apeldoorn (1998).

23 For the US–American case, see Huntington (1981); Lipset (1996). Due to recent changes in the composition of migrants in the US the Protestant salvation and frontier myth can no longer serve as a unifying theme of civil religion; hence the emergence of multiculturalism as a potentially new content of civil religion – from the point of view of the old myth a threat to the national identity of the US (as Schlesinger 1993 believes).

24 The 'deconstruction' of space has been noticed already much earlier, for instance by Martin Heidegger in his book *Prolegomena zur Geschichte des Zeitbegriffs* (Heidegger 1979), but also by Marshall McLuhan in *Understanding Media*: 'The principal factors in media impact on existing social forms are acceleration and disruption. Today the acceleration tends to be total, and thus ends space as the main factor in social arrangements' (McLuhan 1965: 94).

25 See the hidden agenda of the Gulf war of 1991 which was not only about the restoration of the territorial sovereignty of Kuwait (Ismael and Ismael 1994)

26 Territory is important for the identity of states: not because 'territory is the essence of state' as Forsberg argues (Forsberg 1996: 367), but because territory (next to descent) is an essential indicator of citizenship in nation states.

27 Similarly, in 1957 Herz anticipated 'the passing of the age of territoriality' (Herz 1956/7: 475).

28 See the arguments against the 'post-modernist' devaluation of territory in Forsberg (1996: 365–72).

4 European welfare state transformation and migration

Magnus Ryner

Introduction

This chapter accounts for the dynamics of contemporary welfare state transformation in Europe and relates these to migration politics. The chapter complements contributions to the book that focus on migration politics, allude to the significance of welfare policy, but leave as implicit the question of the nature of welfare state dynamics. In other words, whereas other chapters in this book focus primarily on migration, this chapter focuses primarily on the welfare state and draws out some implications for social citizenship and migrant inclusion. The chapter addresses the kinds of issues, questions, and problems that migration dynamics pose for welfare state restructuring.

The chapter views the current transformation of European welfare states against the backdrop of the crisis of the post-war Keynesian welfare state (KWS). The nature of the KWS is the focus of the chapter's first section. This is followed by an account of the crisis tendencies of the KWS that were evident during the 1970s and the responses that this crisis provoked in the 1980s and the 1990s. The concluding section focuses more explicitly on the question of migration and attempts to discern how welfare state restructuring and migration condition one another in EU member states and how this then affects our understanding of contemporary forms of social citizenship.

By focusing on the interrelationship between the systemic reproduction of the political economy, the social integration of subjects, and power mobilisation of socio-political actors I develop the argument that the inclusion of migrants in what T. H. Marshall called 'social citizenship' remains problematic. The nationally oriented 'post-war settlements' of the KWS were never intended to include 'foreigners' such as immigrants. However, 'generality' in liberal institutions coupled with the mode of functioning of welfare states meant that it was not possible to exclude legally resident 'guest workers' and their offspring from benefits. This was because the KWS institutionalises general social rights like health care, unemployment insurance, and pension schemes designed in such a way that they did not allow for exemptions. The inclusion of migrants into these welfare measures was unavoidable, but politically accepted on the basis of the assumption that migration was a process that was politically controllable and could be reversible by the state. It was not foreseen that inclusion into welfare provisions was producing rights for immigrants that restricted and finally eroded the potential to politically control and reverse immigration processes.

Nevertheless, the unintended consequences, ironies and paradoxes continue: the extension of social citizenship to immigrants – one aspect of the general welfare state expansion of the 1970s – contradicted the imperatives of a capitalist socio-economic system in crisis. The neo-liberal paradigm shift that has been evident since the early 1980s has subsequently redressed the systemic crisis of capitalism, but the consequence has been a serious attenuation of social citizenship that, within the present trajectory, may well continue. If so, then it is doubtful whether it is meaningful to talk about social citizenship at all in relation to social welfare provision. Social services and insurance that previously were delivered and managed according to the norms of universal public entitlement, are increasingly privatised and/or managed according to business criteria for those with adequate purchasing power on the market. Public 'welfare' is increasingly a lower quality product, subject to means tests, and is reserved for the 'deserving poor', who cannot afford private provision and/or pose an 'unacceptable risk' for private providers. In this context a welfare state may still exist, but it is doubtful that social citizenship does. These kinds of privatised, market-provided, insurance fall under the classical liberal category of civic (or perhaps better 'economic') citizenship. Means-testing, with its *ipso facto* particularism and state discretion has very little to do with citizenship at all. Despite its 'social dimension', it is this type of social welfare regime that the current patterns of European integration contributes towards, with the emphasis placed squarely on economic rights, a medium degree of civic rights, and a low degree of social rights (*pace* Streeck and Schmitter 1991).

Again, the role of migration and migrants is paradoxical in this context. Migrant labour is a crucial input in the 'flexible neo-liberal' pattern of post-Fordist economic development. A particularly important effect of policies designed to restrict immigration has been the development of diversified forms of migration that evolve as a result of restriction. These include family migration, asylum seeking, illegal immigration, contract labour and migration arising from EU freedom of services provisions. Apart from upper middle-class professionals, migrants are also social subjects standing in an ambivalent relation to social citizenship norms. They tend to be subject to discretionary state power and discrimination in selective means-tested welfare regimes. On the basis of this, one could make the case that migrants ought to be 'natural allies' for 'traditional' welfare state constituencies of the KWS. Yet, migrants are also more likely to be willing to accept lower levels of payment and working conditions, as well as informal or illegal employment since in many cases this offers them the chance to earn much more than they could in their countries of origin. Their chances do appear to rely in some sense on inequality and not equality and citizenship with important implications for the 'welfare state constituencies' and their relation to neo-liberal pressures on national welfare states that I discuss in my concluding section. Xenophobia and social divisions immanent in the patterns of socio-economic and political restructuring also feed into each other and drive these social groups apart, thus generating sub-optimal outcomes for both.

It may well also be the case that welfare state restructuring has made more visible the extent to which welfare states rely on closure and that they are national welfare states. This can help explain the diversification of migration and the ambivalent relation of migrants to welfare states. Migrants often require welfare provisions, but they are also likely to attempt to realise opportunities resulting from their marginal position in relation to welfare states. In my conclusions, I suggest that the Scandinavian 'social democratic' welfare regimes might provide a way out of this dilemma. However, the future viability of this type of welfare regime requires quite another construction of the EU architecture than the present one, shaped as it is by the EMU monetarist convergence criteria.

The Keynesian welfare state

The KWS was institutionalised in western European nations through the 'post-war settlements' that occurred after the Second World War and can be defined with reference to a number of central policy realms that presupposed and depended on one another. Together, they secured the means–ends functional requisites of the KWS, as defined by the post-war settlements:

- In the social policy realm the KWS was characterised by a system of publicly provided or guaranteed social insurance and transfer payment- and service-programmes. These programmes included pension plans, unemployment insurance, health insurance, child benefits, health care, housing and education. The premise behind this system was that it was the responsibility of the state to provide its citizens with basic security against certain life-risks. Moreover, the premise was that it was the role of the state to guarantee aid in certain vulnerable phases of the life cycle.
- In the industrial relations realm, the KWS was associated with the formation of collective bargaining regimes. These were constituted through compromise accords between organised labour and capital. Trade unions accepted the right of management to manage and codified restrictions on the usage of the 'strike weapon', in exchange

for the recognition of trade unions as workers' representatives in wage bargaining. The latter meant that strikes could legitimately be called, when due procedure had established that agreement on wages could not be reached, thus ensuring a counter-weight to the power of employers to dismiss their workers. The significance of this was that, what previously had been in the private sphere of absolute discretion of the owners of the means of production, was now partially subject to public procedure. Moreover, labour markets were regulated and labour as a production factor was partially protected from market discipline (de-commodification).

• In the economic policy realm, the KWS implied a commitment by the state to intervene in the market economy in order to minimise unemployment, and to ensure economic stability. A premise, rooted in the experience of the 'Great Depression' and the Keynesian paradigm shift, was that *laissez-faire* could not 'automatically' achieve these results.

None of the policy elements of the KWS were 'new' in the late 1940s. They had appeared individually, or in different mixes, in varied attempts – democratic, and authoritarian, liberal, socialist and fascist – to deal with economic instability and the 'social question', since at least the famous Bismarck reforms in Germany in the 1890s (Flora and Heidenheimer 1981). However, for the first time following the Second World War these elements crystallised into the rather stable institutional framework that generated an unprecedented dynamic of economic growth and diffusion of prosperity among the broad mass of the population in the capitalist democracies.

Analysis and explanation of these welfare state developments have often been framed in terms of a polarised debate. On the one hand, the welfare state has been viewed as essentially about social control by the state, imposed 'from above', on (especially subordinate) groups and individuals. This theme runs through much of the neo-liberal (e.g. Hayek 1944, 1960), as well as neo-Marxist (e.g. Habermas 1975: 68–143; Hall 1979; Panitch 1979; Offe 1985: 88–118) and post-modernist (Foucault 1969) writings on the welfare state. On the other hand, it has been argued that the welfare state represented the realisation of aspirations for social rights and entitlements that were required to make modern capitalist society compatible with democracy. According to this version, the KWS expanded representation in capitalist society, through the notion of social citizenship (Marshall 1950). This postulated dualism between the 'repressive' and 'progressive' perspectives on welfare state development is rather unhelpful since the two characteristics really are different sides of the same coin.

Welfare policy did indeed emerge as a response to functional pressures, and in response to perceived threats against social order. These pressures emerged in the context of the 'Second Industrial Revolution' in the late 1800s. This phase of capitalist development was centred on the 'core products' of steel, chemicals, and later automobiles, and Taylorist production processes arising from the technological possibilities of mechanisation (especially the conveyor belt). Given the increased importance of sunk costs, asset specificity and economies of scale, the capitalist economy became more prone to booms and busts, successive phases of under-consumption and overproduction, and uneven development, which contributed to social as well as geo-political conflict.

Social order was also threatened because of the partial breakdown of traditional family and community structures that previously had provided a framework of moral socialisation, social belonging, and a buffer against material life-risks. Rapid modernisation, urbanisation and proletarianisation undermined these, generated increased material insecurity, life-risks, and what in classical sociology became known as 'anomie' and 'alienation'. This development was problematic for capitalist society, since many of its motivational inputs (such as 'work ethic', and respect for authority) presupposed this traditional infrastructure (Habermas 1975: 24–32).

In Europe, political class struggle would prove to be the primary outcome of these contradictions in the late nineteenth century, as indicated by the emergence of the socialist labour movement. The 'worker question' was prominently on the agenda of European political society. Traditional and corporative institutions that had, in the past, integrated peasants were undermined, and, in their place, emerged working-class organisations that proved to be a revolutionary threat, or at least were thus perceived. In addition the 'great transformation' (*pace* Polanyi 1957) of the countryside provoked conservative responses by farmers, whose grievances were a fertile terrain for Fascism and then later for Christian Democracy. The KWS is plausibly interpreted as a rather successful response of social integration to these challenges to capitalist society that emerged after a decade of instability and conflict including Fascism, Stalinism and two World Wars with attendant genocides.

One important achievement of the KWS was that it resolved the problems of 'systems integration' of the capitalist economy. Keynesian demand management, collective bargaining, and public sector expansion proved to be effective means of counteracting tendencies towards under-consumption/overproduction and overly extreme booms and busts. The result was a more predictable framework for corporate planning, and more confidence that sunk costs could be underwritten through stable and expanding markets. Particularly important in this respect was that productive potentials of mass production and the refinement of Taylorist mechanisation could be better realised through regulatory mechanisms that ensured mass consumption *ex ante* ('Fordism'). 'Dynamic' productivity increases, resulting from increasing returns to scale and production-process innovation, more than offset static diseconomies caused by tax and wage increases. This meant that profit rates could be sustained, despite real wages increases.[1] This provided the material basis for a 'positive sum game' in the negotiations between labour and capital from which both sides could extract benefits. Moreover, it created the tax revenue base for welfare state expansion. Hence, capitalist systems integration and the material conditions of T. H. Marshall's (1950) social citizenship co-evolved and could simultaneously be achieved.

The subjection of individuals to bureaucratic forms of discipline and 'normalisation' is without doubt also part of the story of the KWS. And, as emphasised by neo-Marxists, in a political sense, this implied above all mediation and neutralisation of working-class demands. At the same time, this integration necessarily implied important qualitative changes that, to a degree, opened the state up for social representation of these subordinate groups and their organisations. Welfare state reforms were real changes that rather successfully appealed to the aspirations of working-class organisations and other social forces that demanded social protection from the discipline and turbulence of 'self-regulating markets' (e.g. Ross and Jenson 1986: 25–8).

It is by no means a straightforward exercise to determine the 'mix' of discipline and representation entailed in welfare policy. One fruitful approach is to juxtapose the degree to which social subjects are included as beneficiaries in a manner that reflects their self-understanding of their interests with the degree to which policy imposes upon them regulation and surveillance of their behaviour (Jenson 1989). A key distinction in this context is means testing *versus* universalism. Means testing, by its very nature, implies top-down imposition. The state decides who are the 'deserving', and what conditions one has to fulfil in order to be classed as deserving. Universalist programmes imply less surveillance and control of clients, and are thus more compatible with the idea of rights. Although, if universal benefits are to be adequate, they are usually very expensive, and require high levels of taxation (Rothstein 1998).

In addition to this, the question of whether a state disciplines or represents is a subjective one, and depends on how subjects internalise ideological doctrines. A welfare state with high taxes and a high level of public benefits can be seen as more representative if a society or class have a more collectivist ethos, and more disciplinary if an individualist ethos prevails. If an individualist ethos prevails, welfare services are more likely to be representative if they are organised as private insurance. This is also generally the case in 'residual' liberal welfare states (Titmuss 1974), where the 'safety net' of the state is the domain in which the marginalised are cared for, through means testing, while the social mainstream is provided for through the private insurance form. Note, however, the limited relevance for 'social citizenship' in the residual welfare state. Means testing is particularist and a question of state prerogative, hardly a state of affairs compatible with the notion of citizenship. Moreover, for the 'mainstream' of society, life-risks are hedged through private providers and the market-mechanism. This is hardly distinguishable from the norms associated with the traditional liberal 'economic rights', as opposed to 'social rights'.

In the context of this discussion, one should note important variations between different KWSs. These variations can be usefully categorised in terms of Gøsta Esping-Andersen's (1985b, 1990) three ideal typical 'welfare policy regimes'. He distinguishes between:

- *The 'residual' liberal welfare state regime* prevailing in North America but also, albeit in a less pure form, in the UK. Reflecting the strength of liberalism as an ideological force and the market as social institution. Markets remain the chief mode of social organisation. Private insurance and service arrangements are the norm. Public welfare plays a role as safety net, and tends to target benefits through means test. (An exception for Britain is the NHS.) The organisational density of the labour market is low, and collective bargaining regimes are weak and fragmented. Full employment policies are highly restricted according to 'the limits of the possible' in a market economy.
- *The 'conservative' status-oriented welfare regime* tends to prevail in areas where Christian Democracy is strong, i.e. continental Europe. Traditional corporatism and status-relations informs welfare policy, and entitlements are determined according to status. The state nevertheless, intervenes heavily and sets a framework of compulsory benefits. Corporatist arrangements also prevail in industrial relations, where the parties are understood as 'factors of order' in the political economy. Policies are designed to reproduce the sanctity of family. Hence, traditional forms of provision are encouraged, implying that social service expansion is discouraged. Welfare state expansion tends to be restricted to status-based transfer payments (pensions, UI and health insurance benefits).
- *The 'social democratic' regime* is associated with Scandinavia. Here, the labour movement became a hegemonic force, and managed to make universal social-citizenship entitlements the norm, covering the benefit needs of 'society as a whole' (and hence cementing different classes to a more collectivist image originating with the labour movement). These programmes are financed through high taxes. Full employment is crucial to the regime, and is backed by a dense network of policies and regulations. As in the 'conservative' case, corporatism prevails in industrial relations, but arrangements tend to be more favourable to organised labour than in the former case.

Whatever variations there might have been, however, between the different types of post-war settlement, these were all distinctly national accords. The KWS was embedded in the institutional forms of national sovereignty. Social policy, industrial relations, and economic intervention required national state autonomy. Moreover, particularist nationalist 'imagined communities' (*pace* Anderson 1983) framed their discourses of legitimacy. Following E. H. Carr (1945), one can aptly characterise these accords as a simultaneous socialisation of nationalism and nationalisation of socialism.

The connection between welfare and the 'national question' is perhaps most explicitly clear in the 'conservative' policy regimes. Bismarck's reforms were based on the idea of integrating and organising German workers into the national project. (As Bommes indicates in his chapter, welfare norms were closely related to national belonging in the Federal Republic of Germany after its creation in 1949.) In consociational states, like The Netherlands, welfare arrangements are closely associated with national reconciliation of religiously divided societies, through 'pillarisation'. In 'liberal' regimes, like Britain, the post-war settlement was also closely associated with national belonging and a common national experience, based on the sacrifices in two World Wars (Krieger 1992: 42–3). Even in Sweden, where the post-war settlement was discursively constructed explicitly in terms of the more abstract category of class and universalist inclusion, and in opposition to the romantic nationalism of the nineteenth century, nationalism was more relevant than what superficially seems to be the case. As recent research has indicated, this welfare state was encoded by a particular and monistic conception of 'normality'. This conception tended to be conflated with 'Swedishness', and displayed little tolerance for deviance and outsiders (Matl 1997).

Yet, while the KWS was based on nationalist sovereignty, it also had a crucial international dimension. This is of course the case with the sovereign state in general. Paradoxically perhaps, one of its defining characteristics is international recognition in an 'anarchical society' of sovereign states (Bull 1977). But in addition, the *modus operandi* of the KWS – indeed, its very capacity to act as such an entity – was dependent upon the multilateral framework constructed under American hegemonic leadership after the war. Especially important in this context was the Bretton Woods system.

Bretton Woods created what Ruggie (1983) called a 'double screen', where multilateral free trade could coexist with the discretionary capacity of individual states to intervene in the economy so as to ensure welfare goals such as full employment. Hence, the most favoured nation principle and reduced tariffs in trade, currency convertibility, and a multilateral agreement on fixed exchange rates, were balanced with mutual recognition of capital- and foreign-exchange controls, as well as with currency swap networks in case of balance of payment difficulties (Helleiner 1994). This was essential to ensure adequate scale of Fordist capital accumulation on the one hand, while ensuring sufficient policy autonomy on the other.

From a European perspective, it might be worthwhile to note that the European Economic Community (EEC) was to play a subordinate and auxiliary role in this 'double screen framework', where the locus of activity was on the national and trans-Atlantic levels. The 'Luxembourg Compromise', which affirmed scope for the use of national vetoes in the collective decision-making of the EEC's Council of Ministers, confirmed this state of affairs. This is not to say that European integration did not provide important contributions to transnational governance. The 'Schuman Plan' effectively restructured the 'input industries' of steel and coal – economically as well as politically (these industries had been core supporters of Hitler) – and thus facilitated Fordist economies in Germany and France (van der Pijl 1978). The EEC also served as a catalyst for tariff reductions, when GATT lagged behind. But Euro-federalism was at this time effectively contained and subordinated to Atlanticist structures, centred around the OEEC and OECD on the one hand, and on the other, the intergovernmentalism that was a product of the Luxembourg Compromise. Hence, I agree with Ross' (1992) characterisation of the EEC, as a 'convenient help maiden' to the nationalist (and Atlanticist) settlements of this period.

What relevance did the KWS in Europe hold for migration dynamics and vice versa? Immigration policies targeting skilled labour provided a means to offset inadequate provisions of the 'public good' of vocational training associated, above all, with liberal/residual regimes. Most importantly, however, immigrant 'guest workers' became important for the Fordist economy in the post-war period as a 'secondary' labour force at the very peaks of the business cycles. They were brought in on temporary resident contracts as what were considered to be relatively transient 'birds of passage' that could be laid off at downturns (Piore 1979). Hence, the introduction of guest workers became a convenient solution to problems of labour shortages under boom conditions, especially in the conservative regimes that discouraged increased participation rates for women. Hence, migrant workers served an important function in the KWS. They even contributed to financial consolidation of transfer systems by paying taxes and 'pay-as you-go' contributions, without, it was assumed, being able to claim benefits, since they would return to their home countries before retirement, or leave the country if they became unemployed. This was, of course, not to be the case because many of the 'guests' actually stayed. This permanent settlement by labour migrants and the acquisition of legal residence by 'foreigners' raised questions about forms of inclusion for non-national labour migrants, such as guest workers in Germany. This was particularly so since national welfare states had been closely linked to the practices and discourses associated with the institutionalisation of national citizenship and forms of social belonging oriented towards nationals (see also Jost Halfmann's argument in the preceding chapter).

Crisis tendencies, responses and transformations of the KWS

The KWS displayed remarkable stability in its 'golden age' during the 1950s and the 1960s. In the 1970s, however, it was subjected to pressures and tensions that hardly could be resolved within the existing institutional framework. Hence, it is justified to talk about a 'crisis' during this decade. Welfare policy has subsequently undergone significant transformations in the 1980s and 1990s.[2] The crisis was multifaceted, and is not captured by reductionist explanations and the isolation of independent variables. Nevertheless, one central theme of the crisis has been the contradiction between the formal commitment in liberal democracy to universalism and generality, and substantive pragmatism and particularism associated with positive welfare state intervention. Paradoxically, as suggested by a comparison of conditions before and after the Second World War, these interventions seem to have been necessary for a mass integration of the population into capitalist liberal democracy in the first place (Unger 1976).

This contradiction was immediately relevant to social policy and immigration in Europe in the 1970s. Particularism characterised the explicit policy towards guest workers in the KWS. They were assumed, by state regulation and the constituent societal groups of the post-war settlement, to be 'outside' the boundaries of social citizenship. To put it bluntly, the 'role' ascribed to guest workers was to be a variable in counter-cyclical positive economic state intervention, to be excluded from the benefits of nationally specific transfer payment and insurance systems, even when they contributed to their financing. However, as Guiraudon and Hollifield (this volume) document, the consequences of labour migration – i.e. permanent settlement and legal residence – demonstrated that the demands of economic regulation and means-end rationality contradicted the liberal democratic principles of the rule of law and equality before the law. National courts have been bulwarks for the extension of social citizenship entitlements to immigrants in Europe, drawing on the principle of 'equality' between legal *residents*. As labour shortages prevailed in the 1970s (especially in conservative welfare regimes, discouraging female participation rates), 'guest workers' settled more permanently, qualified for residence and benefit entitlements, and brought in dependants who were also entitled to welfare state benefits, such as health care, education and training. Could such a shift from immigrants as an exploitative resource to 'social citizens' be underwritten economically and fiscally in the capitalist market economy? And, could such an extension of rights to 'foreigners' be rendered socially legitimate, given the nationalist aspects of the post-war settlements? As the contributions by Guiraudon and Hollifield to this book demonstrate, the inclusion of migrants into the welfare regulations (for reasons associated with the functioning of these regulations themselves) produced precisely these kinds of rights for migrants. It was not just liberalism, the rule of law and equality before the law that produced these inclusive effects since this does not answer the question of how migrants grew into the position of equality. States still differentiate between citizens and migrants. Migrants are not equal in all kinds of respect, a fact that no court has ever denied. The equality of migrants was to a large extent an effect of the working principles of the KWS itself. What has become apparent is that national welfare states have learned this lesson and that they are trying to avoid these effects (as the contributions by Roland Bank and Andrew Geddes on the denial of access to 'normal' welfare state entitlements for asylum seekers demonstrate).

This extension of social rights is only one example of a broader movement towards entitlement and benefit extension, which resulted from the pressure from 'new social movements', and social policy professionals in the 1970s. The mobilisation for this was based exactly on the theme that the myth of general inclusion in the 'affluent society' did not correspond to a reality that excluded a broad range of 'minority groups' (for overviews, see Mishra 1984: 3–5; Ross and Jenson 1986: 31–3). However, this expansion coincided with, and perhaps partly contributed to, economic stagnation as the Fordist phase of capitalist development reached its frontier of expansion. Hence, the reforms could not be underwritten economically and contributed to 'stagflation' and fiscal crisis.[3]

This is not to imply that migration can be 'blamed' for the economic crisis. The causes for this are rather to be found in diseconomies of Taylorist labour practices and industrial relations that emerged at this time, with the oil crisis contributing further momentum (Lipietz 1987: 32–40).[4] It is merely to suggest that the movement for an extension of social-citizenship rights that included migrants could not be underwritten in the context of capitalist stagnation, thus contributing to the crisis of the KWS.

It is important to underline that the theme of contradictions between particularism and universalism/generality is not only relevant with reference to questions of legitimacy, but also the means–ends rationality of public administration. Ironically, the attempts to respond to demands for expansion and universalisation of social entitlements themselves became a key problem here, generating what Samuel Huntington (1975) called 'excess democracy' and an 'ungovernability crisis'. Especially, it has been argued, the internal integrity of the institutions and medium-functions of rule of law (Unger 1976: 192–223; Teubner 1985) and money are being eroded. The latter took the form of systematic and enduring inflation.

Different welfare state regimes have displayed varying capacities to mediate problems of capital accumulation, social steering, legitimacy and welfare state expansion. Corporatist regimes of industrial relations, associated with the conservative welfare-policy regimes of continental Europe, as well as the social democratic regimes in Scandinavia, displayed a higher capacity to mediate employment and price-stability goals, than the liberal Anglo-Saxon ones (Lehmbruch 1979; Cameron 1984). Nevertheless, this only indicates that there were variations within a general trend towards higher inflation.

The dynamics of welfare state transformation

The pressures on 'governability' resulted in a counter-mobilisation of elites closely connected to business and state apparatuses charged with economic regulation. Their agenda has been, above all else, and at almost any cost, to eliminate inflation and to restore the institutional integrity of the money medium. If this restoration has clashed with the extension of benefits, as demanded by the principle of general equality, then the answer has been a general equal reduction of benefits. The subsequent hegemony of monetarist doctrine and policy practice has indeed resulted in price stability, which indicates that this counter mobilisation has been successful. The result, however, was mass unemployment and hence a clear departure from one of the central pillars of the KWS.

Monetarism was part of a broader movement. During the recession of the early 1980s, business adopted an increasingly antagonistic stance against the KWS in all its aspects, and successfully launched a shift towards more market-driven 'neo-liberal' governance. 'Thatcherism' and 'Reaganism' were the most famous expressions of this. The impact has, however, been much broader. Perhaps most importantly, there has been a paradigm-shift in economic thinking and policy that also includes Christian and Social democrats. These have perhaps not bought the neo-liberal doctrine lock, stock and barrel, but their practices do emphasise the importance of the market as a disciplinary device for economic (especially price) stability and for scaling down expectations for social protection. The economic policies of the governments of Helmut Schmidt and Helmut Kohl in Germany, James Callaghan and now Tony Blair in Britain, the Socialist admini-strations in France, those in Sweden after 1985, as well as the Dutch 'Purple Coalition', are all more or less ambivalent examples of this (see *inter alia* Esser, Fach and Simonis 1980; Clarke 1987; Hay and Watson 1998; Visser and Hemerijck 1997; Waringo 1999). Within this framework, there has been a radical corporate transformation, based on the paradigmatic adaptation of computer technology and informatics to economic processes. It is no exaggeration to talk about a 'third industrial revolution' generating economies by breaking down information bottlenecks in a complex division of labour (Kaplinsky 1988). The logic of 'post-Fordism' is fundamentally based on the strategic adoption of a mix of the following corporate techniques:

- Flexible production and specialisation: general-purpose machines, and a re-articulation of conception and design, increase the scope for demand-sensitive production differentiation, that at the same time is not productivity inhibiting. This requires a more skilled workforce able and willing to take on a broader range of tasks and that flexibly adjusts the execution of tasks, as the circumstances require.
- 'Just-in-time' production: this is a variant of flexible production that focuses specifically on the time horizon. Products are supplied (and demanded) when they are needed. Hence, costs relating to turnover time, stockpiling, and excess capacity can be reduced.
- 'Space-time compression' in economic organisation. New technology makes it possible to optimise the organisation of production over a

larger space. Low-wage production of certain components in the periphery, can be combined with more skill-intensive high-wage production in the core, and final assembly in the proximity of consumer markets, at a lower cost. This is the fundamental logic behind the 'internationalisation of production'.

• Finally, there are economies of increased capital intensity.

The 'third industrial revolution' has changed the terms for economic systems integration. It has reduced the incentive of business to cooperate with Fordist regulation, integrating mass production and mass consumption. Arguably, competition based on economies of scope and flexibility has increased the self-regulating capacities of markets in capitalism. Internationalisation of production has also increased the capacity of business to use the leverage of 'exit', when regulation is not to its liking. As a result, the autonomy and countervailing power of the nation state *vis-à-vis* capital has decreased structurally (Gill and Law 1989; Strange 1988; Harrod 1998).

This increased structural power should not be confused with the popular, but technological determinist and falsifiable idea, that neo-liberalism is a necessary and inherent effect of the logic of the new technology. Neo-liberalism and welfare state retrenchment certainly constitutes the predominant trend. But post-Fordism is in fact a more open-ended phenomenon, and more than one form of post-Fordism could be conceived. Flexibility does not necessarily imply market-determined wage flexibility as long as functional flexibility in the production process and adequate skills are ensured. Here, one can conceive of advantages of 'social citizenship', such as a public commitment to training and active labour market policy, co-determination, and income maintenance (Boyer 1995; Freyssenet 1998; Sandberg 1994). Indeed, there is evidence that the old Keynesian and Fordist formula of integrating mass production and mass consumption, could have a positive (so-called 'Kaldor-Verdoorn') effect on economic dynamics in a reconfigured mode of economic regulation. This could ensure adequate investments, and stable environment and longer time horizons for the development of 'learning by doing' (Boyer and Pascal 1991; Boyer 1995).[5]

Nevertheless, tight macroeconomic policy combined either with labour market deregulation (especially in Britain) or stillborn 'progressive post-Fordist' experiments or neo-Taylorism and high unemployment (in the rest of western Europe) prevails. The result is a kind of economic restructuring that is not particularly impressive in terms of productivity growth. Nevertheless, it has managed to resuscitate growth and profitability, through an extension of markets, and a deepening of market relations (especially in the service sector), an extension of private debt, speculation and risk management, and a lowering of the wage share in relation to the value added (Harvey 1989).

What have been the effects of this on the welfare state? Aggregate figures of social expenditure/GDP in the OECD countries clearly indicate that social policy is far from extinct. In fact, after close to two decades of neo-liberalism these figures display a remarkable stability (Esping-Andersen 1996). This is a partial validation of the 'irreversibility thesis', that welfare policy provides some essential functions that advanced capitalist society cannot do without, because the informal networks that once provided these functions have been undermined (Offe 1985). However, the rate of welfare state growth has been halted. Furthermore, there have been shifts of distribution between different kinds of expenditure, which indicates that there have been important qualitative changes in the welfare state. Unemployment-related expenditures have increased as the full employment commitment and the idea of employment as a 'citizen right' has eroded. For the conservative regimes especially, increasing pension expenditure resulting from early retirement that was intended to contain unemployment increases, helps account for the 'stable' expenditure. Means-tested and conditional benefits (workfare), especially for youth are on the increase, and the level of transfer-payment entitlements has been reduced (Clayton and Pontusson 1998).

This trajectory of welfare state transformation raises the question of whether the social-citizenship principle is in the process of serious erosion, despite stable expenditure levels. The abandonment of employment as a 'citizen right' seems a decisive step in the direction of erosion. The same applies for the shift from general to means-tested programmes (for reasons stated earlier in the chapter). If the current trend prevails, it is also likely that the state will withdraw further from pension commitments. This would mean that private providers – who are key players on the global financial market that disciplines the welfare state, and who are notorious for following the most speculative hedge-funds in their investments – will step in and support those who can pay. But again, this is not social citizenship but classical liberal citizens operating on the market. Alternatively, insofar as employers will take the pension-tab for its core employees, 'enterprise corporatism' (Harrod 1998) would be an apt term.

On the labour market one can observe trends towards re-commodification. That is, supply, demand and price (wages) of labour power are again increasingly determined by market forces, as the economic policies and the structures of welfare entitlements of the KWS are dissolved. One indication of this is the reduced elasticity of wages to consumer prices in most OECD countries (Boyer 1995, graph 2). Especially in the Anglo-Saxon cases, there has been erosion of the post-war collective bargaining regimes, and a deregulation of the labour market. This trend is uneven, allows for variations between more or less neo-liberal and 'competitive corporatist' strategies (given variations of path dependence of institutions and the location in the international division of labour in individual states). Nevertheless, the direction of the general tendency is clear: high unemployment and spiralling pension expenditures operate as powerful forces, compelling the 'conservative' and 'social democratic' regimes towards further market deepening, in order to expand precarious employment in a private service sector (Esping-Andersen 1996; Stephens 1996). It is, however, unlikely that all will find adequate solutions to their life-risk problems and other welfare needs (such as education and child rearing) in the new post-Fordist and post-industrial economy. Many of the new jobs are in low productivity activities, and hence result in low wages. Given the hollowing-out of welfare provisions governed by social-citizenship norms, this means that a growing portion of European society faces increased social precariousness.

The impact of European integration

Transnational relations are assuming an ever-increased importance in the new form of neo-liberal governance. Within this broad trend, macro-regional governance is increasing in Europe, as indicated by the revitalisation of the EU in the late 1980s and early 1990s following the successful launch of the single-market programme and the formulation of a plan for economic and monetary union (EMU). This is not only, or even primarily, a question of a quantitative increase of transnational economic transactions, and a shift of the locus of activity to transnational organisation. Perhaps more importantly, the qualitative practices have changed. I would argue that the new central principle of transnational governance, contrasting sharply with the Bretton Woods principle of the 'double screen', is 'new constitutionalism'. Whereas the double screen ensured the capacity of states to manage aggregate demand and mitigate market-generated social disruptions, new constitutionalism deliberately reshapes state market boundaries so as to expose states to international capital markets and implies a deliberate abdication from discretionary state action that violates market norms. The metaphor of Ulysses tying himself to the mast is often invoked. Thereby, the classical liberal separation between state and economic forms is politically enforced. The purpose is to create a buffer against demands for protection against market effects, and to discipline social actors to conform to market constrains and criteria (Gill 1998). An important effect of this is that a neo-liberal variant of post-Fordism is promoted, as, for example, unemployment generated by austerity policies reduces the bargaining power of organised labour (Ryner 1998).

   New constitutionalism informs the practices currently recommended by IMF 'Structural Adjustment Programmes', the Bank of International Settlements (BIS) on macroeconomics, the new World Trade Organisation (WTO), and the new Multilateral Agreement to Invest (MAI). But it also informs the (core) EU's core agreement: the principles of mutual recognition and subsidiarity are very much in line with subordinating all else to the creation of a macro-regional market-space. Moreover, at EU level, the Financial Services Directive, the Convergence Criteria, the mandate of the new European Central Bank (ECB), and the Dublin Stability Pact confirm that the EMU will follow new constitutional norms impeccably (Gill 1998).

By contrast, the 'voluntarist' and 'inter-governmental' character of the EU's social dimension hardly constitutes a counter-weight to the dominant neo-liberal trend (Streeck 1995b). True, the existence of a social dimension, as evidenced by the Treaty of Maastricht's Social Chapter, indicates that the EU process cannot be seen as a neo-liberal conspiracy. There are other forces at work, other considerations have to be factored into institution building, and there are unintended institutional consequences once these have been cemented that might be exploited by contending political forces. But this does not deflect from the fact that the disciplinary neo-liberal and monetarist project prevails, and that thus far the complex and contra-dictory dynamics of regionalisation have been successfully managed and co-ordinated. Most notably, although monetarist Central Bankers were worried about Keynesianism slipping in through the back-door through the abandonment of the EMS in favour of the EMU, the Stability Pact indicates that disciplinary neo-liberalism has prevailed.

With regards to European social policy, Leibfried and Pierson (1995b) have made an important contribution by showing that analysts like Streeck have underestimated the force of transnational norms. But this must not be confused with a counter-tendency to the neo-liberal post-Fordist trend, and a pre-emption of social dumping. They emphasise the role of the European Court of Justice, and its expansionist interpretation of market compatibility requirements and labour mobility principles. With the possible exception of health and safety norms, these developments are likely to undermine the fragile national institutional arrangements that underpinned the continental-European transfer-payment system. Hence, the tendencies observed by Leibfried and Pierson threaten to undermine the coherence of national social welfare systems, for the sake of market integration. What is more, there is no compelling evidence that a new coherent configuration on a regional level is emerging, that would be powerful enough to provide countervailing social protection against market forces, *qua* the KWS. Hence, just as the label 'market compatible requirement' suggests, it is economic citizenship, not social citizenship, that is promoted.

The dilemmas of social mobilisation for social citizenship

It is vital to emphasise that there is nothing economically or technologically inherent in the neo-liberal trajectory of welfare state transformations that are the consequence of a deliberate and coherent strategy of governance that prioritises the re-institutionalisation of self-regulating markets. Recent electoral defeats of neo-conservatism, such as in the UK in 1997, indicate that this development does not enjoy comprehensive popular support. But those who wish to defend social citizenship have to mobilise and counteract neo-liberal governance at its co-ordinating centres. This is, indeed, a 'Gordian knot' for welfare state constituencies because not only are these centres increasingly located on a transnational level (although it is that too), welfare state constituencies – for better or worse – are increasingly fragmented within societies. Probably for the better, the male nationalist blue-collar working class is no longer the dominant welfare state constituency in this context. It has fragmented from within, and shares 'the space' with among others unemployed, elderly, women and, indeed, immigrants and their descendants (Soysal 1994) as conscious subjects. Although as I have also pointed out, the internal differentiation of migration types means that the relation of immigrants to the welfare state is internally highly differentiated dependent on their legal/residential status, labour market position, etc. The idea of mobilising an adequate solidarity among these 'strangers' is a daunting task. In the absence of this, they approach the problem instrumentally, and are likely to face a situation that resembles 'Prisoners Dilemma' with regards to welfare state retrenchment and their mutual relations to each other. In other words, they are constituted as different 'client groups', which compete with one another. Hence, they can actually be mobilised for welfare state retrenchment as they are pitted against one another, or the fear of such competition makes them turn to the market for protection. As retrenchment proceeds, these centrifugal effects are likely to gain further momentum (Offe 1996: 72–88, 105–20, 147–82).

As illustrated by the contributions to this volume, immigration and the welfare state is a very interesting example in this context. When unemployment is high, they are unlikely to find solidarity among the old welfare nationalist constituencies. At the same time, as Hunger demonstrates in relation to the EU provisions for freedom of movement for services, skilled and non-skilled immigrants contribute to a neo-liberal post-Fordism (including the growing service sector) by providing important 'inputs' on the labour market, that allow this form of restructuring to continue. Skilled migrants make up for public goods shortages resulting from inadequate labour market policy, and they are still a source of precarious labour willing to take on tasks that (still relatively protected) domestic labour is unwilling to take.

Hence, while the evidence suggests that migration has contributed to 'welfare gains' rather than welfare losses (in the narrow economic sense), immigration from less economically developed countries seems to contribute to the neo-liberal transformation. Migrants, excluded from social citizenship entitlements they would like to be able to claim and tend to support (as Banting, this volume, pp. 13–33, demonstrates), willingly take the opportunities that neo-liberalism provides. It is also likely to be the case that the internal differentiation of migrant types provide some opportunities particularly in relation to the other side of welfare state regulations where forms of migration occur that arise as a consequence of the reduced capacity of welfare states to control access to their territory. Immigrants find their way to the territory of these states as asylum seekers, refugees, family migrants and 'illegals' and use the opportunities they can find. For those reasons one could also argue that immigration has consequences that actually support neo-liberalism. This then this seems to create xenophobic resentments among national welfare state constituencies, since migrants make possible the retrenchment they are trying to resist. Hence, rather than forging alliances to counter the neo-liberal project of economic restructuring, immigrants and nationalist welfare state constituencies are pitted against each other, and this generates sub-optimal outcomes for both groups, and adds further to the momentum of neo-liberalism.

The only possible way out of this sub-optimal situation would be to reconstitute the *universal* welfare state, which would have to include '(re-) de-commodification' of the labour market. This would include a return to full employment (or some form of guaranteed annual income) as a 'citizen right' combined with a social accord that guarantees a 'share in the dividend of progress'. Such a reconfiguration would unburden unemployment expenditure and contribute to pension fund and tax revenue, and hence provide an alternative way out of fiscal imbalance – a requisite for welfare state universalism and social citizenship. The main danger of such reform is that it would prove to be inflationary. But the important implication of Boyer and Pascal's (1991) research on 'Kaldor-Verdoorn' effects, is that the expansion and stabilisation of demand that is implied, would enhance productivity growth and hence tendentially dampen inflation.

As Banting indicates, the full employment 'social democratic' regimes (as they were until the 1980s) are comparatively less prone to 'welfare chauvinism', and more successful in incorporating immigrants into the welfare state. The challenge for such states would be to divorce the principle of universal entitlement from a monistic conception of 'normality', and combine universalism of entitlement with a pluralism of delivery. In other words, such a project would build on the extension of entitlements granted to immigrants since the 1970s by national courts invoking basic liberal democratic principles. However, to cement such a project in the broader civil and political society, it would be necessary to further divorce the idea of universal entitlements from nativist conceptions of 'national belonging'.

Yet, it must be emphasised, such a project would have to include a fundamentally different type of economic regulation of post-Fordist transition, than the one that is pursued in Europe right now. This is because a fully fledged welfare state regime based on public universalism is incompatible with the trajectory of economic development. 'Social democratic regimes' are in serious trouble. Monetarist economic governance has been the central cause of the unravelling of the 'solidaristic' wage regulation that was their cornerstone (Ryner 1994, 1998; Stephens 1996). Contemporary fiscal realities are such that public universal entitlements would not cover life-risks. The result is a dualisation and fragmentation of social groups, between those who can insure themselves privately and then demand lower taxes, and those that have to rely on means testing. Again, this brings us back to the sub-optimal social outcome.

The consequence is that there is a crucial link between the migration and welfare state problematic and the 'co-ordinating centre' of disciplinary neo-liberalism – which in the European context means the present content of EMU – and whether it would be possible to conceive of alternatives capable of realising the potential for a more egalitarian form of post-Fordism. As long as the prevailing policy content of the EMU is not challenged, the objective of integrating immigrants into an economically sustainable 'social-citizenship state' is very unlikely to be realised. The plan for EMU is, however, embedded in a transnational institutional architecture that is a human artefact. This means – although it is beyond the scope of this paper to suggest how – the disciplinary neo-liberal EMU might be challenged. More broadly the EU is also a contradictory unity, that not only exerts discipline, but that also potentially offers new and novel sites for social representation. Could these new sites of representation contribute towards a challenge to the EMU criteria while achieving a reconfiguration of social citizenship, suitable for a 'post-nationalist' age?

Notes

1 Most OECD countries experienced an unprecedented phase of productivity growth after the Second World War (the exceptions are the USA, with high growth for a century and the sluggish development in the UK). Output increased on average by 3.8 per cent per head in the advanced capitalist economies between 1950 and 1973 (1913–50 the figure was 1.2, 1870–1913: 1.4 and 1820–70: 1.0) (Armstrong, Glyn and Harrison 1991: Table 8.1, p. 117 cf. Maddison 1982: 91). Between 1955 and 1970, productivity increased by 60 per cent in the advanced capitalist economies, and product wage increases had an almost identical development (ibid. Figure 8.3, p. 121). Profit rates remained between 25 and 30 per cent of invested capital between 1955 and 1968 (except for 1958, when the rate dips to 21 per cent) (ibid. Figure 8.2, p. 120). Apart from the close to identical development of productivity and wage increases, it is notable that wage elasticity to prices was exactly 1 in all G-5 countries as well as Italy, Austria, and Sweden during the post-war period up until the early 1970s. That is, a perfect *indexation* with respect to consumer prices. In the nineteenth century the corresponding figure was 0.1–0.2, and as we shall see, it has changed markedly since the 1980s. This means, according to Boyer (1995) that the wage no longer is a pure market variable. It '[took] into account a minimum standard of living' and the idea of a 'sharing of the dividend of progress', as opposed to merely being a function of the developments of labour supply and labour demand.

2 I work here with a concept of crisis, as defined by Habermas (1975). According to Habermas, through systems theory, social scientists derive a notion of crisis from biology, wherein crisis is defined 'as a state of illness, in

which it is decided whether or not the organism's self healing powers are sufficient for recovery'. Social scientists also derive a notion of crisis from classical tragedy where crisis refers to 'a fateful process that, despite all objectivity, does not simply impose itself from outside, and does not remain external to the identity of the persons caught up in it.... Fate is fulfilled in the revelation of conflicting norms against which the identities of the participants shatter, unless they are able to summon up the strength to win back their freedom, by shattering the mythical power of fate through the formation of new identities. Both notions of crisis are relevant to the crisis of the KWS in the 1970s. Systems dysfunctional signals could not be managed by the standard operational procedures of the KWS, but could only be managed by the formulation of new instruments and procedures (e.g. the 'paradigm shift' in economic policy). The contradictions and antagonisms generated by the crisis, shook up the 'post-war settlement' accords to such an extent that even the identities of social subjects (employers' associations, unions, political parties and so forth) had to be radically altered in the 1980s and the 1990s.

3   GDP growth slowed down in OECD-Europe from an annual average rate of 4.7 per cent 1960–73, to 2.2 per cent 1973–89, despite marked increases in inflation (Armstrong, Glyn and Harrison 1991: Table 14.1, p. 234 cf. OECD *Historical Statistics and Economic Outlook*, various issues). Productivity growth declined from an annual average rate of 4.3 per cent 1960–73 to 1.9 per cent 1973–87 (ibid., Table 14.7, p. 245). Recurring budget deficits in the 1970s led to a doubling of government debt/GDP ratio in the OECD countries 1973–86, from 16 to 33 per cent (ibid.: 256).

4   Lipietz shows that decreases in productivity gains started before other crisis symptoms as early as the mid-1960s. They were originally 'counteracted' by an increase of the value of capital per head, which had an adverse effect on the profit rate. Oligopolies could initially 'pass on' the welfare loss to its consumers through mark-up procedures, but the result of this was inflation. The cause for the slowdown in productivity, in turn, is to be found in the successful resistance of workers to, and the increasingly expensive organizational overheads of, further Taylorist refinement of the production process.

5   However important the economies of scope discussed are as microeconomic principles, as Robert Boyer (1995: 23) has argued, this is not enough to ensure a new type of capital accumulation. They do not in themselves ensure adequate investment levels. Their potential does not in and of itself guarantee a stable environment in which the diffusion of 'best practices' (primarily through 'learning by doing') could be realised. Rather, this requires a wage relation that integrates a 'supply side productivity regime' with an adequate demand regime that generates growth, via compatible social wage, 'normal' profit-rate, savings, finance, and investment relations. This thesis is given empirical substantiation in Boyer and Pascal (1991: 50–5, 61–2). Their argument is that the unchanged aggregate productivity growth rates of the 1970s and the 1980s are consistent with the idea that there is a change of productivity regime, but without a change in accumulation regime. By pooling time series and cross-section data for manufacturing for OECD economies 1950–88, they observed a break in the so-called 'Kaldor–Verdoorn relationship' in the 1970s. (That is, the cumulative–causal relationship between demand expansion, generating growth, that allows for productivity increases based on increasing returns of scale and process innovation.) The slowdown in the rate of growth in the 1970s ought to have led to a more pronounced decrease in productivity growth. This is consistent with the idea that technological change and production process improvement retained pro-

ductivity levels despite a slowdown in demand growth. In the 1980s production/productivity links suggest that the Kaldor–Verdoorn relation has been re-established, but without an increase in aggregate productivity rates. But this has, then, been a period of sluggish and uneven growth and contraction of demand, as well as unstable and uncertain relations between norms of consumption, profits, finance productive investment and wages. This is consistent with the idea that a more stable and expansionary demand regime would allow for increased productivity rates, that would underwrite demand expansion.

5 The Marshallian triptych reordered

The role of courts and bureaucracies in furthering migrants' social rights[1]

Virginie Guiraudon

Introduction

When studying the incorporation of migrants into national welfare states in western Europe, it seems that foreigners enjoy the same access to welfare provisions and education as nationals. Sociologist Yasemin Soysal (1994) believes that this illustrates the advent of 'post-national membership' in post-war Europe, whereby the enjoyment of rights is no longer linked to nationality. In her view, this evolution stems from the diffusion of norms based on residence and 'personhood' crafted by international institutions and transnational collectivities. This chapter offers a different interpretation of the convergence of migrants' access to welfare provisions in Europe.

Some chapters in this volume underline the transnational dimension in their analysis of migration and the welfare state, in particular in the light of the European integration process. They include the European Court of Justice jurisprudence on freedom of movement, freedom of services, and association treaties or the status of contract workers in the German construction industry. Notwithstanding, the extension of welfare benefits to foreigners preceded these developments. It took place within national contexts where state institutions played a crucial role, in particular, bureaucracies and courts. This chapter therefore sets out to study the importance of these institutions in non-nationals' access to social citizenship.

Modern citizenship defined as a set of rights and obligations relating the state and the individual in a bounded political unit is a notion that expanded during the past two centuries to include larger segments of the population and a wider array of rights. As T. H. Marshall's famous lecture on citizenship rights argued (1965), first came the advent of civil rights protecting the individual against the arbitrary of the state and consecrating equality before the law. With universal suffrage, political rights developed. Finally, came *social rights* with the birth of the welfare state and universal and compulsory education. His framework is useful to disaggregate the different ties between the state and the individual, and to understand citizenship as an on-going historical process that expands and contracts (Bendix 1977; Turner 1986).

Marshall underlined that the development of citizenship coincided with the building of national communities. It found its origins in 'the first stirrings of a sense of community membership and common heritage' (1965: 93).[2] Yet, foreigners residing in western Europe enjoy many of the rights of nationals (Brubaker 1989a; Layton-Henry 1990; Soysal 1994). Tomas Hammar coined a word for this historical evolution by referring to settled legal immigrants as 'denizens,' waiting in the antechamber of full citizenship (1990). The extension of civil, political, and social rights to foreigners took place in an order that reverses T. H. Marshall's: welfare benefits were secured early on while political rights remain contested (Bauböck 1995).[3] This is true in both northern and southern Europe.

How and why have non-nationals acquired social rights and welfare benefits since the 1970s? I have sought to answer this question through a comparative study of the evolution of the rights of foreigners in France, Germany and The Netherlands since 1973, when post-war foreign labour recruitment ended officially. I proceed in three steps. First, I explain why the reversal of T. H. Marshall's model of citizenship rights in the case of foreigners is puzzling given existing theories about migration or welfare and I examine the shortcomings of plausible existing hypotheses. I then describe the legislation with respect to social rights in the three countries. Finally, I develop an explanatory model that emphasises the importance of the location of debate with respect to reforming foreigners' rights. This means focusing on the rules that govern the allocation of debate and the characteristics of the organisations (or venues) where decision-making is allocated.

Given the negative biases harboured by public opinion, the media and anti-immigrant parties whose voices can be heard in a large-scale debate, rights are more likely to be granted when they are confined to bureaucratic or judicial venues. I argue that welfare benefits could be granted through regulations after a bureaucratic debate or were the object of court decisions, in venues biased in favour of equality before the law. This is not the case for other types of rights. For example, the granting of political rights such as the right to vote requires constitutional reform or at least legislative debate. Spillover in a wider electoral arena is more likely.

The Marshallian triptych reversed: a puzzle

First, the equal social rights enjoyed by foreigners seem counter-intuitive given the restrictionist policy goals of European governments regarding migration flows after the first oil crisis. The consolidation of welfare entitlements made immigration a more attractive prospect for immigrants. Second, the economic logic of these reforms is not self-evident. They went against the logic of post-war labour migration as a mobile army of cheap labour since they narrowed the difference between native and foreign workers. This logic conceived of migrant workers as 'birds of passage' creating a dual labour market, acting as shock absorbers in capitalist economies and preventing the inflation of wages (Piore 1979). The consolidation of their labour and industrial rights as well as of their residence status contributed to persuading the birds of passage to stay 'here for good' (Castles 1987). Why governments submitted to changes that led to a rapprochement between foreign and native labour is what we must understand. Third, the inclusion of foreigners in the welfare state after the long boom is also puzzling. During the first waves of labour migration, it was in the interest of European states to do so because migrant workers were mostly young, healthy men, who contributed more than they received from welfare services. This ratio changed as family regrouping took place and welfare provisions extended to family dependents. Yet, the move towards inclusiveness continued. The granting of welfare rights is not only counter-intuitive given the quantitative implications of the present context of immigration but also given welfare state theory. The principles of the welfare state require non-members to justify a departure from free-market mechanisms through a community-based solidarity (Freeman 1986). Unlimited migration would undermine the high level of benefits in advanced industrialised countries; thus, the replacement of porous geographical borders by a guarded entry to the welfare state would seem logical.

If we compare social and political rights, there is a stark difference between the incorporation of aliens into welfare and education benefits and the small headway that they have been allowed to make in terms of rights of political representation. This cannot be readily explained. Why would social rights that involve costs create less political controversy than more symbolic rights of representation, especially in a period when the welfare state came under fire for ideological, demographic and economic reasons? In fact, while only parties of the extreme right and a handful of right-wing radical mavericks speak of denying provisions to aliens, opposition to the political participation of migrants is much more accepted and widespread.

In 1980s France, many Socialists criticised Mitterrand's occasional calls for municipal voting rights. The Gaullist RPR (not the National Front) launched a petition against granting voting rights to foreigners in 1989. The mainstream right-wing MPs for their part, passed a law in 1993 that reformed citizenship law to prevent second-generation migrants from obtaining French nationality automatically when they reached voting age. In Germany, the conservative parties have launched a petition against a SPD/Green reform proposal that would allow for dual nationality and ease citizenship requirements on grounds such as the creation of ethnic parties.

How can we account for this sequencing of rights extension? Yasemin Soysal, when trying to understand why social rights have been extended more generously to aliens than political rights points to the importance of the timing of immigration in western Europe (1994). Immigration occurred long after political and civil rights were codified in a strong nineteenth-century nationalist context but it took place as welfare states expanded and provided a powerful source of consent. Thus, foreigners may have borne the fruits of the social aspects of the post-war settlement. This general conclusion is appealing yet close historical scrutiny suggests that it needs to be amended. If we take the case of France, a case where there already were important levels of immigration in the nineteenth century, welfare was not reserved for nationals before the late-nineteenth century.[4] Foreigners were not excluded from the provisions of the mutual assistance law of 1850 and local welfare bureaux ignored the nationality criterion in giving out aid (Noiriel 1988).

There is a partly ideational explanation for this: at that time, social rights were still understood as 'Christian charity' – and also materially the Church still played an important role – and this implied that, as God's creatures, the poor did not have a homeland (Houzé de l'Aulnoit 1885). Moreover, in an odd alliance, the rise of economic liberalism also favoured a lifting of restrictions on rights. It is only at the turn of the century that discriminations on the basis of nationality appear: some laws such as the 1893 law on free medical care and the 1910 law on state pensions did not apply to aliens (Noiriel 1988). So, in effect, the granting of welfare rights to aliens is not an invention of the post-war settlement but a deviation from the founding principles of the modern welfare state.

There might a cruder reason for the different patterns of rights extension. Stated bluntly, a government cannot have people starving on the streets while you can have them not vote. In other words, governments bought out the social peace that was needed for their stability by granting aliens welfare provisions. This point of view is also compatible with writings that portray migrants as passive citizens and equate their lack of political rights with political quiescence. They emphasise passive rights as opposed to active ones. The argument is not altogether satisfying, given that European governments seem not to have been concerned by the socio-economic problems of foreign populations who suffered from unemployment in rates higher than the native labour force, and who lived in dire housing conditions. These situations led and still lead to social unrest and tensions between aliens and natives without governments showing signs of feeling threatened.

A final approach that would explain the difference between political and social rights would be to focus on migrants' participation in the welfare state. The use of welfare services by migrants has been at the centre of a political and academic controversy in the US in recent years. These debates have not been prominent in Europe, except perhaps in Germany, yet the cost/benefit ratio of aliens' participation in the welfare state cannot be overlooked when considering the extension of social rights to aliens. The issue is very complex and there are so many ways of calculating pluses and minuses that no two studies will yield similar conclusions.

What is known is that during the post-war recruitment period and the 'guest worker era', aliens contributed more in taxes and social contributions than they received because of their age, family situation, and because of the conditions laid down in laws and agreements regarding benefits. In fact, the German State Secretary in the Ministry of Labour, Kattenstroth, emphasised in 1966 guest workers' net contribution to the welfare state:

> [F]oreign workers in the Federal Republic pay income tax and social security deductions according to the same rules as indigenous German workers. Given the age of the foreign workers, this has a very favorable effect, at present especially in connection with old age insurance, because far higher revenues are taken from the foreign workers than are currently paid out in pension benefits to this category of individuals.
>
> (quoted in Herbert 1990)

The German welfare state had all to gain from these young and healthy *Gastarbeiter*[5] as long as they did not stay too long nor grow old in the Federal Republic, as long as they stayed so little that they could not be eligible for the benefits enjoyed by Germans once they had stayed ten or fifteen years in the same firm (leaves, spa cures, early treatment).[6]

There was a change when family reunification changed the demographics of the population, when the number of foreign unemployed grew, and when foreign workers reached retirement age. The percentage of foreigners who were part of the workforce sharply dropped. Family allowances are very important because aliens have, on average, more children and fewer resources. Given that the birth rate has been declining in Europe, family policy (especially France's population growth policy) is organised so that benefits are higher for families of three children and more.

Beyond the issue of costs, welfare benefits are seen as a pull factor for migration and, thus, counterproductive *vis-à-vis* migration control policy. For instance, at his party's *états généraux* on immigration in the spring of 1990, Jacques Chirac declared: 'The situation regarding welfare benefits is apt to break all the barriers that we could elevate against increases in immigration. It is a vacuum pump phenomenon ... we are not going to give a certain number of welfare benefits to people who risk being too attracted by our country.' The Assises de la droite (Assembly of the right-wing parties) had just proposed that social rights 'could legitimately be linked to conditions of length of residence, nationality, and reciprocity'.[7] In The Netherlands, academic advisers to the government have recently proposed linking the duration of residence with welfare state access so as to create internal gateways of entry into the Dutch system for newcomers.[8]

A final line of analysis would focus on the calculus of political parties. Who benefits from granting rights to aliens? The record so far indicates that working-class parties, social democratic parties, are likely to get most of the migrant vote. This can be deduced from what has already happened in countries such as Scandinavian countries and The Netherlands where they vote locally and, also, from looking at the electoral behaviour of naturalised migrants or citizens from ex-colonies (Layton-Henry 1990; Leveau 1989). Still, in the case of The Netherlands, all mainstream parties voted to grant foreigners social and political rights and even centre-right parties such as the CDA are getting some electoral feedback (Rath 1988). Either political calculus isn't everything or politicians are acting irrationally.

In brief, the granting of social rights to aliens is not self-evident and requires further scrutiny. The next section examines legal provisions regarding welfare benefits and access to education in detail in three countries studied, and contrasts them with provisions for political rights before I turn to the factors that explain this pattern of outcomes.

The evolution of social and political rights in France, Germany and The Netherlands

In all three countries, nationality is generally irrelevant for the enjoyment of benefits whereas residence and its legality can be important conditions. Exceptions are few and becoming fewer. Aliens can also export benefits when they return home. Illegal aliens have few rights (besides emergency medical care) and asylum seekers have a different status. A 1987 study of aliens' access to social services in six European and North American countries came to the same conclusion (North, Wihtol de Wenden and Taylor 1987).

Welfare provisions

France

In France, the text of the Constitution does not distinguish between nationals and aliens in the area of welfare provisions. Specifically, the 1946 Preamble to the Constitution states that 'the nation guarantees to all, notably to the child, the mother, and to the old workers, health care, material security, rest and leisure.' In a 22 January 1990 decision, the Constitutional Council had the occasion to affirm the principle of non-discrimination on the basis of nationality in this area. Three years later, when examining the constitutionality of the Pasqua-Méhaignerie laws, the Council made clear, however, that the legality of the stay of aliens was a prerequisite for the enjoyment of equal social rights.[9]

If one focuses on family provisions, known as *allocations familiales*, aside from the fact that foreigners need to prove that they reside legally in France,[10] they have the same access to family provisions as nationals.[11] If the children reside in the foreigners' country of origin, they have to show that they work the equivalent of 18 days of work per month. The exact modalities then vary according to the type of bilateral agreement that France has entered into with the foreigners' homeland[12] although, in all systems, aliens receive much less than if the children lived in France.[13] A number of other family benefits act as complements or substitutes to family allowances. Three are known as 'legal social aid' and are handled by national and regional welfare agencies (aid to families, social aid to childhood, military service benefits). For the last one, residence in France is not required; the others do not set a minimum length of residence. There is also 'optional social aid' that can be decided by authorities at any level (communal, regional, national). They include benefits to pay for childcare, or housing. Nationality is not a decisive condition to receive these benefits according to a 1986 administrative court decision.

Foreigners contribute to the unemployment insurance system and are entitled to the same unemployed benefits as nationals or, if they wish to, grants given to start a company. Nationality is not a legally permissible criterion for the granting of additional locally managed unemployment benefits (Prétot 1990). In addition, the 1945 Ordinance on aliens protects them from seeing their residence permit not renewed should they become unemployed. Regarding pensions, there is no nationality criterion for employees' pensions or those for non-salaried residents. If the alien does not reside in France, s/he will receive a pension through systems set up in bilateral agreements or EU law (Chenillet 1990). In addition, resident aliens have access to all additional benefits for the aged, poor or sick persons except the Fonds National de Solidarité that is reserved for nationals and 'l'allocation aux adultes handicapés, l'allocation aux vieux travailleurs salariés et l'allocation aux vieux travailleurs non salariés' (Lochak 1991). The Constitutional Council ruled in 1990 that this situation was not constitutional but a revision of the Social Security Code would be needed for aliens to enjoy these benefits. Since aliens pay taxes, the fact that these supplemental incomes are non-contributory benefits was not seen as a legitimate reason to exclude aliens. A report commissioned by the Prime Minister in August 1997 suggested that the Code be reformed to allow aliens access to these benefits (Weil 1997).

Access to the health-care system is not based on the nationality criterion but on the legality of residence since the 1993 law except for emergency health care and, for some minor benefits, the legality of the entry on French territory of the alien's family. Should a foreigner go back home on holidays or need care for his/her family at home, international conventions apply. Only a definite transfer of residence would lead a foreigner to losing his right to medical insurance on the basis of the territoriality principle. As C. Nguyen van Yen points out, the poor medical facilities in many countries of origin more than the fear of losing coverage deter aliens from transferring their residence legally (1990).

Germany

The German Basic Law states that the 'pursuit of a just social order' is a state prerogative. This *Sozialstaat* principle has been applied to foreign residents as well as to nationals. The field of social legislation uses the principle of territoriality as the basis of rights (Hailbronner 1989: 572). The Social Security Code 'essentially makes no distinction between Germans and foreigners, but is geared to the residence of the beneficiaries in Germany' (Federal Government's Commissioner for Foreigners Affairs 1994). Indeed, residence is a key criterion, not nationality. Equality of treatment regards unemployment contributory benefits and additional assistance, sickness, and accident benefits. It also concerns:

- Old-age pensions as provided by the Federal Republic's statutory pension insurance funds: foreigners can derive entitlements in expectancy in pensions insurance from the times they spent bringing up their children if parents and child were in Germany throughout the period.
- Health insurance: the members of the statutory health insurance scheme's families are covered by family insurance provided they have their habitual residence in Germany.
- Child benefits: for children living in home countries, Germany has signed bilateral agreements and parents receive adjusted child benefits that are lower than for children residing in Germany.[14] To receive child benefits, one must be in possession of a residence permit or a right of unlimited residence.
- Federal child-raising assistance: state-level allowances exist. Some *Länder* (Bavaria and Baden–Württemberg) do not grant foreigners child-raising allowances when the corresponding Federal allowance comes to an end while others do (Berlin, Saxony).

In addition, resident aliens can receive certain non-contributory benefits pursuant to the Federal Act on Social Assistance (*Bundessozialhilfegesetz*) such as subsistence aid, help during illness, help for expectant mothers, women in childbed and nursing aid. Yet, receiving subsistence aid can be a basis for the non-renewal of an alien's residence permit. Finally, although the field of social legislation uses the principle of territoriality as the basis of rights, it should be said that aliens can 'export' some benefits (pension insurance benefits, health or accident insurance),[15] so that residence is not always required for the enjoyment of social rights. The Federal Republic has signed agreements with home countries to facilitate these money transfers.

The Netherlands

The Dutch system is divided into three parts: workers' insurance, national insurance and national assistance. Workers' insurance handles the financial consequences of unemployment, sickness, and disability. Insured people are paid irrespective of nationality. Illegal aliens are excluded from unemployment benefits unless they come from Turkey following a 1990 court case (Minderhoud 1994) but they can receive sickness and disability benefits. National insurance provides child benefits, old-age pensions, and pensions for widows and orphans. All residents are insured. This includes legal aliens but, in some cases, illegal aliens as well. The Dutch Health Insurance Act contains elements of the workers' and national insurance and covers aliens.

The only act that makes a clear distinction between Dutchmen and aliens was the National Assistance Act (*Algemene Bijstandswet*) adopted as the tailpiece of the social security system. It excludes illegal aliens from the right to welfare allowance. Moreover, receiving welfare allowances is considered a sign of 'insufficient means of support' and, therefore, can be a reason for the non-renewal of a temporary residence permit. The difference between the 1970s and now is that this rule lapses for aliens with a permanent residence permit or who have resided for 10 years in The Netherlands.

Discriminations on the basis of nationality nevertheless existed in practice in the 1970s, as was the case for unemployment benefits until the intervention of legal aid groups led to a reaffirmation of equal treatment in this area. The Dutch have also been alert to regulations that put aliens at a disadvantage even if they did not contain a nationality criterion. They were listed in a 1983 report (Beune and Hessels 1983). For instance, a worker could receive benefits while on holiday only if he was abroad for less than 20 days. Aliens often went for longer periods. The directive is no longer applied. Another disposition that no longer applies regarded an extra once-only benefit for people with a minimum income. To receive it, you could not leave the country for longer than six to eight weeks and, because the month of August was the month of reference, immigrants did not receive the benefit (Böcker and Minderhoud 1991). Equality of treatment *vis-à-vis* social security is thus guaranteed in The Netherlands and efforts have been made to eliminate provisions that discriminated against aliens even if not nominally.

Equal access to education and training

In France, education is an obligation since 1936, not a right. In 1973, a decree opened up high school education grants to young foreigners under the same conditions as French youths (decree No. 73–1054 of 21 November 1973).[16] A circular in 1982 was issued as a reminder that education is for all including illegal aliens. Moreover, a 1982 Council of State decision stated that 'the equal access of children and adults to education' written in the 1946 Preamble to the Constitution, France's 'bill of rights,' also applies to higher education (Council of State, 26 July 1982).[17] Since 1989, court cases

involving veil-wearing foreigners' daughters who attended public schools
have led to a consistent jurisprudence that prevents their expulsion from
school unless they proselytise or disrupt school activities, even though a
September 1994 Ministry of Education circular bans 'ostentatious signs of
religion'.[18]

In Germany, education for all is a state mandate written into the Basic
Law (Article 3). The Federal Law on Financial Assistance for Students
(section 8, subsection 1) and the Employment Promotion Act (section 40)
include provisions that give foreign nationals who have grown up in
Germany and reside there permanently an equal right to educational
financial assistance. Moreover, in 1985, the 7th law amending the
Employment Promotion Act gave foreigners more opportunities to benefit
from allowances for vocational training.[19] In a few cases involving foreign
girls who refused to attend physical education classes, the mandate of the
state to provide education came into conflict with the right to practise one's
religion. The Federal Administrative Tribunal and other lower courts seem
to give freedom of religion priority (Federal Government's Commissioner
for Foreigners' Affairs 1994: 50–1). In February 1998, a Berlin court ruled
that Moslem pupils should be offered classes about Islam in German with
the same format as their Christian counterparts.

In The Netherlands, education is compulsory until age 16 and some
form of formal education is required at ages 17 and 18. Aliens have access
to financial assistance as well. The main difference between The Netherlands
and the other two countries lies in the possibility offered to aliens to
register their children in state-funded denominational schools (e.g. Moslem
and Hindu).[20] In light of the high rate of unemployment among ethnic
minorities in The Netherlands, there has also been an accrued effort in the
area of job training.

Political rights

Out of three cases examined here, the only country where aliens have
gained electoral rights is The Netherlands. For the first time in 1986, aliens
who had been legally residing for three years could vote and stand as
candidates in local elections. Beforehand, foreign residents had been
allowed to participate in elections for neighbourhood councils, which had
been introduced in big cities such as Rotterdam and Amsterdam. Another
right traditionally considered to be reserved for nationals, the right to work
in the public sector except in 'sensitive posts' (*vertrouwenfuncties*), was also
extended to aliens after a bill was submitted in 1985 to repeal the Act of
1858 on this matter.[21]

In Germany, since 1982, all parties except the CSU and the extreme-
right accept foreigners as party members. They had first been allowed to
do so in 1967 (Dohse 1981). Foreigners also participate in a number of
consultative committees. Yet, there are a number of constraints on the

political activity of aliens. Aliens cannot vote or stand as candidates in local, regional and national elections. The only exception regards EU nationals in local and EP elections. The constitutional court voided an attempt by two Ländern to grant resident aliens the right to vote in local elections in 1990. In this respect, 'the tension between cosmopolitan and ethno-nationalist constitutional norms that were originally incorporated in the Basic Law has not disappeared to this day' (Oberndörfer 1991). A revision of the Basic Law would be necessary to allow resident aliens to obtain electoral and eligibility rights. The constitutional court argued that the inclusion of migrants in the political sphere could be achieved by passing a law easing naturalisation requirements.

In France, prior to 1981, many aliens who were trade union activists or human rights workers were expelled on the grounds that they had not 'respected the political neutrality to which any foreigner residing on French territory is bound' (Wihtol de Wenden 1988). The grounds for expulsion was 'breaching public order'. There even were restrictions on political participation for aliens that had become French citizens. Until 1981, naturalised aliens could not vote or be eligible for a period of five years. They had to wait ten years to be granted electoral rights or work in the public sector until a law passed in April 1975 (Weil 1991). Aliens cannot vote in local or national elections in France. The only constitution that allowed it was the short-lived Constitution of 1793. The exercising of political authority extends to the administration. Civil service is reserved for nationals in France (article 5, paragraph 1 of 13 July 1983 law) although exceptions have existed since the late 1970s.[22] Some EU citizens now can since the passing of the law 91–715 of 26 July 1991 following France's condemnation by the European Court of Justice (for not respecting article 48, paragraph 4 of the Treaty of Rome).[23]

Overall, there have been improvements in the status of aliens and the rights that they enjoy yet the process of rights extension has not gone as far in all countries for all types of rights.

When rules facilitate the stealth of the executive

The rules that govern reform go a long way towards explaining why reforms extending certain types of rights are bound to spill over from the executive arena (political rights) whereas others will not (social rights). Granting voting rights to foreigners entails constitutional revision and thus legislative passage by a large coalition. This means that a public discussion on the issue is almost inevitable and bound to be long and divisive as all sorts of larger debates will resurface (e.g. on the definition of the nation) thus hampering chances for reform.

Welfare benefits do not obey the same rules as political rights. In their case, regulatory changes often suffice; or they can be extended by the passing of a bill that includes many social measures so as to divert attention from the benefits attributed to foreigners.[24] In any case, they only need to be adopted by a simple majority. In a number of cases, legal texts are neutral as far as nationality is concerned. The issue is to render effective rights that exist only on paper or inversely to stop applying old regulations rather than to adopt new laws. It is less likely that reforms that only require a clarification in the form of an information note to welfare providers or a circular will need the approval of other ministries. These are in some sense circulars that do not circulate. These facts facilitate the adoption of social benefits. It should be noted that rules here vary across types of rights rather than across countries.

Still, one may ask why state bureaucracies favour equal social rights for aliens? Starting in the 1970s, there was a concern with the costs of special programmes for migrants. What transpires from policy documents in the three countries studied, however, is that equality in law is important because it replaces special services and is thus less costly.

Furthermore, although each country had a different attitude towards the inclusion of migrants in society, they all converged around the idea of equal social rights. In Germany, equal social rights for foreigners conform to the territorial principle on which the national welfare system is based. Moreover, incorporating migrants into existing legal and bureaucratic structures seems more politically acceptable than setting up special programs and special rules for migrants as part of an incorporation policy. Having an incorporation policy would have meant acknowledging that Germany was an *Einwanderungsland* which governments have refused to do. In addition, it would have been difficult to realise given German federalism, a system that leaves the states leeway in the area of social and cultural policy. France does not deny that it is an immigration country yet balks at instituting policies that emphasise the right to difference. Equality of rights is, therefore, a more acceptable solution than differential treatment of populations and is compatible with the overarching Republican paradigm. The Netherlands set up a multiculturalist framework in the early 1980s. Notwithstanding, the expert report on ethnic minorities that inspired it and the government document that followed insisted that non-legal discrimination on the basis of nationality was a prerequisite (WRR 1979; Opwet-Minderhedennota 1981). In summary, for different reasons, equal social rights fitted with the dominant norms on migrant incorporation and afforded bureaucracies a solution that required less organisational costs.

Therefore, welfare benefits have been less discussed in a large public sphere than have political rights and have largely remained a bureaucratic problem. There is an interesting 'false exception' to this general dynamic: child allowances. This benefit stands out as having been at the centre of politically charged discussions in all three countries studied and one of the rare welfare provisions that clearly distinguishes between aliens and citizens. Except in The Netherlands, aliens receive a lesser amount of allowance if their children stay in the alien's country of origin. In The Netherlands, however, there is regular debate about the issue. Whenever the budget is discussed in parliament, someone raises the issue, an occurrence Ruud Lubbers contextualised as part of the restructuring of the Dutch welfare state and the discourse on the abuse of the social security system by natives and migrants alike.[25] Budget discussions are one of the few moments when one can truly predict issue salience: every time a new budget is under scrutiny. We would expect allowances to be reduced for children abroad if it is politicised in a context of fiscal austerity and welfare bashing. In The Netherlands, however, reform has been delayed for lack of consensus although it is important to note that the Left and the Right have both changed their position.

The effect of linking the amount of child allowances and their place of residence is not a clear-cut issue. When the German government in the 1970s said that they would diminish *Kindergeld* for children residing abroad, they spurred a wave of family reunification. Therefore, from the standpoint of migration control agencies (at the Ministry of Justice),[26] it is counterproductive to give less money to aliens. It is now, in fact, those responsible for integration policy who want to use benefit differentials so that aliens bring their children sooner: this way children can adapt and do better in the host society educational system. These arguments are outcome-oriented and typical of a bureaucratic perspective. They differ from those inspired by political rhetoric and ideology. In politicians' debates, the arguments oppose those who argue for equal benefits and stress the importance of equality before the law and those who favour unequal benefits and argue that 'children allowances should not be paying for the development of entire villages in Turkey'.[27] In brief, this is a case where there might be a contradiction between desirable policy outcomes and lucrative political discourse. It further shows that whether a state bureaucracy or an assembly of political party representatives is responsible for policy decisions yields opposite results. No ideological camp can have their cake and eat it too, this situation hampers reform.[28]

In cases where rules allow flexibility in the way in which policy change is enacted, the expansion of debate is more likely to come from the existence of conflict among policy-makers since 'where there is little or no conflict, policies tend overwhelmingly to be made by small groups of experts in specialized policy communities far from the view of the public' (Baumgartner 1989: 213). In the case at hand, this refers to the governmental agencies in charge of immigrants. It is in their interest to do their work stealthily. It is significant that the main mode of change has been the enactment of unpublicised decrees and circulars. Stealth becomes arduous, however, when agencies have competing aims, for instance, between ministries in charge of social issues and ministries in charge of border controls as we have seen in the case of family allowances. Still, social rights are much less politicised than political rights thanks to legal rules for reform.

The role of the legal sphere

Another venue that has been conducive to guaranteeing equal rights for aliens is the courts. For example, in France, the Council of State and the Constitutional Council have been instrumental in consolidating the welfare rights of foreigners. In 1985, the Paris municipal council headed by Jacques Chirac, as part of its pro-fertility policy, decided to grant a new non-contributive benefit (*l'allocation municipale de congé parental d'éducation pour le 3ème enfant*) only to nationals. The administrative tribunal of Paris tribunal cancelled the decision on 19 March 1986 and, when it was appealed, the Council of State confirmed the judgement of the tribunal on 30 June 1989.[29] Both jurisdictions insisted on a strict application of the universality of rights. On 22 January 1990, the Constitutional Council struck down a legislative measure that extended a non-contributive benefit (*l'allocation adulte handicapé*) to non-nationals but only to EU nationals. It reaffirmed that exclusion of foreigners from welfare benefits is against 'the constitutional principles of equality'. All along the judicial chain, the principle of non-discrimination was further strengthened.

In Germany as well, high courts have affirmed the principle of equality before the law in the area of social rights for aliens. The landmark case dates back to 1979, when the Federal Constitutional Court ruled on a case involving pension payments to a Brazilian and a Guatemalan (decision of 20 March 1979, in *Entscheidungen des Bundesverfassungsgerichts* 51: 1). Under the Salaried Employees' Social Security Act, pension payments were suspended if a former employee or his/her surviving spouse left voluntarily the FRG unless s/he was German or a national of a country that had signed a reciprocity agreement. The government justified the statute as a bargaining lever during the international negotiations of social security treaties. The Court did not find the argument convincing and invalidated the federal statute. The substance of the case involved social protection, and German constitutional law sets as a government goal 'a just social order' and the court underlined the importance of social insurance law. Yet, it is precisely on that account that the decision is interesting: the 'social state principle' that defined post-war Germany was also in the eyes of the court to be enjoyed by non-Germans.

In The Netherlands, legal aid groups for migrants fought in the 1970s through the courts and through lobbying to overturn successfully discriminatory practices in the area of welfare benefits. Until the mid-1970s, immigrant workers only received unemployment benefits for six months and it was a customary administrative practice to take away their residence rights and expel them if they had not found a job after three or six months. Dutch workers are entitled to two and a half years of benefits but unemployment legislation stated that legally employed foreigners were a special category (Groenendijk 1989). Moreover, municipalities would distribute benefits *à la tête du client* rather than the full legal amount – 300 or 400 guilders instead of 1,000 for instance.[30]

The role of courts in upholding aliens' rights has not been limited to social rights. Since the 1970s, administrative and constitutional courts have issued rulings that significantly circumscribed bureaucratic discretion regarding the entry and stay of aliens, and reaffirmed consistently the principle of non-discrimination on the basis of nationality in cases involving civil rights. This has been the case even in France where courts are often considered a weak and dependent junior partner in the hierarchy of powers. This positive bias towards foreigners' rights derives from the distinct *modus operandi* of courts. Scholars in comparative politics have begun to 'bring the courts back in' (Stone 1992) as full-time actors in social reform echoing an older debate in American legal studies about the role of the courts as agents of societal change (Horowitz 1977; Rosenberg 1991).

Alec Stone has argued that European courts 'were less determined and more insulated from both concrete social interests and from political struggle taking place in other state institutions' (1992: 13). Given this insulation of courts from electoral politics, their attitude confirms my hypothesis that foreigners' rights are best discussed behind closed doors than in a media-covered electoral arena where xenophobic voices can be heard. Moreover, high courts have a positive bias towards equal rights of foreigners because of their mode of functioning.

A crucial element if courts want to establish their legitimacy is consistency. In other words, if they treat different groups/constituencies differently, they will not be credible as neutral arbiters. Martin Shapiro has argued that the 'triadic model of justice' implies that judges must act neutrally to insure their legitimacy (1981). All the decisions on aliens are presented and debated in the courts as a balancing of state interests and individual freedom based on the notion of proportionality. This mode of reasoning specific to the legal world contrasts with the power relations that migrants may face in the sphere of politics.

There was also a legal basis to further migrant social rights. Constitutions often use expressions like 'every one', 'all' when outlining rights. Therefore, once the courts had been solicited, they disregarded nationality as a criterion for the attribution of rights.[31] Moreover, courts are also responsive to 'public interest' ideas (Schuck 1998). They apply principles such as due process and equal treatment to fill in the law when basic texts are not explicit. For example, as aliens' length of residence increased, German courts opened up rights that were reserved for aliens on the ground that aliens had nowhere else to go (*Rechtsschicksal der Unentrinnbarkeit*) and, in this way, narrowed the distinction between citizen and human rights. European high courts have also drawn upon norms of constitutional and administrative legal norms that had long been established in other areas.

The role of the courts will remain crucial as guarantors of the social rights of aliens during the age of welfare retrenchment and strict migration control policy. Recent developments where courts applied EEC association treaties with Turkey, the Maghreb, and ACP/AP countries to acknowledge certain welfare rights for migrants show that international and national legal texts can have great resonance once the juridicisation of immigration politics has occurred. Even in the case of posted workers in European countries,[32] in particular project-tied workers, whose status seemed to exclude them from national social security and labour law protection, courts have tended towards integrating them in the receiving country's welfare state system and labour market (Groenendijk and Hampsink 1994).

Conclusion

As we have seen, the inclusion of legally residing foreigners in the welfare state has been quite extensive during the last decades in spite of the fact that it ran against some of the policy goals of migration control policy and against the closed logic of the welfare state. It is also counter-intuitive that the rights that entailed redistributive costs were granted more easily than regulatory ones. The reasons for such inclusiveness lie in the institutional trajectory of reforms. Unlike other rights such as voting rights, rules allowed for a lower visibility of the reform process. This implies that the voting public who might have felt the diffuse costs of the inclusion of foreigners in the welfare state was largely unaware of them. Moreover, the organisations where debate on the issue was allocated such as courts and social bureaucracies, seem to have been positively biased in favour of equal treatment for reasons that originate in their own functioning. Put simply, bureaucracies standardise operations and courts seek coherence in the application of legal principles. This helped migrants gain access to welfare benefits. In this respect, the conclusions presented here concur with studies of social policy such as Hugh Heclo's that have underlined that much policy-making is elaborated away from the public eye (Heclo 1974; Heclo and Wildavsky 1981).

Moreover, they are relevant in the area of welfare state studies at a time of transformation and/or retrenchment.[33] In a word, welfare rights reforms can be labelled 'unpopular' implying that parties in power can expect to be penalised at the next election for passing them. Therefore, they inscribe themselves within a much larger set of policies where one would expect policy haters to outweigh the beneficiaries and supporters of policy change in the current 'politics in hard times' or 'age of high unemployment' in Europe (Pierson 1994, 1996b; Esping-Andersen 1985a).[34]

If they want to maintain their chances of re-election or avoid social unrest, political leaders find it in their interest to avoid being blamed for the passing of unpopular reforms. Some scholars have identified a number of strategies to achieve 'blame avoidance' (Weaver 1986). They include playing constituencies against one another, compensating vital ones, and making it hard for voters to trace the responsibility either by seeking a wide consensus or by lowering the visibility of reform. In the case of foreigners' rights, these strategies include shifting debate to venues that are sheltered from electoral fallout and whose functioning is biased towards programme or norms expansiveness.

Notes

1 I am indebted to the participants of the European Forum conference on Migration and the Welfare State in May 1998 in Florence, Italy, for their comments and, in particular to Andrew Geddes and Michael Bommes for their careful reading of the draft of this chapter.
2 Or, as Jürgen Habermas wrote, 'nationalism … founded a collective identity that played a functional role in the implementation of citizenship' (1994: 23).
3 For a discussion of this aspect of T. H. Marshall's model and its applicability to current developments in Europe, see Crowley (1998).
4 There might be interference in the argument with T. H. Marshall's account of the evolution of citizenship rights since his focus is on Great Britain – a country that stigmatised social welfare much earlier than its continental counterparts (Esping-Andersen 1990).
5 The labour contracts did not specify social welfare provisions. It was made clear, however, that aliens had the duty to pay taxes in Germany and generally had the right to send earnings home, for contract samples see Schill (1965).
6 Neglecting housing conditions for guest workers also made considerable savings.
7 *Le Monde Diplomatique*, May 1993. My translation.
8 Han Entzinger's 1994 proposals to the Dutch government. Interview, ERCOMER, Utrecht, 1995.
9 In fact, the appearance of the condition of legality of stay dates back to a 1986 law on family provisions and it was extended in the 24 August 1993 law to health, family, invalidity and life insurance, as well as pensions. It is only after that law that the Constitutional Council clarified its stance.
10 Article 512–2 of the Social Security Code (modified by the law 86–1307 of 29 December 1986 to add the legal status of children older than 16 as a criterion for receiving provisions).
11 Article 512–1 of the Social Security Code states that 'toute personne française ou étrangère résidant en France, bénéficie pour ses enfants des prestations familiales dans les conditions prévues par le présent livre'.
12 For a summary, see 'L'immigré et sa famille: les prestations familiales des immigrés' in Alfandari (1990).
13 This inequality is partly remedied by the facts that Fonds d'Action Sociale is funded in part by the money that aliens contribute without being able to get benefits in return.
14 The figures for benefits differ as follows: DM10 as opposed to DM70 for the first child; DM25 as opposed to DM130 for the second; DM60 as opposed to DM220 for the third (Federal Ministry of the Interior 1993).
15 They cannot export unemployment benefits, however, since they are only paid if the receiver is available for work in Germany.
16 The family of the youth has to reside in France, according to an internal letter of instructions (Lochak 1991).
17 The case was brought by GISTI and the CFDT (Heymann-Doat 1994: 132).
18 For an extensive presentation of the existing jurisprudence, see Commission Nationale Consultative des Droits de l'Homme (1996).
19 The Federal Law on the Promotion of Education and Training was amended

in 1986 to include a similar improvement (10th Act to amend the Bundesausbildungsförderungsgesetz, June 16 1986).

20 In addition, one should mention that certain aspects of migration policy affect the education of foreign children but they are not individual or group rights. One would be extra funds allocated to schools with a certain percentage of immigrant children (in The Netherlands and in French ZEPs (Priority Education Zones) since the 1980s). The other regards education in the language and culture of foreign parents.

21 The actual act was published on 20 April 1988 (Stb 1988, n14231). See Groenendijk (1989). In fact there already were foreigners working for the state (in hospitals, schools, the railway system and cleaning services) but in contractually precarious positions whereas, with the new law, they obtained civil servant status with all the attached benefits. See the 1993 Ministry of Interior Survey *Ethnische Minderheden bij de Overheid*. If this was symbolically important as an example of the de-linking of nationality and citizenship rights in the *res publica*, it was also significant as a way of enhancing socio-economic opportunities for migrants given that the public sector employed 825,000 people at the time (1984 statistics, excluding the army, Groenendijk 1989).

22 This means that one may find foreign teachers, doctors or public employees in France who do not enjoy the same status as French public sector workers in terms of job guarantees, pay and benefits.

23 In Germany, access to the public service is to a large extent reserved for nationals.

24 French Minister of Health Simone Weil resorted to this technique in the 1990s to give equal professional rights to foreign doctors. In Germany, including the question of child benefits for aliens in a wide ranging tax reform of 1975 is another example of diversion.

25 Interview, Ruud Lubbers, Former Prime Minister of The Netherlands, Cambridge, MA, April 1996.

26 In The Netherlands, civil servants of the IND in the Ministry of Justice remember the German example. Interview with Mr de Boer, Natalie Jonkers, Nicolas Franken, Ministry of Justice, The Hague, February 1995.

27 Example of discourse given by Ruud Lubbers in interview op. cit.

28 One has to choose between (1) less family reunion but more benefits for aliens or (2) equal benefits for aliens but unsuccessful integration.

29 See *Plein Droit*, February 1989 and November 1990 issues.

30 Interview, Kees Groenendijk, Faculty of Law, Nijmegen, June 1995.

31 There again, the contrast with political rights is striking, since domestic constitutions but also international human rights texts such as the European Convention of Human Rights and Fundamental Freedoms (Article 16) reserve political rights to nationals.

32 This is in the case of posted workers that the tension between freedom of services and European social policy is most at odds and where ECJ rulings seem to favour the former. See Eichhorst (1998).

33 Just how much retrenchment has taken place is obviously a matter for debate among welfare state analysts. See van Kersbergen (1997) for a review. See Alber (1996) and Pontusson and Clayton (1998) for proponents of the retrench-ment thesis. See Pierson (1996b) and Stephens, Huber and Ray (1996) for comparative analyses emphasising the resilience of the welfare state.

34 For an interesting study on elite strategies and success at imposing welfare reforms in Spain and Portugal, see Glatzer (1997).

6 National welfare state, biography and migration

Labour migrants, ethnic Germans and the re-ascription of welfare state membership

Michael Bommes

Introduction

In modern society individuals are not 'members of society'. The chances to become included in different social realms – the economy, law, politics, education, health and the family – are no longer based on descent, or belonging to a social strata, or to an ethnic or religious group. It is individuals themselves that principally achieve inclusion in these different social realms and the risks of failure are high. Consequently, if we understand modern national welfare states as organisational complexes which try to heighten the chances of inclusion and minimise risks of exclusion for their citizens, then one central structural form of providing inclusion has been the institutionalisation of *the modern life course* (Kohli 1985). In this chapter, I discuss the reasons why this institutionalisation of the life course and the safeguard within it of individuals with a structured biography have become central for the mode of operation of welfare states. I then show that migrations that transgress state borders highlight some very specific social preconditions of these arrangements for inclusion. If biographies are understood as the result of a sequential process in which chances for social participation, supported by welfare states, are accumulated, then migrants are likely to be structurally poor because of their specific relation to national welfare states.

The chapter then develops these core observations with a case study of the immigration of ethnic Germans and labour migrants in Germany. It demonstrates that migration makes some of the structural preconditions of the modern life course regime visible. It also shows that migration can be taken as part of a process that erodes the classical arrangement by which welfare states provide an ordered life course for the members of the national community, i.e. for their citizens in exchange for political loyalty.

The 'social construction' of biographies through organisations

The participation of individuals in modern society is no longer based on a unitary principle of inclusion and exclusion. The social conditions of inclusion, i.e. the mode by which individuals become engaged, are defined by the differentiated social systems of society: the economy, the law, politics, education or health. If individuals fulfil the functionally specific requirements of these systems then they are included. Individuals are perceived in relation to their relevance to these social systems, everything else is left out of the account. This means that social inclusion in modern society presupposes the exclusion of individuals as 'totalities' from society in the sense that they are not predefined by social bonds or some principle of belonging (Luhmann 1989, 1995b). Instead, in modern society, individuals become socially defined by their personal histories of inclusion and exclusion in different social realms.

Inclusion occurs as a result of their biographies. These are an invention unknown to former societies differentiated by strata, which defined individuals by inclusion and social belonging. A central point is that if traditionally it was social belonging that defined the social options of the individuals, then in modern society it is biographically accumulated social options that define social belonging. The definition of an individual becomes self-referential in that the individual is what he or she has become. The identification of individuals thus changes from the observation of social belonging to a temporal form of observation that can be characterised as the development of the individual in time (Hahn 1988). As an effect of this shift, the past of individuals – their biographies – carry the information, which allows the building of expectations about their future options. For instance, whether or not an individual is suited for future inclusion in economic, educational, scientific or legal processes.

An early historical experience of modern society was the high risk of failure of social participation connected with these new structural conditions of inclusion. There was no automatic inclusion of individuals in society. Pre-modern stratified orders of inclusion had ascribed the individuals to the strata of society and dealt with the poor, i.e. the 'fallen' individuals who were seen as a constant threat to social order, by a mixture of mercy and violent repression (Fuchs 1997). The breakdown of this order and of the corresponding local poor relief systems provided historically one of the most relevant contexts for the expansion of the modern nation state which eventually sought to deal with the political mediation of the socially restructured chances of inclusion and exclusion (de Swaan 1988; Bommes 1999). The effect was that national welfare states became the worldwide institutionalised form of organisation of the political system and, with their emergence, they have evolved as international 'thresholds of inequality' (Stichweh 1998). This means that they have provided for the *internal loyalty* of their citizens by a welfare policy that promotes chances for inclusion

based on *external closure* and exclusion. Historically, welfare state organisations have been established as a reaction to the political claim for not only
formal, but also substantial equality for all members of the national
community. This claim was founded in the political form of membership,
i.e. of citizenship (Marshall 1950). Since then, however, the political
semantics of solidarity and substantial equality have been eroded. Empirically, it is clear that social differentiation and individualisation processes
rather than equality have been promoted by welfare states (Pierson 1993,
1995).

A central part of this promotion of differentiation and individualisation
– as a precondition and as a result – was the institutionalisation and
safeguard of a modern life course, of individual biographies, and, related
to this, the concept of a 'career'. These social forms permitted observation
of the personal past that was then usable for building expectations about
the future. When exclusion and the freedom from inherited social bonds
becomes the precondition for inclusion in functional systems and
organisations, then security of expectations in relation to individuals and
their behaviour can no longer be gained from their social descent and
belonging. It can only be gained from their lived sequences of inclusions.
This can be conceptualised as the life course with related social biographies
and identities. Biographies can be told and individuals are expected to
present themselves and their identities in a biographical form.[1] This
institutionalisation of the life course, of individual biographies and careers
are a result of the way in which modern organisations recruit members and
of the moderation of these organisational processes of social inclusion and
exclusion through the welfare state.

Finding employment in modern society involves offering competence
and specific services to an organisation in exchange for payment and other
rewards. As a particular type of social system, organisations rely on the
formal definition of membership that distinguishes between members and
non-members. By engaging individuals as members, *organisations* distribute
conditions and chances for the inclusion and exclusion in other social
spheres. For instance, the recruitment of personnel and the allocation to
them of positions and careers in organisations are linked with the
distribution of money, reputation and influence or – in the words of
Bourdieu – economic, cultural and social capital. Organisational memberships that are based on careers open up and mediate differential chances
for individuals to receive services and resources as, for instance, consumers,
patients, clients, pupils and electors. These organisational ways of
allocating positions and incomes are one central frame of reference for
welfare state policies, which aim to increase and, especially, secure the
transferability of chances. That is, to seek to ensure that organisational
membership equips individuals with the necessary means and rights to
provide options for participation in the differentiated social realms of the
economy, education, law, health, politics and the family.[2]

One main form to secure this transferability was the institutionalisation of the life course. The life course can be understood as a complex of social rules that order the time dimension of an individual life viewed as a sequential program (Kohli 1986). 'Biography' and 'career', both of which are central elements of the social concept of a life course, are historically formed by the interplay of modern organisations recruiting members, and the welfare state establishing social preconditions for the possibility to find and recruit members with an expectable life course.[3] The introduction of social insurance schemes had the effect of organising around the employment of individuals in organisations the temporal accumulation of social entitlements. This depended to a large extent on the duration of employment, changes in the conditions of employment and dismissal, the institutionalisation of public education, the provision of family and education allowances. All these welfare state measures can be understood as structural elements of the institutionalisation process of the life course. From this perspective it becomes clear that life becomes socially conceptualised as a sequential program partitioned into three general stages: childhood/education, foundation of a family and working life, and retirement. Related to this structuration of life the family then takes on the form of the modern nuclear family.

Welfare state measures orient individuals towards the structures of a life cycle. The core institutions of the welfare state are structured in a way that implies the expectation that individuals are prepared and willing to prepare themselves for a biographically ordered sequence of inclusions in different social realms and their organisations. The enforcement of this expectation is historically successful since it provides social requirements for both organisations and individuals.

For organisations the welfare state creates the social preconditions allowing individuals that fulfil the necessary requirements to then be observable in the form of a 'career' (Corsi 1993). The welfare state backs up the likelihood that careers can be built. The 'career' maintained by organisations relies on the assumption that a 'normal biography' can be realised. This means participation and access to education, work, the family, as well as to economic, legal, political and health resources. Participation in each single context implies the fulfilment of certain preconditions that are provided elsewhere. For example, education presupposes that pupils have families, have access to economic means to fulfil their needs (through their parents), have a right to be educated and are healthy. Moreover, the education system has gained universal competence for this task and the specification of educational problems. The same is valid for other realms such as the economy,[4] law and health, which rely on the assumption that different problems are dealt with in other social contexts. The less this is empirically the case then it is more likely that there will be exclusionary chain reactions. Modern welfare states can be understood as institutional arrangement attempting to intervene in this kind of 'spillover' effect[5] by establishing and accompanying the life course in order to provide the necessary conditions for the chance to build an ordered course of life.

For individuals the social expectation that they lead their lives oriented to a biographical order structured by the social conditions of inclusion and related welfare state programmes, offers the chance of social continuity and orientation. The duty to be an individual with a specifiable and personal biography and identity (see also Strauss 1959) is equipped with a social form. In this way, welfare organisations not only constitute the life course as a social form but they provide a structure for the life-long relation between the state and the individual. This relation is founded in the specific inclusion form of the political system, which is national citizenship. National citizenship designates a relation between the individual and the state which is exclusive, immediate and permanent (Grawert 1984). A core element of the successful establishment of state sovereignty over the population on their territory – circumscribed as a national community – has been the acknowledgement of state responsibility for the assurance and structuration of the chances to lead a life as a member of that community.[6] The institutionalisation of the life course and its variations in different welfare states can be taken as the result of the specific historical formation of the relation between each state and its citizens.

What effects does international migration have on an arrangement in which national welfare states provide chances for their citizens to realise an ordered life course? Recent migration research has concentrated on the question of whether migration undermines the capacity of national welfare states to control their territory and to maintain levels of provision. In this context, the ways in which political and legal restrictions seek to reduce the capacity of migrants to collect social entitlements has been analysed (Miles and Thränhardt 1995). This chapter's focus on the relation between the welfare state, biography and migration addresses three questions. First, what kind of positions do migrants have in the life course regimes of welfare states? Second, what kind of effects does immigration have on the structure of institutionalisation of the life course provided by national welfare states? Third, does immigration change the relation between the welfare state and the collectivity that has been historically constructed as the national community of legitimate welfare receivers? Before we shift to the empirical example of the immigration of labour migrants and ethnic Germans (*Aussiedler*) in Germany, it is necessary to provide a more general consideration on the relation between migration, biography and the welfare state.

Welfare states and the 'social deviation' of migrants

The constitution of biographies and their moderation by the welfare state makes the deviation of the biographies of migrants very likely. Deviation means that their life courses and biographies do not fulfil the institutionalised expectations of normality. Consequently, migration puts in view some of the social preconditions of the relation between differentiation and the individual biography/career as a social form. If we understand biographies and related careers as the accumulation of structural participation chances, then migrations make this precondition visible since migrants are presumably structurally poor or deprived and it cannot be assumed that careers with the required elements have been built. Consequently, those things that under 'normal conditions' are treated as given can no longer be presupposed. In other words established abstractions need revision. This becomes obvious if one looks at some common deviations of migrants in three biographically central dimensions: education, labour and participation in pension schemes.

- Education: migrant children have access to schools in many countries even when they do not have a residence permit. This permits analysis of the legal and political conditions of education and the education system's assumption that families of children are settled. Migrant children (with or without legal status) may not speak the official language and, in this way, question institutionalised assumptions about normal socialisation processes, as well as linguistic and cultural competencies as central preconditions for the ability to learn something. Moreover, careers of migrant children built at school in their countries of origin may not be accepted by the education system in the immigration country. This may close important paths of educational success and increase the likelihood of failure.
- Employment: labour migrants are less likely to be able to offer socially established biographies and careers of education and work. This excludes them from competition in large segments of the labour market. It should be noted, however, that the absence of careers and related social claims were in many respects the precondition for the immigration of labour to western European countries during the postwar period. In this case the absence of a career provided the chances of social inclusion for labour immigrants on those market segments which were in need of unqualified workers. The same holds true for major parts of illegal immigration.
- Retirement: migrants can access welfare entitlements even if they are not citizens. Older migrants, however, are likely to have low pension incomes since many have not been included long enough in pension insurance funds to accumulate adequate entitlements.[7] For those reasons it is likely that many will rely on public assistance.

These three brief examples go to show that the modes by which migrant biographies may deviate from expectations guaranteed by welfare states, and the social meanings and consequences this may have, cannot be purely

theoretically derived. The social observation of deviation and its consequences depends upon the various kinds of expectations of normality
supported by different types of welfare state. Moreover, immigration takes
on different forms in immigration countries and migrants have varying
legal status and welfare entitlements linked to their immigration path.
Finally, as a result of the different histories of immigration in the various
national welfare states we find specific combinations of welfare and
immigration regimes.

To illustrate these points, the discussion moves on to an empirical
example of the immigration of ethnic Germans (*Aussiedler*, literally
'outsettlers' or 'resettlers') after the Second World War and to compare
their structural position in the German welfare state with the position of
the labour immigrants of the *Gastarbeiter* period. Are both groups included
in the provisions of the German welfare state to an extent that allows these
migrants to develop some security of expectation concerning their future
life course? This is found not to be the case, which means that differences
and explanations for the different paths of immigration and the social
conditions linked to them need to be accounted for. One effect of these
different positionings of migrants has been the re-composition of the
political community defined as legitimate welfare receivers. This case study
does not allow for simple generalisations about the relation between
migration, welfare state and biography, but throws light on the specific
relation of migrants to the welfare state and the established life course
regime and on the structural effects of migration on this regime. Further
comparative research can discuss similarities and differences in other
countries in order to build on a more general theory on the relation
between migration, welfare and biography.

Ethnic German immigration and changing welfare state positions

Ethnic German (EG) immigration became a subject of general migration
research following the collapse of the socialist countries and increased
immigration of EGs to Germany since the late-1980s. EGs have been
immigrating to Germany continuously since the Second World War, but
until the late 1980s they were mainly the subjects of historical studies or
social policy-oriented research on social integration (Bade 1987), the
reasons for which are assessed later.

We commence from the observation that the structural position of EGs
in the German welfare state has changed dramatically since 1990. They
have been the targets of major expenditure reductions and lost many of
their former social entitlements. The extent of these reductions will not be
the focus here, rather the shift of the structural position of EGs in the
welfare system linked to these reductions will be examined. In order to
understand this shift it is important to clarify the position of EGs in the
German welfare state before 1989. This category does not include refugees

and expellees who came to West Germany after 1945, but does include the immigration of Germans from Poland, the Soviet Union, Hungary and Rumania after 1950, legally defined as EGs (see Table 6.1 and Figure 6.1). This group is then divided into those who came before and those who came after 1988.

Table 6.1 Immigration of ethnic Germans 1950–88

Year	Total numbers	Main countries of origin		
		Poland	*Rumania*	*Soviet Union*
1950	47,165	31,761	13	—
1951	21,067	10,791	1,031	1,721
1952	5,537	194	26	63
1953	8,296	147	15	—
1954	10,390	662	8	18
1955	13,202	860	44	154
1956	25,302	15,674	176	1,016
1957	107,690	98,290	384	923
1958	129,660	117,550	1,383	4,122
1959	27,136	16,252	374	5,563
1960	18,171	7,739	2,124	3,272
1961	16,414	9,303	3,303	345
1962	15,733	9,657	1,675	894
1963	14,869	9,522	1,321	209
1964	20,099	13,611	818	234
1965	23,867	14,644	2,715	366
1966	27,813	17,315	609	1,245
1967	26,227	10,856	440	1,092
1968	23,201	8,435	614	598
1969	29,873	9,536	2,675	316
1970	18,590	5,624	6,519	342
1971	33,272	25,241	2,848	1,145
1972	23,580	13,476	4,374	3,426
1973	22,732	8,902	7,577	4,494
1974	24,315	7,825	8,484	6,541
1975	19,327	7,040	5,077	5,985
1976	44,248	29,366	3,764	9,704
1977	54,169	32,861	10,989	9,274
1978	58,062	36,102	12,120	8,455
1979	54,802	36,274	7,226	9,663
1980	51,984	26,637	15,767	6,954
1981	69,336	50,983	12,031	3,773
1982	47,993	30,355	12,972	2,071
1983	37,844	19,122	15,501	1,447
1984	36,387	17,455	16,553	913
1985	38,905	22,075	14,924	460
1986	42,729	27,188	13,130	753
1987	78,488	48,419	13,990	14,488
1988	202,673	140,226	12,902	47,572

Source: Bundesausgleichsamt Registrierverfahren (Federal Office for Social Compensation, Procedure of Registration 3/1989); quoted in Blaschke 1989: 238; Reichling 1995: 41ff.

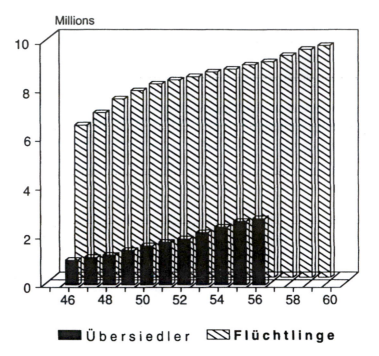

Figure 6.1 Immigration of refugees and expellees (Flüchtlinge) from east European
countries and refugees from the former GDR (Übersiedler) 1946–60.

The post-Second World War immigration of expelled persons, refugees
and EGs in Germany was a result of highly conflictual state building
processes in central and eastern Europe since the nineteenth century. The
attempt of Germans since 1945 to migrate[8] from eastern European
countries to Germany resulted from enduring internal national conflicts in
their countries of origin and from sovereignty claims by the German state
which, since the end of the nineteenth century, regarded them as part of
the German nation. The end of the Second World War, the resultant
division of Germany, and the forced migration of refugees and expellees,
were the high peak of these nationality and state-building conflicts
(Lemberg 1950). The post-1988 immigration of EGs is a late outcome of
this historical constellation.

The reinvention of citizenship in West Germany based on the principle
of *ius sanguinis* ('blood' descent) was a reaction to the post-war situation.
West Germany as one part of the diminished and divided former Germany
claimed to be the only legal and legitimate successor of the former German
Reich. The new German state's introduction of citizenship based on the *ius
sanguinis* principle and the category of the German *Volkszugehörigkeit*
('belonging to the people') happened in order to maintain access to

citizenship for German refugees from east European countries. The country was diminished and divided and a large part of the population of the former state was living outside the territory of both German states. In the immediate post-war context, politically there existed no real alternative to the principle of *ius sanguinis*.

EGs were defined as German *Volkszugehörige* ('members of the people') affected by 'a fate of expulsion' (*Vertreibungsschicksal*) as a consequence of the Third Reich and the war. The 'Law on the Affairs of Expellees and Refugees' (the so-called 'Federal Expellee Law') in 1953 and the subsequent 'Federal Law for the Regulation of State Membership Questions' in 1955 (Heinelt and Lohmann 1992: 55ff.) included EGs into the category of *Volkszugehörige* even if they lived in countries like the Soviet Union, Yugoslavia or Rumania, i.e. outside the borders of the territory of the German state in 1937.[9] In this way access to German citizenship for the EGs was secured.

The granting of citizenship to EGs was a political reaction to the outcomes of the Second World War, when, in reaction to the nationalist war politics of the German state, Germans living in east European countries were subject to all kinds of discrimination. This was especially the case in the Soviet Union, where many EGs were deported to the eastern parts of the country. The inclusion of EGs in the national refugee policy of the 1950s was, therefore, viewed publicly as an act of national solidarity with those who had to suffer from the disastrous politics of the German state. The laws of 1953 and 1955 granted access not only to citizenship for these groups but also to a range of social rights, services and supports which had been set up as part of the so-called 'compensation for burden' suffered by refugees, expellees and EGs alike. In the early 1950s, when the devastating effects of the war were still present and unemployment was high, the 'compensation for burden' was politically legitimised as an act of national burden sharing and solidarity. The inclusion of EGs was seen as part of this act.

Between 1950 and 1988 around 1.6 million EGs immigrated to West Germany. During this period the numbers of immigrants varied between around 20,000 and 40,000 per year, with the exceptions of 1957/8 and 1977–82 when numbers were considerably higher (see Table 6.1). These relatively low numbers of immigrants were the effect of the cold war and the denial of freedom of movement for individuals in the socialist countries. But this is only half the story. The immigration of EGs became possible only as a result of political bargaining processes between states principally dissenting about the national belonging of certain parts of the population. Countries like Poland, Rumania or the Soviet Union never acknowledged any right of the EGs to live in Germany. They allowed the emigration of EGs depending on their political interests in improving bilateral relations or receiving economic support. Until 1989 Germany was an incomplete nation state[10] and was engaged in these kinds of negotiations and conflicts about the legitimacy of competing sovereignty claims over parts of state populations. These kinds of political dissent are once again observable between numerous eastern European states (Brubaker 1994).

The rapidly growing numbers of EGs immigrating to Germany since 1987 was both part of and an indicator of a major change of social context in which this type of migration was situated. The collapse of socialist regimes eroded the former constellation of dissent about national belonging between Germany and eastern European states. The establishment of freedom of movement in eastern Europe allowed EGs to leave their countries if they wished to do so. 'Belonging to the German people' became a privileged option of migration in the countries of origin. The entitlement to enter the German state territory and to claim citizenship was widely used and soon met with immigration restrictions introduced by the German state.

The so-called 'social integration' of EGs in the period of the post-war history until the end of the 1980s was politically and socially a big success which (only seemingly paradoxically) made the EGs socially invisible as an immigration group. After the war until the end of the 1950s, research was politically funded and conducted to monitor the ways in which refugees and expellees were socially included, and the potential for conflict with the indigenous population (see Lemberg and Edding 1959). In the context of the 'economic miracle' (*Wirtschaftswunder*) of the 1950s these fears proved to be wrong. Refugees and EGs lost their political and scientific attraction as a major research topic. Subsequent migration research in Germany since the 1960s concentrated on labour migration and few studies on EGs were conducted. The main result of these studies on social integration were that EGs were successful in terms of education, income, employment and property and that they did not differ significantly from the indigenous population in socio-structural terms.[11] This success is best summarised in the observation that until the end of the 1980s no 'second generation' of EGs socially appeared in Germany. By the beginning of the 1980s, immigration of EGs was viewed as a politically manageable process (Zurhausen 1983). This was in stark contrast to the intensive public debates about settlement by labour migrant families, their possibly restricted capacity for 'social integration', and the political invention of the 'problem of the Turks' (Thränhardt 1988).

For an interpretation of this result a closer look at the welfare programmes for EGs established in the 1950s and, with certain modifications, valid until the end of the 1980s is illuminating. The central structural provisions of these programmes entailed:

• An unemployment insurance system that included the EGs immediately after their immigration as though they had spent their whole former working life in Germany. An EG claiming to be a skilled worker was, for example, entitled to receive the amount of financial support equivalent to an unemployed indigenous skilled worker. Parallel occupational integration programmes then secured the (re-)adaptation of skills of these immigrants.

- The inclusion of EGs in the pension schemes as if they had contributed to these funds during their working life.
- Direct access for EGs to health insurance systems.
- Added to these inclusions into the general social insurance systems of the welfare state were: extended language training programmes, general educational programmes, specific compensatory educational programmes for pupils, increased grants for children in school and university, reduced taxes, preferential consideration of self-employed EGs for public contracts, public housing programmes for EGs, provision of the means for purchase of household equipment, compensation for lost property, cheap credits with low or zero interest rates.[12]

This overview makes the working principle of welfare for EGs and its mode of securing their chances of social participation visible. EGs who immigrated until the end of the 1980s were treated as if they had spent their whole life in Germany, i.e. as if they had accumulated biographically the chances of inclusion which made further social inclusions likely. The welfare state 'repaired' the deviating biographies of the EGs by simulating and ascribing the structurally required elements for social participation. The effect of the additional compensatory welfare programs was the equipment of the immigrating EGs with attributes, capacities and material means, which enabled them to fulfil competently the social roles open to them as a result of the biographies ascribed to them by the welfare state. The treatment of the EGs in this way corresponded to the principles and traditions of the conservative corporatist German welfare state, which aims at the maintenance of the standard of living of different social status groups. EGs were provided with the resources to participate in the way of life of the social status group they claimed to belong to.

I have argued that modern welfare states can be understood as an institutional arrangement of organisations trying among other things to avoid chain reactions of exclusion by establishing and accompanying the life course to provide the conditions for an ordered course of life. This life course regime then structures the life-long relation between the state and the individual citizens. The structural fundament of this relation is the specific political form of inclusion: national citizenship. The result of the political and legal ascription of membership in the national community to the immigration category of EGs was that EG immigrants acquired the structural qualifications and properties for participation and membership in the various social realms and organisations. Equipped by the German state with the necessary elements of a biography and a life course attached to their self-descriptions, they could then be observed as competent persons. This involved both formal entitlements and the substantial sense of competencies and means for fulfilling the roles connected with these biographies.[13] Since EGs were defined as members of the nation they were treated as if their relation with the state had existed for their whole life.

This description outlines the conditions of immigration for the EGs until the end of the 1980s, when the character of the immigration process of EGs changed rapidly. Following the collapse of the socialist countries most of the political restrictions upon the freedom of movement were suspended. The effects were dramatic. Between 1988 and 1993 about 1.6 million EGs immigrated to Germany (see Table 6.2). The German state reacted promptly by introducing means of control that are well-known in immigration countries. In 1990, a legal procedure for the immigration of EGs was installed. EGs were no longer allowed to enter the state territory unrestricted and to claim their 'belonging to the German people' in Germany. They had to enter a formal procedure in their countries of origin in order to be accepted as Germans. Only after their official acceptance as Germans do they receive immigration permission. By the end of 1992, as part of the asylum compromise, the number of EGs allowed to enter the country was limited to 220,000 per year. A newly introduced legal status of *Spätaussiedler* ('late resettler') restricted access to those persons born before 1 January 1993 and who could prove that they either had been affected by measures of expulsion themselves or were descendants of such families. The family members of these 'late resettlers' were excluded from this status if they were not 'late resettlers' themselves. Since this time a large number of them have immigrated as 'foreigners'.[14]

This legal amendment indicates that the entrance of EGs had become politically perceived as immigration and that it was to be dealt with as such. Parallel to this legal shift in their status and immigration rights, the attending welfare programmes for EGs, i.e. their social rights, were heavily reduced (Bommes 1996). The decisive changes were the exclusion of EGs from unemployment benefits, reduced responsibilities for the labour

Table 6.2 Immigration of ethnic Germans 1988–95

Year	Total numbers	Main countries of origin		
		Poland	Rumania	Soviet Union
1988	202,645	140,226	12,902	47,572
1989	377,036	250,340	23,387	98,134
1990	397,073	133,872	111,150	147,950
1991	221,924	40,129	32,178	147,320
1992	230,565	17,742	16,146	195,576
1993	218,888	5,431	5,811	207,347
1994	222,591	—	—	—
1995	217,898	—	—	—

Source: Bundesausgleichsamt (Federal Office for Social Compensation 1993; quoted in Nuscheler 1995: 123; figures of 1994/95 in: Info-Dienst Deutsche Aussiedler, No. 75, January 1996, p. 3.

administration, and the cessation of a number of the compensatory welfare programmes. Step by step, entitlements were reduced. Since 1993, EGs have relied on public assistance paid by local governments if they cannot find a job. Language training programmes were heavily reduced. The professional qualifications of EGs were in many cases no longer regarded as equivalent to German job definitions. Simultaneously, the budgets for occupational training were drastically cut and, in many cases, local governments had to pay for them. The unbalanced distribution within Germany of immigrating EGs during the first half of the 1990s and their concentration in certain areas of Germany led to public complaints from a number of local governments about their exploding social budgets. In reaction to this the 1996 residence assignment law (*Wohnortzuweisungsgesetz*) reduced the freedom of movement of EGs for three years after arrival in case they became dependent on public assistance. EGs are no longer allowed to reside in places of their choice but are tied to the place of residence assigned to them by the administration.[15]

Ethnic Germans, labour migrants and changing relations between the state and community of welfare receivers

In stark contrast to the situation between the 1960s and the 1980s, EGs have a high unemployment risk (Bommes 1996: 224; Thränhardt 1998: 34ff.). They have also become an immigrant group of major political and scientific concern. The political and scientific 'integration-discourse' has again taken notice of the EGs. Political and scientific observers have discovered the so-called second generation of EGs as a target group (e.g. Auernheimer 1995).

The empirical long-term development is difficult to assess, but this chapter's focus is on the potentially systematic effects of these recent developments on the relation between migration and the welfare state. An interesting starting point for a theoretical interpretation is the public 'silence' over the most relevant reductions of the welfare entitlements of EGs. These political decisions had been taken as part of general budget restrictions during the early 1990s. The public debates about these restrictions concentrated on the general topics concerning the amount of unemployment benefits and the conditions of reception. In comparison to these publicly intensive debates the decisions affecting the EGs were taken rather silently in the neo-corporatist negotiation systems where bits and pieces for reduction were collected that were acceptable to the parties participating in the incremental mode of decision finding. The administrative details of these kinds of decision were of no major public interest and the EGs themselves formed no relevant pressure group participating in the decision game.

In the 1950s, the inclusion of the EGs in welfare schemes had been viewed as a political requirement of national solidarity. EGs were seen as part of the nation and its 'fate', the catastrophe of the Second World War and its burdens had to be shared in a solidary manner by the whole nation. At the end of the 1980s, however, even in the context of the German unification process, national semantics of this type no longer possessed their former mobilising potential. The devalorisation of ethnic and national semantics in Germany during the 1970s and 1980s (Bommes 1995) provided the background by which the welfare rights of EGs could be reduced in the corporatist systems of the German welfare state without being publicly debated (Bommes 1996). The exclusion of immigrating EGs from core provisions of the welfare state mobilised almost no public concern about the legitimacy of treating German citizens in nearly the same way as foreign immigrants. Rather, this became an explicit demand within certain factions of the Social Democratic and the Green Party. EGs have become an immigrant group, which, for historical reasons, possesses a right to citizenship and to enter the territory, but which at the same time are deprived of central welfare state provisions.

The meaning and relevance of this change can best be assessed by comparing the situation of the recent German immigrants with the conditions for labour migration of the 1960s and 1970s. The immigration of the *Gastarbeiter* was initiated as part of a labour-market policy of the national welfare state. As in other European countries, the state still acted like the sovereign supervisor of the national economy and its labour market (Scharpf 1996). Part of this supervision was the legal inclusion of migrants in the welfare regulations of the labour market. After some 30 years of employment in specific segments of the labour market, labour migrants had by the end of the 1990s accumulated social rights which guaranteed them a living standard on a low, but fairly secure level (Thränhardt, Dieregsweiler and Santel 1994; Seifert 1995). In this sense, the labour migration of the 1960s and 1970s and the subsequent settlement of the migrant families has been part of the immigration history of a successful national welfare state. Once their immigration proved to be irreversible, the political frame of reference became the 'integration paradigm'. Migrants were to be 'integrated into society' by means of the national welfare state and in the end to become 'its members'.

Labour migrants differ from the pre-1990 EGs because welfare activities for labour migrants were mainly defined by their position in the labour market, i.e. as a structural outcome of the German welfare state structure centred around employment. The main differences between the EGs and the labour migrants become visible in view of, first, the fact that in socio-structural terms most of the labour migrants are part of the lower strata of Germany's social structure (Geißler 1996). The history of their immigration and its political preconditions seem to tie them to this position. They have not disappeared as a category in the general social structure like the EGs. Second, labour migrants were different from the EG migrants because they were not supported by a similar commitment by the educational and vocational system to the success of the labour immigrants' children. Welfare programmes for EGs were targeted at all age groups and were committed to substitute the missing life-long relationship between the individual and the national welfare state. In contrast, a large number of the children of labour immigrants failed to reach educational levels that could open attractive career perspectives for them. Labour migrants are heavily under-represented in the dual vocational training system and their fathers (and partly their mothers) have only, to a very limited degree, gained positions at their work places allowing them to open access to memberships in factories (Faist 1995b). Unemployment among immigrant youth is therefore extremely high (Thränhardt 1998). The limited and 'retarded' commitment of the welfare state to labour migrants seems to affect mainly certain strands of their children.

Nevertheless, it remains true that the welfare state aimed at integrating the immigrants 'into society' and that missing that target was and is seen as a political failure. The national welfare state of the 1970s and 1980s had become responsible too for the chances of labour immigrants to lead a decent life and to legitimately claim certain social rights and expectations. Violent attacks of right-wing political groups were, therefore, almost unilaterally rejected in German politics. By the end of the 1980s, the former national community of West Germany of the 1950s had changed into the community of legitimate welfare receivers which included the major part of Germany's substantial foreign population.

Against this background, immigrating EGs, even if their right to enter was seldom publicly denied after 1989, were no longer perceived as legitimate welfare receivers since they had not contributed to the GNP. After 1989, the federal government legitimised changed welfare programmes by arguing that there should be no privileges for EGs. What had been originally conceptualised as compensation for the forceful separation and exclusion from the national community came to be seen as an illegitimate advantage. In the changed context of the early 1990s, the new community of welfare receivers provided legitimacy for the welfare state to get rid of social responsibility for newly arriving immigrants. This legitimacy no longer relied on national rhetorics, but nevertheless affirmed the undissolvable basis of the welfare state: closure and the maintenance of a threshold of inequality.

Conclusion

Analysing the comparative positions of EGs and the former '*Gastarbeiter*' in the German welfare state demonstrates how the ways that different immigrant groups are included in the life course regime of the welfare state has long-term effects for their socio-structural position and their chances of social inclusion. The labour migrants of the 1960s and 1970s were included in the structural provisions of the welfare state mediated by the political form of recruitment for the labour market. After thirty years they were able to accumulate a certain amount of entitlements and to develop slowly a career structure which allowed them to reach a living standard on a low, but fairly secure level. The EGs of the 1990s are immigrating in Germany on the basis of their political status. Whether they manage to enter the labour market and the welfare provisions centred on employment remains to be seen given that their 'deviant' careers are no longer repaired by the welfare state through the substitute ascription of a complete biography.

Analysing the comparative position of labour migrants and EGs also allows us to view the reconstruction of the community of legitimate welfare receivers. In the 1950s belonging to the nation still defined this community, by the end of the 1980s it was more or less composed of those who had contributed to the GNP. This includes the foreign population of the labour migrants and excludes to different degrees asylum seekers, refugees, contract labourers and EGs (in the eyes of a large part of West Germans even the East Germans). One can summarise this by saying that the welfare state redefines its addressee in relation to its technical purposes. To do this it substitutes the national frame of reference by the criteria of legal residence and participation in the labour market. In the case of Germany, this becomes visible by the changing welfare positions of German and foreign immigrants.

Since 1989, migration policies in Germany have been generally characterised by the effort to limit strictly the right of access to and settlement on the state territory for newly arriving migrants. The state seeks to allow only time-limited and reversible labour immigration under severely restricted conditions, for example, contract labour. It also seeks to reduce welfare provisions for those who are in a legal position to acquire permanent residence permits. For these migrants, including the EGs, the welfare state accepts only restricted responsibility. It provides the means of subsistence, but to a much lesser extent, the social conditions of beginning a career, entering a structured life course and accumulating elements for an accountable biography. Further research will have to clarify if immigration after 1989 can also be interpreted as part of a general 'de-institutionalisation of the life course'.

Does the case of the EGs merely reflect a specificity of Germany with no relevance for other countries with differently organised welfare states? The case not only makes visible the specific mode in which the close relation between national welfare states and their citizens has been structured through the institutionalisation of a life course regime, but also throws light on the erosion of this arrangement through immigration. The relevance of the case needs further clarification through comparative research that analyses the position of different immigrant groups in the life course regimes of the different types of welfare states. This will provide the basis for a more solid answer to the question of if, and in what sense, different forms of immigration in Europe may be part of a general de-institutionalisation of the life course. That is, a process which erodes the historically established arrangement by which the welfare state took over the responsibility in relation to its citizens for the assurance that a structured life course linked with biographical expectations and prospects could be realised. One result of the restrictions of sovereignty of the national welfare states by so-called globalisation is the evolution of more groups who can no longer rely on the welfare state as an institutionalised safeguard of the social preconditions for an ordered and expectable life course. Migrants are likely to be among these groups.

Notes

1 This is why 'identity' and 'self-realisation' become a problem (...) one cannot know who one is but has to find out if one's own projections do find social acceptance' (Luhmann 1997: 627).
2 Residualistic welfare states perceive the safeguard of transferabilities only in a limited sense as a political duty. The 'conservative' type of welfare states however aims at the maintenance of the standard of living, whereas the 'social democratic' type is based on the concept of 'social citizenship' as interpreted by Marshall (see Esping-Anderson 1990).
3 This 'interplay' would need more sociological specification concerning the different forms of power created by organisations and the political system which cannot be done in this paper. Organisations gain power based on positive sanctions, since they offer income for labour to individuals who depend on this payment because of their 'risk of unprovidedness' (Weber 1972); the power of states is based on negative sanctions, on the mono-polisation of the means of physical violence, the ultimate foundation of their capacity to produce collectively binding decisions (Easton 1968). The relation between states and organisations circumscribes a field of tension between the indispensable organisational power, on the one hand resulting from the form of membership, and the state power on the other hand relying on this modern form of organisation itself but intervening for welfare reasons in organisational power by modifying preconditions and consequences of organisational decision processes.
4 Marx's argument about the commodification of the labour power was precisely an argument about social abstraction.
5 If inclusion cannot be secured, welfare states create also secondary orders of exclusion by providing scripts of failure (defined for instance by the rules of insurances) and organisations, e.g. of social work which deal with the social accountability of exclusions (Bommes and Scherr 1996).
6 It remains the central insight of Marshall (1950) that the form 'citizenship' establishes the expectation as legitimate that politics has to further and increase the chances of inclusion of their citizens.
7 Most pension insurance funds in European welfare states make entitlements dependent on the time period spent on state territory and/or the time period of employment and contribution (Dörr and Faist 1997). This demonstrates the life course oriented relation between the welfare state and its citizens.
8 The immigration of EG is politically defined as 'remigration', 'an effort of Germans to come home'.
9 The constitution of 1949 defined those as Germans who belonged to the German people and lived inside these borders of 1937. The main difference

between refugees, expellees and EG, the *'Aussiedler'*, exists between their places of origin: refugees and expellees were defined by their 'belonging to the people' and their place of origin laying inside the borders of Germany on the 31 December 1937; EGs were assumed to be German and to be affected by measures of expulsion because of their 'belonging to the German people'.

10 1989, the subsequent unification process and the treaties with various countries established for the first time the identity of territory and population which the German state claims sovereignty about.

11 See Bade (1987), Lüttinger (1986, 1989) and for a summary of the results of this research see Bommes, Castles and Wihtol de Wenden *et al.* (1999: 78f.).

12 This is an incomplete list. For a more detailed overview see Otto (1990) and Bommes and Rotthoff (1994).

13 Looking at education it made a striking difference that the assumption of the individual ability to learn and to participate in education was the basis for the decision to put the children of EGs to the equivalent school level they had been visiting in their countries of origin. The presupposition of competence was backed up by additional education. In contrast the starting assumption for the education of Turkish pupils was the expectation of major social problems and minor cultural and cognitive abilities to assimilate (e.g. Schrader, Nikles and Griese 1976). As one EG put it in an interview: 'I came here as a pupil 12 years old and spoke no German. They put me in a gymnasium, taught me German and then I made the *Abitur.* I can't speak Polish anymore.' The ascription of cultural belonging or difference and the expectations of success or failure linked obviously define in a crucial manner the starting social conditions for individual chances to accumulate the required elements of a successful social career.

14 This change can be seen as part of the readjustment of the German concept of citizenship. In 1990, 1993 and 1999 amendments of the foreigner and citizenship laws had installed legal access for labour migrants and their children to German citizenship. The restrictions of the legal status of EG can be interpreted as part of the strengthening of territoriality as criterion for the granting of citizenship and of the weakening of the *ius sanguinis* tradition. This is another indicator that this tradition is best understood on the historical background of the German state-building process ending in 1989.

15 It appears ironic that the immigration of members of the 'national community' provides the occasion for reintroducing elements of the traditional *'Heimatrecht'* ('home law') of local governments. This traditional law was abandoned by the Prussian state in 1842 in order to undercut the local governments' refusal of immigrants whom they suspected of being ill equipped to care for themselves and to rely on poor relief. The abolition of the *'Heimatrecht'* and the introduction of a poor relief system through the central state can be regarded as one major step of the development of the modern welfare state (Reidegeld 1998; Halfmann and Bommes 1998). It is certainly not exaggerated to regard the introduction of the residence assignment law in 1996 as symptomatic for the structural effects of migration on the welfare state.

7   Immigration and the politics of rights

The French case in comparative perspective

James F. Hollifield

Introduction: immigration and immigrant policy

The last decades of the twentieth century saw a marked convergence in strategies for immigration control and immigrant incorporation in the major receiving states of Europe and North America. The new strategies can best be summarised as a 'grand bargain' between anti- and pro-immigration forces in liberal democracies. In most immigrant-receiving democracies in western Europe, legal immigration has been restricted in exchange for stepped up efforts to incorporate foreigners already settled in the host societies. In the United States, however, the grand bargain entails stopping illegal immigration (closing the back door) in order to maintain a fairly high level of legal immigration (keeping the front door open). In the 1990s, welfare for immigrants and foreigners in the USA has been restricted, in keeping with the American strategy of trying to eliminate as many pull factors as possible.

A simple assumption lies at the heart of these grand bargain strategies: that it is possible to use immigrant policy as an instrument for making immigration policy. By changing the package of rights and benefits available to foreigners, states are trying to alter immigration flows. In western Europe, social (or welfare) policy is viewed as a positive instrument for incorporating immigrants, whereas in the USA social policy is viewed as a negative instrument (a social safety net) preventing members of society from falling below the poverty line. Foreigners/immigrants are not supposed to become public charges. This chapter explores the impact of changing immigrant policies on immigration flows. The focus is on the evolution of civil, social, and political rights for immigrants and foreigners in France, with comparisons to the United States and Germany. The principal question underlying this study is how far can liberal democracies go in limiting rights of foreigners as a strategy for immigration control?

I should like to begin the analysis by advancing eight hypotheses concerning the limits of immigration control in a liberal polity, especially the important role of ideas, institutions, and civil society.

- All things being equal, liberal states will opt for external strategies of control, placing the most stress on border control, or control of territory. The reason for this is simple: territorial closure and sovereignty are essential to the maintenance of the social contract and the rule of law, and this cannot be questioned without questioning the authority and legitimacy of the state itself.
- If a liberal state has the capacity for extraterritorial control, it will opt for further externalisation of control, extending its authority to the high seas, to the territory of neighbouring states, or to the territory of the sending states themselves. The Schengen Agreement is a classic example of extraterritorial control. It has helped to create buffer states, and to shift some of the burdens and dilemmas of control outside the jurisdiction of the liberal states of western Europe.
- If control cannot be efficiently externalised, then a series of internal control policies will come into play, raising questions about how far liberal states can go in imposing such controls on individuals and groups in (civil) society, and whether foreigners and immigrants should be considered members of civil society? The argument advanced in this paper is that ideas, institutions, and culture, as well as certain segments of civil society, which may resist encroachments by the state on negative and/or positive freedoms, impose limits of control.
- In most of the countries of continental Europe, there is a strong statist, administrative, and/or social democratic tradition; therefore regulation of the labour market is likely to be the first strategy for internal control. A strong welfare state functions as a double-edged sword: it may facilitate immigrant incorporation, but it also can function as an efficient mechanism for immigration control. Conversely, in countries like the USA, which have a strong liberal/*laissez-faire* tradition and a weaker welfare state, regulation of the labour market is not a viable strategy, because of weak state capacity, the resistance of civil society, and the reluctance of politicians to impose limits on *negative freedom,* arising in part from free markets.
- In countries like the USA, which have no social democratic tradition and a weak welfare state, the first strategy for internal control is likely to be a roll back of social rights, i.e. the restriction of *positive freedom.* Conversely, in countries like Sweden or Germany, which have a strong social democratic tradition, social rights are likely to be preserved for all members of society, denizens as well as citizens; and the preferred strategy for control will be external control of borders, strict regulation of labour markets, and limits on negative freedom.
- In countries with a strong liberal-republican tradition, such as France, the USA, and Germany, rolling back civil rights (due process and equal protection) as a strategy for internal control and limiting negative freedom will be difficult and contentious. The extent to which this is a viable strategy will depend heavily upon the strength and independence

of the judiciary, which may act as an institutional constraint on both the populist impulses of the legislature or parliament, as well as the administrative or police powers of the executive. Separation of powers acts as a constraint on the ability of states to roll back civil rights and take away negative freedoms. In this respect, Britain has both an institutional advantage (no separation of powers) and an ideological/cultural advantage (no republican tradition) in pursuing internal control strategies. Still, the British judiciary has shown considerable independence and a willingness to intervene in issues concerning the rights of immigrants and refugees.

- The ultimate strategy for internal control, which is the most difficult to pursue in a liberal republic, is to roll back political rights and thereby to limit citizenship. Such a strategy requires governments to change laws governing nationality, which often means amending constitutions and tampering with founding traditions. The relative ease with which the Thatcher government changed British nationality laws in 1981 stands in stark contrast with similar attempts at reform in France and the USA. Britain has no republican tradition that can act as an ideological or institutional check on Parliament.

- In the context of the Westphalian system, which is based on principles of sovereignty and non-interference, there are few limits on the capacity of states, liberal or otherwise, for pursuing strategies of external control. But, with respect to internal control, liberal states are constrained institutionally, ideologically, culturally, and ultimately by their civil societies. Strategies for internal control bend to these constraints. Otherwise, the legitimacy of the state itself is threatened.

Limiting rights: a comparative perspective

In France, Germany, and the United States in the 1990s, we have seen a not-so-subtle shift in strategies and tactics for restricting immigration, away from a reliance on the classic instruments of (external) control of borders and (internal) regulation of labour markets to a new strategy of limiting the rights of foreigners. In each of these liberal societies, external control of borders – with an emphasis on territorial sovereignty and the sanctity of law – is preferable to internal control of society, which may entail infringements of individual, civil liberties. But neither the French, German, nor the American governments have abandoned the classic instruments of border control.

On the contrary, they have reinforced them, especially in the American case in recent years where the liberal concept of negative freedom, implying a minimalist state and freedom to do whatever one wants within the broad confines of the law, has had a much more powerful influence on politics and public policy.[1] The Clinton administration has placed great emphasis on (external) control of borders, as well as (internal) regulation of labour markets. But the power of the American federal state to regulate the domestic labour market is constrained by the lack of a national identification card. Precisely because of their attachment to negative freedoms, Americans are wont to give the state such sweeping power to intrude in their daily lives. In France and Germany, on the other hand, the state has long had the power to intervene directly and forcefully in the labour market. Yet in none of these cases has the state been able to stop immigration, at least not to the satisfaction of the government or the people, if public opinion polls and election results are to be believed (Freeman 1995).

There is, however, evidence in the recent reforms in all three cases of the willingness on the part of politicians and the public to allow the erosion of negative freedoms, so that the state can better manage legal immigration, and stop illegal immigration. The increased power of the police, both internally and at the border, to detain and deport individuals has eroded civil liberties in France, Germany, and the USA. Limiting appeals by asylum seekers and others threatened with deportation strengthens the hand of the state in dealing with illegal immigration, but it is difficult for liberals to accept, because it means more state control and less (negative) freedom. In both France and the USA the state is more powerful and the individual is weaker because of these reforms. Liberal lobbies like the ACLU in the USA, the GISTI in France, and Caritas in Germany have fought restrictive immigration reforms on the grounds that they erode the civil liberties of all members of society.

What makes immigration legitimate?

Even though France has a long tradition of immigration and was the first European state to grant citizenship to Jews, at the time of the Revolution, it was not until the culmination of the Dreyfus affair early in the twentieth century, under the Third Republic, that the main tenets of republicanism – *laïcité* or separation of church and state, equal protection of all before the law, a universalist conception of human rights, and popular sovereignty – were finally accepted by a majority of the French people. It was also during this period around the turn of the century that the French state began to lay the legal foundations for citizenship and naturalisation, which would be based on the birthright principle of soil (*jus soli*) rather than exclusively on blood (*jus sanguinis*) as in Germany (Noiriel 1988; Weil 1991; Brubaker 1992). Thus the republican tradition found its expression in a more open and expansive notion of citizenship, similar (but not identical) to the birthright principle enunciated in the Fourteenth Amendment of the US Constitution ('All persons born or naturalized in the United States, and subject to the jurisdiction thereof, are citizens of the United States') and in stark contrast to the more narrow, ethnocultural vision of citizenship evolving in Germany of the Second Reich. While Germany was struggling with the issues of national and territorial unification and would continue to do so – one could argue – until 1989–90, France was becoming more comfortable with its revolutionary and republican heritage, as reflected in an increasingly expansive policy of immigration and naturalization.

In contrast with the United States – the other great republic founded at the end of the eighteenth century – France was not a nation of immigrants. The first period of intensive immigration in France did not begin until the 1850s, long after the Revolution of 1789. Hence immigration in France was never part of any type of founding myth, as it was (and still is) in the United States. Even though immigration and integration are closely associated with the French republican tradition, they are not crucial to French national identity, except for French Jews for whom the Revolution represents political and legal emancipation (Birnbaum 1995). Sustaining an open and legal immigration policy is more difficult to do in France than in the United States, but much easier than in Germany, which also has a republican tradition, albeit a young one dating from the founding of the Bundesrepublik in 1949 (Hollifield 1997).

For much of the post-Second World War period, French governments of the Fourth and Fifth Republics pursued expansive immigration policies, essentially for three reasons. The first justification – as can be seen in the various five-year plans – was primarily economic. During the period of reconstruction of the 1950s and 1960s (sometimes referred to as the *trente glorieuses*, or thirty glorious years of economic growth and low unemployment), France, like Germany, was in desperate need of labour. The second rationale for an open and legal immigration policy was the long-standing desire to boost the French population. Having gone through its demographic transition much earlier than other industrial societies, France was believed to have a huge demographic deficit and immigration was seen as one way to overcome this weakness. Finally, as I have argued elsewhere, policy-makers and politicians had great confidence in the ability of French society to absorb and integrate the newcomers, because of the strength of the republican tradition (Hollifield 1994). Therefore, an expansive, legal immigration policy was coupled with the most liberal naturalisation policy in Europe, quite similar in many ways to that of the United States.

The consensus for an open immigration regime held until the early 1970s, when the *trente glorieuses* abruptly ended in 1973–4 with the first big recessions of the post-war period. Moreover, decolonisation and the granting of independence to Algeria in 1962 radically altered the ethnic composition of the immigrant flows, as North African Muslims replaced the largely Catholic flows from Italy, Spain and Portugal. The presidency of Valéry Giscard d'Estaing (1974–81) was a radical and dramatic shift away from the open immigration regime of the earlier Gaullist years towards a more closed regime. The most important consequence, which was certainly not unique to France, was to freeze the foreign population in place. By simply decreeing an immigration stop, France, like other European countries, inadvertently accelerated the processes of settlement and family reunification.

Restrictive immigration legislation indicates the lengths to which liberal states are willing to go in rolling back the rights of foreigners, and thereby abandoning some aspects of negative freedom and the minimalist state, in order to restrict immigration. A somewhat easier target – more so in the USA than in France – is positive freedom revolving around the welfare state and flowing from laws designed to help the individual take advantage of the opportunities afforded by negative freedom in a liberal society.[2] The whole range of welfare benefits, from education to health care and pensions, has become a target for those wishing to restrict the rights of foreigners as a way of controlling immigration. Such actions taken by liberal states against foreigners would seem to be less threatening to citizens, depending upon the extent to which citizens are attached to social rights and determined to protect them for all members of society, even for the most marginal, disenfranchised groups, like children, immigrants, and foreigners. The French are certainly more attached to social rights (*les acquis sociaux*) than are Americans, but less so than the Germans, Dutch, or Scandinavians. Thus it is somewhat easier for the Americans and the French to cut welfare benefits for foreigners than it would be for the Germans or the Swedes, for example.

Looking at T. H. Marshall's (1950) classic trilogy of rights (civil, social, and political), we can see that France – like other liberal, republican, and social democracies – has acted to constrain the civil (equal protection and due process) and social (welfare) rights of immigrants and foreigners. If we follow this policy (of limiting the rights of non-citizens) to its logical conclusion, then the ultimate rights that can be denied to foreigners are political (or voting) rights, which are tied to naturalisation. To roll back these rights in a liberal republic requires tampering with founding myths and nationality law.

Table 7.1 summarises some major legislation concerning immigrants' and foreigners' rights in four liberal democracies, indicating whether each law had an expansive (+) or a limiting (−) effect on rights. Britain is clearly the most restrictive of the four, in large part because of the absence of a more universalist, republican tradition, and also because the courts in the British political system are much weaker than in the other three liberal republics, each of which has an element of separation of powers. With the exception of the IIRIRA of 1996, which rolled back immigrant social rights and some civil rights, the United States has the most expansive tradition of rights-based politics. The French case shows a very mixed pattern, with sharp restriction of rights during periods of right-wing rule (from 1993 to 1997), and a modest expansion of rights with the left's return to power from 1997 to the present. In Germany, we see a somewhat similar partisan pattern, but with a much more intensely rights-based politics, which has been expansive under both the left and the right.

Table 7.1 A typology of immigrants' rights

	Civil rights (due process)	Social rights (welfare)	Political rights (citizenship)
United States	IRCA, 1986 (+) Immigration Act, 1990 (+) IIRIRA, 1996 (−)	IIRIRA, 1996 (−)	No change, but expansive tradition based on *jus soli* (+)
France	Pasqua I, 1986 (−) Pasqua II, 1993 (−) Chevènement Law, 1997 (+)	Pasqua I, 1986 (−) Pasqua II, 1993 (−) Debré Law, 1996 (−)	Pasqua II, 1993, weakened *jus soli* (−) Guigou Law, 1997, reasserted *jus soli* (+)
Germany	Amendment of Article 16 of the Basic Law, 1993 (−)	Reduction of social rights for asylum seekers/refugees (1993, 1997) and ethnic Germans (1990–8) (−) Expansive social democratic tradition (+)	Naturalisation Law, 1990 (+) Citizenship Law, 1999 (+)
Britain	Race Relations Act, 1965, 1968, 1976 (+) British Nationality Acts, 1948 (+), 1981 (−)	Asylum Laws, 1993, 1996 and 1999 (−)	British Nationality Acts, 1948 (+), 1981 (−)

The trend with respect to citizenship and political rights has been positive in most cases, except Britain, where a series of steps were taken beginning in the 1960s and culminating in the British Nationality Act of 1981, to cut off immigration from the so-called New Commonwealth countries and to severely restrict non-white immigration to Britain. Changing or amending nationality laws in a republic in order to deal with immigration or integration is exceedingly difficult and fraught with many political dangers, as we have seen in France, the USA, and especially Germany. Reform in this area often means opening up difficult, moral debates about national identity, with many political, historical, and constitutional overtones. In France, it means changing the universalist and nationalist republican model, as it has evolved since 1945 (see below). In the USA, it would mean amending (or at least reinterpreting) the Fourteenth Amendment to the Constitution. In Germany, the problem of control is inextricably linked to the Holocaust and the crimes committed during the Third Reich, and to the problem of integrating a large, permanent foreign population. By changing the 1913 nationality law, the Schroeder government has brought Germany more fully into the club of liberal republics. It would be ironic if the American or French republics were to move in the opposite direction by weakening the *jus soli* principle, which lies at the heart of nationality in both countries.

Infringing individual and group rights or tampering with the social contract, the constitution, and national identity as a means of controlling immigration are fraught with danger for liberal and republican states, because the state or government runs the risk of undermining its own legitimacy, and alienating and/or endangering its own citizens. Moreover, otherwise liberal politicians may inadvertently (or unwittingly) provoke a nationalist, xenophobic, and even racist backlash, which could rebound against these same politicians and undermine the state (and rule of law) itself (Thränhardt 1997). But, in France and the USA, which have long histories of liberal and republican governance, there are institutional and ideological checks that work to protect the state and politicians from themselves. In France, as in other liberal republics such as the USA and Germany, the courts play a crucial role in this regard. Even though the French *Conseil d'Etat* has no real powers of judicial review and its opinions are only advisory, it is one of the most powerful *grands corps* – second only to the *Inspection des Finances*. It has great moral, political, and legal authority, and governments ignore its views at their peril (Stirn 1991). Moreover, decisions of the Conseil d'Etat may presage a ruling by the Conseil Constitutionnel, which does have powers of judicial review and may stop the implementation of any law deemed unconstitutional.

To combat the judges, the Interior Minister, Pasqua, turned one aspect of the republican tradition (popular sovereignty) against another (birthright citizenship). Claiming that the people, having spoken through their representatives, want immigration reduced, he called for a constitutional

amendment that would prepare France for entry into a border-free Europe
and give the State the power to turn back asylum seekers without hearings
or appeals. As provided by the Constitution, the amendment was voted in
an extraordinary congress of the Parliament (the Assembly and the Senate)
at Versailles in January 1994. Pasqua proclaimed that there would be no
'government by judges' in France, as in the USA, where many anti-
immigrant measures such as Proposition 187 in California have been
blocked by the Federal judiciary. Ultimately the US Supreme Court can
rule on the constitutionality of American immigration control policies,
especially when they impinge upon basic civil rights and liberties. The
question remains open, however: how far can a liberal-republican state go
in rolling back rights of individuals in its effort to control immigration? At
what point does the liberal-republican model begin to break down? What is
the appropriate balance between internal and external controls? Between
negative and positive freedom? Between immigration and immigrant
policy? Is the 'grand bargain' a viable strategy for escaping these political,
legal and moral dilemmas?

How to stop immigration?

While the issue of control (immigration policy) would continue to be hotly
debated in France throughout the 1980s and into the 1990s, the issue of
integration (immigrant policy) surged on to the national agenda (Hammar
1990). The realisation that millions of North Africans were settling
permanently in France led governments and political parties to reconsider
their approach to immigration and integration. Political parties, the party
system, and the electorate were increasingly polarised on both issues. The
election in 1981 of a socialist President, François Mitterrand, and the first
truly left-wing government since the Popular Front of 1936, set the stage
for some important policy shifts, which can be described as a kind of liberal
trade-off, or what some analysts have called a 'grand bargain' (Martin
1997).

   The socialists decided to maintain tight (external) control of borders and
stepped up (internal) control of the labour market to inhibit the
development of a black market for undocumented workers (*travail au noir*).
Regulation of the labour market was easy enough to accomplish by the use
of *Inspecteurs du travail*, who could make snap visits to firms and impose
sanctions on employers caught using undocumented workers (Valentin-
Marie 1992). But at the same time, the socialist government, led by Prime
Minister Pierre Mauroy, offered a conditional amnesty to undocumented
immigrants and longer (ten-year) residency and work permits for all
immigrants. Anyone who had entered France prior to 1 January 1981 was
eligible for a temporary residency permit, valid for three months, which
would give the individual time to complete an application for an adjustment of status (*régularisation exceptionnelle*). By the end of the amnesty

period (in 1983), over 145,000 applications had been received (Weil 1991).

Many high-immigration countries as the best compromise in the battle to control immigration have accepted the idea behind this 'liberal policy'. The US also enacted an amnesty in 1986. In a liberal and republican polity, strict control of entries together with an amnesty for illegals came to be seen as a good way to integrate permanent resident aliens, or as Tomas Hammar (1990) calls them, denizens. In addition to the amnesty, to make foreigners residing in France more secure, the first socialist government under Mauroy (1981–4) relaxed prohibitions against associational and political activities by foreigners. Prohibiting the police from making arbitrary identity checks of foreign-looking individuals protected the civil liberties of foreigners. But no changes were made in the nationality law or in naturalisation policy, leaving this key element of the republican tradition intact. Foreigners would be welcome within strict guidelines of labour market rules and regulations; they would be integrated on the (republican) basis of respect for the separation between church and state (*laïcité*); and they would quickly assimilate.

Having thus reaffirmed the previous right-wing governments' commitment to strict immigration control, while at the same time taking steps to speed the integration of foreigners in French society, the socialists, it seemed, were forging a new consensus on the contentious immigration issue. But the issue literally exploded in everyone's face (on the left as well as the right) in 1984 with the municipal elections in the city of Dreux, an industrial town just west of Paris. The Front National – a grouping of extreme right-wing movements under the charismatic and flamboyant leadership of Jean-Marie Le Pen – won control of this city, on a platform calling for a complete halt to immigration and for the deportation of African immigrants. The electoral breakthrough of a neo-Fascist, xenophobic, and racist movement profoundly changed the politics of immigration, not only in France but throughout western Europe. For the first time since the end of the Second World War, an extremist party of the right was making itself heard and finding a new legitimacy, garnering support from large segments of the French electorate across the political spectrum. Within a matter of years, it would become, in the words of the political analyst Pascal Perrineau, 'the largest working class party in France' (Perrineau 1995). From the beginning, the *Front National* was a single-issue party, taking a stand against immigration, and its leader, Le Pen, called for a physical separation of the races. His discourse mixes xenophobia, extreme nationalism (*La France aux français*), and anti-Semitism, with appeals to the economic insecurities of the French working class. How did the breakthrough of the Front National affect French immigration policy and the republican consensus?

The rise of the Front National contributed heavily to a sense of crisis in French politics and public policy, with immigrants at the centre of the maelstrom. Suddenly, immigrants were seen as the cause of the economic and cultural decline of the French nation, provoking a loss of confidence in the republican model, especially on the right. Immigrants were accused of taking jobs away from French citizens, thereby contributing to high levels of unemployment, and Muslims were deemed to be inassimilable and hostile to republican values.

Mitterrand cynically manoeuvred to exploit the rise of the Front National for political gain. From his perspective, not only did the Front National divide the right-wing electorate, but by getting many working-class votes, it also weakened the Communist Party, another traditional adversary of the socialists. Yet on a liberal note, in 1984 following the elections in Dreux, Mitterrand called for granting voting rights to immigrants in local elections, thereby forcing the parties of the traditional right (RPR-UDF) to take a stand on immigration and immigrant policy. But then, on a more cynical and Machiavellian note, the socialist government led by President Mitterrand and Prime Minister Laurent Fabius, changed the electoral system from a majoritarian, single-member district system to one based on proportional representation, just in time for the legislative elections of 1986. The immediate effect of this rule change was to reduce the magnitude of the inevitable victory of the right and to allow the Front National, with roughly 10 per cent of the vote, to gain 35 seats in the new Assembly. For the first time since Vichy, the extreme right had representation in parliament, and a new debate over French national identity was under way.

The first step of the right-wing coalition of neo-Gaullists (RPR) and liberals (UDF), led by Chirac, was to change the electoral system back to the traditional Fifth Republic dual-ballot system with single-member districts. Under the old system, it would be nearly impossible for the Front National to win seats in future elections. But the damage to the right had already been done, and the task remained of recapturing Front National voters. To accomplish this, the government set about reforming immigration and naturalisation policy, handing the entire dossier to the tough Corsican Minister of the Interior, Charles Pasqua, whose name would become synonymous with immigration reform over the next decade. Pasqua's approach to immigration control was quite different to any of his predecessors. As Minister of the Interior, he viewed control primarily as a police matter, so he moved quickly to reinforce border controls by giving sweeping new powers to the *Police de l'Air et des Frontières* (PAF) to detain and immediately deport anyone who did not have proper papers. He also reinforced the power of the (internal) police forces to conduct random (and arbitrary) identity checks of any foreign or suspicious-looking individual. In 1986, a wave of terrorist bombings in Paris, connected to the Middle East, specifically Iran, helped further to legitimise the new get-tough policy with respect to foreigners. The immediate effect of these measures was to restrict the civil liberties of foreigners, specifically North Africans, thereby launching a psychological campaign against immigrants and immigration. The policies were explicitly designed to win back supporters of the Front National, and to prevent any further loss of votes to the extreme right on the issue of immigration. However, they also heightened the sense of crisis and contributed to the growing debate over a loss of national identity.

If we look at the numbers (flows), which measure the outcome of French control policies, what we find is considerable continuity. Total immigration hovered between 200,000 and 100,000 persons annually, throughout the 1980s (see Table 7.2). The only noticeable increase in flows, as in other European states, was in the number of asylum seekers, which peaked at 61,372 in 1989. With the end of the Cold War and the gradual implementation of the Schengen Agreement in the 1990s, the rate of rejection of asylum applicants rose from 57 per cent in 1985 to 84 per cent in 1995 (see Table 7.3). So, if flows were not raging out of control, what was the purpose of the first Pasqua Law of 1986? The most important and controversial aspect of the reform was the attempt to weaken the birthright principle of *jus soli*, by putting an end to the practice of 'automatically' attributing citizenship at age 18 to the children born in France of foreign parents. In effect, this reform, which was intended to placate right-wing nationalists and win back Front National voters, was more symbolic than real. The thrust of the proposal was to require young foreigners to affirm their commitments to the Republic by formally requesting French nationality and taking a loyalty oath. What effect such a change might have on immigration flows was unclear; but the message was quite clear: the acquisition of French citizenship is a privilege, not a right, and it should be withheld from those who have not made a clear commitment to the French nation and society. Regardless of the intention of the reform, the first government of cohabitation succeeded in provoking a political firestorm of protest, as various civil and immigrant rights organisations, such as the GISTI, SOS-racisme, France Plus, and others, mobilised against the reform, leading Pasqua and Chirac eventually to withdraw the bill from consideration.

The withdrawal of the bill constituted a political failure for the Chirac government, which had unwittingly provided the increasingly active French civil rights movement with a new rallying cry: *Ne touche pas à mon pote!* (Don't touch my buddy!) Thousands marched in Paris under this banner. But, in addition to altering the political landscape, launching a new debate about French citizenship and national identity, and creating new political opportunities for the left (Ireland 1994; Feldblum 1999), the attempted reform brought the power and prestige of the Council of State to bear. In ruling on the legality and constitutionality of the bill, the Council of State put the government on notice that the rights of individual foreigners and the republican tradition must be respected. This was a lesson in immigration politics and law, which Minister Pasqua would not soon forget. In 1993, he would have a much stronger hand to deal with the judiciary (see below). But in this round of reform, the right-wing government was forced to

Table 7.2 Immigration in France 1946–95 (thousands)

	1946– 55	1956– 67	1968– 73	1974– 80	1981– 87	1988– 92	1993– 95
Workers	325.2	1205.9	801.3	192.9	195.1	118.6	55.8
Annual rate	32.5	109.6	133.6	27.6	27.9	23.7	18.6
% of total	49	44	39	14	17	20	21
Seasonal workers	247.6	1126.9	821.9	857.3	664.2	258.5[a]	31.0[a]
Annual rate	24.8	102.4	137.0	122.5	94.9	51.7	10.3
% of total	37	41	40	61	59	43	12
Family members	91.7	404.2	423.2	351.0	260.6	169.9	68.8
Annual rate	9.2	36.7	70.5	50.1	37.2	34.0	23.0
% of total	14	15	21	25	23	28	26
Total	664.4	2737.1	2046.5	1401.2	1120.0	601.1[b]	269.0[b]
Rate	66.4	248.8	341.1	200.2	160.0	120.2	89.7
%	100	100	100	100	100	100	100

Notes
a As of 1992, the Spanish and Portuguese are no longer counted among seasonal workers.
b Note that, beginning in 1988, total immigration includes other groups, such as refugees, not listed here. The annual rate for the years 1988–95 are inflated by the inclusion of flows not counted in previous years. For a breakdown, see the annual SOPEMI reports on France by André Lebon, *Immigration et Présence Etrangère en France* (Paris: La Documentation Française, various years).

Table 7.3 Asylum seekers in France 1985–95

Year	Number	Rate of rejection (%)
1985	28,809	56.8
1986	26,196	61.2
1987	27,568	67.5
1988	34,253	65.6
1989	61,372	71.9
1990	54,717	84.3
1991	47,380	80.3
1992	28,873	70.9
1993	27,564	72.1
1994	25,964	76.4
1995	20,415	83.7

Source: OFPRA.

compromise and the decision was made to appoint a special Commission to hold hearings on the possibility of reform of immigration and natural-isation policy.

After hearing the testimony of many immigration experts, the Commission simply reaffirmed the importance of the republican tradition by defending the birthright principle of *jus soli*, while at the same time stressing the importance of integrating foreigners into public and civic life

(Long 1988). Moreover, one of the principal unintended consequences of tougher control policies in France was the revaluation of citizenship, speeding up the process of naturalisation (see Table 7.4) and integration of the foreign population, and inadvertently reinforcing the republican tradition. The same thing happened again in the mid-1990s in France and in the USA, where anti-immigrant policies were pushed through the Republican-led Congress in 1996, contributing to a wave of insecurity among foreigners and a tremendous surge in naturalisations.

The liberal and republican right (UDF and RPR) lost its battle to eliminate the Front National and it also lost the elections of 1988. Jacques Chirac was defeated in his bid to unseat François Mitterrand, who won a second, seven-year presidential term; and the right also lost the legislative elections, as the socialists, led by Michel Rocard, regained control of the Assembly, albeit with the necessity of forming a minority government. With a score of 14.5 per cent of the vote on the first round of the presidential elections, Le Pen continued to cause problems for the right. Public opinion polls at the time (1988–9) showed that approximately one-third of the electorate had sympathies for the Front National's position on immigration.

The new left-wing government, led by Mitterrand and Rocard, essentially returned to the policies of the early 1980s, increasing regulation of the labour market, campaigning against illegal immigration, and taking steps to help integrate immigrants. To this end, Rocard created the Haut Conseil à l'Intégration, to study ways of speeding the integration of the foreign population, which still constituted over 6 per cent of the total population (Haut Conseil à l'Intégration 1991). For the period 1988–93, socialist governments fell back on a 'grand bargain' strategy of strictly

Table 7.4 Naturalisations in France 1984–95

Year	By decree (a)	By declaration (b)	Total (a + b)	Ratio (a/b)
1984	20,056	15,517	35,573	1.3
1985	41,588	19,089	60,677	2.2
1986	33,402	22,566	55,968	1.5
1987	25,702	16,052	41,754	1.6
1988	26,961	27,338	54,299	1.1
1989	33,040	26,468	59,508	1.2
1990	34,899	30,077	64,976	1.2
1991	39,445	32,768	72,213	1.2
1992	39,346	32,249	71,595	1.2
1993	40,739	32,425	73,164	1.3
1994	49,449	43,035	92,484	1.1
1995	40,867	18,121	58,988	2.3
1973–92 (average)	30,740	19,911	50,651	1.5

Source: André Lebon, *Immigration et présence étrangère en France* (Paris: La Documentation Française, various years).

controlling inflows in order to integrate those foreigners already in the country. The hope was to depoliticise the whole issue and defuse the national identity crisis. But no sooner had the left returned to power than it found itself confronted with a highly symbolic controversy when three school girls of Moroccan descent attended a public *lycée*, wearing Islamic scarves (*foulards*), in direct violation of the principles of separation of church and state (*laïcité*), one of the core principles of the republican tradition. Prime Minister Rocard and then Minister of Education, Lionel Jospin, took the decision to allow the girls to wear their scarves, so long as they agreed not to proselytise or in any way disrupt classes. As happened frequently with the issue of immigration and integration, when the rights of individuals *vis-à-vis* the state were in question, the Conseil d'Etat was called upon to help resolve the controversy. In this case, the Conseil d'Etat simply ratified the compromise position taken by the Rocard government. But the compromise did little to allay the growing fears of Islamic fundamentalism among the French public, and the *foulards* affair, as it came to be known, raised a new spectre of multiculturalism (*à l'américain*), seen as yet another threat to French unity and national identity, exemplified by the 'One and Indivisible Republic'. At the same time, *le droit à la différence* (the right to be different) became the new rallying cry of those defending the rights of immigrants (Roy 1991).

Despite the almost continuous atmosphere of crisis in French politics over immigration, integration, and national identity, dating back at least to the early 1980s, very little had changed, either in terms of policy outputs (actual policies for controlling immigration) or in terms of policy outcomes (Hollifield 1994). In the end, the first experience of *cohabitation* (1986–8) did little to alter the republican model and the rules of the game, as spelled out in the Ordonnances of 1945. France continued to be open to legal immigration, with no quotas or ethnic/racial preferences (in contrast to the American model), even though everything possible was done by the left and the right to discourage purely economic (or worker) immigration.

From a 'threshold of tolerance' to 'zero immigration'

When asked about immigration policy in 1991, President Mitterrand suggested that every society, including France, has a 'threshold of tolerance' (*seuil de tolérance*), beyond which instances of xenophobia and racism are likely to increase. But he refused to specify what exactly that threshold might be in the case of France. On the other hand, Charles Pasqua, soon to be (for the second time in his career) Minister of the Interior, stated bluntly that 'France has been an immigration country, but she wants to be no longer.' Like any good nationalist and populist, Minister Pasqua claimed to be speaking in the name of the French people. However, as a powerful member of the second government of *cohabitation*, elected by a landslide in the Spring of 1993, Pasqua made clear what the immigration policy of the new government would be: 'the goal we set, given the seriousness of the economic situation is to tend towards zero immigration'. This explicit linkage of immigration to the severe economic recession – which began in 1991–2 and would push unemployment in France to post-war highs of well over 10 per cent – was again aimed to appeal to the 12.4 per cent of French voters who supported the Front National in the first round of the 1993 parliamentary elections. Immigration and integration policies were still very much at the centre of French politics, and would remain so throughout the 1990s.

Faced with a badly weakened, divided, and demoralised socialist opposition, and having won an overwhelming majority in Parliament, the new right-wing government, headed by Edouard Balladur, had a virtually free hand to pursue draconian policies for: (1) stopping all immigration, (2) reducing the number of asylum seekers to an absolute minimum, and (3) reforming the nationality code to block naturalisation of as many of the resident foreigners as possible. These new policies represented a clear break from the old socialist 'grand bargain.' Even though Mitterrand was still President (and would be until 1995), he was clearly a lame duck and quite ill with prostate cancer. Hence, he was in no position to oppose what looked to be a truly dramatic shift in immigration policy. Only the courts potentially could block the change, therefore the Balladur government wasted no time in launching a sweeping reform of immigration and refugee policy, designed to move France as close as possible to zero immigration. To discourage further settlement of foreigners, the nationality law also would be changed.

What distinguishes this round of reform (in 1993) from earlier attempts to limit immigration (in 1974 or 1986, for example) is the clear focus on rolling back the rights of foreigners across the board. The Second Pasqua Law presented a direct challenge to the republican model, as defined by the 1945 Ordonnances. Equal protection and due process (civil rights) were denied to foreigners by cutting off possibilities of appeal for asylum seekers and by giving the police much greater powers than ever before to detain and deport foreigners. Social rights also would be severely restricted by denying foreigners access to the benefits of the social security system, especially health care. On this point, however, a rift developed within the government between the Minister of the Interior, Pasqua, and the Social Affairs Minister, Simone Weil, who argued for maintaining emergency health care for foreigners.

The debate in France over social rights for immigrants parallels a similar debate that was gathering force in the USA, especially in California, where voters approved a measure (Proposition 187) in November 1994 to cut public and social services for illegal immigrants. Barely two years later (in 1996), the US Congress, under Republican control, would adopt similar laws to cut social services for legal as well as illegal immigrants, and the rights of appeal for illegals and asylum seekers would be sharply curtailed.

Also in the US, prominent right-wing politicians, such as Governor Pete Wilson of California, made proposals to limit birthright citizenship, so that the children born of foreign parents would no longer be automatically entitled to American citizenship. Similarly in France, the second Pasqua law (like the first) sought to change naturalisation procedures by requiring children born in France of foreign parents to make a formal request for naturalisation, between the ages of 16 and 21.

Civil disobedience and the limits of control

Immigration continued to agitate French politics and society during the mid- and late-1990s, during the presidential election of 1995 and especially during the legislative elections of 1997. The election of Jacques Chirac as President of the Republic by a narrower than expected margin over the left candidate, Lionel Jospin, did little to change French immigration policy, even though Le Pen received a record number of votes (15 per cent) on the first round of the presidential elections. The new UDF/RPR government, led by Alain Juppé, controlled 80 per cent of Assembly seats. But one big difference was the absence of Charles Pasqua from the government. Pasqua had supported Chirac's rival, the former Prime Minister Edouard Balladur, for the presidency. Jean-Louis Debré replaced him as Minister of the Interior and quickly made a name for himself by proposing further, draconian steps to limit the rights of foreigners in France and crack down on illegal immigration. The Debré Law of 1997 would test the limits of strategies for (internal) immigration control, leading to civil disobedience, more court rulings, new elections (thanks to the political blunders of Chirac and Juppé), and finally a resurgence of the republican left.

In the summer of 1996, the tough control policies (described in the preceding section) were challenged by a group of Africans, mostly from Mali, who were caught in the web of the Second Pasqua Law (unable to obtain a residency permit, even though many of them had resided in France for many years and could not be legally deported) or whose applications for political asylum had been rejected. The *sans papiers*, as they were called, occupied a church in Paris, demanding that they be given an adjustment of status (*régularisés*), and several of them launched a hunger strike. The highly public *épreuve de force* with the new government was indicative of the willingness of immigrants openly to resist the government's policy and of the sympathy they were able to generate among certain segments of French civil society. Over 10,000 people marched in Paris in solidarity with the *sans papiers*, and even more embarrassing for the government were appeals by the clergy not to remove the immigrants from the church by force. None the less, the police were ordered to storm the church, arrest the protesters, and break up the hunger strike. The government also proudly published statistics indicating that deportations for the first six months of 1996 were up substantially (by about one-third) over the similar period for 1995. Any sign of weakness or wavering by the government in the face of immigrant resistance and civil disobedience was immediately condemned by Le Pen and the Front National.

Apart from occasional acts of civil disobedience by the African *sans papiers*, which continued throughout 1995–7, whether in the form of occupying churches or, in one case, the offices of UNESCO, the civil war in Algeria also had an impact on French control policy. French involvement in Algerian politics led to a number of terrorist attacks by Islamic militants against public targets in France. These attacks forced the Juppé government to increase security throughout the country. The security sweeps by the police and the military, known as operation *vigipirate*, focused public attention on the Muslim (and African) communities in France, bringing the full power of the French state to bear in an effort to catch the perpetrators. In October 1995, the police shot and killed one of the bombers – a young second-generation Algerian man – in the outskirts of Lyon. In the press, his life story was covered in detail and held up as an example of the failure of French society to integrate some segments of the young, Maghrebi population. These dispossessed youths, with no loyalty to the land of their birth, had joined radical Islamic groups and turned against the French Republic.

As in the 1950s, French foreign policy and relations with former colonies, especially Algeria, became a driving factor in immigration and refugee policy in the 1990s. The government felt compelled to grant asylum (or at least temporary residence) to many members of the Algerian political and intellectual class, while at the same time stepping up pressure to keep other Algerians out, and carefully to surveil the established Algerian community in France. This atmosphere of crisis and public insecurity together with continuing pressure from the Front National led the Juppé government late in 1996 to propose a new law, which came to be known as the Debré Law, designed to resolve the ambiguous status of some of the *sans papiers*, particularly the French-born children of illegal immigrants and the foreign spouses of French citizens. These groups could not be deported, but under the Pasqua Law they were not eligible for an adjustment of status. Under the proposed new law, the 'foreign' children under 16 years of age would have to prove continuous residence in France for ten years, and 'foreign' spouses would have to have been married for two years in order to be eligible (like the children) for a one-year residence permit.

Even though the Debré Law had some liberal intent, it became the focal point of controversy and protest because of a provision added to the bill by the conservative National Assembly that required all private citizens to notify local authorities whenever they received in their homes any non-EU foreigner. Moreover, mayors would be given the authority to verify that a foreign visitor had left the private citizen's home once the visitor's visa had expired. What is most interesting about the Debré Law is not so much the effect (or lack thereof) that it had on immigration control, but the response it received both from certain French groups in civil society and institutions of the liberal-republican state. Debré, paraphrasing his predecessor Pasqua, stated that 'I am for zero illegal immigration.... The state must be given the means to deter foreigners who want to enter France without resources, papers or jobs.' The focus in this statement is on those clearly outside the law, i.e. illegal immigrants; but public attention was focused on the effect that the Law would have on private French citizens, who would (by law) be compelled to inform on foreign visitors. Such an intrusion by the state into the private lives of individuals and families was deemed by many to have crossed the invisible line beyond which liberal states are not supposed to go. The Debré Law was denounced as an infringement of (negative) freedom and a threat to the basic civil liberties of all French citizens. The European Parliament even went so far as to pass a resolution condemning the Law and equating it with Vichy-era laws that required French citizens to inform on their Jewish compatriots, so that the Germans could deport them to death camps.

Over the objections of the Conseil d'Etat, which warned the government that requiring citizens to inform on foreigners might be unconstitutional, the Assembly approved the Debré Law in February 1997, but with some important modifications. The amended version required the foreigners themselves to report their movements and whereabouts to local authorities. This compromise illustrates quite well the limitations on the power of the liberal state to pursue strategies for (internal) control of immigration that cross the invisible line between infringement of the liberties of citizens and those of foreigners. It is important to note also that the Law exempted Europeans and visitors from thirty other countries from the reporting requirements, targeting undesirable African immigrants who were more likely to overstay their visas.

Not only did judicial or institutional checks come into play, the reaction to the Law from certain elite groups in civil society was swift and severe, causing the government considerable embarrassment. Fifty-nine film directors launched a campaign of civil disobedience by publishing an open letter in *Le Monde*, declaring that 'we are guilty, every one of us, of harbouring illegal foreign residents ... we ask therefore to be investigated and put on trial.' A rally in Paris to protest the new Law attracted 35,000 people, but the French public, according to polls published at the time, was heavily polarised, with a clear majority (59 per cent) supporting the government's position. Earlier in February, the Front National again scored an electoral victory in municipal elections, as Catherine Megret, wife of the number two in the party, Bruno Megret, won the mayoral race in Vitrolles, a small town north of Marseilles. The victory gave the Front National control of four French cities: Marignane, Orange, and Toulouse, in addition to Vitrolles.

The Debré Law also seemed to violate the liberal principle that an individual is innocent until proven guilty. In order to renew their ten-year residence permits, foreigners would be required to prove that they were not a threat to public order and that they had maintained a regular residence in France, thus shifting the burden of proof from the state to the individual. This provision of the Law, along with another that would have given police access to the fingerprints of all asylum seekers, were subsequently struck down by the Conseil Constitutionnel, which, unlike the Conseil d'Etat, has powers of judicial review. Here again, the precarious relationship between the individual and the state, which is so important in a liberal polity and which is the subject of constitutional law and interpretation, was threatened. But in a republican political system, which stresses popular sovereignty, the will of the people *qua* citizens (desirous to stop immigration, if opinion polls are to be believed) must be respected. As we have seen in recent American experiences, one way to get around this dilemma, which opposes the liberal against the republican half of the polity, is to focus the regulatory and police power of the state on illegal immigrants, thus leaving some legitimacy for legal immigration and the right to seek asylum.

The final version of the Debré Law was passed by the French Parliament (Senate) in March 1996. Provisions concerning notification of the whereabouts of foreigners had been watered down or eliminated altogether. The Law required African visitors to prove that they have adequate accommodations and funds necessary to live in France during their stay and to return home afterwards. Throughout this period of policy reform, a major concern of the French government was to devise a system for controlling entries by Africans (and other foreign visitors coming from developing countries), but without imposing American-style quotas on visas, entries, or immigrants. The resistance to quotas is born of (1) the republican desire to maintain an egalitarian approach to the issuing of visas (where all or most applicants, coming from developing countries, would be treated equally) and (2) a desire to construct a system that would not be overtly discriminatory towards individuals coming from former French colonies in West and North Africa. But regardless of intent, the effect of both the Pasqua (1993) and Debré (1997) Laws has been to severely restrict legal immigration of Africans.

A 'new republican pact'

To the surprise of many, Chirac dissolved the Parliament and called early elections in May–June 1997. Having been elected on a promise to heal the *fracture sociale* and lower the record high levels of unemployment, running at 12–13 per cent in 1996–7, Chirac and Juppé found themselves caught in a political and economic bind, unable to stimulate the economy because of their commitments to EMU, but unwilling to abandon French workers to their fate in a more competitive European and international economy. As a result, Chirac decided to seek a new mandate for his government and his presidency, a huge political gamble, which he lost. The French socialists and their allies (a mixture of communists, radicals, and greens) won control of the National Assembly, launching the third period of cohabitation (divided government) in a little over a decade, only this time the right would control the presidency and the left would control the parliament.

The change of government had major implications for French immigration policy. As in past elections, the Front National received about 15 per cent of the vote in the first round, but thanks to the dual ballot electoral system, it won only one seat in the Assembly, held by Jean-Marie Chevallier, Mayor of Toulon. What was different about this election was the refusal of the FN to co-operate with other parties of the right (RPR and UDF) by withdrawing its candidates – who had received the constitutionally required 12.5 per cent of registered voters on the first round – from the second round of voting. This set up over seventy *triangulaires* (three-way contests) in which the Front National candidate essentially split the right-wing vote on the second round, thus helping to elect a candidate of the left. In effect, the Front National had a big hand in bringing down the Gaullist-liberal government, and putting the socialist-communist left back in power. If the Front National persists in this strategy in the future, it will intensify pressure on right-liberal and Gaullist candidates to strike electoral deals with the Front National, which could lead to a further polarisation of the electorate and the party system on the specific issue of immigration.

In his opening speech to the new Parliament on 19 June 1997, Prime Minister Jospin announced that he would establish a 'new republican pact' with the French people, returning to the 'roots of the Republic' while striving to 'modernise French democracy.' In outlining his government's program, the first two policy items were (1) the school, which he called the 'cradle of the Republic' where values of citizenship are taught (the most important being *laïcité*), and (2) immigration. With respect to the latter issue, Jospin laid out quite a detailed republican vision of immigration policy, reminiscent of earlier periods in French immigration history, from the turn of the century, to the 1920s, to the Ordonnances of 1945, to the early Mitterrand years in the 1980s. To quote Jospin: 'France, with its old republican traditions, was built in layers that flowed together into a melting pot, thus creating an alloy that is strong because of the diversity of its component parts. For this reason, birthright citizenship (*le droit du sol*) is inseparable from the French Nation (*consubstantiel à la nation française*). We will re-establish this right. Nothing is more alien to France than xenophobia and racism ... Immigration is an economic, social and human reality, which must be organised and controlled. France must define a firm, dignified immigration policy without renouncing its values or compromising its social balance' (*Libération*, 20 June 1997).

To accomplish this goal, Jospin called for: (1) a new republican integration policy, which welcomes immigrants, respects their human rights, but combats illegal immigration and black labour markets, thus returning to the 'grand bargain' strategies of earlier socialist governments (see above); (2) a new policy of cooperation with the sending states to help control immigration at its source; (3) a complete reform of immigration policy, including the repeal of the Pasqua and Debré Laws and a comprehensive review of immigration and nationality law, to be carried out by an interministerial task force, chaired by the immigration scholar, Patrick Weil. The Weil report was presented in the form of a bill in the first session of the Parliament in September 1997. Finally, (4) steps will be taken to review, on a case-by-case basis, the situation of all undocumented foreigners (*sans papiers*) caught in the maze of regulations and contradictions surrounding the Pasqua–Debré Laws. The government issued orders to the prefects immediately to begin reviewing as many as 40,000 cases, and foreigners who had waited for months or years for their dossiers to be reviewed, suddenly found a new willingness on the part of administrative authorities to help them by issuing temporary residence permits.

By giving such a high priority to reform of immigration and nationality law, the Jospin government signalled its desire to confront this issue head on; and by appealing to French republican values as a way of resolving the immigration crisis, the government clearly hopes to return to the earlier 'republican consensus,' diffuse the issue, and seize the political and moral high ground (Hollifield 1994). Attempts by right-wing governments to 'steal the thunder' from Le Pen and the FN by cracking down on immigrants and thereby appealing to insecurities and xenophobia of the electorate – what might be called the Pasqua–Debré approach to immigration policy – seemed to do little to reduce levels of support for the FN. If anything, this strategy has led to an increase in support for the far right, which won its most votes ever in the first round of legislative elections in 1997. Whether the socialists and communists can reconstruct the republican consensus will depend in part on their ability to reach out to elements of the liberal and republican right.

What does this new 'republican' strategy mean for French control policy and what will its effect be on actual flows? The emphasis will shift from internal controls – designed to limit and roll back the (civil and social) rights of resident aliens, what Tomas Hammar called denizens – back to a 'grand bargain' strategy of relatively tough, external control of borders, careful, internal regulation of labour markets, combined with a liberal policy for integrating and naturalising immigrants. The effect on flows is likely to be modest. They should return to the annual averages of the 1980s and early 1990s (around 100,000, see Table 7.2). Moreover, France under the socialists is likely to become a more co-operative partner in building a border-free Europe, in the context of the Schengen agreement and the Amsterdam Treaty's provisions on free movement, immigration and asylum.

Conclusion: shifting strategies for control

It is important from the standpoint of the politics and policies of immigration control to understand how early waves of immigration were legitimised. In this respect, France looks less like her European neighbours, and more like the USA. In both cases, immigration was legitimised through an appeal to republican ideas and ideologies. From the very earliest days of the Republic to the various post-war governments of the Fourth and Fifth Republics, politicians have appealed to republican ideals of universalism, egalitarianism, nationalism, and *laïcité*, as a way of legitimising immigration and integrating foreigners. Thus it is not surprising to hear the Prime Minister, Lionel Jospin, calling in 1997 for a new 'republican pact' as a way of solving the latest social and economic crises, especially immigration. The republican model is alive and well and living in Paris.

But immigration, like republicanism, remains contested in France, more so than in the USA. Again, to paraphrase Prime Minister Jospin, immigration is not consubstantial with the Republic.[3] Immigration is not a 'founding myth' of the French Republic, therefore we cannot say that France is, like the USA, Canada, or Australia, a nation of immigrants (Freeman and Jupp 1992). Yet the Prime Minister is correct in asserting that immigration and birthright citizenship are inextricably linked with the evolution of republicanism in France, from the Third to the Fifth Republics (on this point see Noiriel 1988). Attacking immigrants and their rights is to some extent tantamount to attacking the Republic. Conversely, one of the best ways to defend immigrants is to cloak yourself in the values and symbols of the Republic.

Immigrants and immigration did come under attack in the 1970s, in large part because of the shift in the composition and ethnic mix of the flows, from predominantly Christian and European, to Muslim and African. In the early 1970s, the justification for stopping immigration was primarily economic: France had and still has high levels of unemployment, so the reasoning went: if we can stop immigration, this will solve the problems of unemployment. But this Malthusian and economic reason for stopping immigration – although still present today – quickly gave way in the 1980s to the arguments advanced by Jean-Marie Le Pen and others, that France was being transformed and destroyed by an influx of inassimilable African immigrants. In this view, Muslims could never be good citizens of the Republic, because of their inability to separate church and state, and to keep their private, religious views separate from their public life. Their growing numbers were ostensibly causing a crisis of social cohesion and national identity (cf. Kepel 1991 and in a similar vein in the US, Brimelow 1997). Politicians began to play on these fears as a way of changing immigration control policies and as a way of getting votes (Thränhardt 1997; Viard 1996). Throughout the 1980s and 1990s, the tactic of appealing to xenophobic fears and instincts led to further polarisation of the electorate on the issue of immigration and contributed to the rise of the FN. Whether these fears (on the part of the French electorate) are rational or irrational is obviously open to debate, but there is no doubt that they were exploited by politicians for political gain (Weiner 1995).

By the 1990s, strategies for immigration control in France and other liberal democracies began to change dramatically. Instead of relying exclusively on the mechanism of external, border controls (which were none the less being reinforced and further *externalised* and Europeanised through the Schengen system) or on the more classic mechanisms of internal regulation of labour markets, the first right-wing government of the 1990s, led by Edouard Balladur, began to roll back and limit the rights of immigrants, first by attacking civil rights and liberties (due process, equal protection, and the like), then by going after certain social rights, specifically health care. Finally, political rights, naturalisation, and citizenship were challenged, through a reform of the nationality code and the erosion of the principle of birthright citizenship. From a social science standpoint, here is where the story gets interesting; because it is not clear how far a liberal republic can go towards limiting rights of immigrants and foreigners as a way of controlling immigration. We may not yet have a complete and satisfactory answer to this question.

In France, we can see quite clearly the progression of control strategies and the evolution of the relationship between immigration and immigrant policy. First came the imposition of external controls (in the form of new visa regimes) in the early 1970s, then the restriction on hiring foreign workers (in 1974), followed by attempts to roll back the 'right' to family reunification in the late 1970s. The socialist years of the 1980s saw increased regulation of the labour market, and attempts to crack down on *le travail au noir.* In 1990, there was a return to external strategies of control with implementation of the Schengen Agreement and new limits on social and civil rights later in the decade (the First and Second Pasqua Laws, as well as the Debré Law). Finally, attempts were made to limit citizenship by changing the nationality law (the First and Second Pasqua Laws). When the state crossed the invisible line between immigration control (on the one hand), to the point of becoming a threat to civil society and being at odds with the founding (republican) principles of the regime (on the other hand), institutional/judicial, ideological, and social checks came into play. As in other liberal republics, immigration control in France is not purely a function of markets, economic interests, or national security. It is heavily dependent on the interplay of ideas, institutions, and civil society.

Notes

1 In *The Leviathan*, Thomas Hobbes describes freedom as 'the silence of the laws.' Isaiah Berlin describes negative freedom as 'an area within which a man can act unobstructed by others' see Berlin (1969). Finally, Friedman (1962)

defines freedom in terms of the freedom of choice afforded by the market-place.

2 Positive freedom can be defined as having the ability (as well as the liberty) to act. See the works of T. H. Green, such as *Prolegomena to Ethics* or *Principles of Political Obligation*, as well as Rawls (1971).

3 The exact quote, cited in English in the penultimate section of this paper, is *'le droit du sol est consubstantiel à la nation française'*. This is a marvellous and ironic mixing of metaphors, equating birthright citizenship with the French Nation, using the Christian (or more specifically Lutheran) expression/doctrine of consubstantiation to illustrate the point. When only a few sentences earlier, the Prime Minister is extolling the republican virtues of *laïcité*!

8 Denying access

Asylum seekers and welfare benefits in the UK[1]

Andrew Geddes

Introduction

In the UK, a strong executive, relatively weak courts and a largely subservient legislature have been a recipe for stringent immigration control legislation. During the 1990s, increased powers to monitor and control the behaviour of asylum seekers through welfare state-related measures have been acquired that marginalise asylum seekers, reduce the possibility for social integration, and seek to prevent settlement so that asylum seeking deemed to be bogus can be reversible. Yet beneath the surface veneer of executive power and legislation aimed at immigration control lies an asylum policy riddled with practical policy implementation difficulties.

This chapter charts recent asylum policy development in the UK and pays close attention to the introduction of welfare state measures designed to deter asylum applications by marginalising asylum applicants and reducing the possibility of social inclusion. The chapter's first section charts the contemporary politicisation of asylum in the UK to show that asylum has been incorporated within an immigration policy *problematique* with an emphasis on shrinking the numbers of people entitled to enter the UK. The supposition is that most asylum seekers are 'bogus' in the sense that they are really economic migrants seeking to circumvent the drastic narrowing of the economic migration channel into the UK that has occurred since the early 1960s. The chapter's next section analyses how this policy developed during the 1990s to include internal welfare state-related measures designed to separate asylum seekers on the grounds that they were suspicious and a prevailing sense that they were bogus applicants. This separation began with the provisions for fingerprinting of asylum seekers in the 1993 Asylum and Immigration Appeals Act and spread to welfare state benefits via secondary legislation introduced under the Social Security Act (1995). The Conservative government's Asylum and Immigration Act (1996) removed access to welfare benefits to 'in country' applicants, as opposed to those lodged at air or seaports of entry. The consequence of this legislation was that local authorities in London and the south-east of England – where most asylum seekers settled – were forced to pick up the tab for costs of reception of in-country asylum applicants. The chapter's final section analyses the Labour government's Immigration and Asylum Act (1999). The 1999 legislation accepted the rationale of the 1996 legislation: that welfare state benefits attract asylum applicants to the UK. The 1999 Act also sought to address the inadequacies of the 1996 legislation by introducing a voucher system to replace cash-paid welfare benefits and a national dispersal scheme to send asylum applicants all over Britain. Underpinning all these developments, however, have been major administrative and bureaucratic failings that necessarily qualify perspectives on executive omnipotence. Despite ever more stringent legislation and the introduction of internal welfare state mechanisms for population control, the numbers of asylum applicants increased in the late 1990s with no evidence to suggest that capacity to process asylum applications had increased.

The politicisation of asylum

Successive pieces of immigration legislation since the Commonwealth Immigrants Act of 1962 have eschewed the imperial grandeur of a bygone era (Spencer 1997). The 1971 Immigration Act emphasised ancestry – 'patriality' – as the basis for entry to the UK and removed the remaining vestiges of rights of entry for Commonwealth citizens. The 1971 Immigration Act did, however, enter into force on 1 January 1973, the same date as UK accession to the EC and Britain's incorporation within the EC's free movement provisions. Since the early 1960s, executive power combined with a prevailing anti-immigration discourse has facilitated the development of stringent immigration laws for non-EC nationals. Asylum legislation in 1993, 1996 and 1999 swelled executive authority and was loaded with the traditional assumptions of UK 'race relations' policy – restrict numbers of immigrants and asylum seekers in order to maintain 'good race relations' (Favell 1998b).

Executive authority has been exercised through both primary and, perhaps more importantly, secondary legislation. The latter is far more difficult to scrutinise, consolidates executive authority, and empowers executive agents such as the immigration control authorities. Successive governments have been able to present 'blank cheque'[2] immigration and asylum bills to Parliament in which the general framework of legislation is outlined to be filled in by secondary legislation that is far more difficult to scrutinise. In opposition, the Labour party condemned the Conservative governments' immigration and asylum legislation for 'playing the race card' by stoking up anti-immigration/immigrant sentiment and for the abuse of executive authority through the issuance of secondary legislation. Yet, in government, the Labour home secretary, Jack Straw, presented legislation with similar secondary legislative provisions. The 1999 Immigration and Asylum Act contained 50 such provisions for secondary legislation and gives significant power to the immigration authorities. The Labour government elected in 1997 has maintained core elements of existing policy, which should come as no surprise given Labour's historical fearfulness of being seen as 'soft' on immigration.

Yet, there is also an *ad hoc* air about UK asylum policy because asylum legislation has been bolted on to existing immigration legislation (MacDonald and Blake 1995). The reduction of asylum seeking to 'a trickle' in the early 1990s was viewed as exemplifying executive power (Joppke 1997). Yet, numbers seeking asylum rose in the late 1990s. Restrictive measures introduced in the early 1990s had appeared to stem asylum applications. A plethora of restrictive devices at the UK's external frontiers sought to restrict the chances for asylum applicants to enter the UK. These included carrier sanction penalties on airlines and shipping companies (extended to include coach drivers, truck drivers and the operators of the Eurostar trains through the channel tunnel), rules on 'manifestly unfounded applications', designated 'safe countries' of origin to which applicants could be returned, and visa requirements for those from source countries such as Sri Lanka (Cohen 1994; Harlow 1994; Randall 1994; Ward 1994; Joppke 1998: 128–34).

Britain was also an enthusiastic participant in European co-operation on immigration, asylum and internal security instigated following the Single European Act (1986). UK governments have been keen to participate in EU co-operation that rests on executive power with weak judicial and legislative oversight – the recipe for immigration control established in the UK since the 1960s. The UK has, though, refused to participate in supranationalised immigration and asylum policies because this would question the UK's method of external frontier control and give the Commission, the European Court of Justice and European Parliament powers over British immigration and asylum policy with the power to check executive power.[3] Moreover, from behind the well-guarded ramparts of 'fortress Britain', the prospect of 'fortress Europe' appears a chimera resting as it does on the unlikely realisation of strict (i.e. to UK levels) control policies on the EU's eastern and southern flanks (Geddes 2000). As constituted during the 1980s and 1990s, European integration has offered the possibility for intergovernmental, restriction-oriented co-operation free from oversight and scrutiny, but supranational integration means the empowerment of other actors such as supranational institutions with the effect that member states could lose control over policy outcomes.

Agreement on the 'European dimension' is another indication of the strong bi-partisan consensus between the Conservatives and Labour on restriction of the numbers of migrants dating back to 1964.[4] British immigration controls have been racially discriminatory and directed towards dark-skinned immigrants from the new Commonwealth and Pakistan. The fact that many asylum seekers share the phenotypical or cultural markers of previously excluded groups has heightened a perception of racialised asylum policy. In the 1990s, asylum seekers from former Yugoslavia such as Bosnians and ethnic Albanians from Kosovo have also encountered hostility (the most infamous example being in the south coast town of Dover, discussed below).

Despite the devices for control and the bi-partisan consensus on the 'asylum problem' asylum seeking increased from the mid-1990s. Until the late 1980s, there were very few applications made for asylum in the UK. The number rose in the late 1980s from around 4,000 a year during 1985–8 to 44,800 in 1991. More stringent external frontier restrictions led to lower numbers of applications in 1992 and 1993, but applications rose from the mid-1990s. In 1997 the UK received 41,500 applications rising to 46,015 in 1998 and 71,000 in 1999. People from Somalia, Afghanistan, Turkey (mainly Kurds), Sri Lanka and former Yugoslavia featured regularly in the groups seeking asylum in the UK. It is important to put these figures into perspective. Less than 1 per cent of the world's refugees move to Britain and the UK ranks only tenth out of EU member states in the number of asylum applicants per capita. Indeed, when the ratio of refugees to the average GNP is considered, only Germany of EU states ranks among the world's top 50 countries and then only as forty-second. Nevertheless, the vivid language of 'swamping' and 'alien invasion' can appear in reporting of the asylum issue because of the connection made between asylum seeking and the 'threat' of immigration.

In terms of implementing restrictive policies, it appeared that the great expectations of restriction of Whitehall and Westminster were dashed at the Immigration and Nationality Department in Croydon (Pressman and Wildavsky 1973). The Labour government inherited a poisoned chalice from their Conservative predecessors in the form of an asylum system that was fundamentally ill equipped to deal with asylum applications. Asylum legislation had developed in piecemeal fashion attached to the 1971 Immigration Act. The legislation introduced in the 1990s had calamitous effects. The 1996 Asylum and Immigration Act's withdrawal of rights to benefit for in-country asylum applicants meant that in-country applicants sought support from local authorities within the provisions of the 1948 National Assistance Act. This followed a landmark ruling in the Court of Appeal in a case brought in 1997 by the Joint Council for the Welfare of Immigrants. The Court of Appeal found the deprivation of social security rights to be *ultra vires*, arguing that Parliament could not have intended to place asylum seekers at risk of destitution as such an intention would be barbaric. The result of the judgement was that local authorities in London and the south-east of England picked up the tab because it was in these parts of the country that most asylum seekers lived. 'Asylum brokers' also emerged who would act on behalf of London authorities and 'off load' asylum applicants on to seaside towns such as Eastbourne where there were plentiful small hotels and bed and breakfast accommodation.

In addition, the IND went into bureaucratic and administrative meltdown in the late 1990s when a new computer system purchased from Siemens by the Conservative government in 1996 combined with a move to new HQ building led to near administrative collapse. A 1999 management consultant's report identified an 'IT black hole' into which had fallen more than 90,000 asylum and immigration cases. In May 1998 there was backlog of 52,000 asylum applications, of which 10,000 were over five years old. There were also 32,000 pending immigration appeals, of which 70 per cent were asylum cases (HMSO 1998). On top of this were reports of files located in basements that staff were not allowed to enter because of health hazards and of 1,000 of the daily 5,000 telephone calls to the IND office in Croydon, south-west London, remaining unanswered. The IND was reduced to little more than short-term crisis management (*The Guardian*, 1 November 1999). The adjudication system also appeared incapable of acting quickly in what may literally be 'life or death' situations. In the mid-1980s, for instance, an Iranian was sent back to Iran and then shot dead in front of a BBC TV camera crew. These kinds of events tend to live long in the minds of officials, although similar errors have occurred since with Tamil and Zairean asylum seekers (Harlow 1994; Ward 1994).

In the 1990s there was a gap between the discursive and legislative focus on controls and the increased numbers of asylum seekers (Cornelius, Martin and Hollifield 1994). As usual, the response to this gap was the ratcheting-up of anti-immigration rhetoric with little indication that restrictive capacity could match this rhetorical commitment to control. In the UK, asylum became viewed through the prism of already existing immigration laws coupled with efforts to promote 'good race relations' and was politicised in these terms. Media coverage – particularly in newspapers – of the asylum issue has been viewed as playing an intermediary role in 'an orchestrated government campaign to downgrade the public perception of refugees in 1990–1 and 1992–3 to control the numbers entering the UK' (Kaye 1998: 177–8). Even liberal-inclined newspapers were seen as perpetuating the 'genuine-phoney' construct in their writing and thereby casting doubt on the validity of many asylum claims (Kaye 1998: 178). Asylum was to be restricted on the basis of the supposition that many asylum seekers were in fact disguised economic migrants.[5]

In the late 1990s, external frontier controls appeared incapable of addressing 'unavoidable' – because of international and domestic legal obligations – asylum seeking. The UK government could, however, seek to ensure that once in the country applicants would be denied the opportunity for social participation in an attempt to ensure that this form of migration would not lead to permanent settlement. In this sense, recent asylum legislation rests on a familiar assumption that has served as a rationale for British immigration control legislation: that Britain is a small, crowded island that is an attractive location for migrants (Layton-Henry 1994). This kind of reasoning is implicit within the 'numbers game' that is familiar to students of British immigration history and politics: if Britain's borders are not secure then the country could be 'flooded' by unwanted immigrants. There are actually around twice as many labour migrants entering the UK each year than there are asylum seekers, but labour migrants can be regulated prior to entry whereas asylum seekers are spontaneous and the extent of arrivals cannot be easily predicted.[6] It is the unpredictability and management difficulties associated with flows that motivates restriction efforts as well as the supposition that most asylum seekers are 'bogus'. The UK government has sought to separate asylum seekers, to disperse them, to deny them access to cash-paid welfare benefits and to deport those whose claims are not accepted (the acceptance rate in 1999 was 22.8 per cent). Asylum seekers have been cast to the margins of the British welfare state in the belief that most are disguised economic migrants seeking to circumvent stringent immigration legislation. In Britain, as in the rest of Europe, the potent myth of the welfare-scrounging bogus asylum seeker has polluted contemporary immigration-related political discourse. Asylum is organised as a political discretion rather than a human right and incorporated within an immigration *problematique* within which policies are geared towards restriction of asylum applications (Layton-Henry 1994; Joppke 1997). 'Bogus asylum seeking' is viewed as the main challenge to maintaining tight external frontier controls and 'fortress Britain' even though bogus asylum seeking can be viewed as the underside of restrictions on labour migration. The substantive causes of movement of people – economic inequalities, conflict, war, oppression – have not gone away even though barriers to entry in destination countries have got progressively higher.

These considerations of the politicisation of asylum emphasise the importance of analysing the construction by receiving states of highly differentiated categories for migrants as a result of immigration control policies. Whatever their reasons for migration, those individuals who cannot place themselves in one of these categories become by definition 'illegal' or 'abusers' of the migration system. Despite asylum seekers not being immigrants *stricto sensu*, it is fair to say that asylum has become the immigration issue in contemporary Britain. Alongside family reunification, one of the remaining methods of legitimate immigration into the UK is through the granting of refugee status. In this respect, the UK experience is similar to that in other European countries that have restricted labour migration and left family migration, asylum seeking, as well as 'deregularised' informal or illegal employment as the main channels for migrants.

Asylum seekers and access to welfare benefits

The restrictive measures introduced to curb asylum applications had some intended restrictive effects in the early- and mid-1990s, but the causes of instability in sending states remained and applications rose to record levels from the mid-1990s onwards. Attempts to speed up the process had not worked. The advocates of restriction shifted their attention to welfare benefits, which, according to the logic of the 1996 and 1999 asylum legislation, acted as an incentive for bogus asylum applicants. The result of the 1996 Asylum and Immigration Act was expenditure on asylum seekers, according to the 1998 government White Paper on immigration and asylum policy, of around £400 million in 1997–8, estimated to rise to £800 million by 2001/2 (HMSO 1998). These costs fell unevenly on those local authorities in London and the south-east of England who were forced to pick up the tab for policy failure. The 1996 legislation had other consequences that broadened both the scope of immigration control, the type of implementing authorities and had implications for UK race relations. The legislation obliged employers to report suspected illegal immigrants to the immigration authorities. A Commission for Racial Equality enquiry found that no prosecutions had occurred, but also employers became more reluctant to employ people from ethnic minorities.

Hostility towards asylum seekers was nowhere more evident than in the south-coast towns of Folkestone and Dover in the county of Kent. In December 1998 the police warned the editor of the *Folkestone and Dover Express* that he could face prosecution following the virulent racism in an October 1998 editorial which 'argued' that: 'Illegal immigrants, asylum seekers, bootleggers and scum of the earth drug smugglers have targeted our beloved coastline. We are left with the back draft of a nation's human sewage and no cash to wash it down the drain'. This in a town, it is important to remember, that in 1999 according to the Kent county social services department had 790 asylum seekers, 0.06 per cent of the total population of the county of Kent. Kent was also the scene of violent confrontations between asylum seekers and local youths, as well as increased activity by the extreme right-wing British National Party and other hate organisations. The parallels between the attacks (discursive and physical) on asylum seekers in Dover and hostility towards earlier black and Asian immigrants to the UK are hard to avoid.

This sad Kentish vignette illustrates the problems caused by the 1996 Asylum and Immigration Act and the marginalisation of asylum seekers on the supposition that their claim is bogus and that welfare benefits are an attraction. Most asylum seekers arriving at Dover were discovered by the immigration authorities hiding in lorries with the effect that they were classified as 'in-country applications' and therefore not eligible for benefit payments. They thus became the responsibility of Kent social services and entered a painfully slow asylum adjudication system that could take up to two years to process an application. Asylum seekers cannot work until they have been in the UK for 6 months, which left the choice for many of either wiling away the hours in their accommodation or standing in the street. This occurred in a town where the support facilities for asylum seekers such as language training and interpreting, legal advice and community support, were very limited. In addition to this, the Refugee Council found that almost 500 refugee children had been refused schooling in Kent because the schools did not have sufficient funds. A cartoon in *The Guardian* newspaper depicted an immigration checkpoint where the poster on the wall reads 'you don't have to be mad to seek asylum here, but it helps'.

The 1999 Immigration and Asylum Act

The 1998 immigration and asylum policy White Paper stated that: 'people that have not established the right to be in the UK should not have access to welfare provisions on the same basis as those whose citizenship or status gives them an entitlement to benefits when in need' (HMSO 1998). This was not a new direction for policy. The previous Conservative government had pursued a similar policy. The Labour government's expressed intention was to create a 'safety net' scheme for asylum seekers to be administered directly by the Home Office and separately from the existing benefits system. The intended effect was also to greatly enhance powers to control, observe, monitor and anormalise the lives of asylum seekers by ensuring their exclusion from normal social life during their application adjudication process.

The experiences of other European countries were used as a justification. The government noted that other EU member states made payments 'in kind' to asylum applicants. For instance, Germany made almost all payments in kind, while The Netherlands, Belgium and Denmark provided accommodation in reception centres for asylum applicants. In countries where cash payments were made (such as France and Italy), the period of payment was limited. The Labour government agreed with their Conservative predecessors that welfare benefits were an incentive for asylum seekers to come to the UK and that most asylum seekers were actually 'bogus'.

The two core asylum-related elements of the 1999 Immigration and Asylum Act were the introduction of vouchers in place of cash-paid welfare benefits and a national dispersal system. The legislation also outlined an ambitious plan to instigate by 2001 a six-month asylum adjudication process – two months for a decision and four months for an appeal. Asylum seekers were to be excluded from cash-paid welfare benefits during a relatively short adjudication process lasting for a maximum of six months, or at least that was the plan.

The rationale for policy appeared to be that the state interfered too little with the life of asylum applicants in the UK. Once in the country, there was latitude to settle where they chose, to access welfare state benefits, and to work after six months. Asylum seekers could live normal lives with a possibility of settlement that the government was determined to remove. The 1996 and 1999 legislation increased the power of the state over asylum seekers to determine where they would live and their access to the essentials of life. The regime of control was extended from the external frontiers where they had traditionally resided to the internal space. The utilisation of the welfare state as a device to deter asylum seekers added a new weapon to the armoury of post-war immigration controls and redefined the relationship between migrants and the welfare state. Asylum seekers are not citizens and there is the strong suspicion that many are 'abusers' of the asylum system and undeserving of membership of the community of legitimate welfare receivers. This power to marginalise is a relatively new weapon because most immigrants who came to the UK after the Second World War were entitled to the social entitlements of full British citizens or were citizens of the Republic of Ireland with special welfare-related provisions.

The assumption that welfare state benefits do attract asylum applicants is empirically dubious. In a comparative study of asylum seekers in the EU, it was found that in the majority of cases the choice of a country is not actually a 'conscious rational choice' based on comparison of the advantages and disadvantages of various options. More often an asylum applicant finds their country of destination forced on them because of factors such as the availability of travel options (Böcker and Havinga 1998: 79). For those asylum applicants able to exercise some choice then the existence of kith- or kinship connections in the UK would be important, as were colonial ties and the English language. Prior to the 1996 legislation, asylum seekers in the UK encountered very few restrictions on where they lived or in accessing welfare state benefits. The unavoidability of asylum because of international and domestic obligations prompted the UK to construct internal controls governing the reception of asylum seekers and the adoption of policy instruments similar to those in other European countries where population registration systems linked to welfare benefits have played an internal supervisory role. The supposition that welfare benefits – which could hardly be characterised as lavish – were an incentive was questioned in the House of Commons during the 1999 asylum legislation's scrutiny process. It was argued that the long delays in processing applications could serve as an equal if not greater attraction than welfare benefits for asylum applicants given that in May 1998 10,000 asylum applications were over five years old (*Hansard*, 22 February 1999). For a policy to achieve its intended effects it needs to be based on a valid theory of cause and effect (Gunn 1984: 196–218 quoted in Richardson 1996: 280–5). If a policy is based on a misunderstanding of cause and effect then it is likely to fail. If welfare benefits do not cause asylum applications (economic inequalities, conflict, war and oppression or simply a lack of conscious choice about country of destination seem equally plausible possibilities) then welfare restrictions are unlikely to address root causes. Indeed, they may contribute only to a net increase in the sum of human misery among asylum applicants encountering stringent external barriers reinforced by internal social exclusion.

The welfare-related dimension of the UK asylum system was designed to hinder the possibility for asylum seekers to live a 'normal social life' because to provide this opportunity could produce social integration and settlement. Vouchers and dispersal secure and reproduce a constant anormalisation of social life designed to hinder social integration and make it possible for the migration process to be reversed. As in other European countries, asylum seekers are not only made visible as illegitimate welfare receivers as a reassurance for the community of legitimate welfare receivers, but the welfare state operates in a negative mode. Instead of trying to secure chances for inclusion and participation, the welfare state provides asylum seekers with the means of survival (a 'safety net') in a manner that attempts to preclude future chances of participation to ensure potential for the reversibility of migration (see also Roland Bank's chapter).

The voucher system

The 'safety net' voucher scheme makes provision for asylum seekers to receive vouchers redeemable only in certain shops and supermarkets. When the scheme was introduced in 1999 these amounted to the following:

- Single parent aged under 24 – £35
- Lone parents – £55.30
- Child under 16 – £17.75
- Child over 16 – £21.20

The vouchers were worth between 70 per cent and 90 per cent of income support levels and provided for only basic subsistence. The government faced opposition in the House of Lords during the passage of the legislation because the delays within the asylum adjudication system could leave asylum applicants in a cashless society for 20 months (despite the ambitious plans for a six-month process by 2001). In October 1998, the Lords proposed an amendment postponing the voucher system until the six-month process was up and running. The government rejected the amendment, but in the wake of opposition from the Lords, provisions were made for a £50 voucher to be paid every six months for claims not processed (giving a family of four entitlement to vouchers to the value of £200 every six months).

The voucher system also faced strong criticism for two other reasons. First, as the government admitted, there was no administrative experience of operating a voucher system. It was likely that a cash system would be easier to implement, but cash payments attracted asylum applicants, or so it was thought. The new system was also likely to be costly to administer – the costs of a system aimed at politically organised social exclusion. The government initially claimed that the new system would require one to two hundred staff. In response to a written parliamentary question this figure was revised to around five hundred staff at an annual cost of £11.5 million

(*The Guardian*, 1999). The second criticism was that refugees could be stigmatised when trying to use their vouchers. The Labour MP, Diane Abbott, noted research from the Children's Society conducted in east London which found that families and children who depend on vouchers were often subject to racial harassment and discrimination (*Hansard*, 22 February 1999, Cmn. 92). This stigma could be viewed as an effect of the 'anormalisation' of social life for asylum seekers resulting from their heightened welfare state visibility.

If an asylum application were to be successful or an applicant was granted Exceptional Leave to Remain (ELR) then they entered the 'new deal' welfare provisions of the Labour government which centre on the soundbite of 'work for those who can, welfare for those who can't'. For instance, a recognised refugee would be entitled to claim the 'Jobseekers Allowance'. After claiming the Jobseekers Allowance for six months then refugees would be able to join the 'New Deal' employment programmes and access education and training opportunities.

The dispersal scheme

The dispersal scheme was designed to distribute asylum seekers around the country and ease the strain on resources in London and the south-east where the majority of asylum seekers were located. Housing and accommodation are in shorter supply in London than they are in other parts of the country. The dispersal scheme offered accommodation on a no-choice basis to asylum seekers. The scheme was supposed to be introduced in April 2000, but pressures on the south-east and London forced the introduction of an interim scheme on 6 December 1999 with designated cluster areas for asylum seekers. Home Office guidance specified the following criteria as the basis for designation of clusters: suitable accommodation, the existence of a multi-ethnic population or appropriate infrastructure, the possibility of establishing links with existing communities and using support from voluntary and community groups. These guidelines were non-binding. Indeed, the proper assessment of these criteria would take time that the government and implementing authorities did not have.

The interim dispersal scheme in England and Wales was to be administered by nine regional consortia: the North-West, Yorkshire and Humberside, the South-West, South-Central, East England, West Midlands, East Midlands and Wales. Two clearing houses in London and Kent were to manage the dispersal. The plan was for around 6,500 asylum seekers a month to be dispersed across the nine regions. This would break down as follows (with an estimated family size of four persons):

- 600 families per month on benefits seeking housing assistance;
- 700 families per month seeking accommodation and assistance with essential living needs;

- 1,300 single adults per month seeking accommodation and assistance with essential living needs.

The dispersal scheme immediately encountered problems, although whether these were teething difficulties associated with the short notice interim scheme or more deep-seated is yet to be revealed. The chairman of the north west agency stated that 'There has been no thought as to how this will work and the problems it will create in regions when very large numbers of people turn up together' (*The Guardian*, 6 December 1999). Asylum seekers were likely to face isolation. If an asylum seeker left their designated area then all support would be withdrawn. Moreover, the dispersal scheme offered the possibility of asylum seekers being without proper support, particularly legal advice, language assistance and interpreting. The voucher system and cash allowances were not designed to cover the costs of phone calls, stamps and other forms of correspondence. There was also the risk that the isolation of asylum seekers could be compounded by vulnerability to racist attacks if asylum seekers were placed on low-standard, difficult to rent, 'sink' housing estates. Another concern was that asylum seekers would be open to exploitation from unscrupulous private sector operators. In the 1950s and 1960s, the name of the slum landlord Rachman became synonymous with venal exploitation of immigrants. There were fears that the asylum dispersal schemes could also allow unscrupulous landlords to profit at the expense of asylum seekers.

Conclusion

The treatment of asylum seekers in the UK (and across Europe) clearly arises from a perception of the asylum issue constructed as a problem caused by increased numbers of bogus asylum seekers trying to dodge controls on labour migration. Asylum seekers in the UK are subsumed within an existing immigration *problematique* and viewed as a challenge to community relations because the asylum issue has been refracted through a race relations paradigm that construes tight control of migration as the precursor of good race relations. Recent asylum legislation has also demonstrated the addition of an internal control dimension to the array of immigration control measures. Asylum seekers are assumed to be suspicious and not to have a legitimate claim on welfare resources. The welfare-related provisions of the 1996 and 1999 asylum legislation greatly increase the power of the state to monitor, control and anormalise the lives of asylum seekers. The receipt of welfare has become salient in relation to asylum seekers because stringent external frontier controls have been questioned and apparently undermined by unpredictable asylum seeking that is difficult to avoid. Moreover, welfare state restructuring and the criteria for membership of the community of legitimate welfare receivers have been central issues for the Labour government. The welfare state measures marginalise undeserving 'abusers' while ensuring that migration can be reversible by denying access to chances for social integration.

The extension of the control regime to include the denial of access to welfare state benefits to tackle the potent myth of the welfare-scrounging asylum seeker has been the key development in the UK. This welfare state option was unavailable to British immigration control authorities in the past because the majority of immigrants arrived as a consequence of colonial connections or from Ireland and were entitled to welfare state benefits. The 'challenge' of asylum has prompted the denial of access to cash-paid welfare state benefits as an explicit component of restrictive policies designed to reduce the attraction of the UK as a destination for asylum seekers. The empirically dubious presumption that welfare benefits are the magnet appears belied by the fact that the incorporation of welfare state provisions into the regime of control since 1996 has actually coincided with record levels of asylum applications to the UK.

Strong executive authority in the UK has allowed the development of a stringent framework for immigration control. Yet, despite this, the UK immigration and asylum system has not coped with asylum applications. The 1999 Act promises a speedier process, but faces significant administrative and bureaucratic obstacles that necessarily qualify any perspective on the omnipotence of executive authority in the UK. The paraphernalia of restrictive policies are in place. Primary and secondary legislation has given the UK some of the most stringent immigration and asylum control legislation in Europe. Moreover, the exercise of authority is largely unchecked by legislative or judicial scrutiny. Yet, this exercise of state sovereignty has not stemmed asylum seeking. This has prompted new attempts by the state to exercise authority at the external frontier and via the welfare state over asylum applicants to ensure their marginalisation as a deterrent *pour encourager les autres*. Yet the causes of movement remain while the UK asylum system has also proved itself incapable of dealing with anything more than a trickle of asylum applications.

If the policy introduced in the 1999 Act succeeds in attaining its objectives – isolation from the welfare state and speedy adjudication – then the likelihood of life and death mistakes arising from refused applications also increases. If it fails, and adjudication remains slow, then asylum seekers face long periods of time during which they would be denied access to chances for social participation while being visible targets for discrimination because of dispersal and use of vouchers. Alternatively, as currently constructed, European co-operation on immigration and asylum could allow the UK to participate in construction of a buffer zone of states around the EU within which systems for temporary protection would accommodate refugees on the EU's borders. European co-operation combines executive authority with weak judicial and legislative authority. But deeper European integration – as distinct from current intergovernmental co-operation – also raises the possibility of the European Court and European Parliament checking the kinds of executive authority that has proved a recipe for stringent immigration control legislation.

Notes

1 I am grateful to Roland Bank, Michael Bommes and Elspeth Guild for their comments on earlier versions of this chapter.
2 This was a term used by Jack Straw when he was Shadow Home Secretary to criticise the Conservative government's 1996 Asylum and Immigration Act. The exact same criticism was then applied to the 1999 Immigration and Asylum legislation that Straw himself introduced to the House of Commons (*Hansard*, 22 February 1999).
3 The UK opted out of the free movement, immigration and asylum provisions of the Amsterdam Treaty. This was a Conservative government policy preference adopted with equal fervour by their Labour successors. The UK has also refused to participate in the Schengen agreement that was incorporated into the EU by the Amsterdam Treaty.
4 This dates from the notorious Smethwick contest at the 1964 general election when the Conservative candidate triumphed on the back of an overtly racist campaign. The lesson Labour drew was that it risked alienating its core support if it was seen as soft on immigration (Deakin 1965).
5 The treatment of economic migrants and absence of an immigration policy framework (aside from the pursuit of restriction) is a separate issue with which I do not deal, although see Cairncross and Masani (1999). There is no significant pro-immigration lobby in the UK.
6 At an October 1999 conference organised by the Confederation of British Industry the Labour government's Immigration Minister, Barbara Roche, stated that Britain was open for 'genuine economic migrants' and that in the preceding year almost 90,000 word permits had been issued (I am grateful to Elspeth Guild for this information).

9 Europeanising the reception of asylum seekers

The opposite of welfare state politics[1]

Roland Bank

Introduction

The rapid growth in numbers of asylum seekers during the 1980s and 1990s has made the conditions governing their access to welfare state benefits an extremely important issue. These debates used to be located at national level with the European Union (EU) best viewed as an arena for cautious co-ordination of national policies. This situation changed following the entry into force in May 1999 of the Amsterdam Treaty, which sets out an entirely new framework for a common European policy on refugees and asylum. 'Minimum standards on the reception of asylum seekers in Member States' are among the issues to be tackled under Community law within five years of the Treaty's entry into force (by 2004). The subsequent secondary European Law will then determine the conditions and social status granted to asylum seekers during the time between their arrival and a decision being made on their claim throughout the twelve member states participating in the policy area (currently not including Denmark, Britain and Ireland). As a result, in future, these important welfare state questions will be governed by European law covering the restriction of certain liberties, such as free movement within the host state, free choice of residence, and the economic, social and cultural situation encountered by asylum seekers in receiving states.

Two factors are likely to be the cornerstones for emergent European laws. First, member states' obligations under international law where it is important to emphasise that the Amsterdam Treaty gives the Geneva Convention (1951)[2] and the European Convention on Human Rights (ECHR, 1950) a reinforced position in European law on refugees and asylum. Whereas texts adopted in the framework of the European Union under the third pillar of the Maastricht Treaty were supposed to be in line with both of these conventions they were, in reality, not open to judicial review. Member states have decided to subject asylum policy to full judicial control as far as compliance with the 1951 Geneva Convention and the ECHR is concerned. Second, existing national rules and practices will have an impact on emerging European law. Both of these factors will be examined in this chapter with regards to provisions for the reception of asylum seekers and issues associated with Europeanisation. The four countries selected for an analysis of the national situation – Germany, France, Belgium and Austria – which are among the most important EU member states regarding the number of asylum seekers and *de facto* refugees received, provide excellent examples for a variety of different approaches in the reception of asylum seekers. Moreover, as full participants in Amsterdam's provisions, they shed light on the relation between the Europeanisation of asylum and welfare issues.

The chapter shows that, despite important differences in national laws and practices which will require major efforts if harmonisation is to be attained, a tendency towards restriction can be observed arising from deterrence and financial motives. The limitation of possibilities for integration and access to economic, social and cultural benefits also underpins restriction. Receiving states seek to avoid developments that could hinder expulsion of asylum seekers if claims are rejected. Consequently, treatment accorded to asylum seekers points in the opposite direction of welfare benefits because the treatment of asylum seekers during the reception phase actively seeks to impede integration. By excluding asylum seekers as far as possible from participation in the normal life of the host society, states attempt to ensure that law enforcement against rejected asylum seekers is not impaired by the development of strong social ties.

European law on the reception and treatment of asylum seekers between their arrival and the final decision being made on their claim will be dominated by the tension between two contrasting aims of reception policies. First, securing the exclusion of asylum seekers from European societies. Second, maintaining the human dignity of asylum seekers as demanded by the values of modern liberal states. National governments and legislators have not always kept a keen eye on respect for human dignity, national constitutional norms and convincing arguments justifying amendments to existing laws. It is a key challenge for the work to be done at European level to safeguard the principles of European law stemming from the EU's commitment to the rule of law and the common tradition of fundamental constitutional rights. The task of safeguarding these principles is made more difficult because the provisions of international law impose few limitations on these restrictive tendencies.

Securing law enforcement and comprehensive exclusion: retention and detention

The retention of asylum seekers at airports, borders or maritime ports upon entry aims to secure law enforcement by allowing border authorities to send back persons before they have entered the territory if their claim lacks any prospect of success. Retention can be distinguished from 'detention', which always involves the deprivation of personal liberty carried out in detention centres or in prisons within the territory of the country. Retention avoids the possibility of asylum seekers not being deported after a rejection of their application because they have 'disappeared'. At the same time, this refusal of access to the territory represents the most comprehensive way of avoiding integration. Retention creates total dependence on services provided by the state, such as accommodation and food and removes the possibility for access to welfare state benefits linked to presence on the territory.

Whereas detention during these procedures is not applied by Austria, Germany, and France and, while retention in facilities at borders is rare, the national laws of these countries allow for retention in the 'transit zones' of airports. Provisions vary, however, with regard to permissible reasons for retention and maximum periods. In France, asylum seekers may be retained in cases of 'manifestly unfounded applications' (Article 35 *quater* Ordonnance 1945 on conditions of entry and stay of foreigners in France, version 1998). The French government attempted to introduce a law allowing the retention of every asylum seeker entering through airports or maritime ports, but the Conseil Constitutionnel (decision of 25 February 1992) ruled that retention was only constitutional in cases of manifestly unfounded applications (Oellers-Frahm and Zimmermann 1995: 259). Without using this term, Germany is applying a similar concept by retaining asylum seekers coming from countries deemed 'safe' as determined by a list attached to the 1997 law. Furthermore, in Germany, asylum seekers without valid documentation are retained.

In this respect, Belgium is the most draconian because prolonged periods of detention in special centres upon arrival are allowed. Asylum seekers will be transferred to a closed centre near the airport if they do not possess valid documentation or if they arrive from a country with low recognition rates (France Terre d'Asile 1997: 11; Aliens Act 1980, Article 74/5). Detention is deemed to last for the entire period of the admissibility decision (initially for two months, which can be prolonged by decision of the authorities on three occasions to a total of eight months). In practice, admissibility decisions are usually taken within two months.

In Austria, France and Germany, the laws provide strong limitations upon maximum duration of retention at airports. French law strictly limits retention in airport premises to short periods. The border police are entitled to order retention for 48 hours and to renew the order once, after which a court may order another 8 days of retention which can be renewed once. After 20 days, asylum seekers in France have to be released. This period is strictly adhered to which means that if the asylum seeker cannot be returned after that period, he is free to enter French territory and to submit an asylum application to the responsible authorities.

Asylum seekers in Austria can be retained at the border or airports for one week after control at the border in order to avoid entry by persons whose claim is inadmissible because of the safe third country rule or rejected as 'manifestly unfounded'. The period may be prolonged for a further six days if the applicant submits an appeal against this decision (*Asylgesetz*, 1997, Articles 19, 39 and 32 (1)).

In principle, German law also limits the period to be spent in airport premises but does so on a different basis to the Austrians and French. In Germany, an application for asylum can be dealt with in an accelerated procedure in cases of persons from a safe country of origin or without valid documentation.[3] The Federal Office can reject a claim within two days as 'manifestly unfounded' while the applicant is kept in the airport 'transit area'. The difference is that German law does not impose limitations on the duration of retention, but on the procedure, which may take not more than 19 days. If the application is not rejected during this time period then the asylum seeker is admitted to the territory. If, on the other hand, the court rejects the claim to be granted access to the territory and the applicant cannot be deported to his country of origin, it can take months for the applicant to be either readmitted to their country of origin or granted entry to Germany on a discretionary basis.[4] In one case, an Algerian asylum seeker was not admitted to the territory but was also denied readmission by the Algerian authorities who claimed that he was actually Moroccan. He then spent eight months in the transit area of Frankfurt airport (Migration News Sheet (MNS), July 1996: 8). Courts have since ruled that retention beyond 19 days of a rejected asylum seeker in the airport zone is unconstitutional (VG Frankfurt a.M., *Neue Zeitschrift für Verwaltungsrecht* (NVwZ) 1996: 76–9). In reaction to this jurisprudence, applicants refused entry at an airport and rejected in the airport procedure may either stay in airport premises on their own decision until they can be taken back or a judicial order for detention (*Abschiebehaft*) is issued.

The French and the German situations show that the opportunities for securing law enforcement and exclusion of allegedly fraudulent asylum seekers may be limited by the national constitution and legal system.

International law recognises the right of nation states to decide to whom to grant entry to their territory. Further, it does not disallow the retention or detention of asylum seekers; rather it imposes certain limitations with regard to their use and duration. For instance, the Geneva Convention recognises the right of states to take 'measures which it considers to be essential to national security in the case of a particular person' in exceptional circumstances such as war (Article 9). Furthermore, only 'necessary' restrictions on the free movement of asylum seekers who have entered the country or are present illegally are permissible (Article 31 (2)). The UNHCR Executive Committee did not interpret the 1951 Geneva Convention as only permitting retention and detention under the conditions mentioned in these two articles. It actually concluded that 'detention should normally be avoided' and, if necessary,

> may be resorted to only on grounds prescribed by law to verify identity;
> to determine the elements on which the claim to refugee status or

asylum is based; to deal with cases where refugees or asylum seekers have destroyed their travel and /or identity documents or have used fraudulent documents in order to mislead the authorities (...); or to protect national security or public order.

(UNHCR Executive Committee 1986)

In view of these provisions, it is difficult to imagine a situation in which detention would be impermissible *per se* under UNHCR standards. On the other hand, the Executive Committee recommended that detention measures 'should be subject to judicial or administrative review' (UNHCR ExCom 1986: 128).

The ECHR has had more influence than the UN convention on limiting states' powers for the retention or detention of asylum seekers, although it only provides protection if the treatment is not merely a 'restriction of liberty' but is designated as a 'deprivation of liberty'. The difference between the two is a matter of degree and intensity, but not of nature or substance. ECHR jurisprudence shows that this question depends on the type, duration, effect of the treatment and on the way it is carried out (ECHR Amuur v. France, 25 June 1996: 42), as well as on the possibilities for social contacts (Kälin 1997: 35). Interpretations by the European Court of Human Rights shows that retention at airports under certain circumstances may amount to a deprivation of liberty and therefore give rise to protection under Article 5 of the ECHR. The mere possibility of leaving the country where the applicant is seeking asylum does not exclude a 'deprivation of liberty'. The Court hints, in particular, that the guarantee to leave one's own country, protected by Protocol 4 of the ECHR, and the possibility to leave the country where the asylum application is lodged, become merely theoretical if no other country with a comparable level of protection is inclined or willing to receive the applicant. Mere diplomatic assurances given by a government potentially receiving the returned applicant are not considered to be sufficient, at least for states not bound by the 1951 Geneva Convention (ECHR Amuur v. France, 25 June 1996: 48).[5]

Apart from the legal basis for the deprivation of liberty and the observance of lawful national procedures, the ECHR requires the observance of the principle of proportionality (Trechsel 1994: 53). This means that the deprivation of liberty has to serve one of the purposes outlined in the ECHR, such as the prevention of someone from entering illegally or because a person is subject to proceedings concerning his or her expulsion (Article 5 (1) lit. f of the ECHR). These permitted aims of detention are to be strongly adhered to: a deprivation of liberty in the form of a retention at an airport after the end of an accelerated procedure cannot serve the purpose of any longer preventing illegal entry, but turns into a detention for securing expulsion. Such detention is not permitted when it is evident that deportation is not possible (Trechsel 1994: 48). Thereby, the ECHR imposes certain limitations on member states' powers to secure exclusion of asylum seekers by retention at airports and subsequent deportation detention.

By retaining individuals in airport or border premises states create a situation in which the fulfilment of all basic needs depends on the state. Poor conditions in retention centres at airports and borders have been frequently reported (Anafé 1997: 8–23). At the same time, outside scrutiny of these retention/detention facilities has been inadequate (MNS June 1995: 5; MNS November 1997: 6), although in Germany accommodation is provided by charitable organisations such as the German Red Cross or German Caritas. International law actually gives little guidance on minimum requirements but can provide for protection in extreme cases, at least if the treatment is considered to be a deprivation of liberty. The Geneva Convention is silent on detention conditions. The UNHCR Executive Committee has, however, emphasised that conditions must be 'humane', and that asylum seekers shall, whenever possible, not be accommodated with common criminals (UNHCR ExCom 1986: 128). In addition, it recommended that detained asylum seekers be provided with the opportunity to contact the UNHCR. This may be interpreted in such a way that the UNHCR must be granted access to detention centres.

Article 3 of the ECHR clearly prohibits inhuman or degrading conditions of detention (Bank 1996: 222–5) but it should similarly apply against appalling conditions for retention in airport or border premises. However, ECHR institutions – while accepting in principle the possibility that detention conditions may violate Article 3 of the ECHR – have been reluctant to find violations in the cases submitted. This indicates that they are applying a very high threshold in this respect.[6] On individual occasions, there have been decisions of national courts finding a violation of the ECHR arising from poor detention conditions (Tribunal civil (Ref.)-Brussels, 25 November 1993, *Revue du Droits des étrangers*, No. 76, November–December 1993: 604).

In addition to the prohibition of torture, inhuman and degrading treatment by Article 7 of the International Covenant for Civil and Political Rights (ICCPR) provides in Article 10 (1) for a positive obligation on member states to provide treatment respecting the humanity and dignity of persons deprived of their liberty (Nowak 1993: 186 ff.). State parties are obliged to provide detainees with a minimum of services to satisfy their basic needs such as food, clothing, medical care, sanitary facilities communication, light, opportunity to move about, privacy, etc. (Nowak 1993: 189).

Cutting opportunities for social integration: restrictions on liberties and economic rights after admission to the territory

Free movement, the free choice of residence and the right to work are central to individuals leading an independent, self-determined life as full members of a society. Consequently, restrictions on these rights limit opportunities for integration and the creation of irreversible structures that could constitute obstacles to law enforcement against rejected asylum seekers by expulsion and deportation. Such irreversible structures can be formed by family ties, the integration of children in society, or through contacts with employers who may be interested in employing an asylum seeker even after rejection of his or her claim.

Austria, Belgium, France and Germany all impose restrictions to a varying degree on free movement, choice of residence and working opportunities. The exclusion of asylum seekers from the host societies generally applies with regard to refusal of work permits. Moreover, restrictions on free movement and choice of residence can also be found in most of the countries examined. Whereas measures applied in Austria, Belgium and France in this context display certain elements with exclusionary effects the measures applied in Germany, however, constitute a pattern suitable for systematically securing comprehensive exclusion of asylum seekers from integration into the host society. International law actually imposes few limitations on possibilities for restrictive policies.

Freedom of movement within the host states' territory

Restrictions imposed on free movement by asylum seekers once they are admitted to the territory vary. In France and Belgium, there is no possibility to impose restrictions except for national security reasons. Austrian law was used to allow the authorities to limit the preliminary stay permission that asylum seekers receive after submission of their application. Permission could be limited to or exclude certain parts of the territory if this was necessary for reasons of equal distribution of asylum seekers or to avoid concentration of asylum seekers in certain areas of the country (*Asylgesetz* 1991, Article 7). Austrian law did not impose these opportunities for restriction in order to impose obstacles to social integration, but to foster equal distribution. However, the 1997 asylum law (Article 19) abolished this distribution of asylum seekers by the authorities with the effect that asylum seekers in Austria now enjoy freedom of movement.

In contrast, German law provides another example of efforts to avoid the integration of asylum seekers. Stay permits are limited by law to the district of the local office for foreigners (*Asylverfahrensgesetz*, Article 56). The applicant is only entitled to leave the district by specific permission of the authorities or, without permission, in order to appear before a court or a public authority. Respect for the geographical limitations may be enforced by means of detaining applicants. Violations may also be prosecuted and penalised with fines or deprivation of liberty (*Asylverfahrensgesetz*, Articles 59 and 85). Complicated provisions give guidance on use of discretion by the authorities concerning the granting of permission to leave the specified area. As a rule, permission should be granted for counselling visits and other 'compelling reasons' (*Asylverfahrensgesetz*, Articles 57 and 58).[7] Once the obligation to live in a reception centre has ended, the authorities may also grant permission for reasons of public interest or to avoid 'unintended hardship' (*Asylverfahrensgesetz*, Article 58). The latter term has imposed limitations on the discretion of the authorities in pursuing the aims of a restricted stay permit. Courts have ruled that 'unintended hardship' can pertain to situations such as impeding full participation in school activities outside the district or rendering impossible visits to close family members living outside the permitted district (Marx 1995: Article 58, 10). Such decisions illustrate that opportunities for imposing restrictions are limited by the respect for family life, which is not only protected by the German constitution but also by Article 8 of the ECHR, although aside from that, international law does not afford any further protection to asylum seekers.

The right to free movement within the territory of a state is recognised by international law not only for citizens but also for aliens lawfully present in the country. However, the provisions do not constitute far-reaching rights for aliens because the 'lawful' stay of a foreigner within another country's territory depends on the national law of the receiving country. Therefore, if the national law defines the scope of the permission of stay as being limited to a certain area, it defines the 'lawful' stay of the foreigner and is not an infringement of the freedom of movement. In other words, the freedom of movement of a foreigner is limited to the area defined in his or her stay permit. This interpretation is valid for the relevant provisions of the ECHR (European Commission on Human Rights, S. Udayanan and S. Sivakumaran v. Germany, Decision of 1 December 1986) and ICCPR (Nowak 1993: 201). Similarly, the Geneva Convention obliges a member state to accord to 'refugees lawfully in its territory' (which includes asylum seekers who have been admitted to the territory) the right to move freely within its territory subject to any regulations applicable to aliens generally in the same circumstances (Article 26). Bearing in mind the interpretation of 'lawful stay' in the other human rights treaties, the Geneva Convention will have to be interpreted in the same way.

Choice of residence

In a similar way to the restrictions imposed in different countries on free movement, the laws and practices concerning the choice of residence display exclusionary patterns in Germany and, during the admissibility stage, in Belgium too. In contrast, impediments to free choice of residence imposed in Austria until 1997 (resulting from eventual restrictions of free movement) and in Belgium during the period after admission of a claim to the procedure remain limited to the equal distribution of applicants. In France no restrictions apply.

Asylum applicants in France may stay with relatives, friends, on their own means or in a reception centre for asylum seekers until the final decision on the application is taken. However, exercise of this 'freedom' may encounter practical obstacles if the procedure takes more than one year as after this period payments cease for asylum seekers not living in reception centres.

In Belgium, the situation differs according to the stage of the procedure. During the admissibility stage, asylum seekers dependent on social assistance are obliged to stay in a reception centre to which they will be assigned.[8] Those who have sufficient means at their disposal may stay where they wish if they have not entered the country illegally (France Terre d'Asile 1997: 11). Once the claim has been admitted to the procedure, asylum seekers will be assigned to a *commune* according to a distribution plan. They then must register with the local Centre Publique d'Aide Social (CPAS), which will be responsible for them. This does not mean that asylum seekers are obliged to live in the *commune* they are assigned to, however.

In Germany, asylum seekers are even more limited in their choice of residence. There is an array of complex regulations that impose the obligation to live in a reception centre for a certain period and allow the authorities to impose an obligation to reside in collective accommodation after that period. Consequently, asylum seekers are separated from society with regard to their daily life, which obstructs the possibility of social integration. Between six weeks and three months, applicants are generally obliged to reside in a reception centre (*Asylverfahrensgesetz*, Article 47). A choice of location is possible to a very limited extent if the applicant is not bound by a command made by the border or other police. Also, the reception centres must have vacancies within the quota applying to the relevant Land and be in accord with the sub-office's decision that the reception centre is able to deal with cases from the applicant's country of origin (*Asylverfahrensgesetz*, Article 46). In other cases, a central office for the distribution of asylum seekers will assign the applicant to a specific reception centre. This decision is mainly taken on the basis of a quota for asylum seekers established for every Land and the available capacity. A third factor is that the readiness of sub-offices to examine applications by asylum seekers of certain nationalities may be taken into consideration. Moreover, if the family did not arrive together then the authorities need not take family ties into account, although, if the family is divided for this reason, the obligatory period spent in a reception centre is kept as short as possible (Marx 1995: Article 46, 27). A potential danger is that the law's commitment to quotas also prevents the authorities from taking into account the risk arising from extreme right groups in certain Länder and the potential for racist and xenophobic violence directed against asylum seekers. Before the amendment of the law had entered into force assignments to reception centres in high-risk areas had been declared inadmissible occasionally (Marx 1995: Article 46, 13). The system seeks an equal use of capacities and implementation of the idea of 'short distances' because reception centres will be equipped with a sub-office of the Federal

Office for the Recognition of Foreign Refugees at which asylum seekers must submit their application.

Following the period in a reception centre, the applicant will be assigned within the Land of the reception centre to a specific authority in the district where he or she must reside. The discretion of the authorities in such cases is limited by several factors, including that the decision reflects public interests, such as housing shortages and security risks and that the interests of the asylum seeker are protected. The decision must also respect the principle of proportionality, which may place limitations on the permissible length of obligatory residence (Marx 1995: Article 53, 15–19).

What does international law have to say about these issues? Similar to free movement within the territory of the host state, the free choice of residence is to be guaranteed by a member state according to Article 26 of the Geneva Convention applying to 'refugees lawfully in its territory'. This covers asylum seekers with a stay permit. In like manner, international law provides that free choice of residence is granted under the same opportunities for restrictions as pertain to free movement. Consequently, the 'lawful stay' of the alien in the territory of the host state may also define the scope of the liberty of residence (ECHR Fourth Protocol, Article 4; ICCPR Article 12).

There is still the issue of whether or not the obligation to live in a specific centre is covered by the concept of 'lawful stay' because there is no choice of residence. This is in contrast to the concept of a choice limited to a certain area by the lawfulness of stay. Consequently, the obligation to live in a specific centre may be considered to constitute an infringement with the free choice of residence. However, both under the ECHR and the ICCPR, such infringements are justifiable for reasons of public order and for the protection of rights and freedoms of others if they are necessary in a democratic society to that end. The latter criterion includes a review for proportionality of the measure.

Work

Access to the job market is not granted to asylum seekers in Austria, France (since 1991) or Germany (since 1997). The most favourable treatment is applied in Belgium where work permits are issued after the asylum application has been declared admissible, which may take two or three months (France Terre d'Asile 1997: 10). Asylum seekers may receive a work permit valid for between three and six months for a specific job upon application by the employer. In practice, asylum seekers are reported to frequently find jobs for short periods.[9] Until 1993 asylum seekers in Belgium could obtain a provisional work permission for a specific job for the whole period of the procedure.

France restricted its policy in 1991 until when, asylum seekers were allowed to work in any professional sector because the permission to remain in the country during the asylum procedure also included a working permit. Since 1991, asylum seekers are not allowed to work if they have entered the country without the prior permission of the French authorities (Circulars of 26 September 1991). An exception has been granted to ex-Yugoslavs from 'disturbed areas' (Circular of 14 September 1992).

In contrast, Germany reduced the periods banning asylum seekers from work during the first months of the procedure in 1991. Asylum seekers in Germany are not allowed to work as long as they are obliged to live in a reception centre (*Asylverfahrensgesetz*, Article 60). After that period, lasting for a maximum of three months, the authorities may only impose an employment ban by individual orders, with the reasons for such a restriction based on immigration-related considerations. Therefore, a ban may be imposed in order to prevent an influx of persons using the asylum procedures not because of persecution but with the aim of taking up employment. Labour market considerations can lead to a refusal of a work permit, which has to be issued by the labour authorities. Until recently, such permits were issued if neither a German nor another EU national nor another foreigner with stronger status (*Aufenthaltserlaubnis*) was available for the job in question. This practice changed in May 1997, when the Federal Minister of Labour instructed all employment offices to turn down any request for work permits by asylum seekers. Despite this being an order by the labour authorities, the impression given is that the order lacks labour market policy justifications as it is unlikely to produce positive effects on the job market because, even prior to the order, permissions were only given if no German, EU national or other foreigner was available. In fact, the order serves to secure and enhance the effects of deterrence and of exclusion of asylum seekers from social integration.

Restrictive work permit policies for foreigners meet with no strong opposition in international law. Geneva Convention signatory states are not obliged to permit wage-earning employment by asylum seekers, but only to 'give sympathetic consideration to assimilating the rights of all refugees (...) to those of nationals' (Article 17 (3)). States are only obliged to grant asylum seekers exemption from restrictions applied to foreigners after they have resided for three years in the host country or are married to a person or have a child of the host state's nationality (Article 17 (2)). More far reaching obligations, such as granting the right to engage in wage-earning employment equivalent to the most favourable treatment accorded to other foreigners or to grant the same treatment as to nationals in respect of labour legislation and social security, only apply to refugees that have obtained long-term protection (Article 24).

The right to work is recognised in the UN's International Covenant on Economic, Social and Cultural Rights (Article 6). Although this treaty does not contain directly 'binding standards of attainment' it 'requires states to take steps to the maximum of their available resources to progressively realise rights ... in a non-discriminatory way ...' (Hathaway 1991: 110). The prohibition of discrimination is to be directly implemented, which would not allow for a restriction on working possibilities that only applied to foreigners (Hathaway 1991: 111). However, by virtue of Article 4 of the Covenant, states can impose restrictions on this right provided for by law for promoting the general prosperity of democratic society. This justification will apply to restriction of immigration and, therefore, also to restrictions imposed on asylum seekers in order to deter immigration through the asylum procedure.

Refusing state-funded integration: restrictions on access to welfare state benefits

The restrictions on free movement, choice of residence and work reveal effects running contrary to the usual aims of welfare policies. The aim is to prevent the possibility of social integration that could render deportation or expulsion more difficult if an asylum application is rejected. The point at which the distinction between the central purpose of welfare policy and the treatment of asylum seekers becomes particularly apparent is in relation to social policy. Social assistance and health services granted to asylum seekers aim at providing the means for survival during the period in which the claim is under consideration or review. The transitional character of the period together with the statistical likelihood of rejection of an asylum claim are factors that allow for a perception of an asylum seeker's situation that does not necessarily demand integration or inclusion in the host society. On the contrary, social policy towards asylum seekers aims at securing their exclusion underpinned by the differentiation between, on the one hand, asylum seekers and, on the other, nationals and foreigners with a stronger status (in particular EU citizens). While for the latter group, situations of need will be approached in a way seeking to avoid social exclusion, asylum seekers are, at best, supported in a way aimed at securing their survival. This will be shown through analysis of social assistance, health care and cultural rights.

Social assistance

The social assistance concepts and practices applied by Austria, Belgium, France and Germany vary to a great extent, but the bottom line is that exclusionary tendencies are common. Whereas in Belgium and partly in Austria, asylum seekers have no legal claim for any social assistance, Germany and France apply a system giving rights to assistance to asylum seekers that are differentiated according to the period of time spent in the host country. At the same time, the amount of assistance granted is often smaller than that granted to nationals, EU citizens, or other foreigners with a 'stronger' status. Aside from in Germany, the systems do not provide support guaranteeing survival in conditions of human dignity in all cases.

In Austria, social assistance for asylum seekers is granted by the Federal State under the 1991 Federal Assistance Law (*Bundesbetreuungsgesetz*) covering housing, food, medical aid and other necessary assistance, including pocket money. The problem with this law is that asylum seekers have no claim for social assistance and have no possibility for appeal against a negative decision on an application for social assistance. This gives the authorities full discretion with the explicit aim of deterring asylum seekers from entering Austria (UNHCR 1996: 66). Circulars from the Federal Minister of the Interior also exclude certain groups of asylum seekers from social assistance, for instance Polish, Czech and Hungarian nationals, applicants without valid documentation, asylum seekers that have lodged an appeal without suspensive effect, and those without a preliminary stay permit (UNHCR 1996: 63f.). The result is that a majority of asylum seekers are not covered by the Austrian state's social assistance scheme (France Terre d'Asile 1997: 7). So, although asylum seekers without a preliminary stay permit are now issued a permit that is not conditional on submitting the asylum application within a week after entering Austrian territory (Article 7 *Asylgesetz* 1991 and Article 19 *Asylgesetz* 1997), other gaps persist in the Federal social assistance scheme's coverage of asylum seekers. Those not covered depend on charitable aid.

In Belgium the CPAS in each commune is responsible for providing social aid, but only after the asylum application has been admitted to the procedure (MNS May 1996: 7). Until then, social assistance is afforded in kind by the state under the condition that the asylum seeker lives in a reception centre. The costs for social aid provided by the CPAS do not remain with the commune but are reimbursed by the government. Reimbursement to the CPAS depends on the efforts made to help the asylum seeker.[10] Although the mandate is to help any person present in the territory of the commune, the CPAS have been reported to use a commune's refusal to register an asylum seeker as an excuse to not provide social assistance. In other cases, complaints have been voiced that the CPAS has tried to push people out of the commune by granting lower payments than should be expected (Lambert 1995: 116f.).

Asylum seekers in France receive an allowance accorded as 'in kind' assistance in reception centres or as cash assistance for those living outside.[11] Asylum seekers living in a reception centre receive daily pocket money. Food, accommodation and clothes are provided free of charge. 'In kind' entitlements granted in reception centres are not subject to a time limit, but monthly payments for asylum seekers staying outside a centre cease after 12 months after which there is no entitlement for further assistance. This does, of course, entail hardship for people whose procedure is taking more time. Moreover, this assistance is well below levels usually granted to persons in need (whether French or foreigners).

Asylum seekers who wish to live in a reception centre apply to France Terre d'Asile, which will decide on the basis of social criteria on admission and distribution between reception centres. Reception centres are usually of a small size (for around 30 persons), paid for by the state, but managed by a local agency or NGO. Living conditions in a centre have to satisfy the minimum requirements imposed by law, which is identical to that generally applied to *Centres d'hébergement et réinsertion sociale*. Between 10 and 15 per cent of asylum seekers actually live in reception centres. In the case of a sudden rise of inflow of asylum seekers, capacities of reception centres may not be sufficient and there have been situations where asylum seekers were without housing.

The 1997 Law on Social Assistance largely governs social assistance granted to asylum seekers in Germany (*Asylbewerberleistungsgesetz*, AsylbLG).[12] This law has largely replaced cash payments by 'in kind' assistance. Practices differ from one *Land* to the other and sometimes have provoked protest (MNS September 1997: 10). The result is that overall assistance granted to asylum seekers is about 20 per cent lower than the level granted to other persons in need. Since the law came into effect in June 1997, reduced rates have applied to the first three years. This is in contrast to the one year period foreseen in the 1993 version of the law. UNHCR has criticised that this will affect mostly those applicants stemming from countries from which many applicants are accepted as the examination of their claims takes the longest time (MNS November 1995: 7). After 36 months, asylum seekers are entitled to the same social assistance afforded in cash as accorded to all foreigners in need. Since the 1997 amendment, the law also covers foreigners entering Germany by air and refused entry at the airport, and persons having fled from war or civil war and, therefore, granted temporary protection status. In turn, the Länder have agreed to make an annual contribution to a Bosnian Fund for reconstruction of 150 million a year during five years following the adoption of the new law (1997–2002).

As long as an asylum seeker is obliged to live in a reception centre (usually for up to three months), the necessary facilities are provided 'in kind', or through coupons (for clothing). Those concerned can claim for all items necessary to cover the existential minimum (Deibel 1998: 32). On top of that, persons covered by the law will receive a monthly cash sum of DM 80 – as pocket money (DM 40 – for persons under 15) (Article 3 AsylbLG). Pocket money is reduced if persons that have finished obligatory schooling do not fulfil their obligation to carry out work in the functioning of the reception centre, or in public or charitable organisations for DM 2 per hour (Article 5 AsylbLG). Once the asylum seeker leaves a reception centre, the law allows allowances either in coupons or in cash while maintaining the principle of 'in kind' payment. However, the rule is that asylum seekers are living in a centre for collective accommodation and receive assistance in kind. These reception centres and centres for collective accommodation are funded by the respective Land but day-to-day management is usually contracted to charitable organisations, such as the German Red Cross or German Caritas. Regulations on minimum standards for the conditions in these centres scarcely exist. Sometimes there are regulations calculating 6 to 9 square meters of living space for each asylum seeker – however, it seems that these limitations are not adhered to in practice (ECRE 1994: 168). It follows from the German *Grundgesetz* (Basic Law, 1949) that conditions must meet the requirements of human dignity and not be harmful to the asylum seeker's health (Administrative Court Ansbach, Judgement of 12 December 1990). Factors to be taken into consideration include the space that is allocated for exclusive personal use, sanitary equipment, the quality of furniture, and the possibility of using collective rooms. Requirements vary according to the duration and purpose of stay and the particular personal situation of the applicant. Courts usually do not recognise minimum requirements for the size of personal living areas. A court, for instance, did not find a violation of human dignity in assigning a couple with a baby to a room of 11.28 square metres coupled with the possibility of using a collective kitchen of 11.7 square metres and one toilet shared with nine other people (*Verwaltungsgerichtshof Baden-Wuerttemberg*, NVwZ 1986: 783).

The 1997 amendment of the German Law on Social Assistance for Asylum Seekers shows that the legislator has pushed changes through without taking proper account of limitations imposed either by constitutional law or by justifiability. The amendment has prolonged the period of application from 12-months in the 1993 law to 36 months. This prolongation lacks justification if the reasoning in favour of the 1993 law is taken into account. The 12-month period of the 1993 law had been justified by the argument that a short stay in Germany will produce a lower level of needs and therefore allow a reduced level of social assistance. On the other hand, it was argued that the level of assistance had to be increased to the normal level of the Federal Law on Social Assistance if the stay were to be prolonged to more than twelve months. When this period expired, the legislator assumed that a reduced level of needs could not be presumed. The legislative material on the amendments of 1997 contains no explanation for why the period of reduced needs is now three times longer than before (Hohm 1997: 661). In addition to this, the 1997 law violates the obligation to equal treatment as enshrined in German constitutional law (Article 3 of the *Grundgesetz*). As the 36-month period may only start at 1 June 1997, some asylum seekers may be subject to the lower level of social benefits under the Law on Social Assistance for Asylum Seekers for an overall period of four years (12 months under the old legislation and then another 36 months under the new law). There is no legal justification why it should be longer than three years for some people. Therefore, it seems that the aims of cost cutting and deterrence were pursued by the legislator while ignoring problems arising from the constitutional principle of equal treatment. While this may not have been intentional, it may serve as a demonstration for the vigour with which restrictive policies were implemented.

Again, the discretion of national authorities and legislators is hardly hampered at all by international legal standards. The Geneva Convention does not impose any obligations on member states to assure minimum living conditions for asylum seekers. Rules relating to social assistance (Article 23) and housing (Article 21) only apply to 'refugees lawfully staying' in the host country, i.e. to refugees granted a form of lasting protection. The International Covenant on Economic, Social and Cultural Rights acknowledges everybody's right to social security and an appropriate standard of living, including accommodation (Articles 9 and 11 (1)). This also applies to asylum seekers. The right to freedom from forced or compulsory labour (Article 4 ECHR) becomes relevant if asylum seekers are obliged to work, for example, in the reception centre as practised in Germany. In relation to Article 4, the ECHR's Commission has ruled that requiring an unemployed person to accept a job offer under the threat of otherwise losing his or her unemployment benefit does not constitute forced labour (X v. The Netherlands, DR 7 (1976): 161). Similarly, protection under Article 8 of the ICCPR against compulsory labour does not cover situations in which social benefit is cut as a result of refusal to accept a job offer. In such cases, it is argued, 'neither the intensity of the involuntariness nor that of the sanction reaches the degree required for forced or compulsory labour' (Nowak 1993: 151).

Health care

Austria, Belgium, France and Germany do not provide for medical care to be afforded to asylum seekers in every respect. Some states limit treatment to cases of acute illnesses and pain, thereby constituting another striking example of a policy directed at short-term 'survival' instead of long-term care and integration. Austria even does not even grant unconditional emergency treatment for every asylum seeker.

After admission to the asylum procedure in Belgium, the CPAS pay for medical assistance if the asylum seeker is not working. In practice, there have been problems with the reimbursement for asylum seekers who had paid for their medical treatment due to the CPAS' slow administrative process (France Terre d'Asile 1997: 15). During the admissibility stage, the Ministry of Public Health covers medical care and, in any event, full medical care is to be accorded to any alien, including illegal immigrants.[13]

In Austria, health care for asylum seekers is not always guaranteed by the Austrian state, i.e. as was also the situation for social assistance coverage to applicants in need. Only those covered by the federal social assistance scheme can benefit from access to health care (Article 1 *Bundesbetreuungsgesetz*). Others depend on charitable organisations and NGOs (France Terre d'Asile 1997: 9).

In France, medical assistance is differentiated between those asylum seekers in a very early stage of the procedure (those who only have received the first stay permit for one month) and others (with a three months stay permit). Whereas those in the first category are only entitled to hospital care, the second are granted the same access to health care as French nationals. There are some practical problems relating to the complicated and ever changing reimbursement procedures, which, for instance, create obstacles for asylum seekers by asking for birth certificates (France Terre d'Asile 1997: 29).

As for German social services in general, health care for asylum seekers is subject to the 1997 Law on Social Assistance for Asylum Seekers (Article 4 AsylbLG). For the first thirty-six months, asylum seekers are only entitled to medical treatment and hospital care in the case of acute illness or pain, although the special needs of pregnant women must be met. The authorities are also required to guarantee that necessary vaccinations and preventative examinations are carried out. The law's formulation is so vague that the authorities encounter problems actually ascertaining that medical treatment is reduced to that deemed to be absolutely necessary. This situation changes after thirty-six months when asylum seekers are entitled to the same medical treatment as German citizens (Article 36 Bundessozialhilfegesetz).

Once again, the protection of asylum seekers under international law is weak. No provision in the Geneva Convention explicitly refers to health services for asylum seekers. The only article in the 1951 Geneva Convention relating to health services is Article 24 on social security. However, this article only relates to refugees with long-term protection status ('refugees lawfully staying'). The International Covenant on Economic, Social and Cultural Rights acknowledges everybody's right to enjoy the highest possible attainable standard of health, including the obligation for member states to afford to everybody medical treatment in case of illness (Article 12). This could also be interpreted as demanding medical care for acute cases, but not for long-term promotion of health by routine checks.

Cultural rights: education and language training

In the area of cultural rights, including education and language training, we once again, encounter an exclusionary dynamic applying to asylum seekers. While primary education does not form part of the measures aimed at securing the exclusion of asylum seekers in any of the countries examined, language classes are not provided by the states even though they provide important skills for social integration.

In the four countries examined, asylum seekers are covered by compulsory education schemes. This means that primary education is usually free of charge. Small modifications apply in Belgium and Germany. In Belgium, compulsory education until the age of 18 also applies to asylum seekers. In general, education (primary, secondary or higher) is free of charge on the basis of a stay permit but asylum seekers might have to pay registration fees. In some German Länder, asylum seekers or their children are granted access to primary education only after having left the reception centre. In contrast to primary education, language courses are only granted to recognised refugees. However, in some asylum centres language classes are offered on a small scale by humanitarian agencies (Lambert 1995: 119).

The special position accorded to primary education in national law reflects the situation under international law. The Geneva Convention obliges state parties to accord to refugees, including asylum seekers, the same access to elementary education as to nationals, whereas treatment with regard to education other than elementary shall be at least as favourable as that accorded to other foreigners in the same circumstances (Article 22). Language training is not mentioned. The International Covenant on Economic, Social and Cultural Rights guarantees the right to education. In order to implement this right, member states have agreed to make elementary education obligatory and free of charge and to promote the accessibility of higher education (Article 11).

Conclusion

It has been clearly demonstrated that the treatment of asylum seekers during the period while their claims are being processed not only aims to deter potential asylum seekers and save money, but increasingly also aims at impeding the integration of asylum seekers into the host society. Consequently, reception policies follow different goals than welfare policies and mark an important distinction between the treatment of immigrants and their access to social rights – which has been the focus of earlier chapters in this book – and the treatment of asylum applicants. This exclusion is particularly true for social rights accorded to asylum seekers, but also applies for a range of measures relating to personal liberties and economic rights. This use of laws on reception conditions is most evident in the German case where exclusionary rules covering extended periods dominate all areas of reception policies, with the exception only of schooling. To a lesser extent, similar tendencies can be observed in Austria, Belgium and France. In particular, the refusal of access to the (legal) labour market coupled with levels and kinds of social assistance inferior to those granted to nationals is a common feature. Even the seemingly libertarian approach towards freedom of movement and free choice of residence taken in France and, more recently by Austria, is eroded by the absence of any state-paid social assistance for large numbers of asylum seekers, thereby undermining chances for integration and strengthening the effects of exclusion.

A distinct approach can be identified in Belgium, which often applies the harshest restrictionary measures on asylum seekers after their arrival, including extended periods of detention aimed at comprehensive exclusion. These measures are, however, limited to the relatively short period of admissibility proceedings, which usually take two or three months. Subsequently, Belgian law and practices provide more opportunities for integration by granting free movement, reasonable access to individual housing, permission to work, comprehensive medical care, etc. On the other hand, practical limitations such as difficulties in finding jobs or reluctance at communal level to comply with obligations have to be kept in mind.

This chapter's comparison also illustrates the differences in social policies and legal cultures. While in Germany, even under restrictionist approaches, it is unthinkable that individuals or even large groups of people could be left without any social support by the state, this possibility does not seem to pose major problems for the Austrian or French systems. The German approach guaranteeing comprehensiveness in social assistance while at the same time differentiating as much as possible (but perhaps more than reasonable) is reflected in the comprehensiveness and complexity of legal rules governing the area. Particularly remarkable in this context is the French situation that guarantees social aid for a limited period, but after that period has ended provides no further assistance. This model seems to be based on the assumption that a decision on an asylum claim would have been issued within the period that social assistance is granted. It is difficult to see the justification for why the burden for carrying the consequences of procedures that extent beyond the one-year time limit has to be carried by asylum seekers, who are unlikely to be able to meet the cost, than by the French state, which is.

One of the basic problems underpinning the reception of asylum seekers is that the duration of the period between arrival and a final decision on a claim is highly variable. Some asylum seekers only stay for some days or weeks while their claim is being rejected or declared inadmissible in an accelerated procedure for being considered to be 'manifestly unfounded'. On the other hand, the 'normal' procedure for determination of an asylum application may well take several years. Moreover, in 'normal' procedures enormous variations are possible from one country to another[14] and within one country. This depends not only on the complexity of the case but also on increases or decreases in the number of submitted applications in a certain period.[15] Despite these variations, differentiation with regard to the duration of stay with a view to improving access to the host society after a certain time is only made in Belgium and Germany. Even in these two cases, the period applied for pure exclusion differs greatly. In Belgium, improved access is granted after a period of two or three months while in Germany asylum seekers have to wait for three years for a more integrationist treatment. This, however, seems to touch a central question when, bearing in mind the obligation to secure human dignity, how long is it justifiable for a state to limit the opportunities of asylum seekers to mere survival without making provision for them to take part in the host society? The spirit of the Geneva Convention speaks strongly in favour of keeping this period short. Although not containing many explicit obligations for member states with regard to the reception of asylum seekers, it is based on the assumption that the granting of refugee status does not make a person become a refugee (constitutive) but is the act of recognising someone as a refugee (declarative) (UNHCR 1979: 28). The declaratory character of granting refugee status is best respected if states accord to asylum seekers conditions as similar as possible to those of recognised refugees unless the unfoundedness of the claim is obvious.

The challenges for European policy on the reception of asylum seekers will be not only to harmonise the diverging laws and practices in European states but also to safeguard humanitarian values and the dignity of asylum seekers against growing tendencies in European states that emphasise deterrence, cost-cutting and exclusion. Given the important role played by national laws for future European law on reception of asylum seekers, the example of the four countries analysed here suggests a strong danger of arriving at a rather tough European solution, in particular, if tendencies of applying the 'lowest common denominator' approach to this area persisted. On the other hand, the European level offers states the opportunity to cease competing on the basis of providing ever less favourable conditions for asylum seekers as a way of reducing supposed 'pull' factors. While it will be unnecessary for a European solution to harmonise national traditions, such as the national distribution of competencies and responsibilities, a comprehensive European policy will need to fix the point(s) in time at which different exclusionary limitations have to be withdrawn. Excluding asylum seekers from the host society for extended periods would violate the spirit of the EC Treaty, which is underpinned throughout by a commitment to respect fundamental human rights.

Notes

1 I would like to thank Michael Bommes for his comments on various draft versions of this article as well as Monique Blancke (UNHCR, Brussels), Anja Klug (UNHCR, Bonn), Walter Suntinger (UNHCR, Vienna) and Anne Castagnos (France Terre d'Asile, Paris) for the information provided.
2 Standards set out in the 1951 Geneva Convention at least to some extent also apply to asylum seekers. The Convention rather differentiates between three general categories of presence in the receiving country (Goodwin-Gill 1996: 307–9): simple presence, whether lawful or unlawful (some provision refer to 'refugees' without in any way being dependent on their legal situation); lawful presence (that means, the refugee has been admitted to the territory or granted a residence permit according to national immigration or aliens law); and lawful residence (relating to those enjoying asylum in the sense of residence and lasting protection; the terminology is inconsistently varying from 'residing' to 'habitual residence' or 'lawfully staying'). Therefore, the first category comprises asylum seekers; the second category may comprise asylum

seekers, if the national law grants them a legal presence; the last category usually does not comprise asylum seekers as they do not enjoy a status of lasting protection.

3 The justification for an accelerated procedure in the case of safe country of origin is to be found in the assumption that, in general, there is no persecution in the respective country and therefore the examination may be restricted as to whether the applicant can illustrate that there is persecution in his/her particular case. A similar explanation is not in sight for applicants without valid documentation, in particular bearing in mind that in some parts of the world it will be difficult for a genuine refugee to obtain valid documentation in the situation of flight.

4 In 1996, 4,358 asylum seekers went through the accelerated airport procedure. Alone in Frankfurt airport, 199 asylum seekers remained more than 23 days in the transit area, cf. MNS September 1997: 9.

5 The Court concluded that in the case of Amuur, a deprivation of liberty had taken place. For a discussion of the judgement with a view to jurisprudence of the French Conseil d'Etat and the German Bundesverfassungsgericht, cf. Kokott 1996: 569–71. In contrast, the European Commission on Human Rights had argued that the retention at the airport was not a deprivation of liberty because the transit zone at the airport was only closed in the direction of the French territory but open towards the rest of the world. It was said that the applicant had failed to show any dangers awaiting him in Syria or any measures of the French authorities which would have prevented him from entering a plane to Syria (Amuur against France, Commission Report of 10 January 1995: 50).

6 In contrast to the ECHR institutions, the European Committee for the Prevention of Torture has frequently characterised highly problematic detention conditions as amounting to inhuman or degrading treatment (CPT 1993: 90, 93, 97; 1991: 57). As a specialist institution for assessing detention conditions the CPT recommends in general, that point of entry holding facilities – which often have been found to be inadequate, particularly for extended stays – should provide for suitable facilities for sleeping and personal hygiene and should guarantee to persons held there access to their luggage, daily open air exercise, food and medical care. These recommendations of the CPT may only serve as an indicator for what might be considered a respectable standard but do not have any binding force (CPT 1997: 26).

7 Not considered to be a 'compelling reason' is the participation in a political meeting or in religious services (Marx 1995: Article 58, 10).

8 Interview with Monique Blancke, UNHCR Brussels.

9 Interview with Monique Blancke.

10 For instance, if the CPAS does not prove that it has made efforts to find accommodation for the asylum seeker, it will only be reimbursed 50 per cent of the money spent on the rent (interview with Monique Blancke).

11 The data for France are based on a telephone interview with Anne Castagnos, France Terre d'Asile, on 4 May 1998.

12 The AsylbLG first was adopted on 30 June 1993 and entered into force on 1 November 1993, cf. BGBl I 1074. About two-thirds of the asylum seekers were in fact entitled to a more comprehensive care under the Bundessozialhilfegesetz (BSG) in the form of cash payment without the possibility to reductions (as the former Article 120 (2) BSG was deleted when the AsylbLG entered into force), which ran contrary to the aims of the law. The AsylbLG only applied to asylum seekers during their first 12 month of their stay in Germany. As a reaction to these deficiencies in the functioning of the law, the AsylbLG was amended and the new version entered into force on 30 May 1997 (BGBl I, 1130).

13 Interview with Monique Blancke. This was said to be due to bad experiences with under-cared pregnancies which led to deaths of new born children.

14 For instance, the average period for determination of an asylum claim was estimated at three to five years in Belgium (Lambert 1995: 117) and 11 months in The Netherlands (MNS November 1995: 7) around the year 1995.

15 For instance, after a sharp increase in asylum applications, the number of asylum seekers having waited for more than 18 months for a decision on their application in The Netherlands had risen from 3,100 in March 1996 to 10,000 in July of the same year (MNS January 1997: 11).

10 Immigrants' social citizenship and labour market dynamics in Portugal

Maria Ioannis Baganha

Introduction

During the 1980s southern European countries became for the first time powerful magnets for growing numbers of immigrants arriving mainly from neighbouring African countries and eastern Europe. While in western Europe the stock of the foreign population was growing at an average rate of approximately two per cent every year, in southern Europe this same process was occurring at the much higher rate of approximately 10 per cent per year. The legal foreign population within the borders of Italy, Spain, Greece and Portugal increased by almost three-fold between 1981 and 1991.[1]

The existence in southern Europe at the end of the 1980s of close to 1.4 million regular migrants and of an estimated 1.3 to 1.5 million irregular migrants[2] implied that the economic insertion of immigrants in Italy, Greece, Spain and Portugal was intensely taking place in the informal labour market. The simultaneous occurrence of special processes for the mass regularisation of illegal immigrants in Italy, Spain and Portugal in 1992 and 1996 suggests that the informal economy was the primary space of insertion for new arrivals during the 1990s. Immigrants' economic incorporation in the informal labour market thus came to be perceived as a distinctive feature of southern European migratory processes. This chapter's objective is to identify the impact of this mode of economic incorporation on immigrants' access to full social citizenship. The analysis centres on Portugal and is guided by two questions: (1) I ask which system of social entitlements is endorsed by the political mainstream towards extra-communitary (non-EU) migrants? (2) I seek to identify the exogenous factors that may divert governments from fully implementing the system of social entitlements that has been formally endorsed, as well as immigrants from acting in order to ensure the broadest possible access to full social citizenship.

As with other case studies, the specific context in which crucial processes occur necessarily imposes significant limitations on the generalisability of results. On the one hand, the Portuguese case is restrictive because of the distinct historical processes in Portugal that are highly dissonant compared to other EU states. Yet, on the other, it is also didactic because Portugal provides an extremely valuable indication of linkages between migration and welfare in countries with weak welfare traditions. The case of Portugal illustrates the dynamics underpinning different societal behaviour patterns in the EU towards immigrants and the diverse strategies employed by immigrants towards social and economic incorporation. I argue that in countries where welfare traditions are not deeply entrenched and where considerable sections of the population have not fully internalised their own citizenship rights, then there is likely to be less pressure on the state to extend to immigrants social rights that pass from formal laws to everyday reality.

The legal-institutional framework

The access of foreign residents in Portugal to full social citizenship is formally guaranteed in the Portuguese Constitution. The Constitution addresses the rights of resident foreigners under the principle of nationality (Article 15), which means that foreign residents have the same rights and duties as Portuguese citizens and the principle of equality (Article 13), which refers to social dignity and equality before the law. Their constitutional status means that the main human and social rights specified in the Constitution – life, honour, education, health, work, housing, justice and court representation, social security – cannot be curtailed by ordinary law. Yet, while the guarantee of some rights (life, honour, justice and court representation) is universal, the remaining specified rights are reserved. The effect of this is that, although they are disconnected from nationality, social citizenship rights in Portugal are linked to residency status and to the social mode of economic incorporation. The social rights specified in the Constitution – education, health, work, housing and social security – are, in fact, only available to legal residents while entitlements to social security rights such as unemployment benefits or retirement pensions are directly dependent upon formal employment.

In addition to its domestic laws, Portugal has signed all the major international instruments on human rights and on migrant workers' protection. It has also signed bilateral agreements extending social and various political rights to the main extra-communitary immigrants groups in Portugal, namely the Brazilians and the immigrants from the Portuguese-speaking African countries (from now on referred to as PALOP immigrants). Portugal has thus assumed, in the international arena, the responsibility for ensuring the human rights and migrant workers' protection described in these documents. The country has also exercised the political will to discriminate positively towards the nationals of those countries that once comprised the Portuguese colonial empire.

In sum, the legal framework bars access to full citizenship to all immigrants workers and their dependants that are not legal residents and to all those that, independent of their residency status, are incorporated in Portuguese society in the informal economy. Or, in other words, from the legal-institutional point of view, we can say that the degree of exclusion from social rights is a function of the level of irregular permanence and/or of economic informality exhibited by the foreign population in the country.

Permanence and economic incorporation

The foreign resident population

Until the Revolution of 1974, the foreign population was small (around 30,000 immigrants) and relatively homogeneous in its composition. From 1980 onwards, the resident foreign population increased at an average rate of 6 per cent every year during the 1980s and during the 1990s at an average rate of 9 per cent each year.[3] The foreign resident population also became more diverse, not only in terms of countries of origin, but also in terms of spatial patterns of settlement within Portugal, age structure, professional status and occupational structure.

In the late 1990s, the foreign population either with or without a valid resident permit was around 200,000 people. In addition, when the results of the special regularisations of 1992 and 1996 are taken into account, it is possible to say that around 25 to 30 per cent of the immigrant population were illegally/irregularly in the country at some point during the recent past (see Tables 10.1 and 10.2).

For the purpose of this chapter's analysis of immigrants' access to social citizenship, the foreign population in Portugal can be divided into three numerically significant sub-groups: citizens from the former Portuguese-colonies in Africa; citizens from a European country; and citizens from Brazil. The largest of these groups is comprised of the citizens of Portuguese speaking African countries (around one hundred thousand persons) representing more or less 50 per cent of the foreign population; 75 per cent of them live and work in the metropolitan area of Lisbon. The most numerically significant nationality among this group is Cape Verdean.

On economic grounds, the foreign population can be divided into two main groups. The first comes mainly from Europe and Brazil and includes a large proportion of highly qualified people; the second group comes mainly from the former Portuguese African colonies and includes an overwhelming proportion of unskilled people. Accordingly, both Brazilians and Europeans present an extremely biased occupational distribution towards professional, technical and managerial occupations. The percentage of these occupations in total employment ranges from 51 per cent for Brazilians to 56 per cent for Europeans. Between 1992 and 1995, the corresponding figure for this set of occupations was, for the domestic

Table 10.1 Legal foreign residents in Portugal 1980–97

Year	Africa	North America	South America	Asia	Europe[c]	Others	Total
1980	27,748	4,821	6,403	1,153	17,706	260	58,091
1981	27,948	6,018	8,123	1,394	18,931	278	62,692
1982	28,903	6,855	10,481	1,663	19,924	327	68,153
1983	32,481	8,520	13,351	2,219	22,053	391	79,015
1984	37,128	9,887	15,394	2,860	23,896	460	89,625
1985	34,978	7,987	11,567	2,564	22,060	438	79,594
1986	37,829	9,047	12,629	2,958	24,040	479	86,982
1987	38,838	8,623	13,009	3,124	25,676	508	89,778
1988	40,253	8,338	14,645	3,413	27,280	524	94,453
1989	42,789	8,737	15,938	3,741	29,247	559	101,011
1990	45,255	8,993	17,376	4,154	31,410	579	107,767
1991	47,998	9,236	18,666	4,458	33,011	609	113,978
1992[a]	52,037	9,430	19,960	4,769	34,732	621	122,348
1993	55,786	10,513	21,924	5,520	37,154	696	136,932
1994[b]	72,630	10,739	24,815	6,322	41,819	748	157,073
1995	79,231	10,853	25,867	6,730	44,867	768	168,316
1996	81,176	10,783	25,733	7,140	47,315	765	172,912
1997	81,717	10,573	25,274	7,192	49,797	760	175,313

Source: 1980–94: Estatísticas Demográficas, 1980–94; 1995: SEF, Relatório Estatístico, 1995–7.

Notes
a There are discrepancies in the values for 1992 and 1993 in the SEF Statistics.
b The data for 1994 includes results of the Regularisation Process of 1992/93 and around 95 per cent of the foreign residents from Africa are from the PALOP.
c More than 90 per cent come from EU member states (Baganha 1996).

Table 10.2 Special processes of regularisation in Portugal of 1992–3 and 1996 (requests by nationality)

Countries	1992/3		1996	
	Number	%	Number	%
Angola	12,525	32	9,255	26.4
Cape Verde	6,778	17.3	6,872	19.6
Guinea-Bissau	6,877	17.6	5,308	15.1
Mozambique	757	1.9	416	1.2
Sao Tomé e Príncipe	1,408	3.6	1,549	4.4
Total PALOP	28,345	72.4	23,400	66.7
Senegal	1,397	3.6	672	1.9
Morocco	98	0.3	520	1.5
Brazil	5,346	13.7	2,330	6.6
China	1,352	3.5	1,608	4.6
Pakistan	286	0.7	1,754	5.0
India	261	0.7	915	2.6
Bangladesh	139	0.4	752	2.1
Other nationalities	1,942	5.0	3,803	10.9
Total	39,166	100	35,754	100

Source: Serviço de Estrangeiros e Fronteiras. In Baganha and Góis (1999).

employed population, approximately 28 per cent. The relative distribution of the employed population from the PALOP by occupations is, compared to the national average, over-represented in the residual occupational category 'workers in industry, transports, construction, and similar' and under-represented in all the others. The occupational structure of the foreign population when compared to the occupational structure of the domestic population is both biased towards the top (Brazilian and European occupational structures) and the bottom (PALOP occupational structure) of the occupational ladder.

Given that the modern tertiary activities such as financing, insurance and business services are increasing considerably, the labour needs of this group of activities may in part explain the growing in-flow occurring from Brazil and some European countries. The remaining growth in the foreign population – essentially the one from PALOP countries – is not being promoted by the recent evolution of the job market. In fact the job market has been contracting in precisely those activities where immigrants from PALOP countries are concentrated. That is to say, the economic incorporation of PALOP immigrants has not been induced by the evolution of the formal economy because in order to care for themselves immigrants must be working outside the formal economy and consistently and significantly substitute for native labour. The analysis of official statistics can lead to no other logical conclusion (see Table 10.3).

This contention is not totally unexpected since, as already noted, around 25–30 per cent of the immigrant population did at some point reside illegally in the country. Consequently, whatever they were doing to provide for themselves was done either in the informal economy or in the illegal economy, since access to the formal economy is dependent upon the possession of a social security number and a valid resident permit, neither of which illegal immigrants possessed.

Table 10.3 Activities with the highest rate of undeclared workers in Portugal 1991

Activities	Census	Employment survey	Difference in per cent to census
Retail trade	211,412	162,364	23.2
Leisure and culture	24,363	18,118	25.6
Construction	330,935	180,796	45.4
Personal services	92,904	47,512	48.9
Social services	327,917	81,221	75.2
Non-specified industry	47,284	10,860	77.0

Source: Census of 1991 and Employment Survey in Baganha 1996.
Note
The overall rate of undeclared workers was 20.8 per cent.

Immigrants' insertion in the informal economy

During the 1980s, two competing definitions of an informal economy appeared. The first, adopted by the ILO, identified the informal economy with urban poverty and underemployment. The second saw it as the 'irruption of real market forces in an economy strait-jacketed by state regulation' (Portes 1994: 427). These competing notions were devised and developed to cover the realities and behaviour of economic actors and agents considered typical of under-developed societies. The industrial world was supposedly not totally free from economic informality, but the share of the informal economy was considered insignificant, a left-over or residual heritage of pre-modern economic behaviour. Macro- and micro-economic analyses and several case studies during the 1980s demonstrated that the share of the informal economy was far from insignificant in the industrialised world. More than this, it was postulated that informality was not a residual survivor of earlier economic forms of organising labour, production and distribution, but was actually an expanding segment of the economy encompassing both traditional and modern economic sectors and activities.

In this new vein, Feige (1990: 990) defined the informal economy as covering 'those actions of economic agents that fail to adhere to the established institutional rules or are denied their protection'. Alternatively, Castells and Portes (1989: 12) defined it as 'all income-earning activities that are not regulated by state in social environments where similar activities are regulated'. As Feige (1990: 990–2) further elaborated, the informal economy comprises economic actions that bypass the costs and are excluded from the protection of laws and administrative rules covering 'property relationships, commercial licensing, labour contracts, torts, financing credit, and social security systems'. The informal economy generates a fraction of the national income that evades or circumvents tax codes and is not recorded by national accounting systems because the economic actors involved do not comply with the established reporting requirements of governmental statistical agencies.[4]

The existence and extension of economic informality depends essentially on what, at a given time, the state and certain of its agencies, namely the tax revenue bureau and the statistical bureau, define as informal. In this sense, the informal economy is, above all, a politically constructed reality. After this reality comes into being it becomes a social phenomenon that may be characterised in terms of the legal placement of employers and firms, and of the types of employment such placement generates *vis-à-vis* the formal and the illegal segments of the economy. From this perspective, we can represent the constitutive markets of an economy in Figure 10.1.

As Figure 10.1 shows, entrepreneurs and firms functioning only in the formal economy generate protected registered and declared employment (standard and non-standard jobs). Compulsory compliance with the rules

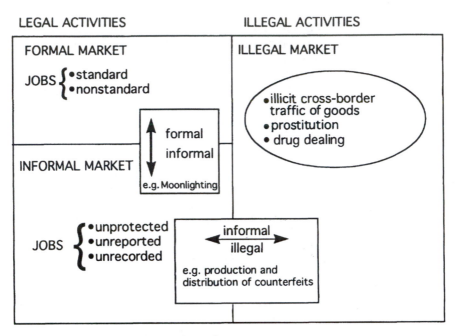

Figure 10.1 The constitutive markets of an economy.

and contracts governing the functioning of this market is guaranteed and ensured by the power of the state and the judicial system. Entrepreneurs and firms functioning only in the informal economy originate unprotected, unregistered and undeclared jobs. Both the state and the judicial system are, in principle, absent from this segment of the market, thus its functional regulation must be ensured differently. Mutual trust on the part of the employer and the intermediary, kinship and community networks, or belonging to a reference group, are usually prerequisites to enter this segment of the market. Compliance with functional norms comes, above all, from social control. Sanctions must be essentially determined by those within the group or network and known by those involved in these arrangements. Entrepreneurs and firms functioning only in the illegal economy also generate unprotected, unregistered and undeclared jobs, but compliance with the rules governing the functioning of this market is usually enforced by the use of violence. Furthermore, while the activities that are carried on in the informal market are in themselves legal, the activities in the illegal market are illicit activities.

Obviously these markets are not mutually exclusive, as Figure 10.1 shows. A firm may well appear to function totally in the formal market while at the same time, by off-the-record hiring or by subcontracting informal entrepreneurs, it may be partially or substantially immersed in the informal economy. It is not only firms that may exhibit 'moonlighting' behaviour, in fact a worker may well have a job in the formal economy and a second job in the informal, or vice versa. Perhaps the fuzziest and most widespread blends of formal and informal are the so-called fringe benefits. These are payments in kind for work done in the formal market and since they simultaneously evade taxes and social security dues they must be considered informal payments.

The structure of each country's labour market, level of efficiency, extent of state controls, and the degree of social acceptance or rejection of economic informality varies from country to country. This creates different social and economic contexts, some of which are more conducive than others to the development of informal economic activities. Not only does the combination of these factors create different national, social and economic contexts, but within the same economy they may or may not promote opportunities for informality, according to the economic sector involved. And, as is obvious, immigrant insertion in the informal economy, the main focus of this chapter, will largely depend on the social and economic context and the economic sectors that, at a given time and place, are involved in the informal economy.

The reports on internal security from the Portuguese Ministry of the Interior repeatedly state that the overwhelming majority of immigrants with an unlawful status of residency are from PALOP countries. For example, the 1991 Report states that: 'So far, irregular immigration in Portugal seems to be, in the overwhelming majority of the cases, more the result of a lack of compliance with formal legal procedures than the result of network of recruitment of clandestine immigrants'.[5] Among the immigrants that are economically active in irregular situations it is Cape Verdeans that form the predominant proportion, followed by immigrants from Guinea-Bissau. The overwhelming number of the immigrants in this situation work in building and construction – men – and in domestic services – women – and live in the suburban areas of Lisbon/Setubal and Oporto, plus from the mid-1980s onwards, in Faro and Braga.[6]

This official portrait of illegal immigrants in Portugal as mainly overstayers from PALOP countries inhabiting the suburbs of the metropolitan area of Lisbon, and working in building and construction (if male) and domestic services (if female) was repeatedly confirmed during our qualitative survey of illegal immigrants. In fact of our twenty-eight male respondents from the PALOP, twenty-three worked in construction while of the fourteen female respondents seven worked in cleaning or domestic services. Perhaps more important than the quantitative results of the qualitative survey, is the fact that all the studies conducted in the last decade on this topic have consistently revealed that to work in the informal market is, indeed, the prevalent mode of economic incorporation for immigrants in Portugal. This is particularly the case for male immigrants from PALOP countries who have been shown to have, regardless of their legal status in the country, an extremely high concentration in construction and building.[7] They also possess a much higher propensity to be incorporated into the informal market than the domestic population or the remaining immigrant population.[8] Thus, for example, a survey of the Oporto metropolitan area found that the percentage of active immigrants working without contract was also over 40 per cent (Luvumba 1997). Other surveys, which, although not totally comparable with the previous example since they target ethnic minorities and not exclusively immigrants, reinforce the point. In fact, a survey of the Cape Verdean population (i.e. Portuguese citizens born in Cape Verde as well as Cape Verde citizens) (França 1992: 130–3) conducted in 1986 found that 26 per cent of the working men and 37 per cent of the working women worked without a contract, while a survey on ethnic minorities inhabiting urban-degraded houses conducted in 1990 (Costa 1991: 62), found that 75 per cent of the active population held unstable jobs, 47 per cent had no contract, and of the remainder, 20 per cent had fixed term contracts. The survey also found that 55 per cent of the men worked in construction and public works and that 64 per cent of the women worked in personal and domestic services, essentially in house-cleaning activities (Costa 1991: 62, 72 and 111). A 1998 survey of economically active immigrants in Portugal revealed that 47 per cent of the men and 21 per cent of the women worked without any type of contract. The percentage of males working without a contract in construction and building attained the astonishing figure of 74 per cent (Baganha, Ferrão and Malheiros 1998).

When evidence on economic activities with the highest rates of non-declared employment is considered, then the insertion into the informal economy of the main extra-communitary immigrants' groups can be summarised as follows. Brazilians working in the informal economy tend to be connected in financing, insurance and business services (particularly marketing), and in retail trade, restaurants and hotels. Citizens from PALOP countries (with the exception of Mozambique) when working in the informal economy do so overwhelmingly in construction and in personal and domestic services.

The building and construction industry: the nexus of the principal migratory dynamic

Given the numerical significance of PALOP immigrants within the Portuguese extra-communitary population, we can conclude that the construction and building sectors are the main locations for the economic insertion of male immigrants. This finding is not in itself particularly interesting since this sector has been repeatedly identified as a main entrance door for newly arrived immigrants in almost all receiving countries. What is interesting in the Portuguese case are the peculiar dynamics that are fostering this process which are, in fact, substantially different from the ones usually described in the literature on this topic and relate to the process of European integration.

Portugal's EU membership after 1986 had two main impacts on building and construction. First, it allowed Portuguese construction and building firms to sub-contract their labour force within the EU space. Since the fall of the Berlin Wall in 1989 this strategy has been driving abroad several thousand workers each year and thereby reducing the available domestic labour force in the country. Second, simultaneous with this accrued demand from abroad for construction workers, Portugal's full EU membership brought substantial structural funds. A very sizeable share of these funds was applied to public investments in infrastructure and public buildings, which temporarily increased the need for labour in this sector.

The combination of these two situations created numerous opportunities for Portuguese firms in the building and construction sectors. Some of these firms sought to profit from the ongoing boom at home and abroad. In Portugal, they resorted to informal hiring and sub-contracting to informal firms. They then sent their formally hired workers abroad. This situation attracted or at least opened up numerous opportunities for incoming or recently arrived illegal immigrants, above all in the Lisbon metropolitan area where immigrants, particularly from PALOP countries constitute a sizeable proportion of all the labour force in this sector and bridge the way for new arrivals.

This perception of the main dynamics that are currently fostering immigration to Portugal was further reinforced by the opinions of a key informer, a trade unionist, who described the functioning of this sector as follows:

> The illegal situation of workers, illegal work and unstable work, and of workers who already were in an irregular situations, makes this industry a 'dumping place'. Interestingly, Portugal within Europe is in a *sui generis* position because workers continue to emigrate to Europe in a new situation called 'workers transfer'. The building and construction workers emigrate to Germany, which becomes host to millions of workers for big public works. This process by which the Portuguese emigrate while Portugal receives immigrants is *sui generis*. What we note is that this constitutes social dumping in the following way – the Portuguese here feel pressed by the arrival of immigrants. They feel pressed in the building and construction sector because their own salaries are affected by the lower salaries that the immigrants are prepared to receive, particularly in unskilled activities and so they emigrate to Europe. In turn, they earn salaries lower than the minimum in the countries where they work temporarily for 3 or 6 months which affects the entire chain and confirms a global lowering not only of salaries, but also of work conditions, hygiene and security at the work sites.
>
> (Baganha 1998: 62)

The result of this situation was a marked growth of informalisation, increasing substitution of the domestic labour force by immigrants, and a growing ethnicisation of this sector of the economy. This ethnicisation has meant that some segments of the informal sector such as subcontracting and unskilled activities are becoming controlled and dependent upon the efforts of ethnic minorities. Tendencies that the prevalent hiring practices, modes of job search and labour paths in this sector tend to reinforce, as exemplified in the following interview extract:

> After arriving in 1989, he went to work in building and construction as a labourer earning 250 escudos per hour. He worked with a Cape Verdean subcontractor. This subcontractor led him to believe that he was contributing towards Social Security (even providing him with a card, but it proved to be fraudulent). He then went to work three months in the Algarve as a helper with another Cape Verdean subcontractor. After this, he went to Germany living clandestinely and working in a car assembly factory (Volkswagen) earning 1,100 marks per month. He had to return because he had no documents. After returning, he went to Luanda (8 months) on holiday doing odd jobs. Then, he got back to Portugal working consecutively for two different Cape Verdean contractors as a labourer without a contract and without discounts, earning 250 escudos per hour. He quit these jobs for various reasons – problems with the subcontractors, transport etc. In 1996, he worked on the Expo 98 construction for 2 months for a subcontractor, earning 900 escudos per hour. This year (1997), he is working as a welder for a Guinean subcontractor 11 hours/day, earning 900 escudos per hour again, without a contract or discounting any money.
>
> (quoted in Baganha 1998: 154)

This example illustrates that entrance and permanence in the labour market are highly dependent upon the immigrant's social capital, which reinforces the tendency to maintain informal labour relations as well as the growing ethnicisation of this economic sector.

The 1992 and 1996 regularisations

Portuguese immigration is essentially constituted by two main groups: those from Europe and Brazil which includes a large proportion of highly qualified people and those from former Portuguese African colonies which includes an overwhelming proportion of unskilled people. The first group, originating from countries with more generous and efficient social security systems and/or able to generate higher incomes should have few or no incentives to belong to a Portuguese system, that is compared to their own, poorer and less efficient. It is to be expected that these immigrants will try to avoid being cut-off from their original social security system or from contributing to a Portuguese system that does not cover them efficiently. The second group, overwhelmingly made up of immigrants from former Portuguese colonies, where the existent social security systems are extremely deficient and incomplete, have clear advantages in belonging to a more developed social security system. The immigrants in this category should be expected to possess the incentive to try to belong to a system that entitles them to a bundle of benefits that their own countries are unable to provide.

As other contributions to this book have already demonstrated, the capacity of liberal states to control immigration should not be exaggerated. Moreover, in the case of a country like Portugal, the social consequences of stringent application of restrictive policies such as repatriation and expulsion would have dire social consequences because of the strong familial connections underpinning immigration into Portugal. The Portuguese government should also be interested in fostering the entrance of these immigrants into the domestic social security system of the country, if, for no other reason, than to minimise the future costs of social exclusion. Given that the probability of becoming socially excluded is greater for unskilled and poorly educated people, immigrants with this profile should be expected to be a target for preferential inclusion into the Portuguese social security system. Since in Portugal, the number of foreigners registered into the Portuguese social security system is numerically insignificant, the relevant factors to uncover are the exogenous factors that are diverting the government and immigrants from acting according to their respective self-interests.

Given what has been described in the previous section on illegality and economic incorporation in the informal economy, it is evident that both the government and the immigrants seem to be acting contrary to their respective self-interests. Although the Employment Survey for 1992–5 has extremely poor coverage and low reliability for the categories of immigrants considered in this chapter, it does clearly indicate that PALOP immigrants are consistently and substantially more excluded from social security than other immigrants. It also demonstrates that the share of the female immigrant population, particularly from the PALOP, with permanent contracts and registered in the social security system is much larger than the correspondent male share.[9] In 1995, 56 per cent of male immigrants from PALOP countries held permanent contracts; the corresponding figure for females was 70 per cent. The proportion registered in social security was 70 per cent for males against 94 per cent for females (INE, Inquérito ao Emprego, 1992–5).

The obvious questions these findings raise are why do such large numbers of people 'prefer' to remain illegal and/or to work informally in the country, and how is such a situation possible? Leaving aside the bureaucratic complexities that may deter some people, and the slowness of public services, some of our key informers argued that several factors contributed to the fact that a significant number of immigrants, who requested their regularisation in 1992 found themselves again in an unlawful situation soon after 1993.[10] First and foremost, is the perception that it is 'easy'. As a key informer stated 'Portugal is not France, where it is difficult to over stay because there are controls'. One of the immigrants interviewed, stated practically the same thing: 'it's comparatively far easier to be illegal in Portugal then in other European countries'. Several key informers did not hesitate to indicate the two situations where individuals are seriously at risk of being detected: travelling on a train without a valid ticket and having a fight in a bar or a disco where police intervention is requested.[11] The opinions expressed by key informers received further confirmation in the statements of the immigrants interviewed. In fact, of the interviewees, to whom we asked if they have ever been asked to show their documents in either a public place or in the work place, only eight of forty-six respondents had been asked. Except for two Chinese respondents, the other six respondents were asked for their documents in one of the situations referred to (on trains or in discos). This indicates that neither random controls of the population in public places nor labour inspections are frequent and/or efficient, which is substantiated by the fact that there is a 0.3 per cent risk of being expelled for unlawful permanence. Consequently, it seems reasonable to reach a first conclusion: it is safe and easy, particularly for immigrants from a Portuguese-speaking country, to live and work in an unlawful residency and work status. It is safe because controls are few and when they do occur they mainly fail to bring sanctions to the immigrants detected in an unlawful situation, as the number of expulsions compared to the number of illegal immigrants in the country abundantly confirms. It is easy because since there is no fear of being detected, no special care (except when travelling on trains without a valid ticket or when getting involved in fights in public places that may give cause for police intervention) is needed. It is also easy because gaining access to the labour market is not dependent on having legal residency in the country or a work permit.

The earlier statement from the 1991 internal security report, which portrays illegal immigrants, if male, as construction workers from PALOP countries, was repeated over and over again during the field research.[12] The overwhelming majority of the male immigrants from the PALOP interviewed were, in fact, working in building and construction. The concentration of male workers in the building and construction sectors arises because many legal immigrants and former immigrants are well integrated in this sector.[13] This means that contacts to get a job for a newcomer are easy and usually done within the inner group, offers are abundant, no legal requirements are made – such as possession of the 'proper papers' – no qualifications are necessary, and there is no fear of being caught by labour inspectors. In fact, there seem to be few objective reasons for fear, since as a former head of the labour office noted, if an illegal immigrant is detected in a construction work site, he just changes to another construction site the next day and the labour inspectors will not find him.

Furthermore, a form of positive discrimination or in other words, the ethnicisation of this economic sector of activity, is taking place, which reinforces the status quo. A key informer from a trade union stated that: 'there is a kind of perverse positive discrimination (in construction and cleaning), which is the preference for immigrant labour in these areas'. Or as a member of Parliament at the time of the 1996 regularisation, who was also the minister responsible for the 1992 regularisation process, stated:

> The labour market issue is far more complicated since the existing law applies to the formal economy not to 'contractors and sub-contractors' that do not exist legally and furthermore are very frequently run by citizens originally from the PALOP, who live illegally and have created an infernal net into which the humanity and the rights of the immigrants vanish.[14]

This statement has two remarkable features, the first is the identification of immigrants insertion in the economy with only one sector, the construction and building sector, and the second is the ethnic dimension given to the perverse functioning of the sector.

The next obvious question is to explore the state's rationale for the apparent lack of efficiency in controlling unlawful permanence and the economic incorporation of immigrants. In more or less elaborated forms the rationales go as follows: 'the government will maintain them (the illegal immigrants) until the public constructions are done', or 'when the country will not need them, they will be kicked out'. The dominant opinion among key informers and immigrants is that the government is not an innocent bystander or a powerless agent but an interested party in the maintenance of the situation. Even the Portuguese government seems to accept this view – in fact the Secretary of State of the Interior during the parliamentary debate that preceded the 1996 regularisation, stated that:

> We need to better understand the needs of our economy in order to be able to establish rational bilateral agreements between the two groups involved (the Portuguese and the PALOP) and to reinforce our own controls, be it in the area of the Ministry of the Interior (borders and permanence) be it in the combating of illegal labour, in the supervision of public construction contracts and in all these fields in which the Portuguese society is compliant and in which, in one way or the other, profits from the undignified conditions that are tolerated in order to take advantage and simultaneously to endorse either repressive or compassionate discourses.[15]

What then was the rationale for the 1996 special regularisation? Was this just a way of monitoring the evolution of the foreign population, or was it a change of political orientation (more in favour of immigrant's rights), or a mix of both? That there was a major change of political mood is clear, whether there was a change of political orientation is probably too soon to say. Our respondents are greatly divided between those who think that the 1996 regularisation was a necessary step in order to close the doors in the future, and those who believed that everything would remain the same. The illegal immigrants of yesterday will be replaced by the illegal immigrants of today and tomorrow. As long as there are major constructions going on and low-wage labour is necessary then new processes of regularisation will take place.

The existence or non-existence of illegal immigrants in Portugal does not, as some of our respondents claim, have to be necessarily dependent on the evolution of the building and construction sector since bilateral agreements for the temporary transfer of labour from the PALOP already exist. If implemented these could solve the conjunctural needs of the economy and potentially benefit everyone involved. The existence or non-existence of illegal immigrants in the country will essentially depend on the effective control of the borders, of a clear and co-ordinated policy on the granting of visas, and on the effective regulation and control of the labour market. Until the government's practice on these matters reveals itself, it will be impossible to know if the 1996 regularisation served only to monitor the foreign population in the country or if it represented a real attempt to change the existing perverse situation and thus corresponded to a real change in political orientation.

It is, however, possible to evaluate the process of 1992. The debate on the 1992 regularisation occurred on 26 March 1992 simultaneously with the debate on Portuguese accession to the Schengen Convention and the debate on the government's proposals for the revision of the law of entry, permanence, departure and expulsion of foreigners. As usual, the first speaker was the Secretary of State for the Interior, who presented the rationale for the several legislative documents under discussion. Some aspects of the intervention of the Interior Minister (Dias Loureiro) are remarkable. In fact, all his intervention was framed from the global to the supranational to the national, and developed in relation to current global dangers (such as drugs traffic and AIDS propagation, and the demographic challenge). These were argued to have a direct impact on Portugal, rendering necessary the implementation of the measures being proposed by the government. The Secretary of the Interior repeatedly equated the trilogy 'immigration' – 'crime' – 'drugs', as the following excerpt exemplifies.

> The government intends to bring out of a clandestine situation many thousand non-EEC workers, particularly from Portuguese speaking countries, who, for many years, have a hidden and uneasy life because they do not have a lawful residency status in Portugal. From a social point of view, the existence of situations of illegality means the

acceptance of marginality and its inevitable consequences, lack of social security, exploitation in the labour market, the growth of marginality, the invitation to delinquency and to crime.

(Diário da Assembleia da República,
Intervenção do Ministro da Administração
Interna (Dias Loureiro) 26 March 1992: 1364–7;
transcribed in Baganha 1998: 181)

For a country where the overwhelming majority of the foreign population are either from the EU or from PALOP countries to use global dangers as political legitimisation to tighten migratory policy seems at best odd. That the main grounds for defending the launch of the regularisation was to reduce delinquency and criminality seems to indicate that the government's main objective was in fact to monitor the foreign population to better prevent delinquency and crime and not to prevent new immigrants from settling in.

In fact, regardless of the apocalyptic tone employed by the government concerning the need for tighter controls in 1992, no efficient measures were actually taken to reduce the number of illegal immigrants in the country, or to detain new ones from settling in. This reality is evidenced by the fact that the level of expulsions remained exactly the same before and after 1992, and receives further confirmation in the statements of our respondents. In fact, the majority of the immigrants we interviewed arrived in the country after 1992. In sum, the perception of Portugal as a country where it is possible to get regularised, where it is easy to reside and work informally corresponds well to the situation between 1992 and 1996.[16]

In summary four main factors determine the prevalent mode of economic incorporation of immigrants in Portugal. First, the perception that it is easier and safer to live and work illegally in Portugal than in other European countries. Second, the web of information and contacts that immigrants and former immigrants retain in specific economic sectors that are characterised by high rates of informality, wage flexibilisation, and precarious labour relations. Third, the transplanting of domestic labour abroad and the vacancies such transplanting entails. Fourth, the state's incapacity to efficiently regulate and control the labour market.

Conclusion

As has been demonstrated, the overwhelming majority of illegal immigrants in Portugal are overstayers from the PALOP. These are immigrants who enter the country with a short-term visa and overstay. They are inserted into a wide network, active at both ends of the trajectory. He/she will simply 'disappear' into a highly concentrated residential area of the metropolitan area of Lisbon where members of his/her inner-group already reside. They are mainly from a rural background and with a poor educational background. This type of immigrant will be economically incorporated in building and construction if male and in personal and domestic services or cleaning services if female.

It is difficult to disentangle whether in the case of 'the over-stayer' the immigrants' profiles are determined by the country's tolerance towards illegal immigrants or by the existence of a large community able to create the opportunities for the newcomers 'to get lost' while securing ample opportunities to work. It can obviously be claimed that such opportunities only exist given the above-mentioned tolerance.

Given the 'ease' of being illegal in Portugal and the functioning of the building and construction sectors, where the overwhelming majority of immigrants from the PALOP are being economically incorporated regardless of their legal status, then it seems reasonable to conclude that the present situation of the exclusion from social citizenship can be linked to four factors. First, immigrants are mainly of rural origin and in the prime years of their active lives and tend to accord very little or no value to the possible benefits to which having lawful permanence and belonging to the formal labour market may entitle them. Second, their economic incorporation in the labour market takes place mainly in the informal economy and prevents them from entering the social security system. Third, a sizeable proportion is in the country illegally, which automatically removes them from several relevant social rights. Fourth, the diffuse future costs implicit in the present situation do not generate sufficient societal pressure to lead the government to change the existing situation, which has clear short-term economic benefits.

In addition to these factors there is another reason that is, in my opinion, at the very root of the present situation, which is the view held by a considerable proportion of the Portuguese about their own right to full social citizenship. In Portugal, sizeable immigration is a recent pheno-menon, but access to full social citizenship is probably an even newer phenomenon. Adaptation to new phenomena requires time and apprentice-ship. The Portuguese are adapting both to the existence within their midst of 'strangers' and simultaneously learning how to claim their rights from the state. Several authors, for example Santos (1990) and Cabral (1997), argue that the existence and spread of dispositions towards economic redistribution and social protection are essentially the result of the social and economic evolution of Portugal and not a natural contractual part of democratic citizenship. An example of this is the way that a large part of the population perceives their rights to social security. As a result of recent changes in the social coverage of the population and due to the fact that a very large proportion of the population was included in the social security system without ever drawing from it, very low benefits were not questioned. In fact they were seen as 'fatherly gifts' that can be taken away 'in a discretionary way by the same omnipotent and distant authority' (Cabral 1997). Consequently, the idea of constituting defensive savings for 'bad times' is still a prevalent feature for a significant proportion of the Portuguese population. Another prevalent feature is the socially accepted principle, that people only pay their dues to the state when it is not possible to avoid doing otherwise. This is, after all, a rational strategy when the state is not viewed as a reliable protector. The first feature continues to drive abroad every year a very significant number of Portuguese, while the second feature helps to explain why the informal economy in Portugal is so widespread and seen as no social stigma. While the Portuguese do not fully internalise their own citizenship rights they are hardly likely to press the state to extend these rights to immigrants from the formal letter of the law to the reality of everyday life.

Notes

1 The figures for 1981 and 1991 are from Baganha (1996). For a more detailed description of the recent evolution, see Fassman and Münz (1994), Castles and Miller (1998) and Appleyard (1991).
2 Figures are for 1988/9, in Diário da Assembleia da República, I Série No. 44, 27 March 1992.
3 During the 1990s the stock of foreign residents increased at an annual rate of 6.4 percent, and became internally more diversified, particularly due to a renewed in-flow from Brazil. Finally, during the last five years, the growth of the foreign population became more intense, on average 9.3 per cent per year, and its composition more heterogeneous.
4 Feige considers the informal economy as a segment of the underground economy, and proposes the following typology for the underground economy: illegal economy; unreported economy; unrecorded economy; informal economy. The typology that is being used in this report differs from Feige's typology because it considers the undeclared and the unregistered economy as characteristics of both the informal and the illegal economies and not as autonomous segments.
5 These reports also referred to the usual practice for PALOP immigrants to enter the country with short-term visas and only after being in the country, when they do not simply overstay, to request a residence permit. This practice was used more frequently than the request for a consular visa. Such a practice, was made possible by the legal provisions that even after they were revoked and residence permits could only be issued by a Consulate abroad, the number of requests in the country was still higher than the number of requests in the Consulates.
6 The 1994 report re-stated the same ideas: 'Immigrants continue to prefer the clandestine path to remain on the national territory, that is they enter with a tourist, a business or a transit visa and do not leave the country at the end of the period of their visas validity'.
7 Members of the Angolan community do not hesitate to estimate that 50 per cent or more of students from Angola complement their incomes by working informally in construction either during a part of the year or all the year around, particularly during periods when remittances from home are difficult or impossible to transfer.
8 Although the extremely poor coverage of the population of interest (note, for example, that according to the SEF registers the number of foreign wage earners with legal residence in Portugal, in 1995, was 67,764, of whom 32,621

where from the PALOP), and the low reliability of the estimators for almost all of the categories considered, highly restricts the analysis, the results for the foreign population contained in the Employment Survey for 1992–5 confirm this point. In fact, PALOP immigrants have lower job stability than other immigrants. The proportion of permanent contracts is higher for the total (the category all foreigners) in all of the observations than the proportion for the PALOP and lower than the proportion for the category 'other foreigners'. In 1995, for example the relevant proportions were 72 per cent (for the total), 64 per cent (for the PALOP) and 82 per cent (for other foreigners).

9 In the Employment Survey, and contrary to what has been noticed, when the surveyed population are ethnic minorities, employed foreign women register a higher share of permanent contracts than the employed foreign men (see, for example, Costa 1991 and França 1992).

10 It is interesting to note on this topic that the Internal Security Report for 1994 has the following statement: 'Only in 1994 were regularisations (from the 1992 process) included in the statistics because many of the situations were not yet regularised due to a lack of care of the foreigners or because inquires to verify eventual situations of fraud. The increase in the number of residents did not correspond with the number of legalised persons put forward by the media (39,166). In fact, during the year of 1994 there was an increase of just 16,091 residents.

11 One of the key informers added to a third situation: attending a hospital emergency service although it seems that no one detected as being without valid documents or undocumented has ever been expelled. We believe that what this statement suggests is that most probably any immigrant with an unlawful residency status will avoid contact with the emergency public health system (the only service where the police are present) as much as he/she possibly can. This arises because of a perceived fear rather than the real danger that such contact would entail.

12 In fact, one of the main findings from our interviews with key informers was that the overwhelming majority of the interviewees equate the terms immigrant and immigration with immigrants and immigration from PALOP countries. Even when the interviewee was knowledgeable about other flows, only exceptionally would he/she volunteer comments and observations on the immigrants and on the migratory flows other than from the PALOP, and only when directly questioned on other immigrant groups would he/she broaden up his/her comments and observations.

13 On this topic see the interview extracts in the previous section and also Monteiro 1995: 39.

14 In Diário da Assembleia da República, I Série, No. 53, March, 1996: 1698.

15 In Diário da Assembleia da República, I Série, No. 53, March, 1996: 1691.

16 For a more developed description on illegal types of immigrants in Portugal see Baganha (1999).

11 Temporary transnational labour migration in an integrating Europe and the challenge to the German welfare state

Uwe Hunger

Introduction

With the end of the socialist development paradigm in central and eastern Europe in 1989–90, the trend towards globalisation in international competition, which began to emerge in the mid-1980s, has accelerated strongly (Rösner 1995: 480). The internationalisation of business proceeds at an unprecedented rate and competition between production locations has become increasingly acute. Investment decisions on the part of business enterprises will, of course, depend on the prevailing economic and political framework. Factors such as the degree of economic and environmental regulation, the extent of labour and social welfare costs and labour relations play an ever greater role (Rösner 1995: 475). Countries find themselves under pressure to create an 'investment-friendly' climate for business, and to compete with other countries for international investors and jobs (Brock 1997: 17).

The impact of this development on the political sphere is enormous. Phrases such as 'loss of national political sovereignty' and 'devaluation of social standards' are used to characterise developments that appear likely to end in a 'policy dictated by the constraints of globalisation' (Beck 1998: 15). In Germany, the consequences of globalisation challenge the foundations of the welfare state and the system of social partnership and consensus that has stood the test since the 1950s. A paradigm change in labour market relations from the Continental European type to the Anglo-American type seems to be emerging.

As in a 'burning glass' (Rürup 1995), the issues raised by globalisation for Germany as a business location have particular resonance in the building industry, which has experienced greatly increased labour migration during the 1990s. In this industry, production is for the most part bound to a particular place and cannot be transferred abroad; instead, low-wage workers are imported. Initially, building workers from the former Soviet Bloc countries of central and eastern Europe were recruited (Rudolph 1996; Reim and Sandbrink 1996). In 1999 there were more than 200,000 employees from European Union (EU) countries working on German construction sites. They invoked the freedoms guaranteed within EU and were posted to Germany on the basis of the free movement of services. As a result of this development, the situation in the German building labour market has changed fundamentally. The labour market is now split, with low-paid foreign workers competing with highly paid domestic counterparts.

The debate over the Foreign Employees Posting Act, which was introduced in Germany in 1996 and which seeks to curb low-paid competition from abroad and to enforce the adoption of German labour and welfare standards for the people concerned, typifies how far the paradigm change has already progressed both in the political sphere and between the two sides of industry. It also shows how the new economic guiding principles of privatisation and deregulation are taking the place of corporatist decision-taking processes (Rösner 1995: 475). The case of the building industry can be clearly seen as an attempt to replace German-style consensus capitalism by an Anglo-American liberal welfare state regime, and thus achieve a further step towards a general system change in labour market relations in the Federal Republic of Germany. Instead of regulated working conditions and collective bargaining a deregulated labour law system and atomised labour market relations dominate. By analysing developments in the German building sector, this article illustrates the effects of contemporary migrations and their effects on Germany's welfare state. The chapter also explores economic and social policy discussions within the German building industry to illustrate the pressures on German-style consensus capitalism.

Posting of employees in the single market

Legal background

The posting of employees to work abroad is a special form of employment (Abella 1997). In the past, employees usually went abroad to work for a company located in that country. During the 1990s the situation has changed because employees are sent (posted) by their home company to a foreign country to fulfil a labour or services contract placed with their home company. On completion of the contract, they return home. The posting companies thereby have access to labour markets in other member states through the fundamental freedoms of services and movement laid down in the EU Treaty.

The crucial question in connection with employee posting is which labour and social welfare jurisdictions should apply to a posted employee during his stay abroad? Are the laws and regulations of the country from which the employee was posted and in which the worker customarily works still relevant? Or, should it, for the duration of his stay abroad, be the laws and regulations of the country in which the employee is temporarily working that apply? Questions like these are usually answered by the bi- or multilateral labour and social welfare law of the countries concerned, but this can differ substantially in interpretation from case to case.

Within the EU, international labour law as part of international private law was harmonised by the Rome Convention of 19 June 1980. This states that the parties to a work contract are free to choose the law by which the employment relationship is to be governed (Article 3 of the Convention). They can therefore opt for the law of the country in which the activity is to be performed (place of production principle) or for the law of the country in which the company is domiciled (country of domicile principle).

The Convention also contains a number of special references, which render particular statutory provisions under the law of the production country applicable regardless of the choice of law. In particular, there are provisions that go beyond the balance of private interests and have an economic and social regulatory function outside the sphere of private contractual relationships. A typical example of this would be state-guaranteed minimum wages and elementary labour protection laws relating to working hours and occupational health and safety, as well as the Personnel Leasing Act (Junker 1992: 117). Collective wage agreements do not create a statutory requirement for intervention, even if they are declared universally valid under Article 5 of Germany's Collective Bargaining Contracts Act (Franzen 1996). This meant that posted workers did not have to be paid the prevailing local wages, which stood in contrast to the principles of guest worker employment since the 1950s.

The question of social insurance coverage for employees temporarily posted to work in another EU country is answered in the EU's Directive 1408/71 of 1971. This proceeds from the principle that employees should be insured in the country in which they are employed. If an employee is temporarily posted to another country, then, analogous to labour law, the law of the posting country continues to apply for the duration of the stay abroad. The precondition for this is, first, that the activity is not expected to last for more than 12 months, and, second, that the employee concerned is not posted abroad to take the place of another employee whose period of posting has expired (Cornelissen 1996). In respect of labour laws, the legal system of the posting company's country of domicile is usually chosen. The effect is that employees who are posted temporarily to another EU country remain, for the most part, subject to the law of their home country.

Economic rationale for intra-Community posting of employees

These social welfare and labour laws result in a simple economic logic for the posting of employees within the EU. Employees from low-wage countries are posted under a service contract to another EU country where the labour and social welfare costs are higher. Both the foreign posting company and the domestic suppliers benefit because companies from low-wage countries can compete internationally through their locational advantage of lower labour costs and thus develop new markets abroad. Companies in high-wage countries are able to take advantage of free movement of services within the EU and operate with cheap, foreign workers thereby offering their products on the basis of significantly lower labour costs. In industries where products are immobile and production plants cannot be transferred abroad such as the building industry, the posting of employees offers a new option for reducing manufacturing costs.

A glance at the different hourly costs incurred for the employment of an industrial worker in Europe clearly illustrates the potential competitive advantages offered by intra-Community employee posting. As shown by Figure 11.1, the costs in 1995 of a working hour in manufacturing industry in West Germany were DM 45.52, in Portugal the costs were only about one-fifth of this amount. These disparities are not new and, have in the past, normally been offset by corresponding differences in productivity levels in the various countries. But when cross-border posting of employees occurs they become fully effective because contrary to the rules for contracts of manufacture or for work and labour, the employees do not work in autonomous entities but are integrated into the operating establishments in the countries to which they are posted. The locational advantages

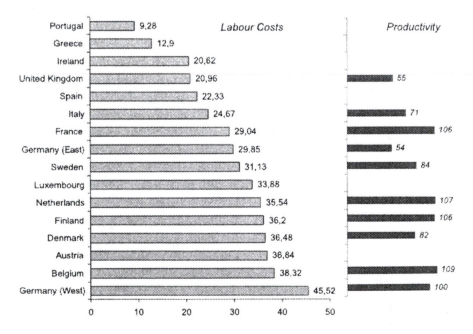

Figure 11.1 Labour costs and productivity in the countries of the European Union 1995.

of the home country, i.e. lower labour costs, are combined with the locational advantages of the host country, such as a highly developed infrastructure, high real capitalisation, highly qualified core workforce, to create competitive advantages (Däubler 1995: 726).

In addition to wage cost advantages, there are other competitive advantages arising from lower social costs. Social security systems in EU member states are, of course, diverse in their nature and organisation. Generally speaking, the social security systems in the countries of western Europe have developed along two different paths (Esping-Andersen 1990). One is the social insurance approach dating back to Bismarckian Germany in the late nineteenth century, the other the need-covering approach devised by Beveridge in the UK during and immediately after the Second World War. Aside from their opposing ideological axioms, they differ above all in the manner of their funding. While insurance-based social security systems are usually financed through contributions of the people insured, need-based social benefit systems are funded through tax revenues. This, together with the fact that the standard of social security provision also differs in EU member states, results in different levels of labour-related costs, as shown in Figure 11.2.

This also has consequences for the competitive position of construction companies in the EU. In the case of Denmark, for example, where the social benefits system is largely financed through value added tax, a building firm can offer its products at a lower price than its German

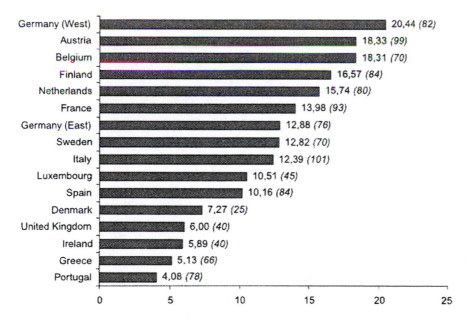

Figure 11.2 Additional labour costs in EU member states 1995 (in DM).

competitors despite the Danish company having higher wage costs. In regions near the Danish–German border, this leads to corresponding shifts in competition.

Moreover, because the social security contributions of posted employees continue to be paid in their home country, and in addition to the wage cost advantages of posting employees from low-wage to high-wage countries, there is also a further cost saving through lower social security contributions. A further competitive advantage arises where an industry makes holiday payments and towards which the companies contribute to workplace benefits. Where no similar provisions are made in the posting countries then these savings make themselves fully felt; but even where contributions have to be made to similar institutions in the other country, there are usually still savings (Köbele and Sahl 1993).

Development in employee postings

Cost differentials within the EU single market have long formed the basis for company decisions about transferring existing production plants abroad or choosing the location for new ones. In the past, the mobility of labour as a production factor remained largely unaffected by disparities in labour and social welfare costs. While it is true that the possibility to take advantage of the differences between the systems by posting employees abroad has existed for a long time, it is only in the last few years that a trend towards bringing in cheaper foreign employees can be observed.

As Figure 11.3 shows, the number of social security certificates issued for employees posted abroad (E-101 forms) has only been increasing since the early 1990s, but that there has also been increasing use made of the possibility of employee posting since then. If the figures for the posting certificates issued in selected states of the EU are compared, it can be seen that the numbers have multiplied several times within the space of only a few years (Donders 1995).

The vast majority of posting certificates was issued for employees in the building industry (Donders 1995: 119). Since the early 1990s, many building firms have employed workers through sub-contractors for deployment on construction projects in Germany. The proportion of foreign-posted workers is now very high in Germany's major conurbations and on its large-scale construction sites. In Berlin, currently the biggest building site in Europe, it is believed that nearly one worker in two originates from a foreign country (Fachgemeinschaft BAU Berlin und Brandenburg 1997: 33; Bauindustrieverband Berlin–Brandenburg 1997).

In the course of this Europeanisation of building production, a complex system of sub-contractorship has developed. Building firms from low-wage countries such as Italy, Portugal or Spain are systematically engaged as sub- or main contractors in high-wage countries such as Germany, Austria,

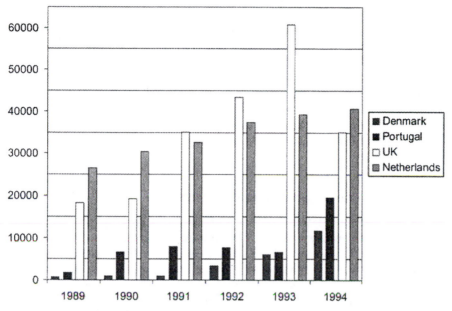

Figure 11.3 Number of E-101 certificates in selected EU countries 1989–94.

France or The Netherlands and now represent a permanent feature in the building production of these countries. Additionally, self-employed building workers from Great Britain or Ireland are employed as quasi one-man subcontractors, and are sent to high-wage countries such as Germany, mostly through agencies based in The Netherlands (Koppelbaas Organisations) (Weipert 1994). In all these forms of employment, there have developed practices and techniques to further exploit the existing legal situation. Some of these are variants that fall within the framework of the law, but most are illegal.

A study by the Dutch Economic Institute for the Building Industry shows that certificates on social security insurance in the home country, which are supposed to document that posting is being carried out in the proper manner, are often issued without significant checks (Ritmeijer 1994). These often fraudulently obtained posting certificates are then used either to fake a posting in order to fall within the 'benefit' of the special regulations under international labour law, or to lessen the burden of social insurance contributions. The effect is that many workers simply go abroad with a blank form but without a contract, hoping to find work when they arrive.

Employee postings in the building industry are also frequently in violation of valid regulations on personnel leasing, which is regulated in different ways within the EU. In Spain, for example, personnel leasing is prohibited altogether while in Denmark it is permitted without restriction (Menting 1993: 168). There can also be special arrangements for the building industry (Ritmeijer 1994). In Germany, for example, employees are only allowed to be leased between firms or plants working in the same branch of industry, and even then only if the companies concerned are covered by the same framework wage and social insurance fund agreements (Sahl and Bachner 1994). This means that commercial leasing firms, like the Dutch Koppelbaas Organisations that arrange employment for British building workers, are not, in fact, allowed to lease any employees to German building firms. Yet, in Germany, 'anyone who knows anything about it ... is well aware that the widespread business practice of engaging subcontractors is often only a well-camouflaged form of personnel leasing' (Fuchs 1995: 29).

Effects of employee posting in Germany

Of all EU member states, the effects of employee posting have been the most significant in Germany because its building sector – worth DM 492 billion in 1995 – was the EU's largest (Hauptverband der Deutschen Bauindustrie 1996: 5). Consequently, it has become one of the main targets for the modern-day form of labour migration. It is only possible to conjecture about the exact number of foreign workers in Germany. The only fact that is undisputed is that since 1993 the number of posted employees has risen extremely rapidly. Whereas in 1994 there were believed to be up to 150,000 EU workers on German building sites, in 1995 the number of posted employees was already estimated to have risen to 200,000. Some sources even put the figure at 260,000 EU workers (Webers 1995: 174). The German National Building Industry Association (Hauptverband der Deutschen Bauindustrie – HDB) calculated a much smaller number. It estimated the figure for 1994 at 137,000, for 1995 at around 161,000, and for 1996, at 210,000 posted workers. But even on the basis of these cautious estimates, the numbers are still impressive. The labour market share of low-wage foreign workers would have doubled in only five years, as shown in Figure 11.4.

As a result of this influx of foreign building firms, the competitive situation on the building market has changed fundamentally. In the building and finishing trades, companies that calculate the costs of their work exclusively on the basis of the wages of their German skilled workers have, in the words of Bernd Eichinger, Vice-President of the Central Association of the German Electrical Craft Trades, 'no chance to compete' (Eichinger 1995: 2). Building firms operate almost exclusively with so-called 'mixed' calculations based both on the wage rates for their own employees and the low wage rates for foreign workers.

This trend affects the firms working in the building industry in different ways. While big companies can respond as necessary to the new situation, small and medium-sized firms tend to lose out. Christian Roth, the President of the German National Building Industry Association (1996:

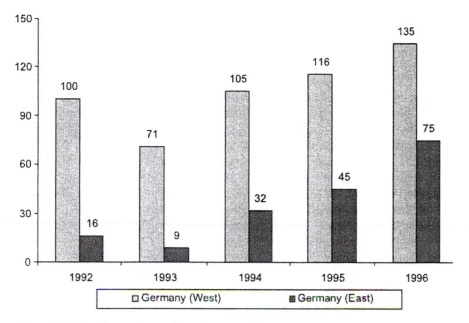

Figure 11.4 Numbers of posted employees in the German building market 1992–6.

164), lists four points that Roth sees as crucial for firms to be able to survive this process of rapid structural change. They are:

- rationalisation and productivity improvements, together with adjustments in personnel capacities;
- specialisation of the firms' production programmes in technically sophisticated building work;
- diversification into the field of construction-related services,
- internationalisation, at least for bigger companies and some small or medium-sized specialists.

Big companies have long since implemented all four points, reducing their core workforce and achieving rationalisation through capital-intensive investment. These companies are increasingly developing away from being simply providers of building work and are becoming modern service enterprises, looking after all aspects of building projects from financing to turnkey completion (Roth 1996: 164). At the same time, they are moving on to foreign markets where they can benefit from the competitive advantages of high-building quality and know-how (Hinrichs 1996).

Opportunities of this kind are much less available to small and medium-sized firms. Neither a capital-intensive rationalisation strategy nor a reduction in their workforce promise greater market opportunities because their capital cover is often not sufficient to allow major investment. Moreover, their core work-force is often already so small that any further reduction would seriously jeopardise their ability to operate (Spillner and Rußig 1996). Diversification towards 'offering complete packages in everything to do with building' (Hauptverband der Deutschen Bauindustrie 1996: 15) is in most cases not a viable option due to lack of an appropriate personnel structure (Regioconsult 1995: 10). The only real alternative for medium-sized firms in the building industry is, therefore, to specialise in work that requires a high level of technical sophistication and craft skill (Eichbauer 1996: 166f.). This is not possible for all SMEs with the effect that they find themselves being increasingly forced into the role of sub-contractors (Regioconsult 1995: 6), where they are increasingly unable to compete with foreign competitors, especially those from low-wage countries. Consequently, the number of insolvencies in the building industry has increased rapidly, as shown in Figure 11.5. The Chairman of the Central Association of the German Building Trades (Zentralverband des Deutschen Baugewerbes – ZDB), Fritz Eichbauer, expressed fears in March 1996 that because of the sustained competition from low-wage countries 'in the long term one in four of the more than 80,000 building firms in Germany' would have to give up (General-Anzeiger, 6 March 1996). This cut-throat competition has been accompanied by a dramatic rise in the unemployment figures in the building industry (Figure 11.6). Despite a rise in building output, the number of people without work has

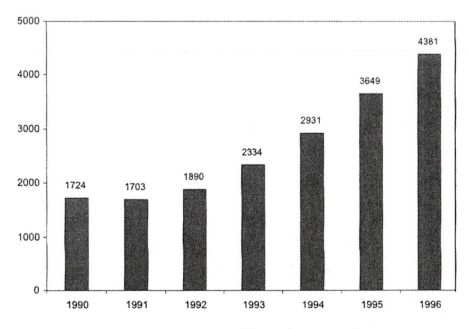

Figure 11.5 Insolvencies in the German building industry 1992–6.

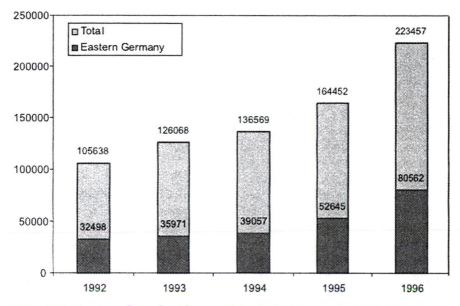

Figure 11.6 Number of people without work in the building trades 1992–6.

increased continuously. In March 1996, the figure was 304,759. This was equivalent to a rise of 57.5 per cent compared with a year earlier.

Although it should not be assumed that foreign workers have replaced all domestic employees, these figures make it clear that a substitution of domestic workers by foreign workers has taken place in the German building labour market (Rürup 1995: 25). This new international division of labour in the German building market also prompts changes in the employment policy of building companies (Syben 1997). The possibility of recruiting foreign workers at lower costs has caused building companies to use substandard employment for not only supplementary functions, to make up for shortages of skilled workers or to cope with order peaks, but to make it a regular part of their recruitment strategy. The effect is that domestic skilled workers are forced out.

This development is already reflected in the training situation in the building and finishing trades. According to the Joint Holiday and Wage Payments Equalization Fund (ULAK) in Wiesbaden, the number of apprentices in their first year of training declined in 1996 for the first time since 1990, and decreased nation-wide by 22 per cent as compared to the previous year. In Berlin it fell by 40 per cent. Besides the change in employment policy as described above, the reason for this is that it is SME firms that have provided most building industry apprenticeships. Their marginalisation and elimination inevitably has a negative effect on the recruitment of young people.

Moreover, and in contrast to other industries, the accident rate in the building sector has risen considerably since 1992 (*Frankfurter Rundschau*, 26 April 1995). The Berlin/Brandenburg State Office for Occupational and Technical Safety gives as the reason for this 'the lack of co-ordination on large-scale building sites and the considerable language difficulties between the people working there (Ministerium für Arbeit, Soziales, Gesundheit und Frauen des Landes Brandenburg 1993; Pernack 1996). However, it must also be noted in this context that, until 1 January 1996, German accident prevention regulations were not part of the mandatory international occupational safety regulations and were, therefore, not applicable to employees posted from other countries.

Posted working does also bring some advantages. In particular, there has been a reduction in building prices. For the first time since 1960, the 1996 price index for building materials showed a downward trend in many areas, with a correspondingly positive effect on the investments of both the public and private sectors.

Besides the economic problems suffered by both workers and companies, there have been social and political consequences resulting from these changes in the construction industry. The use of foreign workers under sub-standard conditions has poisoned relationships between unions and employer confederations as well as among the workers themselves. At the sites, social tensions between indigenous workers and their foreign competition are increasingly giving rise to xenophobia on one side and anti-European sentiments on the other (Köbele 1994: 8).

An additional problem is that German construction workers are now often paid sub-standard wages like their foreign colleagues. This practice is widespread in Eastern Germany. According to the German construction workers' union IG BAU, at some sites only 20 per cent of the German workers receive standard wages (*Der Spiegel*, 37, 1996: 99). The union also reported that in the State of Saxony, this number is about 13 per cent. At some sites in this region they agreed that wages were about 18 DM or 20 per cent below standard (*Süddeutsche Zeitung*, 3/4 August 1996). In certain extreme cases, German workers receive hourly wages of 6.40 DM or 30 per cent of standard. At the same time, the length of the working day of these workers increased in many cases from 8 to 11–14 hours.

The result has been a worsening of the relationship between the construction workers' union and the employer association. In only a few years the German construction industry has transformed itself from a model of consensus labour-management relations in which unions sought compromise within a consensus-oriented partnership model to a scene of conflict in which the requirement for economic survival has prompted lax enforcement of basic workplace regulations.

As a consequence of the dual constellation of labour and social law, a dramatic increase in illegal practices can also be seen. In order to enlarge further the competitive advantages arising from the employment of posted employees, some employers are prepared to act in breach of statutory regulations. Thus, there are frequent reports of 'degrading living and working conditions' for foreign building workers in Germany (Bundesanstalt für Arbeit 1993). The employees are usually accommodated in simple portacabins that often do not meet the lowest hygienic standards (Picareta 1995).

Extreme cases of exploitation are, as yet, exceptions, but they are fundamentally inherent in the logic of the new posting system. First, the specific competitive advantages accruing from the employment of posted workers generally derive not so much from the high level of skills of the employees concerned as from their low labour costs. As there is an almost unlimited supply of this cheap labour available to the companies and, because of their low skill level the individual workers are easily replaceable, the companies see no need either to protect them or retain them.

Second, the dual labour law situation on the building sites and the limited duration of stay of the employees in Germany also fosters exploitation. On the one hand, the German authorities are often not responsible for ensuring compliance with the foreign labour law, and on the other, the foreign authorities do not have a presence in Germany. The result is that the labour laws of neither one country nor the other are applied. The logical outcome of this is that frequently not even the most elementary work safety regulations that should operate under the Rome Convention are actually applied.

Political reaction: the debate on the Foreign Employees Posting Act

At EU level, there has long been discussion about the possibility of regulating or – as many would say – re-regulating the building industry labour market. However, against the background of the general economic policy debate, the complex problem of employee posting in the building industry has acquired a highly explosive character because its solution is primarily seen as lying in the introduction of minimum working conditions, and, especially, minimum wages. Such measures are in fundamental contradiction to the postulates of current economic policy. The introduction of minimum wages would prompt an increased labour cost rise and additional regulation. It could also prompt increased building prices and mean a disadvantage in international competition. Yet, in view of the consequences of the new competitive situation in the European building industry, the following questions can be posed: does this new form of competition make sense in the context of a market economy? Is it tolerable in terms of social policy? Does it lie within the terms of the EU treaties? While free movement can prompt rapid adjustment between the development levels of the individual member countries and is thus seen as desirable (Robson 1987; Straubhaar 1987; Molle and van Mourik 1988), competition in

Europe should, in the view of the responsible authorities in Brussels, also be flanked by adequate social policy regulations (European Commission 1988).

This was why the European Commission announced as early as 1989 in its 'Action programme for application of the charter of basic social rights of employees in the Community' that it would seek to take action against violations connected with employee postings within the EU and draw up a corresponding directive. An initial draft in April 1991 provided that 'irrespective of the law by which an employment relationship is governed, a clearly defined hard core of minimum working conditions should be made mandatory for all employees', including, in particular, the payment of minimum wage rates prescribed by law or under collective wage agreements (COM (91) 230 final – SYN 346).

This proposal and an amended draft of June 1993 (COM (93) 225 final – SYN 346) faced strong opposition from the British, Irish, Spanish, Portuguese, Greek and Italian governments that all opposed regulation of the new labour migration. They benefited from the possibilities of intra-European employee posting and feared economic losses as a result of regulation. The UK government untiringly emphasised that the draft directive was 'incompatible with the principles of the Single Market' and would 'unduly obstruct the free movement of services between the member states' (Council of the European Union 1996: 3). The French, German, Belgium, Danish, Dutch and Luxembourg governments demanded that the directive be implemented quickly in order to contain what they saw as the negative effects of employee posting on their labour markets. In view of this situation, the attempt to resolve the employee posting problem at EU level remained unsuccessful for a long time. Indeed, it was not until mid-1996, after the QMV was introduced, that the Italian President of the Council succeeded in submitting – in the words of EU Social Commissioner Padraig Flynn (*Süddeutsche Zeitung*, 1 April 1996) – 'a historical compromise proposal' to which all the member countries with the exception of Britain and Portugal could agree. However, it was too late to have any direct influence on solving the building industry's problems because the slow EU-level negotiations led some member states to tackle the employee posting problem in their own countries.

In summer 1994, France passed a national employee posting law, making it mandatory for domestic and foreign workers to be treated equally in the French labour market. The Netherlands and Luxembourg also responded soon after this French initiative to labour migration in the building industry by tightening the statutory regulations for the employment of posted workers in their countries (Ritmeijer 1998). On joining the EU in 1995, the former EFTA states of Finland, Austria and Sweden adopted measures to safeguard the labour markets in the building industry. The aim of these measures was to stop developments of the kind witnessed in Berlin before they had the chance to occur. In Belgium and Denmark there had, in any case, always been a statutory requirement for firms to comply with the working and wage standards applicable to domestic firms when carrying out orders at home.

In Germany, the former Labour Minister Blüm announced a national 'go-it-alone' at the end of 1994. As in the other EU member states that acted in this regard, Blüm based this on the argument that the problems in the building industry needed to be dealt with rapidly and therefore could no longer wait for EU approval. It was also hoped that the introduction of national regulations would increase the pressure for agreement at EU level.

The decision about a German employee posting law was taken between the conflict of paradigms of deregulation and the maintenance of welfare state commitments. Contemporary thinking seemed to point towards deregulation and flexibility and reduced influence by the state on economic activity. Yet, the old welfare state conscience began to stir, viewing the practice of intra-European employee posting as a trading practice not in conformity with market principles, but rather – in an original wording by the Labour Minister – as 'dehuman and degrading wage dumping' (Bundesminsterium für Arbeit und Sozialordnung 1995).

While the opposition and large sections of the workers' wing of the CDU and CSU parties came out unequivocally in favour of government intervention and only differed slightly in their views on the intensity and details of a corresponding law, the liberal FDP party voiced their strong opposition. The FDP saw competition on the building labour market as an expression of core principles of the European single market and demanded that there should be no government influence on the building industry. The possibility of recruiting low-cost building workers from abroad was seen by the FDP as an important starting point for lowering building prices and for generally putting 'pressure' on German labour market institutions (*Handelsblatt*, 27 July 1997). The prevention of a national employee posting law was a way of continuing the trend towards general labour market deregulation.

In the view of Graf Lambsdorff, a leading FDP member, the system of collective wage autonomy had resulted in open and hidden unemployment of up to six million people in Germany and could not be allowed to continue. Collective wage regulations such as the 'advantage rule', forbidding unemployed people from offering their labour below tariff were, in reality, a 'disadvantage rule for the unemployed' and should be eliminated as quickly as possible. In his opinion, not only should British and Portuguese workers be able to compete on the German labour market with low wages, but so also should unemployed German building workers. The task of his policy was, therefore, to break up the current 'cartel system of German wage tariff policy' and ultimately to establish a new model of labour market relations in Germany (*Handelsblatt*, 27 July 1997).

In view of the criticism the FDP's opposition provoked from other members of the governing coalition and from the opposition parties, the

FDP gave up their opposition to the introduction of a national employee posting law and supported a joint draft law of the Federal Government. Nevertheless, as tangible representation of their scepticism towards this project, the FDP insisted that the law should only apply to the building trade proper and be valid for a temporary period only. This would give the building industry the time and opportunity to adapt to the new competition situation in the European Single Market while also giving politicians the time and opportunity to eliminate structural differences within the EU.

The law was passed in March 1996 and requires that collective wage agreements in the building industry which are declared universally valid and include a minimum wage shall also apply to firms and their employees posted from abroad. Additionally, building firms which in their home countries are not subject to any holiday fund arrangement must take part in procedures organised under collective wage agreements which have likewise been declared universally valid in Germany and pay corresponding contributions to the relevant institutions.

This combination of statutory and collective wage agreement regulations is the responsibility of the two sides of the building industry. They have the task of ensuring its effectiveness by concluding collective wage agreements that meet the requirements of the Foreign Employees Posting Act and then declaring them universally valid. This is no mere formality, but rather has proved the Achilles' heel of the new law. In practice it has proved extremely difficult to conclude the collective wage agreements between the two sides of industry and then to have these agreements declared valid by the Collective Wage Committee at the Federal Labour Ministry, on which both sides of industry are equally represented. Although the law came into force on 1 March 1996, the corresponding collective minimum wage agreement for the building industry only became effective on 1 January 1997 (Hunger 1998). This delay had considerable repercussions for the effectiveness of the law.

Even during the legislation's first year of existence there were many violations. Besides the problem of even establishing where foreign building workers were deployed, another difficulty has been to prove the suspected violations and determine the wages actually paid (Bundesanstalt für Arbeit 1998). Most building firms were already established on the German market before the law came into force and were able to use various devices such as wage retention clauses, part-payment of wages or charging excessive rates for board and accommodation, to considerably reduce the wages they paid (Hold 1996: 117). It appears virtually impossible to monitor practices of this kind.

The question whether a split labour market will become a permanent feature of the German building industry or whether the developments as described above can be reversed is one that remains open. At present, two possibilities seem to exist. First, the legislature can decide to improve implementation of the law by the adoption of appropriate measures and try to bring the situation, as it has developed on building sites back within the law. Second, the legislature will tacitly accept the present situation by not extending beyond August 1999 the Foreign Employees Posting Act and the universal validity of the collective wage agreements, and by tolerating illegality on building sites in order to preserve labour market flexibility, as has already been the case in, for example, California and in the strawberry fields of southern Norway.

Conclusion

The dispute over the Foreign Employees Posting Act in the building industry is a clear illustration of the extent to which the hitherto existing consensus on economic and social policy in Germany has come under pressure. The battle for the future direction of the German social model has not only begun between the two sides of industry but also in the political arena, where there is no longer agreement as to the instruments of economic and social policy to be used in responding to the challenges of the 'new world economy' (Reich 1993). There is an attempt to preserve and maintain the fundamental features of the system of corporatist wage and consensus formation and to shape the future of the German economy on the basis of balanced distribution structures and co-operative labour relations. Yet, a broad current has developed which advocates departing from the path on which the German model has hitherto developed by placing greater reliance on a supply-oriented, neo-liberal economic policy that seeks to strengthen market mechanisms and roll back the influence of the state as far as possible.

In the building industry, the core issue was an attempt to bring about a creeping but fundamental change in the German labour and social model with the help of new developments in the European single market. In the place of the old, corporatist labour market model, a number of leading representatives of German industry and politics wished to introduce a labour market model along Anglo-American lines. It is true that statutory legislation was finally adopted in 1996, but in view of the evident inadequacies in implementation of these arrangements, the question arises as to how seriously a re-regulation of the building labour market was in fact sought by the legislature and to what extent the idea of restructuring the existing labour market model lurked in the foreground or background? As a result of the Government not taking early enough action and allowing matters to drift, a large number of domestic building firms and jobs were sacrificed. In 1996, for example, within a single year, as many jobs were lost in the building trade proper as corresponds to the total workforce in the German textile industry. To be sure, even if the law had been adopted sooner or the collective wage agreements had immediately been declared universally valid, this massive cut in employment could not have been completely prevented, but the transaction costs of structural change would have been diminished.

There are clear deficits within the German system that require attempts to seek to remedy them. One of these deficits is indubitably – and as critics of the welfare state rightly and repeatedly point out – is that around 50 per cent of unemployed people are poorly skilled. In view of the increasing division of labour between high-wage and low-wage countries as a result of globalisation, it can be expected that the demand for poorly qualified workers in Germany will decline even more strongly in future (Scharpf 1997: 211f.). As far as low-skill activities are concerned, international competition will remain high – and will probably increase even further in the future – with the effect that it will be almost impossible for German wages to compete. Even where these activities have not already been transferred abroad, it will be almost impossible to keep them in Germany.

One solution in this area could be to establish a low-wage sector, although this would have to be co-financed by wage subsidies from the state in order to avoid the problems of the working poor, a burning issue in the USA (Büchtemann 1996; Bosch 1998). Moreover, a reduction in ancillary wage costs and reform of the contribution-funded system of social security would be necessary. As the analysis of the competitive situation in the building industry has shown, foreign competitors have been able to exploit the advantages offered to them by high German ancillary wage costs, and even where wage levels are the same, to offer cheaper ancillary wage costs. This was particularly evident in the case of Denmark where, despite a highly developed welfare state, Danish building firms were able to gain competitive advantages over German suppliers because of lower social security costs. Additionally, a fundamental reform of the tax system is essential: a reduction of tax tariffs for companies and private households and a step-by-step implementation of tax elements into the social security system.

In practice, however, such efforts towards fundamental reform seem unlikely to be crowned by success. Instead, as the example of the building industry clearly shows, the current collective wage system is being hollowed out from the edges and the system of social security bled dry. Migration is playing a major role in this (Rhodes 1998). Especially in industries in which, as in the building industry, the products are immobile, a growing trend can be seen towards importing workers into the country and employing them on terms below the otherwise valid working and wage standards. The result is a situation in which a domestic working population that is seen as static is being increasingly confronted with a labour reserve that is flexible and mobile in every way, thus advancing the deregulation of the whole system.

Outside the building industry, this trend can also be seen above all in the employment of seasonal workers in agriculture and in the hotel and catering trades. Here also employees are paid at rates well below those customary in Germany and thus, as in the building industry, represent a kind of 'internalised low-wage competition' (Faist 1995c) to German employees. In agriculture, the domestic workers have almost ceased to compete for these jobs (Hönekopp 1996; de Bakker 1997). In the transport sector, the principle of 'same wage at the same place' has also been breached. Lufthansa, for instance, has paid foreign stewards and stewardesses in terms of prevailing standards in their home countries (*Frankfurter Allgemeine Zeitung*, 2 February 1996). This example is of special importance as it is precisely the EU's transport sector that is likely to undergo further liberalisation in the foreseeable future.

Transforming the welfare state through migration is, however, a dangerous approach, because there are already signs of a changed attitude towards the employment of foreigners in Germany. While many studies in the past drew attention to the positive effects of migration of foreign workers on the economic development of Germany (Thränhardt 1995; Rheinisch-Westfälisches Institut für Wirtschaftsforschung Essen 1997), this is more difficult for the new form of labour migration. In contrast to the past, where the immigration of foreign workers was largely complementary to economic progress (Kindleberger 1967) and gave the domestic employees economic and social upward mobility, today's form of labour migration is unequivocally substitutional.

The risk grows that new strategies of exclusion of immigrants are introduced and that there emerges a new underclass of foreign workers in Germany as it is the case in the US (Santel and Hollifield 1998; Santel and Hunger 1997). Over the past several decades there was a trend towards inclusion (Hammar 1990; Bommes and Halfmann 1994). Foreigners were integrated into the national health insurance systems and into the welfare state in general. They have been granted substantial civil, social and – to a lesser extent – political rights (Schuck 1989; Hollifield 1992; Soysal 1994) and the once rigid 'ingroup/outgroup' dichotomy *vis-à-vis* indigenous and foreigners has broken down. The foreign workers were able to participate in the economic progress of western Europe and as a result their living situation improved significantly (Santel and Hollifield 1998; Thränhardt 1995).

There can be no question that the mobility of employees has a major role to play in solving the labour market problems in the European Union (Straubhaar 1994). Freedom of movement within the single market is an essential precondition for this. But freedom of movement within the EU does not mean that employees can work anywhere on the conditions obtaining in their home country. On the contrary, every activity is fundamentally subject to the law of the territory where it is carried out. The posting of employees is the sole exception to this rule. So far, it has been possible to justify this by the argument that employee posting only represented an exceptional case in the overall employment of foreigners.

Today, however, the relationship of exception and rule is being turned on its head. In view of the resulting problems, it could be argued that a restoration of the principle of territoriality seems urgently called for, especially as the disparities between levels of development between EU member states will be exacerbated by the planned eastward enlargement of the EU. If the destabilising migrations that have been feared unjustly by critics every time the freedoms in the EU have been introduced or enlarged but that have, with the exception of posted workers, never taken place are to be prevented, it would be advisable at least at core to maintain the principle of equality of treatment for domestic and foreign workers on the labour markets within the EU. With the introduction of the European Posting Directive and the German Foreign Employees Posting Act, a long-term basis has now been created for this. It remains to be seen whether this will be used to preserve and develop the foundations of the continental European welfare state as they have existed to date, or whether the liberal Anglo-American model will prevail.

12 Thin Europeanisation

The social rights of migrants in an integrating Europe

Andrew Geddes

Introduction

The strong national-level resonance of debates about welfare provision, migrant's social rights and social citizenship means that discussions of connections between migration and welfare have a strong territorial dimension embedded in particular national welfare state contexts. Yet, the transnationalisation of economic relations to which in some ways European integration has contributed and to which in others it is a response, introduces a supranational dimension to analysis of migration and welfare centred on the EU's single market with some spillover into a 'social dimension'.

The single market and the social dimension challenge the borders of national welfare states and impinge on discussions of migrant social inclusion with the practical effect that 'Europe matters', but it is also important to specify how and why Europe matters. In this chapter, I seek to build on the discussion in the chapters by Maria Baganha and Uwe Hunger. My aim is to show that the EU's migration and welfare policies are closely connected to market making with some social policy and migrant inclusion implications. These date back to the Treaty of Rome (1957) and have been strengthened by amendments to the Rome Treaty contained in the Single European Act (1986), Maastricht Treaty (1992) and Amsterdam Treaty (1997). All sought development of free movement. Indeed, the commitment to free movement is an integral components of the 'European project' and has brought with it guarantees for the transferability across national frontiers of social entitlements for EU citizens exercising their right of free movement. It is in this limited sense, at least, that European integration affects our understanding of migration and welfare by establishing social entitlements that cross borders coupled with intensified co-operation between member states on external frontier controls. But can it offer more? Can the EU also include currently excluded non-EU citizens (third-country nationals, TCNs)? This question is the focus of my chapter. The question is interesting because it allows us to get to grips with the sources of legal, social and political power connected with European integration. It also allows us to view the relation between external closure and internal inclusion in a European context given the intensifying co-operation between member states on immigration control. Finally, it allows us to view possibilities for Europeanised forms of denizenship that repair incomplete membership by offering European rights independent of prior possession of member states nationality.

Having said that – and laid out three rather ambitious questions – it is important to commence with the observation that, as currently constituted, formal EU provisions relating to migration and welfare apply to EU citizens and exclude around eleven million TCNs. This is what I mean when I refer to 'thin' Europeanisation: the EU offers transferable social entitlements to its own citizens, but very little to settled immigrants and their offspring. This thin Europeanisation has arisen despite (or perhaps because of) the acquisition by TCNs of legal residence in a member state and also applies to second- and third-generation descendants of immigrants.

Given this formal exclusion, we can then ask what relevance the EU's social dimension actually has for TCNs? Can they be brought within its provisions as a result of Europeanising the principle of 'denizenship' so that legally resident TCNs who have acquired social rights at national level can also transfer these rights between member states, as EU citizens already can? If so, then this suggests a supranational form of membership distinct from naturalisation and the acquisition of nationality as routes to social inclusion.

Europeanising migrant social inclusion

Three core issues underpin the chapter's analysis of the scope for Europeanisation of migrant social inclusion. First, the components of the emerging EU migrant inclusion agenda, which I discuss by outlining the development of the EU's social dimension. Second, the new (and limited) political opportunities that arise as a result of EU competencies, which I analyse by examining the development of a migrant inclusion agenda and lobby groups that pursue this agenda. Third, the potential for creation of supranational membership for legally resident TCNs that challenges the EU's 'thin' social inclusion provisions that largely exclude TCNs, which I analyse by outlining the arguments for inclusion that these pro-migrant groups make (and the alliances they seek to build at European level).

The basic position has already been stated: TCNs *qua* TCNs are formally excluded from access to EU-level rights and entitlements unless they are dependants of an EU citizen or covered by an agreement between the EU and a third country (such as that with Turkey). This occurs despite the acquisition of extensive social rights at national level in EU member states as a result of legal residence, i.e. denizenship (Hammar 1990).

It is also important when setting the scene for the analysis to note that pro-migrant political activity in pursuit of the emerging EU migrant inclusion agenda is channelled through an institutional context within which social inclusion and citizenship acquire meaning in relation to EU-level sources of legal, political and social power. The EU's 'institutional repertoire' structures an EU migrant inclusion agenda with the effect that a core insight of institutionalist analysis is particularly pertinent: that certain kinds of EU-level immigration policies and administrative practices lead to certain forms of political action, not vice versa (Ireland 1994; Soysal 1994).

New forms of political action can arise that address Europeanised sources of legal authority and political power to create a European-level political field that shapes the preferences and power of the actors that constitute it (Keohane 1989: 161).

In this context, we can ask whether it makes sense to discuss new 'political opportunities' at EU level? If it does, then new political opportunities may prompt the emergence of 'transnational advocacy networks' that seek expanded EU rights for migrants with the potential to feedback into domestic contexts (Tarrow 1995, 1998; Marks and McAdam 1996; Keck and Sikkink 1998; Danese 1998; Geddes 1998; Favell and Geddes 2000).

Supranationalisation via European integration necessarily involves the creation of power and authority above the nation state backed by EU institutions and law (Mancini 1991; Hix 1999). But does supranationalisation also contribute to 'post-national' forms of membership (Soysal 1994; Jacobsen 1996) that diminish the role of the nation state as the receiver of claims for inclusion? Post-national membership, it is argued, reduces the importance of national citizenship and perhaps even renders it 'inventively irrelevant' (Soysal 1998).

These issues also need to be located within an EU immigration *problematique* where the watchwords have been immigration control and securitisation. Single market development from the mid-1980s brought with it a heightened emphasis on immigration control, restriction of asylum and development of internal security mechanisms for population control (Baldwin-Edwards and Schain 1994; Huysmans 1995; Bigo 1996b; den Boer 1996; Wæver 1996; Papademetriou 1996; Koslowski 1998; Geddes 2000). Most developments have occurred within secretive, intergovernmental forums composed of largely unaccountable national ministers and officials. European integration has brought with it an 'externalisation' of the border control efforts of its member states with a particular focus on southern Europe and potential new member states in central and eastern Europe (Baganha 1997; Lavenex 1998). Policy co-operation has strengthened national executive authority and weakened courts and legislatures at national and EU level because of the limited scope for scrutiny and accountability. Prospects for the Europeanisation of denizenship will be conditioned by and conditional upon the institutional context for migration/

welfare policy, which has a prevailing control and security theme and limited attribution of competence with regards to the rights of TCNs and produces only thin Europeanisation.

The EU context

This section of the chapter explores the origin and development of EU social policy as it relates to free movement, anti-discrimination and transferable social entitlements and as it applies to EU citizens and TCNs. The EU's 'multi-level' polity – with sub-national, national and supranational dimensions – encompasses well-entrenched national welfare states and developing EU responsibilities for aspects of social policy. The horizontal (national) dimension to debates about migration and welfare is likely to remain stronger than the vertical (supranational) dimension. This is because of the difficulty of melding some kind of common response from diverse welfare models and immigrant inclusion policies in member states and, thereby, securing 'positive integration', which involves putting in place new structures at EU level (Scharpf 1996).

Connections between free movement and immigration with consequences for social inclusion means that the distinction between integration in areas of 'high' and 'low' politics may not be 'black and white' but actually constituted by shades of grey (Hoffmann 1966). The 'low politics' of market making have drawn into the EU's remit the 'high' politics of immigration and the welfare states. This is not some straightforward process of 'spill-over' of power and authority to supranational institutions and, thence, to common EU policies. The connection between market making, migration and welfare has not dictated the form taken by a European response. Instead, the outcomes are contingent upon national policy preferences, the accommodation of these preferences at EU level, and the scope once agreement has occurred for distinct supranational legal and political effects to occur. It is helpful to distinguish between inter-state negotiations – the 'grand bargains' – and 'day to day' processes of European integration where supranational institutions (particularly the Commission and ECJ) can play more of a role (Peterson 1995; Wincott 1995; Pierson 1996a; Moravcsik 1998).

European integration has tended to centre on commercial concerns and economic integration, although these have clear social and political consequences and it would be incoherent to suppose otherwise (Meehan 1993). Free movement, for instance, drew in issues associated with the protection of the social rights and entitlements of EU nationals moving between member states. The continued formal, EU-level exclusion of TCNs from free movement and anti-discrimination provisions, despite national denizenship, is a good example of the further social implications of economic integration. This arises because of the importance of possessing nationality of a member state before EU rights can be acquired. The future direction of policy and the scope for migrant inclusion remain contingent upon strong national policy contexts and, as things stand, relatively weak supranational decision-making structures. If arguments for expanded rights are to be made then they tend to derive their force from *extant* legal provisions related to free movement and centre on coverage by EU provisions relating to rights within the single market (free movement, portability of social entitlements, equal treatment, and anti-discrimination).

In general terms, social policy integration has been described as lagging behind economic integration with the risk of being dismissed 'as a pipe dream or as an afterthought to the EU's main project of economic integration' (Pierson and Leibfried 1995: 4). Market-making rather than market-correcting objectives drove the establishment of a supranational framework guaranteeing transferable social entitlements (Eichenhofer 1997). The concern of EU social policy has tended to be with protecting 'the civil right to enter into contract and not with industrial and social rights relating to their outcome' (Streeck 1996: 72). This emphasis on securing the conditions for factor and labour mobility within the common and single markets has meant that EU policy has been largely concerned with 'technical matters' rather than with 'social conscience' (Lodge 1989: 310). EU involvement occurs because of the requirement to establish transferable social entitlements as the buttress of the free-movement framework and in areas of 'encapsulated federalism' (Streeck 1996: 76). This occurs where member states have allowed supranational competence for issues such as gender equality, workplace consultation and working hours because of fears of 'social dumping', where member states compete on the basis of lowering standards of social protection.

For immigrants and their descendants, as the contributions to this book have shown, national welfare states have been the key arenas for social inclusion. These entrenched national welfare state contexts direct attention towards either denizenship or naturalisation as vehicles to repair incomplete membership and promote the social inclusion of immigrants and their descendants. Social entitlements for migrants have arisen as a consequence of legal residence and contributions to national welfare states. Denizenship means that there are around eleven million legally resident TCNs who are not nationals of an EU member state, who have acquired social rights as a consequence of residence, but who cannot acquire rights at EU level. Social spaces have opened at national level, but similar spaces have not opened at EU level because TCNs are not entitled to move freely, benefit from transferable social entitlements or seek EU protection against racist-, ethnic- or religious-based discrimination.

In terms of formal provisions, the connection between market-making, free movement for nationals of member states and social entitlements is clear. The legal framework provided by the EU's treaties and associated legislation configures any discussion of Europeanised denizenship and highlights a distinction between notions of social citizenship as they have been elaborated at national level and the development of economic citizenship associated with the 'regulatory' EU state (Majone 1996). The Treaty of Rome sought the creation of a common market within which workers could move freely. Some attention was paid to social policy, but this was slight because welfare was seen as an issue dwelling in the domain of national competence rather than that of the fledgling EEC. The Treaty of Rome did contain some rhetorical flourishes, such as the section of the Treaty of Rome's preamble mentioning the securing of 'economic and social progress of the member states' and 'the constant improvement of the living and working conditions of their peoples'. Article 2 of the Rome Treaty also contained a commitment to high-employment standards and high levels of social protection, while more substantively, Articles 118–23 contained social policy provisions relating to matters such as gender equality (Article 119) and the creation of a European Social Fund (Article 123). Articles 118–23 later formed the basis for the EC's social action programmes launched in the 1970s when the discourse of a 'people's Europe' became more common.

The Treaty of Rome's Article 51 made clear the connection between free movement and social entitlements. The Council of Ministers was given power to adopt by unanimity measures for social security provision for migrant workers who were nationals of an EC member state. The Treaty of Rome did leave open the possibility that free-movement rights could be extended to TCNs because it did not specify that nationality was a requirement for access to such rights (Plender 1988). But when the Treaty's provisions were given effect in the late 1960s free-movement rights were restricted to workers who were nationals of a member state. Moreover, this legislation made it clear that the aim of EC policy was co-ordination of national provision not harmonisation with implied common policies (Handoll 1995).

There was some scope for inclusion of TCNs within these social entitlement provisions if they were dependants of a member state national or covered by an agreement between the EU and a third country (such as those with the Maghreb countries and Turkey). TCNs who are dependants of EC national migrant workers derive rights under Community law from Regulation 1612/68. The ECJ has acted to guarantee the rights of TCNs who are dependants of nationals of an EU member state, but does not have the power to guarantee rights for TCNs *qua* TCNs. For instance, in Dzodi v. Belgium, the ECJ allowed for spouses to move with the holder of the right, to remain permanently resident in the host state, to be admitted to that state's education system on the same conditions as the nationals of that member state, to have the right to work and have access to social security benefits in the host state.[1] In the Kziber case the social provisions of the Treaty were for the first time interpreted in such a way as to include a TCN as a result of a co-operation agreement with a third country. The ECJ ruled that a Moroccan national covered by the agreement between the EC and

Morocco did have the right to special unemployment benefits for school leavers.

If the role of the ECJ has been relatively constrained then is there scope for supranational leadership or 'entrepreneurialism' in the migration/ welfare policy area? In relation to migrant inclusion, this entrepreneurialism would focus on extended rights for TCNs and enhanced anti-discrimination legislation. Evidence suggests that in the area of immigration and immigrant policies a Treaty base that extends only limited competencies limits the ECJ, Commission and European Parliament. If we look at particular issues we see these limits. For instance, it was the case that the Commission's initial interpretation of the possible scope of the EC's first Social Action Programme (SAP) introduced in 1975 did include migrants who were not nationals of an EC member state, but the Commission then faced opposition from the Council of Ministers. The Council did not share the Commission's expansive understanding of the term 'migrant' and the programme was limited to cover migrant workers holding the nationality of a member state. It was fairly clear that the member states saw conditions governing the social, economic and political inclusion of TCNs as member state issues and the Council was not prepared to countenance an ambitious interpretation of the EC's role that would trespass on national sensitivities. The same problem was encountered by other SAP measures that did possess the potential to affect TCNs, but actually had little real impact. For instance, Council Directive EEC 486/77 on the education of the children of migrant workers watered down a Commission proposal that had included all children (including those of TCNs) within the remit of the proposal.[2] Supranational leadership in the migration/welfare policy area was undermined by the lack of a substantive legal basis which limited the Commission's role while the prevailing immigration *problematique* and associated forms of intergovernmental co-operation have through the 1980s and 1990s steered policy in the direction of control and security.

The increased pace of European integration from the mid-1980s centred on the single market programme also saw renewed efforts to develop the EC's social dimension. The SEA added new social policy articles to the EC Treaty, although without increasing the rights of TCNs. In 1989, the Council adopted the non-binding Fundamental Charter on the Basic Social Rights of Workers (better known as the Social Charter) on 30 October 1989,[3] which 'acts as a gloss on the limited legal basis of social policy law' (Nielsen and Szyszczak 1991: 26). The Charter's status as a non-binding declaration meant that it had effect neither as an international agreement, nor as a Regulation, nor as a Directive. Efforts were further consolidated by the Maastricht Treaty's social protocol that covered issues such as improved living and working conditions, proper social protection and the combating of exclusion, which covered all workers residing in a member state (i.e. TCNs as well). The requirement for unanimity placed a brake on the scope for action, but for the first time the employment rights of TCNs had a

Treaty basis.[4] This becomes relevant when we examine arguments for inclusion made by pro-migrant lobby groups because it can serve as a legal basis for arguments for TCN inclusion. Maastricht also created EU citizenship, although this was only a limited package of rights that largely excluded TCNs because it applied to nationals of member states (Martiniello 1994; Kostakopolou 1998).

The Commission's 1994 social policy White Paper addressed issues associated with the establishment of a European labour market in the light of single-market integration and the criteria for EMU convergence (CEC 1994b). It recognised that legally resident TCNs 'suffered multiple disadvantages' because they were not covered by the same provisions as EU citizens. As a first step, the Commission stated that they should be entitled to necessary health care benefits (CEC 1994b: 28). The white paper also noted that: 'An internal market without frontiers in which the free movement of persons is ensured logically implies the free movement of all legally resident TCNs for the purpose of engaging in economic activity. This objective should be realised progressively' (CEC 1994b: 29–30).

Even though Maastricht's social protocol had established a Treaty basis for TCN's employment rights, the Commission adopted a cautious approach. A 1995 Commission proposal aimed to ensure that member states gave priority to TCNs legally resident in another member state when job vacancies could not be filled by nationals of that member state or by legally resident TCNs. In October 1997 the Commission proposed a Directive which would extend the personal scope of Regulation 1408/71 to all TCNs affiliated to a national social security scheme. The proposal was still under consideration in 1999.[5]

The scope for refocused politics that addresses Europeanised sources of legal, political and social power has been constrained by the limited attribution of formal competence. Moreover, the meaning of EU-level social inclusion will be decisively affected by an institutional context for migration/welfare policy that connects the free movement framework to an underlying market integration ethos and casts notions of inclusion in functional market-related terms. Given this policy context, can new political opportunities be detected, as well as the development of transnational advocacy networks that address the EU as a venue for refocused forms of political action? In the next section the institutional location of this action will be outlined as a way of showing the EU-level institutional channelling of political action in respect of claims for the social inclusion of migrants.

The migrant inclusion agenda

Having examined the origin and development of EU social policy, the chapter moves on to explore the development of an EU-level migrant inclusion agenda. What are the components of this agenda? Does the emergence of an EU-level migrant inclusion agenda point to the development of new political opportunities. How are these opportunities structured? Moreover, how does this agenda relate to the ongoing debate about European citizenship? The location of political opportunities at EU level requires that attention be paid to the policy context configuring the range of policy options (Favell and Geddes 2000). Where competencies have been ceded and where new patterns of co-operation and integration have developed then there is scope for refocused political action. In the area of migration, this has been particularly evident for internal security (Anderson *et al.* 1995; Bigo 1996b).

Refocused pro-migrant activity and a migrant inclusion agenda associated with it are potentially indicative of 'transnational advocacy networks'. Activists bound by 'shared values, a common discourse, and dense exchanges of information and services' constitute these networks. They are able to draw from 'resource rich' international organisations and feed back into domestic contexts where previously marginal actors can be strengthened as a direct result of deployment of transnational resources (Keck and Sikkink 1998: 1). Can these advocacy networks be linked to an EU context that shapes the notion of migrant social inclusion, associates it with forms of economic citizenship and Europeanised denizenship, and institutionally channels political action? There has been a growing body of work on lobbying at EU level that focuses on the activities of groups seeking to influence decision making in Europeanised policy sectors (Mazey and Richardson 1993; Greenwood 1997). Very little of this work has focused on pro-migrant lobbying (although see, Danese 1998; Geddes 1998, 2000) but there are some general characteristics of EU lobbying that are relevant. First, because of its relatively small size, when formulating proposals, the Commission often relies on the kinds of expertise that lobby groups can bring. This can lead to the co-option of expert opinion into a complex system of comitology. Second, and linked to this, lobby groups often seek insider status as a way of securing privileged access and input into decision-making processes. As a result, EU-level lobbying tends to be characterised by co-option of expert opinion into elite-level decision-making processes with a strong technocratic ethos. This does not accord too closely with social movement mobilisation and bottom-up challenges to powerholders (Tarrow 1998). Instead, the inducement, inculcation and encouragement (including financial support) of interest group activity by EU institutions is an important characteristic of EU lobbying. The effect is that EU-level pro-migrant lobby groups can become closely associated with the institutions they seek to influence within an EU political field with its own sources of culture, capital and habitus (Favell 1998a). Many of the most influential and active pro-migrant groups are human rights (Amnesty International, European Council on Refugees and Exiles) or church-based organisations (Caritas, Churches Commission for Migrants in Europe) that carry with them moral authority with associated symbolic capital that they can use to back their claims. Moreover, by operating at European level and identifying European sources of legal, political and social power as the addressee of their claims, these groups reproduce their own relevance and underline the importance of a rights-based dimension associated with European integration.

It is also important to consider the often close relationships that can develop between EU institutions and lobby groups. The Commission seeks to involve lobby groups in consultation and decision-making that can add an element of legitimacy to decision-making processes. For many of the leading pro-migrant lobby groups at EU level, the perceived problem is that there is too little, rather than too much, 'Europe'. As they see it, European integration creates the possibility for establishment of political and legal authority at EU level capable of challenging 'lowest common denominator' restriction and security-oriented immigration policies emanating from the intergovernmental Council of Ministers. The Commission, European Court of Justice and European Parliament can become part of the solution within a Europeanised context where the motivations and alliance-building strategies of lobby groups and EU institutions can become closely connected. That said, the EU's institutional terrain and the immigration problematique that is associated with it clearly provide a difficult context for pro-migrant lobby groups. In turn, this directly relates to the three core issues identified in this chapter's introduction: it places limits on the notion of 'social inclusion', stymies development of new political opportunities, and places supranational constraints on post-national membership.

Even in this difficult institutional environment, there has been a particular increase in pro-migrant lobbying at EU level during the 1990s as the connections between free movement and immigration and asylum became clearer in the aftermath of the Single European Act. During the pre-Amsterdam Treaty intergovernmental conference (IGC), pro-migrant NGOs sought extension of the Treaty framework so that rights of free movement and transferable social entitlements would be extended to legally resident TCNs. The EU-level pro-migrant NGO network[6] brought forward a dossier of proposals that dealt with reforming the control dimensions of immigration and asylum policy, but also included measures relating to the social entitlements of TCNs. For instance, the Churches Commission for Migrants in Europe (CCME) saw unequal treatment as a key issue in urgent need of rectification because of the demotion of TCNs to the status of 'second-class citizens'. In fact, the term 'second-class citizens' is actually a misnomer: TCNs are not citizens in a second-class sense. It is the essence of the particular problem with regards to free movement and social entitlements that, although TCNs acquired rights of denizenship at national level as a result of legal settlement, this has not allowed access to EU entitlements based on Europeanised denizenship. The debate about European citizenship is also interesting because of the distinction that can be made between the limited, technical meaning of citizenship of the Union and the 'constructive potential' it has been viewed as possessing (Wiener 1997). The consequence of this is that EU citizenship can be taken more seriously than its rather limited technical basis would suggest because it prompts association with identified rights, participation and inclusion 'deficits' at EU level. All of these have become 'problems of Europe' to which closer European integration is a possible solution. Not surprisingly, the Commission is quite receptive to this line of reasoning.

This brief discussion of EU citizenship draws attention to an important issue: the EU possesses no legal authority to interfere with the nationality laws of member states, as unequivocally stated by member states in a declaration attached to the Maastricht Treaty. In its submission to the pre-Amsterdam IGC, the CCME proposed that EU citizenship be extended to TCNs, with a five-year qualification period. As they noted of their proposal: 'One of its key features is that it complements rather than replaces the individual's existing nationality. Therefore Union citizenship could easily embrace TCNs resident in the Union without requiring them to possess nationality of an individual member state' (CCME 1996: 2). The EU Migrant's Forum echoed the CCME proposals and proposed an amendment of Article 8a TEU so that it would read: 'Citizenship of the Union is hereby established. Every person holding a nationality of a member state or who has been lawfully residing in the territory of a member state for five years shall be a citizen of the Union' (EUMF 1996: 3). The European Citizens Action Service (ECAS) also proposed the extension of the right of EU citizenship to TCNs legally residing in a member state for five years (ECAS 1996). As EU citizens, legally resident TCNs would enjoy the same free-movement rights and the right to equal treatment as other EU citizens.

The Amsterdam Treaty and its aftermath

The Amsterdam Treaty (1997) raised interesting questions about free movement, immigration, asylum and anti-discrimination. In this section, the Amsterdam Treaty's impact on the migrant inclusion agenda and upon pro-migrant political action is explored. Have the anti-discrimination provisions of the Amsterdam Treaty created potential for the opening of social and political spaces for TCNs? In the previous section, the arguments for inclusion of pro-migrant lobby groups during the Amsterdam Treaty negotiations were analysed. These proposals stood little chance of success because the supranational competencies affecting nationality laws and citizenship were anathema to the member states (Hix and Niessen 1996). Amsterdam was, however, very significant in other ways because it brought immigration and asylum from the intergovernmental 'third pillar' covering Justice and Home Affairs issues created by Maastricht (Monar and Morgan 1994) to a newly created Title IV of the Treaty where they would reside with free movement (Geddes 2000: chapter 5). This 'communi-tarisation', i.e. shifting immigration and asylum from an intergovernmental pillar to the community pillar, created the potential for supranational-isation, although the emphasis on unanimity for at least five years following Treaty ratification could impede the empowerment of supranational institutions.

The Amsterdam Treaty fell short of the aspirations of pro-migrant NGOs. Even though intra- and extra-EU migration were clearly connected there was a reluctance to empower the engines of potential supranational 'spillover effects', i.e. the Commission and the ECJ. The Amsterdam Treaty did not extend the EU's citizenship provisions to cover TCNs. The Council was given power to set out conditions under which TCNs would have freedom to travel within the territory of the member states during a period of no more than three months, but this provision required unanimity and did not cover employment. Maastricht's social protocol did, however, apply to conditions of employment and could serve as the basis for arguments in this respect (Handoll 1995). The Amsterdam Treaty also gave the Council the power to set out the measures defining the rights and conditions of TCNs who are legally resident in a member state and reside in another, but this provision was not covered by the five-year timetable applying to other Title IV measures.

The Amsterdam Treaty was also significant because it expanded the anti-discrimination provisions of the EU Treaty. Previously, discrimination on grounds of nationality between nationals of EU member states was expressly forbidden while action had also been taken to curb gender inequalities covered by Article 119 of the Treaty of Rome. Amsterdam added a new Article 13, which gave the Commission power to introduce proposals to combat discrimination on the grounds of race, ethnicity, religion, age, disability and sexual orientation. This was not as strong as the existing commitment against nationality-based discrimination because the new article did not expressly forbid the forms of discrimination it identified. Rather, it conferred a power of proposal upon the Commission with the proviso of unanimous agreement by the Council. The creation of a legal base raised the possibility for action at EU level on migrant social inclusion, albeit in a difficult institutional context with an emphasis on unanimity and where, in the past, national sensitivities have tended to preclude legal and political development.

Before the ink had dried on the Amsterdam Treaty and long before it would come into force on 1 May 1999, the Commission proposed a Convention on the Rules for Admission of TCNs to the Member States of the European Union (CEC 1997). The Convention was introduced using the outdated 'third pillar' provisions of the Maastricht Treaty (i.e. they had been replaced by Amsterdam's provisions). Consequently, it stood no chance of adoption as proposed, but the Commission announced the intention to re-submit a proposal for a directive under the new provisions of the revised Treaty following ratification of the Amsterdam Treaty. The draft Convention marked an attempt by the Commission to stake a claim for a leading role in shaping post-Amsterdam arrangements for free movement, immigration and asylum policy as a way of attempting to move towards supranationalisation of these policy areas. Again, this raises the issue of supranational leadership, but also shows the limitations in an area such as immigration policy and the rights of TCNs.

The Commission's July 1997 Convention connected with many issues raised by NGOs regarding the rights of TCNs and proposed the creation of a 'Resident's Charter' that would break the connection between nationality, free movement and the transferability of social entitlements within the EU. It would extend to EU level the principle of denizenship, i.e. of social rights and entitlements acquired as a result of legal residence. The UK-based Immigration Law Practitioners Association called the Commission's proposed Convention 'revolutionary stuff indeed' (ILPA 1997: 1). This was certainly the case when compared with the perception of Commission inactivity in these areas. The Convention proposed enforceable rules on employment, self-employment, study and training. It also proposed the creation of a right to enjoy family life. This right would not be extended to the same degree as for EU citizens and member states would still retain an element of discretion over treatment of TCNs that they had long since ceded to the Union for intra-EU migration. Member states would, however, be obliged to justify any use of national discretion on the admission of family members of TCNs (Guild 1998). The draft Convention also contained free-movement provisions that created a right for long-term resident TCNs to move to any member state to take up employment. It also listed a series of basic rights that they would take with them. These included equal treatment with EU citizens as regards employment, self-employment, training, trade union rights, the right of association, access to housing whether in the private or public sector, and schooling.

Among the EU-level pro-migrant NGO lobby, the Starting Line Group (SLG) has sought to exploit opportunities presented by the Amsterdam Treaty to propose strengthened rights for TCNs, who would be granted access to rights of free movement and social entitlements (SLG 1998). The SLG's proposed directive, published in early 1998, derived the force of its argument from the association agreements between the EU and third countries. Turkish citizens, for instance, were covered by the 1964 association agreement between Turkey and the EC which gave Turkish nationals established rights in areas such as employment, the right to residence and social entitlements exceeding those given to other TCNs. The SLG argued that the rights given to Turkish nationals should constitute minimum rights to be accorded to all TCNs. It was proposed that social security rights that had been acquired as a result of legal residence in an EU member state by migrants and their descendants would become transferable within the EU. The proposal for a 'Resident's Charter' would extend to EU level the acquisition of social rights as a result of legal settlement rather than nationality.

In terms of its specific provisions, the SLG's proposal stipulated that after three years legal employment in one member state a TCN would enjoy free access to paid employment or self-employment in any member state. The proposed directive then went on to outline provisions for employment and free movement, the right of establishment, the provision of services and family reunion. The proposed directive mirrored the free-movement provisions of Regulation 1612/68 by allowing qualified TCNs exercising the right of free movement to be issued with a residence permit for five years, with the possibility of automatic renewal. It was also seen as essential that TCNs exercising the right of free movement be granted equal social treatment with other EU citizens. Provisions were, therefore, made for access to employment and self-employment, vocational guidance and training, trade union rights, the right of association, access to public and private sector housing, social welfare, education, health care, and the provision of goods, facilities and services. These provisions would guarantee equal treatment for TCNs within the single market. Of equal importance they would establish the framework for an EU immigrant policy framework with supranational sources of legal, political and social power capable of establishing a framework for migrant inclusion in relation to Europeanised competencies arising in the main from single market integration.

Commission attention has also been directed towards action within the scope of the new, wide-ranging Article 13 that introduces scope for legislation tackling discrimination on grounds of race, ethnic origin, religion, age, disability and sexual orientation. The Commission sought to launch a debate on the use of Article 13 in its 1998–2000 social action programme (CEC 1998). Action in three areas is envisaged:

- A horizontal directive covering all the forms of discrimination mentioned in Article 13 that seeks to combat direct and indirect discrimination regarding employment and occupation. This would relate to access to employment and self-employment, access to vocational training, employment and working conditions (including pay and dismissals), and the membership of professional or trade union organisations.
- A directive with broader scope to counter direct and indirect discrimination on the grounds of race or ethnic origin. This would lay down minimum standards enabling member states to introduce provisions more favourable to the protection of the principle of equal treatment (as defined in Directive 76/207/EEC of 1976 on equal treatment in employment between men and women). The directive would cover the forms of discrimination mentioned in the horizontal directive, plus social protection and social security, social advantages, education, access to the supply of goods and services, and cultural

activities and sports. As in the case of equal treatment, positive action
to overcome existing inequalities would be permitted.
* An action programme to support and complement these proposals.

As yet, it is too early to judge whether these proposals will be introduced in
this form. For one thing, they must secure unanimity among member
states.

Lobbying for migrant social inclusion in respect of the Europeanised
issues of free movement, social entitlements and anti-discrimination occurs
within a 'difficult' institutional terrain where the balance of power lies with
the agents of immigration control and security. There is, however, scope for
development of a migrant inclusion agenda related to the EU's social
dimension and the new Article 13 on anti-discrimination that seeks to
extend economic citizenship and the principle of denizenship to EU level.
In the chapter's next section the motivations, calculations and alliance-
building strategies of institutional actors at EU level are analysed as a way
of drawing attention to institutional channelling and the forms of political
action associated with an EU migrant social inclusion agenda. Particular
attention is paid to pro-migrant lobby groups and those units within the
Commission with responsibility for social affairs.

Arguing for inclusion

As has been seen, the EU-level migrant inclusion agenda, as well as groups
seeking to propagate this agenda, have developed during the 1990s. In this
section of the chapter, the motivations, actions, strategic calculations and
alliance-building strategies of EU institutions, particularly the Commission,
are explored. In particular, the potential for development of pro-migrant
alliances is assessed. Expanded EU migration policy competencies have
also meant that supranational institutions have become policy actors in the
social domain dealing with a range of social problems that have acquired a
European dimension and are viewed as necessitating some form of
European response. The member states have a clearly expressed interest in
building the single market while 'preserving the national foundation of
social rights of citizenship as well as the integrity and political stability of
their respective domestic regimes' (Streeck 1996: 71). The Commission's
scope for 'entrepreneurialism' (Majone 1996) in areas where policy
competencies have been ceded has developed along with the expanded
remit of the EU's social dimension since the mid-1980s.

The rhetoric and commitment to a European social dimension and to
social inclusion has also become more resonant at EU level, but it can be
far from clear what the 'evasive concept' of social inclusion actually means
(Hantrais 1995). Difficulties with the conceptual underpinnings of the
social dimension and notions of inclusion reflect differences at both an
intellectual level and in practical policy terms. Social theorists differ about

the 'meaning' of inclusion and the resultant divergent perspectives are reflected within national policy frameworks in member states that display significant differences regarding the multifaceted nature of the problems of inclusion and appropriate remedies to phenomena associated with exclusion. This has, of course, been particularly evident for migrant inclusion. To meld divergent national responses into some kind of EU inclusion paradigm is likely to be very difficult.

That said, the absence of conceptual clarity might actually provide the Commission with an opportunity because the quest for inclusion has become a Commission task and the continued existence of social phenomena that can be classed as indicative of exclusion is likely to sustain Commission activity. Thus, if we conceptualise the Commission in instrumental terms seeking scope for 'purposeful opportunism' (Cram 1994), then the Commission can seek to profit from social exclusion in the sense that Europeanised exclusion contributes to arguments for extended supranational competencies and the development of scope for policy entrepreneurialism. The quest for Europeanised inclusion can then sustain a political-institutional logic of Europeanisation that is a valuable resource for supranational institutions such as the European Commission. In this context, it can be advantageous that the terms inclusion and cohesion are vague and their meanings unclear because this implies that the quest for social inclusion is likely to be able to sustain itself in the long term and potentially be institutionalised at European level. Rather than seeing 'inclusion' as an objective category that can be applied to social problems of 'exclusion', it is useful to view the definition and operationalisation of a Europeanised notion of inclusion as an instrumental resource that shapes the strategies and motivations of EU-level actors.

This draws attention to the importance of placing a discussion of the meaning of EU-level inclusion in the context of specific institutional competencies as delimited by the EU treaties and associated legislation. It goes without saying that it is important to ascertain the sources of social, legal and political power and the associated capacity to act before seeking to understand the relation between Europeanisation, migration and welfare. This chapter has focused on the relation between the market-making motives underpinning European integration and their social implications. It is in this context that inclusion acquires meaning in relation to free movement, the transferability of social entitlements and expanded anti-discrimination competencies. As currently constituted, the EU extends rights that cross national borders to citizens of its member states, but excludes TCN irrespective of whether or not they are permanently resident in an EU member state. It could be construed as ironic that the supranational EU actually reaffirms the importance of national citizenship for accessing rights and entitlements created by European integration. The future development of a migrant inclusion agenda embodying extended free movement, social and anti-discrimination provisions is a test of forms of supranational social inclusion that transcend national welfare contexts.

Conclusion

The European dimension challenges national welfare states, but does so in particular ways linked to market making, free movement and a prevailing immigration *problematique* with a strong control and security orientation. The scope for Europeanisation of the social rights of non-national migrants – this chapter's focus – is structured by legal, political and social power that directs attention towards Europeanised denizenship that would counteract 'thin' Europeanisation and towards the issues of free-movement rights, transferable social entitlements, and anti-discrimination. This would create scope for a supranational form of membership attached to European integration rather than to naturalisation and national citizenship.

The chapter's introduction outlined three core issues impinging upon scope for Europeanised denizenship. The first was the structuring of the notion of social inclusion by the EU's legal and political context and the ways in which EU-level migrant inclusion acquires meaning in relation to the EU's core objectives. It is important to emphasise that the EU is not replacing its member states as the provider of welfare, but that it does have a social dimension that creates the possibility for Europeanised denizenship. The main effect of EU migration policy developments since the mid-1980s has been a thin notion of migrant inclusion with an emphasis on externalisation of immigration control with few countervailing EU-level inclusion measures. In this sense, European integration challenges the connection between 'immigration' and 'immigrant' policies as part of the liberal 'grand bargain' underpinning the opening of social and political spaces for migrants in liberal states.

Elite patterns of European integration have tended to stimulate elite patterns of migrant interest representation with the inducement, encouragement and inculcation of expert opinion and incorporation of NGOs in an advisory capacity into Commission processes of policy discussion and formulation, albeit in an area where the Commission is not strong. Certain forms of political action and certain kinds of actors are privileged. This new political field in Brussels can in many respects appear detached from 'day-to-day' issues of migrant inclusion as understood at sub-national and national level in EU member states. This does not mean that it is irrelevant, rather that its relevance needs to be made clear in relation to Europeanised social inclusion issues.

In the final analysis, it seems that post-national universalism runs up against the supranational particularism of 'fortress Europe'. The EU has created new forms of Europeanised membership centred on EU citizenship with social rights that cross borders within Europe. The other side of this extension of rights to supranational level has, however, been increased efforts to police the external frontiers of the Union, to co-operate on internal security measures, and to maintain a distinction at EU level between EU citizens and TCNs. Post-national universalism encounters a European regional bloc that rests on Europeanised sources of legal, political and social power. Europeanised denizenship seeks incorporation for TCNs within this regional bloc. These claims for inclusion have centred on inclusion within the consequences of the EU's market making and its social policy consequences. As such, they do not necessarily bear close relation to social citizenship as understood in national welfare states because there are no a priori reasons to assume that the EU is acquiring the responsibilities of national welfare states. Rather, it is important to be specific about what the EU can do and how power relations within it are configured before developing discussion of options, alternatives and strategies.

Notes

1 Joined Cases C-297/88 and C-197/89 (1990) ECR 3783.
2 Official Journal L199/32 1977.
3 The Community Charter of Fundamental Social Rights of Workers, Luxembourg: OOPEC, 1990.
4 The UK government opted back in following the election of the Labour government in May 1997.
5 In its Action Plan for Free Movement of Workers the Commission stated that 'The extension of Regulation 1408/71 to third-country nationals is part of the Commission's long-standing policy to improve the legal status of third-country nationals residing in the Community. It is no longer justifiable that a worker who is covered by national social security arrangements should be completely excluded from the protection offered by the Community co-ordination system simply because he or she is not an EU national' (Commission 1997: 12).
6 The NGO network on European Refugee, Asylum and Immigration Policy was composed of Amnesty International, Caritas Europe, CCME, ECRE, the Migrants Forum and the Starting Line Group. The UNHCR attended meetings as an observer. It received support from other members of the EU's NGO network: ECAS, European Citizen Action Service, Fédération Internationale des Droits de l'Homme, Jesuit Refugee Service Europe, Quaker Council for European Affairs and the Red Cross-EU Liaison Office.

13 Unexpected biographies
Deconstructing the national welfare state?

Valérie Amiraux

Introduction

Islam can provide a framework in which new transnational social options for individuals and collectives grow. As a result of migration, religion can play a more important role in Europe than is allowed for by sociological modernisation theory or theories of functional differentiation. This is connected with the meaning that Islam has acquired for Muslim immigrants. In particular, new transnational dynamics that arise as a consequence of migration equip people with social options that present additional or alternative 'biographical' prospects in terms of the relationship between the individual and national welfare states in France and Germany. In this sense, Islam becomes relevant for its organisational potential and not just as some kind of 'traditionalist' or 'anti-modernist' reaction to settlement in western Europe.

In order to demonstrate this, I explore three key issues as a way of elaborating upon this central observation. First, I define the term trans-nationalism in terms of its usage in international relations and political science and then transfer it to discussion of migration and clarifying the meaning of Islam and Islamic organisations in this context. Second, I analyse the position of religious organisations and associations in Germany and France in terms of the traditionally different relation between state and religion in these countries. Third, I evaluate the meaning of Islamic organisations for the biographical options of immigrants in both countries, i.e. the structured relation between individuals and the state, the definition of a community of 'legitimate welfare receivers', and the potential for creation of 'unexpected biographies' resulting from the dynamics of trans-national settings.

At first glance, addressing the question of European welfare state in connection with the issue of the religious affiliation of migrants (Islam) could be viewed as wrong because it adds a cultural-religious marker to the more usual economic, social and juridical classifications associated with debates about access to social rights. It could push us down the path of considering Muslims as a 'social problem': as competitors, as a drain on resources, as carrying alien traditions, as not fitting into the national landscape and notions of cultural homogeneity, or as threatening the social contract because of questions about their loyalty. It is the mobility of Muslim immigrants that is a core component of arguments about perceived threats and dangers and the supposed challenge to individual and collective loyalty to the state.[1] This can also be connected with a more general discourse that builds migration as a security issue and connects it with a new technology of governing (Bigo 1998). In these kinds of contexts, religious identification can play the role of a cultural marker that offers scope for distinction to be made between actors and for them to be construed as *'classes dangereuses'*.[2] The strong link between the elaboration of a rationale associating migration and the social construction of threat is evident, for instance, in the perceived terrorist potential of Muslim communities organised from European territories.

The position of religion in modern society and the development of the relationship between individuals and their community of belonging are in constant evolution and highly complex. Functional differentiation in modern societies saw religion switch from the public domain to the private sphere (Beckford *et al.* 1989). In this context, secularisation, privatisation and pluralisation are three main aspects of the larger societal frame with which religious matters have to deal. Without going into too much detail, the actual position of religion in European societies could be summarised as 'a functional sub-system in a functionally differentiated society' (Luhmann 1977).

Islam in Europe is directly concerned with these elements while also being confronted with a specific dimension related to the experience of migration. Islam was uprooted from its original setting and transplanted to a radically different environment. Consequently, Islam in Europe must deal with the absence of religious authorities[3] and consequent disconnection from direct social relevance (even though it has become the second largest religion in both France and Germany). This new configuration has very important consequences because it induces a change in the individual way of living the faith (Roy 1998). Being a Muslim is not only a matter of faith; it is also a choice. Culture and religion are no longer imposed structures but are a process of personal choices that are free of dramatisation (Luckmann 1967). This element of choice combines with the reformulation of the religious narratives in a flexible way. As Berger and Luckmann (1964: 337) put it: 'To satisfy the need for 'essential identities' an identity market appears, supplied by secondary institutions. The individual becomes a consumer of identities offered on this market. ... The secondary institutions, the suppliers on this market, are a variety of identity-marketing agencies, some of them in competition with each other'. Thus, while settlement in Europe produces new ways of being Muslim, the generational variable influences the redefinition of religious membership. Being a Muslim is both inherited and conquered, transformed and reinvented, and increasingly it can be likened to the position of an actor in a network. It is this organisational relevance of Islam in Europe that is the particular focus of my analysis as I discuss alternative forms of welfare provision and the provision of alternative biographical options that complement or substitute those provided by national welfare states. I do this by focusing on the case of Muslims in France and Germany. I seek to show the relationship between national welfare states defined in culturally homogeneous terms and the contemporary evolution of Islamic networking in the country of residence. I argue that transnational dynamics provide an alternative space for capitalisation and conversion of resources that allow individuals as well as collectivities to escape an ascribed biography scheme within these national welfare states and present unexpected biographical opportunities as avenues for inclusion. This is especially relevant for the cultural and religious domains 'where the nation state is clearly losing its position as the dominant frame of reference' (Koopmans 1999: 67). I also ask how Islamic associative networks in France and Germany succeed in setting up alternative modes of action to the one provided by the classical inter-pretation of the welfare state as a form of incorporation that is deeply embedded in territorial and national definitions of membership. What are the new biographical configurations for employment, education and politics that arise from these alternative options and opportunities?

The opening of transnational social spaces

My core hypothesis of new types of biographies among Muslims is based on the relevance of a transnational frame of action. State and national territory are no longer the unique and exclusive frames of reference for participation and action. The first step is to clarify the term 'transnational' and link it with the recent development of Islam settled in France and Germany. By putting Muslims at the core of this chapter the focus is not placed exclusively on a discussion of welfare provisions in terms of identity, solidarity, loyalty, or in terms of those entitled to benefit from it while not being citizens (i.e. rights of denizenship). The chapter also deals with the ways in which political actors organise themselves and the ways in which organisation is influenced by the nature of the welfare system in which they are settled and by their own objectives. The second step is to emphasise the specificity of national sets of opportunities. The capitalisation of resources by groups and individuals is facilitated by these contexts. Actors who are temporarily disconnected from national sovereignty can organise the ways and the means of their participation by channels other than that of citizenship.[4] The chapter's final step is to develop an analysis of the relationship between, on the one hand, the logics produced by the standards and the institutions on either side of migratory flows and, on the other, the collective and individual strategies of Muslims in a transnational perspective. This final section focuses on specific domains of action such as education, entrepreneurship and political representation where the welfare state is challenged.

Clearly, given its centrality to this chapter's analysis, the term 'transnational' needs clarifying. It has been used by international relations specialists to account for a shift in world politics from a state-centred to a multi-centred reality (Rosenau 1980). Multi-centredness is marked by the increased complexity of official business and the emergence on the international scene of non-official actors (Risse-Kappen 1995). Transnational developments have also captured the interest of migration specialists (for example: Basch, Glick Schiller and Szanton Blanc 1994; Tölölyan 1996; Faist 1999; Portes 1999; Cesari 1999).[5] Transnationalism has been defined as ' processes by which immigrants forge and sustain multi-stranded social relations that link together their societies of origin and settlement. These processes are called transnationalism to emphasise that many immigrants today build social fields that cross geographic, cultural, and political borders. Immigrants who develop and maintain multiple relationships – familial, economic, social, organisational, religious and political – that span borders are called 'transmigrants'. An essential element of transnationalism is the multiplicity of involvement's that transmigrants sustain in both home and host societies' (Basch, Glick Schiller and Szanton Blanc 1994: 7). Transnational perspectives on world politics have been influenced by new methods of communication and by the growing power of the media and by the fact that social locations cannot so easily be identified and labelled.

The transnational also provides new resources, which demonstrate that political participation and practices need no longer to be activated solely from a national basis to be effective. For example, on 24 December 1995, the Avrupa Milli Görüs Teskilatlari (AMGT, Organisation of National Vision)[6] organised trips for Turks from Berlin, Cologne, Stuttgart, and Munich to travel to Turkey to take part in the elections and to bring their voices to the *Refah*. This testified to the success of the AMGT and to the almost indestructible link between the Turks of Germany and politics in their country of origin. Another example occurred in September 1999, when Algerians living in Marseilles were the first citizens asked to express their opinion in the referendum organised by President Bouteflika.

Migration's transnational dimensions are multiple, although a problem can be that their admission into analysis can mask the absence of a clear definition with the effect that transnationalism becomes a fashionable term for those interested in religious identities connected with migration. Use of the term transnational can cover a multitude of sins including various definitions and different observation scales. It is important to emphasise that the transnational dynamics of Islam are not in themselves new because membership of the community of belief, the *Umma*, is not structured by a territorial geographical principle. That said, it has developed in a different way in Europe as a result of immigration to European countries, although use of the term transnational seldom allows us to determine if this involves bilateral, cross-border or diasporic relations. This adds to the blur of the label. The debate on the transnational can too often be reduced to the status of an alternative to state-centred theories that signals the end of the hegemony of traditional geopolitics. The weakness of this approach is that it neglects to observe individual positioning in various national spaces that exploit the transnational dimension as a resource mobilised for a specific strategy (Badie 1995).

Migration is, of course, not only composed of individuals but of networks that are of great significance for the distribution of information, communication, the movement of people, goods and ideas, and the capitalisation and mobilisation of resources. Even if they are not citizens, legally resident foreigners are usually entitled to social services such as education, health and welfare benefits and social insurance, and guarantees of their civil rights. In terms of religious needs, organisations are at the interface of the relation between national welfare states and individuals. These organisations help establish common interests, reciprocal obligations, and can result in a form of internal integration (Faist 1996a, 1996b). Immigrants build their own associations and form their own communities that provide health, employment and cultural services. These associations constitute the principal resource of transnational dynamics. They reduce the costs of engagement for their members and represent an increase in chances for success in the realms of health, education, employment, cultural fulfilment and political participation. The contacts, coalitions and interactions that are integral elements of these organisations cross national borders and cannot be checked by the central agencies of foreign policy (Keohane and Nye 1972). They therefore occupy a central place in transnational dynamics and make it possible to use 'solidarity' resources as was the case within the Muslim Turkish population in Europe during the Bosnian conflict. Networks and the non-official forms of organisation operate – as do many key aspects of transnational practices – on a collective scale as much as on an individual one. In particular, they offer an alternative in terms of benefits and can even provide a certain regulatory effectiveness (Colonomos 1998). As a direct consequence the exercise of state sovereignty is modified and reformulated by effect of competition between actors 'free of sovereignty' searching for access to negotiation and not for conquest of territories (Bigo 1998: 336). This does not mean the withdrawal of the state as an actor or as a determinant variable in the constitution of transnational networks or that we must endorse the radicalism of Rosenau who denounces the paradigmatic prison of state-centred theories. States and networks may actually interact rather than cancelling each other out. Thus, it makes sense to evoke a transnational space rather than a transnational relationship because it avoids the limitations of exclusively bilateral perceptions. Evoking the notion of transnational space also makes it possible to analyse social practices produced in various national environments and their deterritorialisation in favour of migrants, as well as their institutionalisation or even their incapacity to be brought out of from their original configuration. In particular, considering the transnational perspective as implying social spaces and not exclusively cross-border dynamics, underlines the convertibility of mobilised resources that are used by actors. For instance, symbolic and identity capital cannot be evaluated along the same lines in the country of origin or in the country of residence, being for the acquisition of a house (Caglar 1995) or for the election as deputy (Amiraux 1999b). It also makes it possible to envisage the coexistence and overlap of social processes. This latter point is of considerable interest insofar as these practices resulting from transnational space do not deal exclusively with the economic but can also improve and professionalise political careers.

In the context of a discussion of transnationalism, it is also important to consider the meaning of deterritorialisation as an important aspect of 'globalisation' and its relation to welfare provision. As Cohen (1997: 157) notes: 'deterritorialisation of social identity (is) challenging the hege-monizing nation states' claim to make an exclusive citizenship a defining focus of allegiance and fidelity in favour of overlapping, permeable and multiple forms of identification'. In this context, deterritorialisation represents the new adjacency of territories (Bigo 1996a). It becomes central to a reflection on the transnational, on its operating modes, on its limits as regards to states understood as exerting their sovereignty on a given territory, and connected in their legitimacy and identity with this territorial constraint. The transnational does not signal the end of a territorial definition of state action, but reformulates the action procedure; or rather it associates it with new alternatives. In particular, it re-evaluates local and cross-border dimensions. Moreover, transnational dynamics encourage extension of identity affiliation beyond national borders that are far from the contractual ideal connecting citizens to states.

Transnational spaces are also the product of an effect of composition born from the coincidence of the interests of sending and receiving states with regards to the management of Islam. This conjunction should be envisaged from the point of view of opportunities offered by both of the contexts. Migrants are, of course, not devoid of political or cultural identification. Rather they carry with them representations, symbols and cognitive stocks. These apply in particular to the history of the interface between state and religion. Transnational space can thus be understood as the result of a meeting between at least two sets of opportunities. In the Turkish–German case, it concerns a context inhibited as regards religion and a series of the opportunities arising from the German context in this matter.[7] The transnational setting imports general frames of action and maintains the sensitivity to the political life of the country of origin in particular via the media.[8] In Germany, the state–religion partnership is among the variables that contribute to the development of transnational dynamics. This is in addition to the compensation mechanisms linked with the context of origin. Other variables in the German context include the federal structure and its 'many alternative pockets for participation' (Tarrow 1998: 81), the fragmentation of decision making, the corporatist organisation of institutions, and the structure of civil society.

To summarise this section and to return to the chapter's point of departure, the relevance of the transnational as far as Islam and the welfare state are concerned points us in two directions. The first concerns our understanding of the evolution of the position of religion in Europe and the way that Muslims produce their religious identity (Berger and Luckmann 1964). The religious apparatus can be considered as a social, ideological and symbolic *dispositif* integrating four dynamics: the communitarian, emotional, ethical and cultural. This view contradicts the typical west European view of Islam as a cultural, symbolic and social system differentiated and specific in civil society and distinct from politics (Cesari 1998). In other words, perceptions of Islam usually neglect its relevance as an organisational form that can contribute to alternative patterns of organisation that can contribute to alternative biographical opportunities for Muslims in Europe. One hypothesis could point to Islam as providing these kinds of alternative resources and not just as 'anti-modern' or traditional. The second concerns the ways that the displacement of Islam from the countries of origin to the host countries has important effects because it amends the relationship between the believer and the community of belief at various levels. When a clearly established institution exists, as in the case of Turkey and the Diyanet Isleri Türk-Islam Birligi (DITIB, Office of Religious Affairs), it is the symbolic strength and the authority of this organisation that is affected when it seeks to exert authority over Turks in Germany. The relation has become characterised by the growing autonomy of individuals as though they were in a sense becoming the exclusive protagonists of their own faith. Recent work on Islam in Europe refers to this movement as 'back to individuals', referring in particular to subjectivation and individuation. The phenomenon is not new, but for Islam this process can be assigned another dimension connected with its location in Europe and with the idea that the authority of primary identificational groups, such as the family, is confronted with competition from other primary groups that may weaken them. The generational problem becomes increasingly acute in connection with the fact that Islamic norms and values are not performed by institutions capable of coercion (Roy 1998).

The second aspect is connected with the hypothesis of biographical continuity assumed in the reading of welfare state as constituting an *institutionalisation of life courses* (Saraceno 1993; Bommes, this volume, pp. 90–108). Turks, Algerians and Moroccans arrived in Germany as foreign 'guest workers' as the result of labour market policies, but, of course, they did not remain exclusively as economic actors because they also acquired significance as cultural actors. Welfare states are often considered as amounting to an institutionalised 'threshold of inequality' (to belong or not, to be in or out). Many authors have shown that national welfare states were inclusive of second and third generations during the 1970s and 1980s and that these groups were not excluded for 'class-race' reasons (Hammar 1990; Hollifield 1992). Subsequently, the chances for inclusion have been reduced because of the failure of education which in turn hits employment opportunities and can set into action a chain reaction of exclusion that adversely affects the 'institutionalisation of the life course' and the individual's biographical relation to the national welfare state. The effects of immigration on wages, unemployment, social security, education and social services have increasingly been cast in 'we' versus 'them' distinctions, i.e. along ethnic and racial lines switching from a 'class cleavage' to a 'class-race cleavage' (Faist 1996b: 244).

It is now possible to relate the discussion of transnational spaces to Islamic organisations in France and Germany and then to analyse the meaning of these Islamic organisations for the biographical options of Muslims in these countries. These biographies in Europe are composed of several variables, although they converge towards the same idea, i.e. that national contexts provide different sets of opportunities in which associations, groups and individuals define themselves as Muslims and within which they pick and choose organisational tools. For instance, Islamic associations seeking the recognition and defence of Muslims' rights offer alternative forms of participation to that of citizenship. Not only do transnational dynamics concern collective organisation but they also touch the individuals engaged in it. This individuation process combines with the more general secularisation, i.e. of a changed place for religion, which does not lose all its value in terms of its explanation of the world. These phenomena of hybridisation – of 'creolisation' Hannerz (1992) – benefit from the transnational dimension and from the possibility of individual action simultaneously in several spaces. These hybridisation processes are both cause and consequence of transnational mechanisms, or as Badie (1995: 244) puts it: 'The religious, regional, cultural, linguistic and economic solidarities put the individual in various concurrent spaces, the balance between them being dependant upon the intensity of each allegiance'.

Comparing Islam in France and Germany

Welfare states represent the history of the encounter between private matters and public issues and the ensuing combination of rights and recognition. In this kind of institutionalised national welfare context, the presence of Islam in Europe can be viewed as 'path dependent' (North 1990). For instance, the observance of religious duties will be structured by the interface between religion and society that may cause structural difficulties in the sense of social and legal obstacles constraining equal participation in the host societies (Shadid and van Koningsveld 1991). In turn, this can contribute to economic, social and cultural marginalisation and favour the setting up of religious, cultural and social activities that offer stability and allow Muslims to comply with Islamic requirements. In this compensatory movement, the local and national environment within which these associations are embedded plays a significant role. Three points are particularly crucial:

- church–state relations;
- levels of political decentralisation;
- the legal status of migrants and nationality laws.

Relations between church and state

For many scholars and policy-makers studying the issues connected with the presence of Islam in Europe means assessing the relation between policy and religion and evaluating the institutionalisation potential of Islam.[9] Concretely – and the question is framed in these terms across Europe – this involves the regulation of a Muslim's religious life by an institution representing the interests of all. This would have both symbolic and material costs for host-countries with implications that transcend ethnic and cultural social cleavages. Moreover, secularisation – regarded as the transfer of functions from religious organisations to the secular administration – does not correspond to a similar reality in both home- and host-countries. Turks, Moroccans, Algerians (considered here as Muslims) do not share the same experience of separation between political and religious powers, while France and Germany follow different paths of secularisation. For instance, in Turkey secularisation prompts competition between two antagonistic value systems – Islamism versus Kemalism – while in Germany, secularisation was based on Catholic–Protestant rivalry. In fact, the Treaty of Westphalia (1648) instigated a climate of legal protection with regards to religion that retains relevance. Antagonism towards Islam in Turkey can be compensated by the advantages provided by the German legal environment. The Turkish republican context meant control of religion by politics. Turkish Islamic associations in Germany do, however, use the possibility for organisation and the public recognition of the legitimacy of a partnership reflected in legal status (*Körperschaft des öffentlichen Rechts*) which allows religious groups to decide the content of religious courses, the opening of religious schools and of mosques. They also manage the presence of the spiritual advisers (*Seelsorge*) in public services, such as army, hospitals, police, prison administration and the media. They also benefit from free advertising on public televisions and radios. This German partnership between state and church assumes its importance in the ways that there have, since 1977, been regular requests submitted for official recognition by the public authorities,[10] although this claim has not yet succeeded because there is still no single federating structure that is representative of all Muslims.

In France, the strict separation of church and state since December 1905 determines the avenues Muslims can choose to organise their claims making. To maintain the institutional analogy, the 'path dependence' of Islam in France is constructed differently to that in Germany where the religious neutrality of the state does not impeach the potential for partnership.[11] The position of Islam is conditioned by the French state's *laïcité* dogma, which can be summarised as follows: religious particularism should be restricted to private matters. In terms of juridical possibilities to organise, the liberalisation of the rights of foreign associations since 1981 has given birth to new actors competing with each other and divided along nationalities and political lines, especially those coming from a north African background. This new self-organisation trend was perceived as 'the way to facilitate that evolution and to offer an opening towards social, cultural, economic and, soon, political intermediary functions for which there were few elites available' (Leveau 1991: 123). This creation of intermediary elite groups in order to establish potential partners is a usual strategy of French administrative and political authorities that is testament to 'community-based rhetoric and allegiance to central power' (Leveau 1991: 124) that seeks conformity between a centralised state and the representative elements of specific communities. For Islamic associations in France the key for recognition and dialogue remains a 'keep it discrete' strategy. The French administrative input reached a climax in March 1990 when the Interior Minister, Pierre Joxe, organised the Conseil de Réflexion sur l'Islam en France (CORIF) following the first controversy in 1989 about wearing of the veil by Muslim schoolgirls. This new institution was composed of representatives of the main Islamic associations and sought to dissociate French Islam from the influence of the countries of origin and from other types of foreign support. This wish to cut French Islam's links with its foreign brothers was already significantly present in the new associative movements arising after the 1981 law.

The decentralisation of political power

As a result of the strength and centrality of *laïcité*, the management of Islam in France remains highly centralised even though local administrations and officials are increasingly asked by government to assume policy implementation responsibilities. In the *affaire de foulard*, for instance, the official position taken by the Conseil d'Etat in November 1989 underlined the non-contradiction between wearing the veil and French laicité. The implementation of this decision has fallen under the scrutiny of the *médiateur de la République*, which has been asked to check that the Conseil d'Etat's opinion is actually implemented locally in the schools concerned by such events.

Katzenstein's (1987) famous definition of Germany as a 'semi-sovereign state' coupled with the legitimating value of constitutionalism (Lepsius 1990) helps in understanding the strong impregnation of German political culture by the law. This legal dimension structures the debate on the status of foreigners and of Islam. Analysis of Turkish Islam only serves to confirm the importance of this remark. Indeed, the creation of Turco-Islamic associative networks was the reason for the move to Berlin at the beginning of the 1980s of the Diyanet Isleri Türkiye Islam Birligi. The DITIB was created in March 1924 to promote a certain Islam in conformity with the standards of the Turkish westernisation–secular project. The DITIB manages the relationship between Islam and secularism in the midst of the Kemalist project, or as Cinar (1998: 201) notes: ' the hub of the Western-isation was thus secularisation and the hub of secularisation was the re-definition of Islam in accordance with the new purposes of the State'. The Turkish state sought to maintain its influence in the place of migration, i.e. in a territory over which it was not the legitimate sovereign.[12] More-over, the attempted management of religious activity in Germany and the intervention by Ankara in the religious life of its nationals installed in Germany also resulted from the coup of 12 September 1980 and the wish to prohibit development of Necmettin Erbakan's Refah Partisi (Welfare Party).[13] This attempt to exert control over Turkish Islam in Germany obeys two logics. First, it pursues a Turkish domestic policy agenda as the Turkish state 'delocalises' its action when dealing with religious matters. Second, it formulates a response towards a specific situation in a specific context. In Turkey, 'deviance' from the secular dogma of Kemalist elites is placed, semi-officially, albeit increasingly explicitly, under the authority of the military while in Germany, Consulates and the Embassy are the resources for state action.[14]

Nationality laws

The classic dichotomy that opposes *jus sanguinis* and *jus soli* as the opposing symbols of German and French nationality law and the basis for the construction of a policy towards Islam also passes through other less obvious, but still relevant, channels. This involves identifying the lines drawn between those deemed to be legitimate recipients of welfare, as well as investigating ties of social solidarity, membership and a 'politics of belonging' (Geddes and Favell 1999). This requires investigation of formal rules on nationality and the like, as well as analysis of symbolic processes that organise the perception of minorities and their relation to the perceived community of legitimate welfare receivers. As Breuer *et al.* (1995: 377) put it: 'The relevant options and interdependencies facing citizens in fragmenting solidarities allow actors within welfare systems to behave as "club members"' even though it is precisely the point that 'the club' has lost its meaning as an organisational term for solidarity because of this fragmentation. Muslims, for instance, can enter different classifications: as 'citizens' to the extent that second and third generations can become nationals of the countries they are living in or 'denizens' for 'guest workers' with legal residence.

In this respect, France and Germany share a similar chronology. In the early 1960s, when labour recruitment agreements with foreign countries were signed, it was assumed that people would stay for only a short period. As is well known, for many foreign employees this temporary arrangement became permanent: they changed their plans, brought their families to Europe. In this sense, Islam as a political issue resides at the cross-roads between cultural and social policies understood in the Marshallian sense of the intervention of political power to help the economic system achieve results it could not attain on its own (Marshall 1975). Moreover, in the post-migratory context of western Europe, national spaces lose their obviousness: one does not reside inevitably in the space of one's political participation. New transnational dynamics interact with states.

It is also relevant to relate these reflections on church and state, of centralisation/decentralisation and on nationality laws and the politics of belonging to prevailing approaches to the analysis of Islam in Germany and France. If welfare states create multiple forms of status by matching different types of international migrants to various types of rights, this process does not occur in isolation from broader dynamics contributing to 'ascribed identity'. In France and Germany, Islam has been both ignored and (re)discovered following a similar chronology. The relative indifference of research in Germany – or rather the location of studies of Islam in Germany within anthropology, ethnology and only recently political science, and within certain debates, especially the Orientalist and *Islamwissenschaftler* debates, differs from the French situation. In France, political pressure around Islam perceived as a threat, danger and fifth column has created a 'supply and demand' relationship between policy and scientific research. In this sense, the welfare state can intervene in social scientific discourses by providing funds for specific research. The French 'panic' about Islam does not exist on the same basis in Germany. In any case, German public opinion does not show the same sensitivity towards these topics, in particular because young Turks in Germany have usually not been viewed as electoral clientele in the way that they have in France.

By focusing on the cultural features of the German and French welfare states, i.e. the historical and social processes which give birth to nationally differentiated types of welfare, we can also locate the arenas where the question of 'Islam' is debated and the opening of institutional options. Welfare cannot be exclusively considered as regards to its performances in providing provisions and services but needs to be associated with a specific anchorage in national historical processes, especially as far as the welfare state is considered as the form through which equality and inequality are institutionalised. In this respect, citizenship guarantees a formal equality but remains embedded in national particularities. The cultural determination of types of welfare state articulates inclusion/exclusion mechanisms and national ways of protecting access to citizenship. Two different legitimacy criteria derive from the national manners of maintaining control over territory and population within the scope of sovereignty. While in Germany the nationality law still protects access to the state by imposing time and economic criteria on candidates, the French system places cultural assimilation at the core of participation. In both contexts, mechanisms of closure and protection of the distinction between legitimate users of welfare provisions use various tools and intervene in different arenas. The chapter's main hypothesis focused on the development of alternative biographies relating Muslim immigrants to national welfare states. The analysis has underlined the ways in which perceptions of Islam in France and of nationality in Germany play similar roles in terms of social closure and the legitimacy and possible incorporation into the public sphere of religious difference. In France, the Republican welfare state is based on the idea of a public sphere exclusively devoted to political claims. In this respect, citizenship appears to be the consecration of social and political homogeneity with ethnicisation, communalism and particularism considered as threatening. In this context, transnational dynamics in France inevitably refer to the fight against the financial support from the states of origin for mosques that are built in France and for the terrorist activism (of which the Khaled Kelkal affair was the climax[15]).

In the highly regulated German society, with its high levels of welfare provision and social services, Islamic associative networking is seen as an attempt to set up welfare services as alternatives to those offered by the German welfare state. This pursuit of alternative strategies has three motives, all of which are dimensions of welfare state integration: functional (cost-benefit), ethical (identities) and moral (solidarity and justice) (Faist 1996b). In fact, Islam appears as a kind of meta issue on the basis of which migrant organisations can cover the same three dimensions, reacting towards the politicisation of the social rights of migrants. On a functional and moral level, dealing with mechanisms of solidarity and justice, Islamic associative networks both in France and Germany compensate for deficiencies of national contexts in which they are settled in relation to, for instance, ethnic entrepreneurialism and certain social services. At the ethical level, as mentioned in the chapter's introduction, Islamic associative networks elaborate their activities on the basis of a 'between us' motto which should not be interpreted as an 'against them' logic and be labelled as 'traditional'. Rather, it should be viewed as an attempt to build up a safe space in terms of religious socialisation by keeping alive an identity reference for young generations.

The widening of biographical options through transnational Islam

The settlement of Muslims in Europe prompts the construction and reconstruction of social and cultural identities that are able to provide continuity to individuals, as well as to groups. In this process, secondary institutions such as associations occupy a key position as agencies for socialisation in relation to what can be a precarious social environment. Such institutions, therefore, help bind people into alternative and competing social groups (Turner 1991). The construction of networks and associative activities for Muslims in Germany and France has been helped by the existence of linguistic, cultural, material and technical needs.[16] Religious associations owe their survival to their capacity to provide social services, to offer comfort and support, to facilitate daily life, to maintain community links, and to ensure the production of cultural references to a removed population. In France and Germany, migrant associations have changed their nature since the 1980s, as marked by the increased focus on education and sport. The associative groups have widened their profile to attract younger people and, therefore, widen and diversify their audience and going beyond the 'safety' of observing Islamic rules. What was unexpected was the incredible amount of resources and new perspectives that would be found in both the national and transnational contexts as a result of networking activities. In an important sense, choosing to be active in an Islamic association meant some guarantee of continuity in what could be discontinuous social circumstances caused by social fragmentation and the end of normative lifestyle evaluations as a principle norm for allocation of provisions and services. As Berger and Luckmann (1964: 337) wrote: 'In one area of the social system the individual is functionalised as performer, while in the order he is left to his own devices to discover a presumed "essential identity".' Islam in Europe could be characterised as indicative of *'nomadism'* (Balandier) or *'bricolage'* (Levi Strauss) and as composed of individuals with new cognitive maps, a degree of uncertainty, as well as mobility between reference groups as new elements of the life course. In this more unpredictable context, Muslims can be considered as 'autonomous political actors with the capacity to pursue (at least some of) their own policy options' (Leibfried and Pierson 1995a: 20). If economic exclusion remains the most tangible, it is also important to bear in mind that the symbolic dimension requires some consideration as challenging the normative component of expected biographies.

As Bommes (this volume, pp. 90–108) notes, welfare states intervene in recruiting practices of organisations on the basis of certain rules and practise redistributive and regulatory interventions. Individuals are given social positions that define their options. From this perspective arises the idea that as social concepts 'careers' and 'biographies' are 'a result of the ways in which organisations recruit members and the moderation of these organisational processes of social inclusion and exclusion through the welfare state'. The welfare state thus becomes the principal agent moderating the relation of inclusion within institutionalised life courses. The life-course concept refers explicitly to an 'expectable life course', i.e. an ascribed biography providing sets of competencies and meanings to fulfil. The manner in which Germany and France deal with Islam in their legal and political environments helps us to understand this point, while contradicting the idea of expected biographies understood from a time-sequential perspective and according to participation in specific domains – 'functional contexts' – on the basis of political inclusion as national citizens. Full participation in each of these sub-systems is indexed in relation to certain abilities. In this respect, education plays a central role. The universal aim of education systems in France and Germany is regularly challenged by particular inputs. The education system procures opportunities through institutional regulation and legal entitlements, while still taking for granted the control of migrants' biographies, at least the limit of their mobility especially as far as expression of identity is concerned. In fact, the institutional arrangements for education within the welfare state grant extensive social rights in a polity that is presumed to be ethnically homogeneous. Access to resources remains unequally shared in both an economic sense and in terms of social and cultural capital. Even though they may not be citizens of the state in which they reside, i.e. denizens, migrants can also be assigned an ascribed biography. But while this control is guaranteed in Germany by the law on nationality that protects the state, the French welfare state cannot be dissociated from the nation state and its central pillar, *laïcité*.

If we consider the management of religious life in Germany, the framework of the action produced by the national context contributed to the establishment of compensating mechanisms, in particular competition and collaboration between rival associations. The sharing of a common migratory experience and mobilisations for the defence of the interests of those involved do not necessarily involve acting together, but rather imply the development of sectoral logics. The keenest competition can be seen in relation to the nomination of imams and the building of mosques. Restrictive nationality laws and the legal regulation of links between church and state have, in fact, contributed to the maintenance of the legitimacy of the transnational as a working method, as a resource and as a form of communication. The transnational allows access inside a given territory and to a sense of community. In this context, ethnic communal organisations acquire importance because they can provide alternative forms of welfare provisions and assist individuals to get involved in politics.

In France and Germany, social inclusion of Muslims has to be considered through two main institutions regulating and protecting access to the state. In France there is *laïcité*, in Germany there is the nationality law. With regard to these two institutions, associative networks with a cultural basis founded on Islamic identification give the possibility to migrants of deviating from the expected norm of the 'institutionalised life course' that both nationality law and *laïcité* are supposed to help implement. As 'unexpected biographies', those associative networks provide, for example, educational opportunities demonstrating how new possibilities open that do not take the national welfare state as their frame of reference, but instead draw from resources created by the opening of transnational spaces.

Recently, new types of careers have been appearing in the German and Turkish public spaces. They concern 'new' individual figures who chose politics as their profession. This 'unexpected' biographical element can be seen in the context of the closure of access to German citizenship. These 'new' figures are also present on the Turkish scene, especially since the 1995 legislative elections (Amiraux 1999b). It is certainly the case that constraints and opportunities defined by national institutional structures affect the organisational methods and mobilisation potential of Turkish Muslims. This does not, however, imply the disconnection of mobilisation from the main principles of Turkish domestic policy. On the contrary, these opportunities permit networking on the basis of an identity that exists independently of their position as citizen or non-citizen of the state in which they reside. The profiles of these individuals engaged in politics (through the German parties or the Turkish ones) share a similar socialisation background through Islamic associations. Whether this involves being elected in Turkey or in Germany, the choice of a political career is based on the capitalisation of different kind of resources that mix social status, economic position, control of sources of information, and popularity/reputation. Upon leaving the associative structures as the sole and exclusive frame of their engagement, individuals enter the polity from the perspective of a 'German' experience of Islamic militant socialisation. This occurs in relation to the transition from mobilisations of the community type towards participation as Turks or naturalised Germans in Germany. It is certainly the case that these political careers remain an option for only a minority. Nevertheless, whether they deal with the community as clientele within a local framework – through for instance federal political training in parties or trade unions – or with 'return to the country of origin' – actors accumulate resources and capital in transnational spaces that result from the individual's post-migratory configurations (Amiraux 1999a). Ultimately, these unexpected careers face two obstacles. First, other Turkish–German actors, who do not share the Islamic associative background, but are part of the German game and deny access to the political game to actors they see as threatening their own tacit agreement with Germany based on their profile as *immigrün*. This conveniently ignores the fact that their own election was the result of a German plebiscite rather than of mobilisation by naturalised immigrants.[17] Second, while the German public space did not anticipate the arrival of those individuals at such a level in political competition, the reaction prompts a security discourse linked to perceptions of an internal threat.

Individual success is more easily accepted in business. The interplay of their social positions in two different societies is of particular relevance in, the ethnic business sector. For a long time, the ethnic business sector contributed financial resources to the political associations and, thereby, furnished (immediate) economic and (medium-term) symbolic advantage. These funding activities could also serve as springboards for individual political careers. Ethnic entrepreneurship has been the first step in the consolidation of transnational dynamics among Turkish Muslims. There are two aspects of this entrepreneurship: the goals pursued by the individuals performing economically oriented activities, and the collective resources they offer for the group identified as such.

There are important differences between the ethnic business sectors in France and Germany. In France, the halal business is a consequence of family reunification and settlement while in Germany it was present at the very beginning of migration. In Germany, foreigners had already started their own businesses in the 1960s. These businesses were concentrated in the retail, gastronomic and craft trade sectors, as well as travel, import–export, wholesale food, construction and removals. Although foreign business people still focus on these sectors today, the ethnic business sector expanded into other service-oriented areas such as banking and finance.

The most frequently named reasons for starting one's own business include the desire for independence as a self-employed business person, prospects for better income, more social status as an employer than as an employee, and providing for one's children. Unemployment plays only a secondary role as a reason for starting a business. Faist (1996a) analyses the parallel growth of advances in labour market, educational and political integration coupled with the development of ethnic organisation in terms of an 'ethnic paradox': ethnic identification leads to both ethnic networking and to the empowerment of migrants outside of their ethnic community. The self-employment rate among foreign nationals is also likely to reach the German level by that time as well. The trend toward a growing number of foreigner-owned businesses will be accompanied by a change in the type of businesses. The inclusion of the foreign resident population in terms of education and welfare could present the opportunity for development of businesses that move beyond the ethnic niche. Indeed, the German press has consistently presented such business activity as the principal indicator of the success of the Turks in Germany.

The French interpretation of the welfare state is based on the centrality of the idea of social contract and loyalty. This questioning of individual as well as collective loyalty does not stop with the acquisition of French nationality whether it is acquired automatically or not. The public opinion perception of the *affaire du foulard* and of violence in suburbs attests to the reactivity of this debate. Islam as a mean of organisation and networking for migrants is not viewed as intervening with the same clear compensatory effect as it does in Germany. Without offering alternative biographical options to Muslims, the religious affiliation questions the permeability of certain social spaces that are highly symbolic as far as Republican integrity is concerned (particularly schools). In France, the 'challenge' of Islam is defined less in terms of the nature of unexpected careers than in connection with the social arena where this challenge takes place; the nation and the welfare state cannot be considered as two different settings (Wihtol de Wenden 1998). In France, unexpected biographies are located elsewhere at the very heart of Republican ideology: the public school. In the Republican French context, school remains the main place where what it means to be a citizen is defined. Education is the main site for definition of the condition for being admitted as a 'club member'. The French Republican model basically promises integration and participation to candidates under the condition that they renounce particular identity in the public space. The individual actor is then not allowed to counteract the *universel abstrait* which could be described as a normative cultural model dominating the French public space in which particularism should remain strictly located in the private sphere and public space should be dedicated to 'pure' political business (Khosrokhavar 1996: 114).

Not only is the nation state the regulator of economic and social relations, it is the political instance of universalism to the extent that in France 'secularism in the schools is national policy' (Moruzzi 1994: 653). Education is the arena where various competing sets of cultural constructions meet and it carries the direct heritage from the Third Republic, which first conceived it as the carrier of an emancipatory Republican discourse. Khosrokhavar (1996) describes perfectly the contemporary switch of this discourse from a dynamic of emancipation to repression as far as young Muslims are concerned, in particular young girls wearing the veil. Analysing the different veil affairs since 1989, the conclusion can be reached that the discussion has not been constructed in terms of liberalism, tolerance and multiculturalism, but as a 'threat' to French culture and Republican integrity.[18] The visibility of Islam in schools destabilises the normative view of the public space that defines the public identity of citizen and is aimed at controlling it both inside and outside the public schools. Wearing the veil also means being associated with a cultural community of belonging that escapes any form of state control. In fact, Islamic associations function as agencies for socialisation in the sense that French state schools do not provide religious education.[19] The over-politicisation of the veil affairs also revealed a social culture of the political. This was particularly the case with regards to the ways in which particular identities were promoted in schools and made it clear that social inclusion also works through channels other than the primacy of universalism or particularism. In a way, this doubt about the future career of those individuals carrying visible signs of a particular identity signs the failure of the sacred mission attributed to schools.

Conclusion

This chapter questions the idea of an exclusive and permanent relationship between state and individuals through citizenship and social and political participations with the idea of alternative perspectives defined along cultural and religious lines. The issue of welfare was linked with a symbolic dimension and the limits of acceptance of unexpected individual biographies produced by Muslim settlement in France and Germany. The symbolic dimension appears as a kind of ideal meta-issue with its functional, ethical and moral aspects that responds to or compensates for the failings of the French and German welfare states. Playing with the symbolic dimensions of identification and participation, the transnational dynamics among Muslim populations in Europe question the normativity of political and social belongings as drawn by nation states (Labelle and Midy 1999).

In France and Germany two different configurations can be viewed. The German case tends to work along juridical lines by grounding exclusion on the basis of nationality law while the French case refers systematically to politics in which administration and bureaucracy speak and decide in the name of the Republic. When facing these main frames, collective and individual actors invest differently in alternatives such as those offered by Islamic networks and transnational practices. This means that unexpected biographies are not similarly constructed. Moreover, the growing distance between economic participation and education curricula, and social recognition or identification by the country of residence is nowadays very pertinent when discussing cultural distinction. In a way, this bifurcation triggers the transnationalisation of social spaces within which actors are located while disconnecting their political, economic and cultural participations from an exclusive and unique national frame of reference. The notion of 'space' implicitly refers to the idea of social space developed by Bourdieu combined with ideas about social capital. As Pries (1999) put it: 'The social space serves as an important frame of reference for social positions and positioning and also determines everyday practices, biographical employment projects, and human identities, simultaneously pointing beyond the social context of national societies'. Consequently, transnational spaces deal with several dimensions: legal, material, social, and, last but not least, identificational. The cumulative dimension of transnational activities (Portes 1999) from strict economic activity to broader social and political implications helps in conceiving the social mobility that these new types of transnational spaces make possible. It is clear that bargaining, protection, compensation or separation, and the use of cultural-religious references as producing new frames for action does not systematically lead to communalism. Inclusion within alternative channels of socialisation should not be perceived as a reaction, challenge or threat, but as an alternative. If we consider the welfare state as the central moderator of relations of inclusion by producing occasions and dispositions for inclusion and by processing and ordering the consequences of exclusion, then Islamic organisations may be considered as alternatives and not as mediators between state and individuals. Islam furnishes the tools for 'identity management' of migrants' exclusion to attain a measure of autonomy and enhance the possibility for 'integration without assimilation'.

Notes

1 Building enemies by using the opposition between mobility and settlement is not a new idea and connections between mobility and criminality are well-established. Mobility and its control, in particular with regards to resource allocation and (re)distribution by the state played an essential role in the establishment of legal systems regulating the situation of foreign people. (Lucassen and Lucassen 1997).

2 The building of a '*classes dangereuses*' thematic is not an homogeneous one and the principles of its justification vary from one country to another even if the media coverage is similar. See, for instance, the difference between the historical past: no need to 'symbolically' pay for historical mistakes between Turks and Germans such as between the Maghreb and France.

3 Religious authorities in Islam do not correspond to the Christian institution of church and in *sunni* Islam, there is no clergy. The absence of an official centralised institution does not, however, mean that there are no authorities.

4 The citizenship corresponds less 'to the civic desire to enter into the destiny of an overall community with which one would be identified' (citizenship as 'input') than to the 'rational desire to receive the means of guaranteeing a minimum of safety against the arbitrary of an external power' (citizenship as an 'output') (Leca 1996: 261).

5 The transnational aspects of immigration are particularly evident within the US literature on the subject. The role of networks in the economic transactions of ethnic entrepreneurs is at the core of the work directed by Portes (see, for example, 1995). Peggy Levitt's work stresses the performative function of the transnational in establishing, organising and structuring the aims of migrants at a local level. She elaborates in particular on the concept of 'social remittances', i.e. 'ideas, behaviors and social capital that flow from receiving to sending country communities' (Levitt 1997: 512).

6 The names of associations often change. AMGT is today called the IGMG, Islamic Society-National Vision.

7 Opportunities here are meant as 'consistent – but not necessarily formal or permanent – dimensions of the political environment that provide incentives for collective action by affecting people's expectations for success or failure'. (Tarrow 1998: 76–7).

8 This remark is of particular relevance regarding the Kurdish population. See Bozarslan (1997).

9 The institutionalisation of Islam would mean *recognizing the permanence and settlement of another religion within the national scope.*

10 On a more general level, the possibility for foreigners to organise as foreigners' association (*eingetragener Verein*) allows Turkish Islamic actors sanctioned by or even censured at certain moments in recent Turkish history

to acquire a status and visibility from which they are not inevitably benefiting in the country of origin.

11 In Germany, regional states (Länder) and churches co-operate very closely in education. By delegation of the state, church welfare agencies have also assumed control of social care of southern European migrants while for Muslims, the Arbeiterwohlfahrt has been designated as the social welfare appendix of the Social Democrat Party and the Labour Movement (Puskeppeleit and Thränhardt 1990).

12 The Turkish state actively maintains its management of national interests, for instance the imposition of conscription.

13 He headed the government of the Refahyol coalition (Refah Partisi-Doğru Yol Partisi) between June 1996 and June 1997. The Refah is today called the Fazilet Partisi.

14 In February 1997, the meeting of the National Safety Council fixed the legitimate political framework within which the Islamists of the *Refah*, members of the governmental coalition *Refahyol*, are supposed to evolve. The assigned limits take into account the religious dimension by repressing in particular the *imam hatip lisesi*, colleges of training of the imams.

15 Khaled Kelkal, who was French of Algerian origin, was suspected of responsibility for terrorist bombings in Paris. After having been pursued, he was killed by the police. The French daily newspaper published an interview with Kelkal by D. Loch, a German sociologist who was working on young Muslims in France (*Le Monde*, 19 October 1995).

16 By which is meant the construction of mosques, the opening of halal food chains, the allocation of Muslim sections in cemeteries.

17 This concerns, for instance, success such as that of Cem Özdemir.

18 This defensive attitude intending to protect the 'French Republican values' went through all the political groups, even if the extreme right National Front was the first to mobilise on this chorus.

19 No Islamic schools have been established in France although religious communities are entitled to run their own schools with public funding. Simultaneously, imams and religious educators are still trained in the countries of origin.

14 Conclusion

Defining and redefining the community of legitimate welfare receivers

Michael Bommes and Andrew Geddes

In this conclusion, we draw together the issues identified in the preceding chapters by addressing four key questions that underpin much of the book's analysis of relations between immigration and welfare states. Why have national welfare states supported immigrants even though they have politically declared themselves to be non-immigration countries? Does immigration erode the national welfare state? Are new immigrants being excluded because they are perceived as undeserving of welfare state benefits? Does free movement within the European Union (EU) create new migration that undermines national welfare states?

These questions are, of course, nested within a series of more general issues associated with the development of national welfare states that historically developed to provide scope for social participation for citizens, which in turn tied citizens to the state, its territory and its sovereignty. Yet, as has been shown, chances for social inclusion in national welfare states have also been provided to non-national legal residents via the denizenship path, which 'repaired' incomplete membership for non-national immigrants. The pre-condition for this form of inclusion has, however, always been external closure based on the assumption that immigration can be controlled and restricted according to the interests of nation states.

The classical European nation states never described themselves as immigration countries, even after they changed from being emigration countries to countries that became the destination for immigrants. The emergence of European nation states initiated migrations for national and ethnic reasons, but the state-building process was not based on migration as one of its premises, unlike in immigration countries such as the USA, Australia or Canada. With the expansion of welfare organisations and programmes, European nation states became 'thresholds of inequality' for immigrants. These states permitted labour migration, as well as migration of asylum seekers or civil war refugees, family migration, and migration for educational reasons. During the 1970s, however, nearly all west European states declared themselves to be non-immigration countries. If we take this as the common ground for our concluding discussion then we can return to the four questions mentioned in the first paragraph, which allow us to refocus our results.

Why have 'mature' national welfare states supported immigrants even when they have politically declared themselves to be non-immigration countries? The history of labour migration since the end of the Second World War coincided with the high point of the national welfare state. Politics perceived itself as the sovereign supervisor and was convinced of the possibility to steer central social areas, especially the national economy, by means of state – especially welfare state – instruments of a modern labour market policy. Until the mid-1970s this model proved to be successful (Scharpf 1996). Part of this policy was the recruitment of labour and postcolonial migration, which was to a large extent recruited by the states themselves for national labour markets. This suggests that we can periodise our analyses. The contributions of Keith Banting, Jim Hollifield and Virginie Guiraudon suggest that we can identify a distinct period in recent European migration history during which labour migrants and their families were included within the welfare provisions of the countries in which they resided, irrespective of whether or not they were citizens.

It is also clear that labour migration was differently structured in each European country. France, The Netherlands and the UK exploited colonial connections, whereas states like Switzerland, Germany, Belgium, and also The Netherlands actively recruited labour power, mainly from southern European countries. Labour migration was actively encouraged because of the assumption that the main aim of these migrants was to achieve an income and that their stay in the territory of the state would be temporally limited and reversible. So, even though there are major differences between European labour immigration countries with regards to processes, the extent of immigration, and the duration of political efforts to limit the chances of participation for labour immigrants, they did also share the common experience of stopping labour immigration under the changed economic circumstances of the early to mid-1970s. Yet, this immigration stop – contrary to their original expectations – did not lead to remigration, but to settlement by immigrants. The migrants were followed by their families and grew into the status of 'denizens' (Hammar 1990).

It became apparent that national welfare states became more inclusionary than their political self-descriptions as non-immigration countries suggested they would. This common result of migration is interpreted in different ways. Hollifield (1992 and in this volume, pp. 109–33) sees this as an outcome of the institutionalisation of the liberal state and is concerned about the strength and stability of this institutionalisation in expectable future conflicts about migration and welfare. Guiraudon's interpretation, which establishes a critical distance to Yasemin Soysal's thesis about the decisive impact of universal personhood and post-national membership, entailed a two-fold argument stressing, on the one hand, the importance of the organisational structure of welfare states for the granting of social rights and welfare programmes for immigrants and, on the other hand, differentiation between law and politics. She showed that various court decisions spelt out legal implications of residence and welfare inclusion by granting residence and social security and thus limiting political capacity to manage foreign immigrants solely under premises of political expediency. It became clear that welfare states created rights that limited the ability of states to regulate migration. During this period of large-scale labour migration and family reunification, it is accurate to say that neither permanent settlement nor denizenship was the intention, but that they were the outcome. There was an assumption of temporariness, but this was misplaced because the 'guests came to stay' based on mechanisms for recruitment and settlement. It also seems likely that this particular constellation is unrepeatable in the foreseeable future.

Analysing this period of labour migration, family reunification and welfare state inclusion was vastly significant because of the high percentage of labour migrants and their families in relation to the population in immigration countries such as France, Switzerland, Germany, Belgium and The Netherlands. More than this, though, it is significant because of the structuring consequences these labour migration processes had for later migration. Labour migration formed the basis for family migration so that family membership became a crucial mechanism for the transfer of immigration rights that were difficult for states to limit and control. These countries also became destination areas for later migrations by refugees and asylum seekers because, for instance, refugees from the former Yugoslavia or Turkey can rely on social networks and infrastructures set up by former labour migrants and their families.

Does immigration erode the national welfare state? The opportunity to use migration paths resulting from earlier migrations has led welfare states to introduce diversified categories of migrants linked with different clusters of rights and restrictions. This can be seen as an effort to reaffirm external closure and as the basis for internal inclusion. Migration is perceived as a threat eroding the basis of the national welfare state in various dimensions, including the sovereign control of access to the state territory – as discussed in Jost Halfmann's contribution – and the definition of the community of legitimate welfare receivers that had traditionally been built by the nation (Marshall 1950). Migration is also viewed as a threat to the capacity of welfare states to maintain levels of provision. But migration may also have effects on the willingness of states to provide welfare if it provides an opportunity to undermine the extent to which the provision of welfare can be legitimately socially expected. The perception of erosion is therefore not just a question of the economic costs and benefits of migration.

The contributions to this book make it very clear that the perspective 'migration is a threat to welfare' is much too abstract and general. Migrants are differently perceived and treated dependent on the internal infrastructure of welfare states, different traditions of immigration, diverse legal traditions, etc. Denizenship and (eventually) access to citizenship are certainly a common result of the post-war labour migration processes. But restructuring effects of these processes on diverse national welfare states, on their internal organisational structure, on their structure of rights and provisions and on their frame of reference – the community of welfare receivers – differ widely. It is through analysis of inclusion events arising from settlement by labour migrants and their families that the diverse national settings through which we view the interactions between migration and welfare become clear. And these same settings build the framework for efforts of social closure based on border control, internal immigrant policies and the differentiation of migrant categories and the civil and social rights linked to them. What this demonstrates very clearly is that we need to focus on national settings, on national political-institutional repertoires that structure migration regimes, and on the immigration and immigrant policies that all pave the path to social participation.

By doing this, we can explore both the control dimension of immigration policies and their specific relation to social participation in national welfare states. A key issue has been the gap between various restrictive policies and the in-flow of new migrants as illustrated, for example, by increased numbers of asylum seekers. Asylum seeking, just like family migration, is, in a sense, an unavoidable form of migration for liberal states with domestic and international obligations. These forms of migration and others linked to seasonal or contract labour provide the context for what is described as forms of transnationalism using the structural options provided by national welfare states without restricting themselves to these national frame, as discussed in Valérie Amiraux's chapter. But asylum seekers and refugees are not citizens and national welfare states have made it increasingly clear that they seek reversibility for this form of unavoidable and unwanted migration. To achieve this, they keep these migrants beyond the bounds of 'normal' inclusion in liberal states and subject them to the 'anormalisation' of social life, evident in current policies for the reception of asylum seekers (as the chapters on asylum by Roland Bank and Andrew Geddes show).

Are new immigrants being excluded because they are perceived as undeserving of welfare state benefits? If migration is seen as a threat to the welfare state it is not just registered as a purely factual observation but as a moral or ethical problem. Immigrants appear as illegitimate if they are seen as claiming support from the welfare state and thereby claiming access to resources which are viewed as reserved for members of the community of legitimate welfare receivers. In a sense one could assume that border-crossing migrants are becoming the new 'undeserving poor' from the outside.

Yet, if we look closely at relations between migration and the welfare state we see that migration has become part of a constant process of the definition and redefinition of this community of legitimate welfare receivers. Various contributions to this book demonstrate that not only could the boundaries of this community accommodate non-national residents and that they have done so extensively, but that migration is also part of a process by which the moral fundament of this community and the meaning of the nation may change dramatically, even to the extent of excluding groups formerly seen as part of the nation (as Michael Bommes showed).

An aspect of these processes is that the political redefinition of migration types has reduced the numbers of people entitled to migrate. Many are subject to the suspicion that they use migratory options in order to access 'undeserved welfare' entitlements. The effect has been that the channel of geographical mobility as a means of enhancing chances for social participation has been progressively narrowed. The increase in numbers of asylum seekers and refugees is a reflection of this. Clearly, many are genuine asylum seekers fleeing persecution as defined by the Geneva Convention, others though are fleeing other forms of hardship often linked to economic inequalities. It can be assumed that illegal or undocumented migration as well as certain forms of contract, pendel or seasonal labour are another side of these redefinition and closure processes of the community of legitimate welfare receivers.

Does free movement within the European Union create new migration that undermines national welfare states? A key dimension demonstrated by contributions to this book has been the territorial dimension of welfare state politics centred on social provision in return for loyalty as an important aspect of the social contract in mature European welfare states. One common supposition is that national welfare states are under pressures resulting from the changed global economic and political environment, as Magnus Ryner discusses. How do they maintain levels of provision? How do they ensure loyalty within welfare states that face significant challenges in the era of globalisation? Migration is part of the challenge, but to assess the extent of the challenge – and to avoid simplistic notions of threat – we need to pay close attention to contemporary welfare state dynamics and to migration patterns. This book has emphasised the importance of distinguishing between migration categories and the national contexts into which they occur. Just as different types of welfare states cope differently with the challenges of globalisation (Esping-Andersen 1996) they are differently equipped to cope with future migration.

If migration can be seen as part of a global challenge to the borders of national welfare states in relation to their core roles of provision and loyalty then several contributions to the book ask if European integration is another element of this process providing new forms of mobility that further undermine the national welfare state without any substitute or equivalent being in view at European level. Again, it becomes abundantly clear that differentiation and specificity of argumentation is paramount. EU freedom of movement provisions has not led to increased intra-EU migration. This experience is certainly of major importance for further research on the migratory effects of future EU enlargement and the incorporation of new member states into EU free-movement provisions.

It also clear that the forms of mobility and migration made possible by the EU differ and, as we can see from the chapters by Maria Baganha and Uwe Hunger, it is the combination of specific national welfare state types – their forms of social inclusion and construction of the welfare community, their forms of immigration control and their ways of dealing with illegality – in relation to EU provisions that is a key issue. Clandestine migration, as Maria Baganha demonstrates, needs to be located in the context of European interdependencies that may see workers leave low-wage/low-social protection member states to move to high-wage/high-social protection member states. This can lead to erosion of standards and political debates about welfare in countries that receive these workers, such as Germany. Meanwhile, intra-EU migration draws extra-EU migration from non-EU states into countries such as Portugal to fill labour market gaps. The Europeanisation of relations between migration and welfare and the interdependencies that it provokes illustrate the point that, even though welfare states remain national welfare states, they face distinct pressures arising from European integration. Migration also draws into view differences between national social security and tax systems. A key issue for future research is the political economy of migration in an integrating Europe, migration from both within and outside the EU, and the ways in which interdependencies feed into national debates about welfare provision.

In this book we have sought to explain inclusionary and exclusionary dynamics arising from relations between immigration and the welfare state. To do this has required close specification of forms of migration, of welfare state types and of the core relationship between external closure and internal inclusion in the light of these national welfare state and the challenges they face. Migration's challenge to national welfare states is, of course, bundled up with a series of challenges to national welfare states. We have tried to demonstrate that by focusing on the definition and redefinition of the community of legitimate welfare receivers we can illustrate relations between migration and welfare in diverse national settings and in an era of European integration. We cannot claim to have told the story of welfare state development. We never intended to. What we have tried to do is illustrate the impact that closer understanding of relations between immigration and welfare can have on analysis of welfare state dynamics in contemporary Europe.

References

Abella, M. (1997) *Sending Workers Abroad. A Manual for Low- and Middle-Income Countries*, Geneva: International Labour Office (ILO).

Agranoff, R. (1996) 'Federal Evolution in Spain', *International Political Science Review*, 17: 385–401.

Alber, J. (1996) 'Selectivism, Universalism, and the Politics of Welfare State Retrenchment in Germany and the United States', paper presented at the 1996 Annual APSA meetings.

Albert, M. (1998) 'Die Zukunft der Sozialmodelle', in Streeck 1998a.

Alen, A., Billet, J., Heremans, D. and van Rompuy, P. (1990) *Vlaaderen Op Een Kruispunt: Sociologische, Economische en Staatsrechtelijke Perspectieven*, Leuven: Lannoo.

Alesina, A., Baqir, R. and Easterly, W. (1997) 'Public Goods and Ethnic Divisions', NBER working paper no. 6009, Cambridge, Mass.: National Bureau of Economic Research.

Alfandari, E. (ed.) (1990) *Immigration et Droits Sociaux*, Paris: Sirey.

Amiraux, V. (1999a) 'Les Limites du Transnational comme Espace de Mobilisation', *Cultures et Conflits*, 33–4: 25–50.

Amiraux, V. (1999b) 'Transnational en Puissance, Transnational en acte. Le Rôle de l'Espace Migratoire dans la Mobilisation Politique Islamiste', in G. Groc (ed.) *Formes Nouvelles de l'Islam en Turquie*, Paris: ERISM-INALCO.

Andersen, J. (1992) 'Denmark: The Progress Party – Populist Neo-Liberalism and Welfare State Chauvinism,' in P. Hainworth (ed.) *The Extreme Right in Europe and the USA*, New York: St. Martin's Press.

Andersen, J. and Bjørklund, T. (1990) 'Structural Changes and Cleavages: The Progress Parties in Denmark and Norway', *Acta Sociologica*, 33: 195–217.

Anderson, B. (1983) *Imagined Communities: Reflections on the Origins and Spread of Nationalism*, London: Verso.

Anderson, M. (1996) *Frontiers: Territory and State Formation in the Modern World*, Cambridge: Polity Press.

Anderson, M., den Boer, M., Cullen, P., Gilmore, W., Raab, C. and Walker, N. (1995) *Policing the European Union*, Oxford: Clarendon Press.

Appleyard, R. T. (1991) *International Migration: Challenge for the Nineties*, Geneva: International Organization for Migration.

Armstrong, P., Glyn, A. and Harrison, J. (1991) *Capitalism Since 1945*, Oxford: Blackwell.

Association Nationale d'Assistance aux Frontières pour les Étrangers (Anafé) (1997) *Visites des zones d'attente – rapport 1997*, Paris: Anafé.

Auernheimer, G. (1995) *Einführung in die interkulturelle Erziehung*, Darmstadt: Wissenschaftliche Buchgesellschaft.

Axtmann, R. (1993) 'The Formation of the Modern State: The Debate in the Social Sciences', in M. Fulbrook (ed.) *National Histories and European History*, London: University College London Press.

Bade, K. J. (1987), 'Sozialhistorische Migrationsforschung und "Flüchtlings-integration"', in R. Schulze, D. v.d. Brelie-Lewien and H. Grebing (eds) *Flüchtlinge und Vertriebene in der westdeutschen Nachkriegsgeschichte. Bilanzierung der Forschung und Perspektiven für die künftige Forschungsarbeit*, Hildesheim: Lax Verlag.

Badie, B. (1995) *La Fin des Terrritoires*, Paris: Fayard.

Baganha, M.I. (1996) 'Immigrants' Insertion in the Informal Economy. The Portuguese Case', MIGRINF PROJECT, TSER, ERBSOE2CT95, 3005. First report, Coimbra, CES.

Baganha, M. I. (ed.) (1997) *Immigration in Southern Europe*, Oeiras: Celta Editora.

Baganha, M. I. (1998) 'Immigrants' Insertion in the Informal Economy. The Portuguese Case', MIGRINF PROJECT, TSER, ERBSOE2CT95, 3005. First Report, December 1996, Second Report, February 1998, Coimbra, CES.

Baganha, M. I. (1999) 'Labour Market and Immigration: Economic Opportunities for Immigrants in Portugal', in R. King, G. Lazaridis and C. Tsardanidis (eds) *Eldorado or Fortress? Migration in Southern Europe*, London: MacMillan Press.

Baganha, M. I, Ferrão, J. and Malheiros, J. M. (coords) (1998) *Os Movimentos Migratórios Externos e a sua Incidência no Mercado de Tabralho em Portugal*, Instituto do Emprego e Formação Profissional, Lisbon: Relatório Final.

Baganha, M. I., and Góis, P. (1999) 'Migrações Internacionais de e para Portugal: o que sabemos e para onde vamos?', *Revista Crítica de Ciências Sociais*, 52/3: 229–80.

Bakker, E. de (1997) 'Saisonarbeit in Deutschland: Diskussionen, Gesetze und Regelungen im Gartenbereich. Ein Überblick zur Orientierung', unpublished working paper, University of Nijmegen.

Baldwin-Edwards, M. and Schain, M. (eds) (1994) *The Politics of Immigration in Western Europe*, London: Frank Cass.

Bank, R. (1996), *Die internationale Bekämpfung von Folter und unmenschlicher Behandlung auf den Ebenen der Vereinten Nationen und des Europarates*, Freiburg: edition iuscrim.

Bank, R. (1998) 'Europeanization of the Reception of Asylum Seekers: The Opposite of Welfare State Politics', paper presented at the Conference on Migration and the Welfare State in Contemporary Europe, European University Institute, Florence, May.

Bank, R. (1999) 'The Emergent EU Policy on Asylum and Refugees – The New Framework Set by the Treaty of Amsterdam: Landmark or Standstill?', *Nordic Journal of International Law*, 68: 1–29.

Banting, K. (1987) *The Welfare State and Canadian Federalism*, 2nd ed., Montreal/Kingston: McGill-Queen's UP.

Banting, K. (1995) 'The Welfare State as Statecraft: Territorial Politics and Canadian Social Policy', in Leibfried and Pierson 1995a.

Banting, K. (1998) 'The Past Speaks to the Future: Lessons from the Postwar Social Union', in H. Lazar (ed.) *Canada: The State of the Federation 1997: Non-Constitutional Renewal*, Kingston: Institute of Intergovernmental Relations, Queen's University.

Barbalet, J. (1988) *Citizenship: Rights, Struggle and Class Inequality*, Milton Keynes: Open UP.

Basch, L., Glick Schiller, N. and Szanton Blanc C. (1994) *Nations Unbound: Transnational Projects, Postcolonial Predicaments, and Deterritorialized nation states*, Amsterdam: Gordon and Breach.

Bauböck, R. (1995) *Transnational Citizenship. Membership and Rights in International Migration*, Aldershot: Edward Elgar Publishing Limited.

Bauindustrieverband Berlin–Brandenburg (1997) 'Baudaten Berlin–Brandenburg (Stand 1997)', Potsdam.

Baumgartner, F. (1989) *Conflict and Rhetoric in French Policy-Making*, Pittsburgh: University of Pittsburgh Press.

Beck, U. (1998) *Was ist Globalisierung? Irrtümer des Globalismus – Antworten auf Globalisierung*, Frankfurt-am-Main: Suhrkamp.

Beckford, J. and Luckmann, T. (eds) (1989) *The Changing Face of Religion*, London: Sage.

Bendix, R. (1964) *Nation-Building and Citizenship. Studies of Our Changing Social Order*, New York: John Wiley.

Bendix, R. (1977) *Nation-Building and Citizenship*, 2nd ed., Berkeley: University of California Press.

Berger, P. and Luckmann, T. (1964) 'Social Mobility and Personal identity', *Archives Européennes de Sociologie*, V: 331–43.

Berlin, I. (1969) 'Two Concepts of Liberty', in *Four Essays on Liberty*, Oxford: Oxford UP.

Berman, N. (1994) 'Between "Alliance" and "Localisation": Nationalism and the New Oscillationism', *New York University Journal of International Law and Politics*, 26: 449–91.

Bertels, J., Pieters, D., Schoukens, P. and Vansteenkiste, S. (1997) *De Vlaamse Sociale Zekerheid in 101 Vragen En Antwoorden*, Leuven: Acco.

Betz, H.-G. (1994) *Radical Right-Wing Populism in Western Europe*, New York: St. Martin's Press.

Beune, H. H. M. and Hessels, A. J. J. (1983) *Minderheid – Minder Recht? een Inventarisatie van Bepalingen in de Nederlandse wet- en Regelgeving Waarin Onderscheid Gemaakt Wordt Tussen Allochtonen en Autochtonen*, The Hague: Staatsuitgeverij.

Bigo, D. (1996a) 'Guerres, Conflits, Transnational et Territoire', *Cultures et Conflits*, 21/2: 397–418.

Bigo, D. (1996b) *Polices en réseaux, l'expérience Européene*, Paris: Presses de la Fondation Nationales des Sciences Politiques.

Bigo, D. (1998) 'Nouveaux regards sur les conflits?', in M.-C. Smouts (ed.) *Les Nouvelles Relations Internationales: Pratiques et Théories*, Paris: Presses de Sciences-Po.

Birnbaum, P. (1995) *Destins Juifs: De la Révolution française à Carpentras*, Paris: Calmann-Lévy.

Blaschke, D. (1989) 'Aussiedler – Eine Problemskizze aus der Sicht der Arbeitsmarkt und Berufsforschung', *Arbeit und Sozialpolitik*, 43 (8/9): 238–45.

Bleicken, J. (1978) *Verfassungs und Sozialgeschichte des Römischen Kaiserreiches*, 2 vols, Paderborn: Schöningh.

Böcker, A. and Havinga, T. (1998) *Asylum Migration to the European Union: Patterns of Origin and Destination*, Luxembourg: OOPEC.

Böcker, A. and Minderhoud, P. (1991) 'Immigrants and Social Security: Perspectives of Dutch Implementation Officers and Turkish Clients', paper presented at the International Conference of Law and Society, 26–9 June.

Boer, M. den (1996) 'Justice and Home Affairs: Co-operation without Integration', in H. Wallace and W. Wallace (eds) *Policy-Making in the European Union*, Oxford: Oxford UP.

Bommes, M. (1995) 'Migration and Ethnicity in the National Welfare State', in M. Martiniello (ed.) *Migration, Citizenship and National Identities in the European Union*, Aldershot: Avebury.

Bommes, M. (1996) 'Migration, Nationalstaat und Wohlfahrtsstaat – kommunale Probleme in föderalen Systemen', in K. J. Bade (ed.) *Migration – Ethnizität – Konflikt. Systemfragen und Fallstudien*, IMIS-Schriften, vol. 1, Osnabrück: Universitätsverlag Rasch.

Bommes, M. (1997) 'Von 'Gastarbeitern' zu Einwanderern. Arbeitsmigration in Niedersachsen', in K. J. Bade (ed.) *Fremde im Land. Zuwanderung und Eingliederung im Raum Niedersachsen seit dem Zweiten Weltkrieg*, IMIS-Schriften, vol. 3, Osnabrück: Universitätsverlag Rasch.

Bommes, M. (1999) *Migration und nationaler Wohlfahrtsstaat. Ein differenzierungstheoretischer Entwurf*, Opladen and Wiesbaden: Westdeutscher Verlag.

Bommes, M., Castles, S. and Wihtol de Wenden, C. (eds) (1999) *Migration and Social Change in Australia, France and Germany*, IMIS-Beiträge, 13, special issue, Osnabrück: Universitätsverlag Rasch.

Bommes, M. and Halfmann J. (1994) 'Migration und Inklusion. Spannungen zwischen Nationalstaat und Wohlfahrtsstaat', *Kölner Zeitschrift für Soziologie und Sozialpsychologie (KZSS)*, 46: 406–24.

Bommes, M. and Halfmann, J. (eds) (1998) *Migration in nationalen Wohlfahrtsstaaten. Theoretische und vergleichende Untersuchungen*, IMIS-Schriften, vol. 6, Osnabrück: Universitätsverlag Rasch.

Bommes, M. and Rotthoff, U. (1994) 'Europäische Migrationsbewegungen im kommunalen Kontext', in Konrad-Adenauer-Stiftung (ed.) *Interne Studien No. 100*, St. Augustin: Konrad-Adenauer-Stiftung: 93–148.

Bommes, M. and Scherr, A. (1996) 'Exklusionsvermeidung, Inklusionsvermittlung und/oder Exklusionsverwaltung. Zur gesellschaftstheoretischen Bestimmung sozialer Arbeit', *Neue Praxis*, 26: 107–23.

Borre, O. and Scarborough, E. (eds) (1995) *Beliefs in Government*, vol. III: *The Scope of Government*, Oxford: Oxford UP.

Bosch, G. (1998) 'Brauchen wir mehr Ungleichheit auf dem Arbeitsmarkt?', *WSI-Mitteilungen*, 51: 15–5.

Boyer, R. (1995) 'Capital–Labour Relations in OECD Countries: From the Fordist Golden Age to Contrasted National Trajectories', in J. Schor and J. Il You (eds) *The State and Labour: A Global Perspective*, Aldershot: Edward Elgar.

Boyer, R. and Pascal, P. (1991) 'Technical Change, Cumulative Causation and Growth', in OECD Technology and Productivity Programme, *Technology and Productivity: The Challenge of Economic Policy*, Paris: OECD.

Bozarslan, H. (1997) *The Kurdish Question: States and Minorities in the Middle East*, Paris: Presses de Science-Po.

Breuer, M., Faist, T. and Jordan, B. (1995) 'Collective Action, Migration and Welfare States', *International Sociology*, 10: 369–86.

Brimelow, P. (1997) *Alien Nation*, New York: Random House.

Brock, D. (1997) 'Wirtschaft und Staat im Zeitalter der Globalisierung. Von nationalen Volkswirtschaften zur globalisierten Wirtschaft', *Aus Politik und Zeitgeschichte*, 47, 33–4: 12–19.

Brubaker, R. (ed.) (1989a) *Immigration and Politics of Citizenship in Europe and North America*, Washington, DC: German Marshall Fund and University Press of America.

Brubaker, R. (1989b) 'Citizenship and Naturalization: Policies and Politics', in Brubaker 1989a.

Brubaker, R. (1989c) 'Membership without Citizenship: The Economic and Social Rights of Noncitizens', in Brubaker 1989a.

Brubaker, R. (1992) *Citizenship and Nationhood in France and Germany*, Cambridge, Mass.: Harvard UP.

Brubaker, R. (1994) 'Nationhood and the National Question in the Soviet Union and Post-Soviet Eurasia: An Institutionalist Account', *Theory and Society*, 23: 47–78.

Büchtemann, C. F. (1996) 'Zwischen "Beschäftigungswunder" und "Working Poor": Entwicklungen auf dem amerikanischen Arbeitsmarkt', in S. Empter and F. Frick (eds) *Beschäftigungspolitik als ordnungspolitische Aufgabe*, Internationale Beiträge zum Carl Bertelsmann-Preis 1995, Gütersloh: Bertelsmann.

Bull, H. (1977) *The Anarchical Society*, New York: Columbia UP.

Bundesanstalt für Arbeit (1993) *Stellungnahme zur öffentlichen Anhörung über Mißbrauch ausländischer Werkvertrags- und Saisonarbeitnehmer*, Bonn: Bundestagsdrucksache 12/3299.

Bundesanstalt für Arbeit (1998) *Jahresbericht 1997*, Nuremberg.

Bundesministerium für Arbeit und Sozialordnung [Übersetzung] (1995), *Pressemitteilung vom 30.11.1995*, Bonn.

Cabral, M. V. (1997) *Cidadania, Política e Equidade Social em Portugal*, Oeiras: Celta Editora.

Caglar, A. (1995) 'German Turks in Berlin: Social Exclusion and Strategies for Social Mobility', *New Community*, 21: 309–23.

Cairncross, F. and Masani, Z. (1999) 'They're Good for Us', *The Guardian*, 28 December 1999: 17.

Cameron, D. R. (1978) 'The Expansion of the Public Economy: A Comparative Analysis', *American Political Science Review*, 72: 1243–61.

Cameron, D. (1984) 'Social Democracy, Corporatism, Labour Quiescence and the Representation of Economic Interest in Advanced Capitalist Society', in J. J. Goldthorpe (ed.) *Order and Conflict in Contemporary Capitalism*, Oxford: Clarendon Press.

Canada (1994) *Into the 21st Century: A Strategy for Immigration and Citizenship*, Ottawa: Supply and Services Canada.

Carr, E. H. (1945) *Nationalism and After*, London: Macmillan.

Castells, M. and Portes, A. (1989) 'World Underneath: The Origins, Dynamics and Effects of the Informal Economy', in M. Castels, A. Portes and L. Benton (eds) *The Informal Economy: Studies in Advanced and Less advanced Countries*, Baltimore: Johns Hopkins UP.

Castles, S. (1987) *Here for Good. Western Europe's New Ethnic Minorities*, London: Pluto Press.

Castles, S. and Miller, M. (1998) *The Age of Migration*, 2nd ed., New York: Macmillan.

Castles, F. and Mitchell, D. (1993) 'Worlds of Welfare and Families of Nations', in F. Castles (ed.) *Families of Nations*, Aldershot: Dartmouth.

CEC (Commission of the European Communities) (1994a) *Report on the Education of Migrant Worker's Children in the European Union*, COM, 94, 80 final.

CEC (Commission of the European Communities) (1994b) *European Social Policy: A Way Forward for the Union*, COM, 94, 333 final.

CEC (Commission of the European Communities) (1997) *Proposal for a Decision on Establishing a Convention on Rules for the Admission of Third Country Nationals to the Member States of the European Union*, COM, 97, 387 final.

CEC (Commission of the European Communities) (1998) *Social Action Programme 1998–2000*, COM, 98, 259 final.

Cesari, J. (1998) *Musulmans et Républicains. Les Jeunes, l'Islam et la France*, Paris: Complexe.

Cesari, J. (1999) 'Les Anonymes de la Mondialisation', *Cultures et Conflits* (special issue): 33–4.

Chenillet, P. (1990) 'L'immigré et sa Vieillesse', in Alfandari 1990.

Churches Committee for Migrant's in Europe (CCME) (1996) *The Starting Point*, Brussels: CCME.

Cinar, M. (1998) 'The Republican Character of Islamism in Turkey from the prospect of the Political', unpublished PhD. thesis, Bilkent University (Ankara).

Clarke, S. (1987) 'Capitalist Crisis and the Rise of Monetarism', in R. Miliband and D. Saville (eds), *The Socialist Register 1987*, London: Merlin Press.

Clayton, R. and Pontusson, J. (1998) 'The New Politics of the Welfare State Revisited: Welfare Reforms, Public Sector Restructuring and Inegalitarian Trends in Advanced Capitalist Societies', mimeo, Cornell University.

Cohen, J.L. and Arato, A. (1992) *Civil Society and Political Theory*, Cambridge, Mass.: MIT Press.

Cohen, R. (1994) *Frontiers of Identity: The British and the Others*, London: Longman.

Cohen, R. (1997) *Global Diasporas. An Introduction*, London: UCL Press.

Colonomos, A. (1998) 'L'acteur en réseau à l'épreuve de l'international', in M.-C. Smouts (ed.) *Les Nouvelles Relations Internationales: Pratiques et Théories*, Paris: Presses de Sciences-Po.

Commission Nationale Consultative des Droits de l'Homme (1996) *La Lutte Contre le Racisme et la Xénophobie: Exclusion et Droits de l'Homme*, Paris: La Documentation Française.

Commission 1997 *An Action Plan for Free Movement of Workers. Communication from the Commission*, COM (1997) 586 final.

Cornelissen, R. (1996) 'Die Entsendung von Arbeitnehmer innerhalb der Europäischen Gemeinschaft und die soziale Sicherheit', *Recht der Arbeit*, 49: 329–38.

Cornelius, W, Martin, P and Hollifield, J. (1994) *Controlling Immigration. A Global Perspective*, Stanford, Cal.: Stanford UP.

Corsi, G. (1993) 'Die dunkle Seite der Karriere', in D. Baecker (ed.) *Probleme der Form*, Frankfurt-am-Main: Suhrkamp.

Costa, A.B. da (coord.) (1991) *Minorias Étnicas Pobres em Lisboa*, Lisboa, Dep. De Pesquisa Social do Centro de Reflexão Cristã (mimeo).

Council of the European Union (1996) *Press Releases of 24 September 1996*, Brussels.

CPT (Committee for the Prevention of Torture and Inhuman or Degrading Treatment or Punishment) (1991) 'Report to the United Kingdom Government on the visit to the United Kingdom carried out by the CPT from 29 July to 10 August 1990', CPT/Inf, 91, 15, Strasbourg: Council of Europe.

CPT (Committee for the Prevention of Torture and Inhuman or Degrading Treatment or Punishment) (1993), 'Rapport au Gouvernement de la République Française relativ à la visite effectuée par le CPT en France du 27 octobre au 8 Novembre', CPT/Inf, 93, 2, Strasbourg: Council of Europe.

CPT (Committee for the Prevention of Torture and Inhuman or Degrading Treatment or Punishment) (1997) 'CPT 7th General Report', CPT/Inf, 97, 10, Strasbourg: Council of Europe.

Cram, L. (1994) 'The European Commission as a Multi-Organization: Social Policy and IT Policy in the EU', *Journal of European Public Policy*, 1: 195–217.

Crepaz, M. (1998) 'Inclusion versus Exclusion: Political Institutions and Welfare Expenditures', *Comparative Politics*, 31: 61–80.

Crowley, J. (1998) 'The National Dimension of Citizenship in T. H. Marshall', *Citizenship Studies*, 2: 165–78.

Danese, G. (1998) 'Transnational Collective Action in Europe: The Case of Migrants in Italy and Spain', *Journal of Ethnic and Migration Studies*, 24: 715–34.

Däubler, W. (1995) 'Ein Antidumping-Gesetz für die Bauwirtschaft', *Der Betrieb*, 48 (14): 726–31.

Deakin, N. (ed.) (1965) *Colour and the British Electorate. Six Case Studies: Sparkbrook, Brixton, Bradford, Southall, Smethwick, Deptford*, London: Pall Mall Press/Institute of Race Relations.

Deibel, K. (1998) 'Das neue Asylbewerberleistungsrecht', *Zeitschrift für Ausländerrecht (ZAR)*, 1/1998: 28–38.

Dohse, K. (1981) *Ausländische Arbeiter und Bürgerlicher Staat*, Königstein/Ts.: Verlag Anton Main.

Donders, P. (1995) 'Temporary Employment Across Borders. Posting in Accordance with Regulation 1408/71', in IKA Social Security Institute of Greece (ed.) *Second European Conference on Social Security in Europe: The Free Movement Within the European Union: Posting and the Perspectives of Community Coordination in the Context of the Regulation 1408/71*, Crete: 103–46.

Dörr, S. and Faist, Th. (1997) 'Institutional Conditions for the Integration of Immigrants in Welfare States: A Comparison of the Literature on Germany, France, Great Britain, and the Netherlands', *European Journal of Political Research*, 31, 4: 401–26.

Easterly, W. and Levine, R. (1997) 'Africa's Growth Tragedy: Policies and Ethnic Divisions', *Quarterly Journal of Economics*, 112: 1203–50.

Easton, D. (1968) 'Political Science', in D.L. Sills (ed.) *International Encyclopedia of the Social Sciences*, New York/London: Macmillan.

ECAS (Euro Citizens Action Service) (1996) *European Citizenship: Giving Substance to Citizen's Europe in a Revised Treaty*, Brussels: ECAS.

ECRE (European Council on Refugees and Exiles) (1994) *Asylum in Europe*, London: ECRE.

Eichbauer, F. (1996) 'In der Rezession ist Flexibilität gefragt', *Arbeitgeber*, 48(6): 166–9.

Eichenhofer, E. (ed.) (1997) *Social Security of Migrants in the European Union of Tomorrow*, IMIS-Schriften, vol. 4, Osnabrück: Universitätsverlag Rasch.

Eichenhofer, E. (1998) 'Migration und Wohlfahrtsstaat in der Europäischen Union', in Bommes and Halfmann 1998.

Eichhorst, W. (1998) 'European Social Policy between National and Supranational Regulation: Posted Workers in the Framework of Liberalized Services Provision', discussion paper series, Cologne: Max-Planck-Institut für Gesellschaftsforschung.

Eichinger, B. (1995) 'Gleicher Lohn für gleiche Arbeit – Gegen Lohndumping auf den Baustellen. Rede auf der bundesweiten Entsendetagung der IG Metall am 23.9.1995 in Offenbach', unpublished speech, Bonn.

Esping-Andersen, G. (1985a) *Politics against Markets: The Social Democratic Road to Power*, Princeton: Princeton UP.

Esping-Andersen, G (1985b) 'Power and Distributional Regimes', *Politics and Society*, 2: 223–56.

Esping-Andersen, G. (1990) *The Three Worlds of Welfare Capitalism*, Princeton: Princeton UP.

Esping-Andersen, G (1996) 'After the Golden Age', in G. Esping-Andersen (ed.) *Welfare States in Transition: National Adaptations in Global Economies*, London: Sage/UNRISD.

Esser, J., Fach, W. and Simonis, G. (1980) 'Grenzprobleme des Modell Deutschland', *PROKLA*, 40: 40–63.

EUMF (European Union Migrant's Forum) (1996) *Proposals for the Revision of the Treaty on European Union at the Intergovernmental Conference 1996*, Brussels: EUMF.

European Commission (1988) *The Social Policy of the European Community: Looking Ahead to 1992*, Luxembourg.

Fachgemeinschaft BAU Berlin und Brandenburg (1997), *Bauwirtschaftlicher Jahresrückblick 1996 und Ausblick 1997. Neue Wege in der Tarifpolitik*, Berlin.

Faist, T. (1995a) 'Boundaries of Welfare States: Immigrants and Social Rights on the National and Supranational Level', in Miles and Thränhardt 1995.

Faist, Th. (1995b) *Social Citizenship for Whom? Young Turks in Germany and Mexican Americans in the United States*, Aldershot: Avebury.

Faist, T. (1995c) 'Migration in transnationalen Arbeitsmärkten. Zur Kollektivierung und Fragmentisierung sozialer Rechte in Europa', *Zeitschrift für Sozialreform*, 41(1): 108–22.

Faist, T. (1996a) 'Das ethnische Paradox und die Integration von Immigranten: Zur Bedeutung von sozialem und symbolischem Kapital in vergleichender Perspektive', *Peripherie*, 64: 70–95.

Faist, T. (1996b) 'Immigration, Integration and the Welfare State: Germany and the USA in a Comparative Perspective', in R. Bauböck, A. Heller and A. Zolberg (eds) *The Challenge of Diversity*, Aldershot: Avebury.

Faist, T. (1999) 'Developing Transnational Social Spaces: The Turkish–German Example', in Pries 1999.

Fassmann, H. and Münz, R. (eds) (1994) *European Migration in the Late Twentieth Century: Historical Patterns, Actual Trends and Social Implications*, Aldershot: Edward Elgar.

Favell, A. (1998a) 'The European Citizenship Agenda: Emergence, Transformation and Effects of a New Political Field', paper presented at the 11th Conference of Europeanists, Baltimore, 26 February–1 March.

Favell, A. (1998b) *Philosophies of Integration: Immigration and the Idea of Citizenship in France and Britain*, Basingstoke: Macmillan.

Favell, A. and Geddes, A. (2000) 'Immigration and European integration: New Opportunities for Transnational Political Mobilisation?', in R. Koopmans and P. Statham (eds) *Challenging and Defending the Fortress: Political Mobilisation Over Ethnic Difference in Comparative and Transnational Perspective*, Oxford: Oxford UP.

Federal Government's Commissioner for Foreigners' Affairs (1994) *Report by the Federal Government's Commissioner for Foreigners' Affairs on the Situation of Foreigners in the Federal Republic of Germany in 1993*, Bonn.

Federal Ministry of Interior (1993) *Survey of the Policy and Law Concerning Foreigners in the Federal Republic in Germany*, Bonn.

Feige, E. L. (1990) Defining and Estimating Underground and Informal Economies: The New Institutional Economics Approach, *World Development*, 18(7): 989–1002.

Feldblum, M. (1999) *Reconstructing Citizenship: The Politics of Immigration in Contemporary France*, New York: SUNY Press.

Ferrera, M. (1996) 'The "Southern Model" of Welfare in Social Europe', *Journal of European Social Policy*, 6(1): 17–37.

Fitzmaurice, J. (1998) 'Diversity and Civil Society: The Belgian Case', unpublished manuscript.

Flora, P. and Heidenheimer, A. (1981) 'The Historical Core and Changing Boundaries of the Welfare State', in P. Flora and A. J. Heidenheimer (eds) *The Development of Welfare States in Europe and America*, New Brunswick, NJ: Transaction Books.

Forsberg, T. (1996) 'Beyond Sovereignty, Within Territoriality. Mapping the Space of Late-Modern (Geo)Politics', *Conflict and Cooperation*, 31(4): 355–86.

Foucault, M. (1969) *Discipline and Punish*, London: Tavistock.

França, Luís de (ed.) (1992) *A Comunidade Cabo Verdiana em Portugal*, Lisbon: IED.

France Terre d'Asile (1997) *Reception and Accommodation of Asylum Seekers in Europe*, Paris: France Terre d'Asile.

Franzen, M. (1996) 'Gleicher Lohn für gleiche Arbeit am gleichen Ort', *Deutsche Zeitschrift für Wirtschaftsrecht*, 6(3): 89–101.

Freeman, G. (1986) 'Migration and the Political Economy of the Welfare State', *Annals of the American Academy of Political and Social Science*, 485: 51–63.

Freeman, G. P. (1995) 'Modes of Immigration Politics in Liberal Democracies', *International Migration Review*, 29: 881–902.

Freeman, G. and Jupp, J. (1992) *Nations of Immigrants: Australia, the United States, and International Migration*, Melbourne: Oxford UP.

Freyssenet, M. (1998) 'Reflective Production: An Alternative to Mass Production and Lean Production', *Economic and Industrial Democracy*, 19: 1.

Friedman, M. (1962) *Capitalism and Freedom*, Chicago: University of Chicago Press.

Fuchs, P. (1997) 'Weder Herd noch Heimstatt – Weder Fall noch Nichtfall. Doppelte Differenzierung im Mittelalter und in der Moderne', *Soziale Systeme*, 3(2): 413–37.

Fuchs, R. (1995) *Ausländerbeschäftigung. Dargestellt unter besonderer Berücksichtigung ausländischer Subunternehmen in der Bauwirtschaft*, Stuttgart: Poeschel.

Geddes, A. (1998) 'The Representation of "Migrant's Interests" in the European Union', *Journal of Ethnic and Migration Studies*, 24(4): 695–714.

Geddes, A. (2000) *Immigration and European Integration: Towards Fortress Europe?*, Manchester: Manchester UP.

Geddes, A. and Favell, A. (1999) *The Politics of Belongings: Migrants and Minorities in Contemporary Europe*, Aldershot: Ashgate.

Geißler, R. (1996) *Die Sozialstruktur Deutschlands*, Opladen/Wiesbaden: Westdeutscher Verlag.

Gellner, E. (1983) *Nations and Nationalism*, Oxford: Basil Blackwell.

Giddens, A. (1981) *A Contemporary Critique of Historical Materialism*, London: Macmillan.

Giddens, A. (1985) *The Nation-State and Violence*, Cambridge: Polity Press.

Giddens, A. (1990) *The Consequences of Modernity*, Cambridge: Polity Press.

Gilens, M. (1995) 'Racial Attitudes and Opposition to Welfare', *Journal of Politics*. 57(4): 994–1014.

Gilens, M. (1996) 'Race Coding and White Opposition to Welfare', *American Political Science Review*, 90(3): 593–604.

Gill, S. (1998) 'European Governance and New Constitutionalism: Economic and Monetary Union and Alternatives to Disciplinary Neo-Liberalism in Europe', *New Political Economy*, 3(1): 5–26.

Gill, S. and Law, D. (1989) Global Hegemony and the Structural Power of Capital, *International Studies Quarterly*, 33: 475–99.

Glatzer, M. (1997) 'Rigidity and Flexibility: Patterns of Labor Market Policy Change in Portugal and Spain 1981–1993', paper presented at the Conference on Unemployment's Effects, Princeton University (November).

Goodwin-Gill, G. (1996) *The Refugee in International Law*, Oxford: Clarendon Press.

Gould, S. and Palmer, J. (1988) 'Outcomes, Interpretations, and Policy', in J. Palmer, T. Smeeding and B. Torrey (eds) *The Vulnerable*, Washington, DC: The Urban Institute.

Grawert, R. (1973) *Staat und Staatsangehörigkeit. Verfassungsgeschichtliche Untersuchung zur Entstehung der Staatsangehörigkeit*, Berlin: Duncker and Humblot.

Grawert, R. (1984) 'Staatsangehörigkeit und Staatsbürgerschaft', *Der Staat*, 23: 179–204.

Grawert, R. (1987) 'Staatsvolk und Staatsangehörigkeit', in Isensee and Kirchhof 1987.

Greenwood, J. (1997) *Representing Interests in the European Union*, London: Macmillan.

Groenendijk, C. A. (1989) 'Nationality and Access to Employment in the Public Service: Law and Practice in the Netherlands', *Netherlands International Law Review*, 36(2): 107–30.

Groenendijk, K. and Hampsink, R. (1994) *Temporary Employment of Migrants in Europe*, Nijmegen: Reeks Recht and Samenleving.

Guild, E. (1998) 'Competence, Discretion and Third Country Nationals: The European Union's Legal Struggle with Migration', *Journal of Ethnic and Migration Studies*, 24(4): 613–26.

Guillén, A. (1997) 'Welfare State Development in Spain', in MIRE, *Comparing Social Welfare Systems in Southern Europe*, Paris: MIRE.

Guiraudon, V. (1998) 'The Marshallian Triptych Re-Ordered? Institutional Pre-Conditions for an Inclusive Regime for Migrants Welfare Benefits', paper presented to the Conference on Migration and the Welfare State in Contemporary Europe, European University Institute, Florence, May.

Gunn, L. (1984) 'Why is Implementation so Difficult?', *Management Services in Government*, 33: 169–76.

Habermas, J. (1975) *Legitimation Crisis*, Boston: Beacon Press.

Habermas, J. (1994) 'Citizenship and National Identity', in B. van Steenbergen (ed.) *The Condition of Citizenship*, London: Sage.

Hahn, A. (1988) 'Biographie und Lebenslauf', in H.-G. Brose and B. Hildenbrand (eds) *Vom Ende des Individuums zur Individualität ohne Ende*, Opladen: Leske and Budrich.

Hailbronner, K. (1989) *Ausländerrecht*, 2nd ed., Heidelberg: C. F. Müller Juristischer Verlag.

Halfmann, J. (1995) 'Moderne Gesellschaft und die Konstruktion einer nationalen Solidargemeinschaft. Zur Bedeutung eines neuen Nationalismus in der Bundesrepublik Deutschland', in H. Timmermann (ed.) *Die Kontinentwerdung Europas*, Berlin: Duncker and Humblot.

Halfmann, J. (1997) 'Immigration and Citizenship in Germany. Contemporary Dilemmas', *Political Studies*, 45(2): 260–74.

Halfmann, J. (1998) 'Citizenship Universalism, Migration and the Risks of Exclusion', *British Journal of Sociology*, 4: 513–33.

Halfmann, J. and Bommes, M. (1998) 'Staatsbürgerschaft, Inklusionsvermittlung und Migration. Zum Souveränitätsverlust des Wohlfahrtsstaates', in Bommes and Halfmann 1998.

Hall, S. (1979) 'The Great Moving Right Show', *Marxism Today*, 23: 1.

Hammar, T. (1990) *Democracy and the Nation State : Aliens, Denizens and Citizens in a World of International Migration*, Aldershot: Avebury.

Handoll, A. (1995) *Free Movement of Persons in the EU*, Chichester: John Wiley and Sons.

Hannerz, U. (1992) *Cultural Complexity: Studies in the Social Meaning of Organisation*, New York: Columbia UP.

Hantrais, L. (1995) *Social Policy in the European Union*, Basingstoke: Macmillan.

Harlow, C. (1994) 'Accidental Loss of an Asylum Seeker', *Modern Law Review*, July: 620–6.

Harrod, J. (1998) *Globalization or Corporatization: Labor and Social Forces in the Global Political Economy*, Annual Meeting of the International Studies Association, Minneapolis, USA, March 17–21.

Harvey, D. (1989) *The Condition of Postmodernity*, Oxford: Basil Blackwell.

Hathaway, J. A. (1991) *The Law of Refugee Status*, Vancouver: Butterworth.

Hauptverband der Deutschen Bauindustrie (1996) *Gestern. Heute. Morgen. Bauen setzt Zeichen*, Wiesbaden.

Haut Conseil à l'Intégration (1991) *La Connaissance de l'Immigration et de l'Intégration*, Paris: La Documentation Française.

Hay, C. and Watson, M. (1998) *Rendering the Contingent Necessary: New Labour's Neo-Liberal Conversion and the Discourse of Globalisation*, working paper 8.4, Center for European Studies, Program for the Study of Germany and Europe, Harvard University.

Hayek, F. (1944) *The Road to Serfdom*, London: Routledge.

Hayek, F. (1960) *The Constitution of Liberty*, Chicago: University of Chicago Press.

Heclo, H (1974) *Modern Social Politics in Britain and Sweden: From Relief to Income Maintenance*, New Haven: Yale UP.

Heclo, H. and Wildavsky, A (1981) *The Private Government of Public Money: Community and Policy inside British Politics*, 2nd ed., London: Macmillan.

Heidegger, M. (1979) *Prolegomena zur Geschichte des Zeitbegriffs*, Collected Works, vol. 20, Frankfurt-am-Main: Klostermann.

Heinelt, H. and Lohmann, A. (1992) *Immigraten im Wohlfahrtsstaat am Beispiel der Rechtspositionen und Lebensverhältnisse von Aussiedlern*, Opladen: Leske and Budrich.

Heisler, M. and Heisler, B. (1990) 'Citizenship – Old, New and Changing: Inclusion, Exclusion and Limbo for Ethnic Groups and Migrants in the Modern Democratic State', in J. Fijalkowski, H. Merkens and F. Schmidt (eds) *Dominant National Cultures and Ethnic Identities*, Berlin: Free University.

Helleiner, E. (1994) *States and the Re-Emergence of Global Finance*, Ithaca: Cornell UP.

Herbert, U. (1990) *A History of Foreign Labor in Germany*, Ann Arbor: University of Michigan Press.

Herz, J. (1956/7) 'Rise and Demise of the Territorial State', *World Politics*, 9: 473–93.

Heymann-Doat, A. (1994) *Libertés Publiques et Droits de l'Homme*, Paris: Librairie Générale de Droit et de Jurisprudence.

Hicks, A. and Misra, J. (1993) 'Political Resources and Growth of Welfare in Affluent Capitalist Democracies, 1960–1982', *American Journal of Sociology*, 99(3): 668–710.

Hicks, A. and Swank, D. (1992) 'Politics, Institutions and Welfare Spending in Industrialized Democracies, 1960–82', *American Political Science Review*, 86(3): 658–74.

Hinrichs, K. (1996) 'Perspektiven des deutschen Auslandbaus', unpublished manuscript, Bonn.

Hix, S. (1999) *The Political System of the European Union*, London: Macmillan.

Hix, S. and Niessen, J. (1996) *Reconsidering European Migration Policies: The 1996 Intergovernmental Conference and the Reform of the Maastricht Treaty*, Brussels: Churches Commission for Migrants in Europe.

HMSO (Her Majesty's Stationery Office) (1998) *Fairer, Faster and Firmer – A Modern Approach to Immigration and Asylum*, Cm 4018, London: HMSO.

Hoffmann, S. (1966) 'Obstinate or Obsolete? The Fate of the Nation State and the Case of Western Europe', *Daedalus*, 95: 892–908.

Hohm, K.-H. (1997) 'Novellierung des Asylbewerberleistungsgesetzes', *Neue Zeitschrift für Verwaltungsrecht (NVwZ)*, 1997: 659–63.

Hold, D. (1996) 'Arbeitnehmer–Entsendegesetz Gegen Lohndumping und Illegale Beschäftigung im Baugewerbe', *Arbeit und Arbeitsrecht*, 51(4): 113–17.

Hollifield, J. F. (1992) *Immigrants, Markets and States: the Political Economy of Post-War Europe*, Cambridge, Mass./London: Harvard UP.

Hollifield, J. (1994) 'Immigration and Republicanism in France: The Hidden Consensus', in Cornelius, Martin and Hollifield 1994.

Hollifield, J. (1997) *Immigration et l'Etat Nation: à la Recherche d'un Modèle National*, Paris: L'Harmattan.

Hollifield, J. (1998) 'Grand Bargain Strategies for Immigration and Immigrant Policy', paper presented at the Conference on Migration and the Welfare State in Contemporary Europe, European University Institute, Florence, May.

Hommelhoff, P. and Kirchhof, P. (eds) (1994) *Der Staatenverbund der europäischen Union*, Heidelberg: Müller.

Hönekopp, E. (1996) *Old and New Labour Migration to Germany from Eastern Europe*, working paper no. D 2/ 10–1996, Nuremberg: Institute for Employment Research.

Horowitz, D. (1977) *The Courts and Social Policy*, Washington, DC: Brookings Institute.

Houzé de l'Aulnoit, A. (1885) *Les Ouvriers Belges à Lille. Etude sur les Conditions d'Admissibilité des Indigents Étrangers aux Secours Publics*, Lille: Banel.

Huber, E., Ragin, C. and Stephens, J. (1993) 'Social Democracy, Christian Democracy, Constitutional Structure, and the Welfare State', *American Journal of Sociology*, 99(3): 711–49.

Hunger, U. (1998) 'Arbeitskräftewanderungen im Baugewerbe der Europäischen Union. Problemanzeigen, Regelungsversuche und Schlußfolgerungen für die zukünftige Beschäftigung von Ausländern in Deutschland', in D. Thränhardt (ed.) *Einwanderung und Einbürgerung in Deutschland*, Yearbook Migration 97/98, Münster/London: Lit.

Hunger, U. (2000) *Von Kontinentaleuropäischen zu Angloamerikanischen Arbeitsmarktbeziehungen? Eine International Vergleichende Policy-Analyse zum Paragidmenwechsel in den Arbeitsmarktbeziehungen am Beispiel der Deutschen Bauwirtschaft*, Baden-Baden: Nomos.

Huntington, S. (1975) *The Crisis of Democracy: Report on the Governability of Democracies to the Trilateral Commission*, New York: New York UP.

Huntington, S. (1981) *American Politics. The Promise of Disharmony*, Cambridge, Mass.: Harvard UP.

Huysmans, J. (1995) 'Migrants as a Security Problem: Dangers of "Securitizing" Social Issues', in Miles and Thränhardt 1995.

Immergut, E. (1992) *Health Politics: Interests and Institutions in Western Europe*, Cambridge: Cambridge UP.

ILPA (Immigration Law Practitioners Association) (1997) *European Update*, London, ILPA.

Ireland, P. (1994) *The Policy Challenge of Ethnic Diversity: Immigrant Politics in France and Switzerland*, Cambridge, Mass.: Harvard UP.

Isensee, J. and Kirchhof, P. (eds) (1987) *Handbuch des Staatsrechts der Bundesrepublik Deutschland*, vol. 1, Heidelberg: Müller, Jur. Verlag

Ismael, T. Y. and Ismael, J. S. (1994) *The Gulf War and the New World Order. International Relations of the Middle East*, Gainesville, Fla.: UP of Florida.

Jacobsen, D. (1996) *Rights Across Borders: Immigration and the Decline of Citizenship*, Baltimore: Johns Hopkins UP.

James, E. (1987) 'The Public/Private Division of Responsibility for Education: An International Comparison', *Economics of Education Review*, 6(1): 1–14.

James, E. (1993) 'Why Do Different Countries Choose a Different Public/Private Mix of Educational Services?', *Journal of Human Resources*, 28(3): 531–92.

Jenson, J. (1989) 'Paradigms and Political Discourse: Protective Legislation in France and the United States', *Canadian Journal of Political Science*, 22(2): 235–58.

Joppke, C. (1997) 'Asylum and State Sovereignty: A Comparison of the United States, Germany and Britain', *Comparative Political Studies*, 30(3): 259–98.

Joppke, C, (1998) *Immigration and the Nation State*, Oxford: Oxford UP.

Junker, A. (1992) *Internationales Arbeitsrecht im Konzern*, Tübingen: Mohr.

Kahl, B. (1994) 'Europäische Union: Bundesstaat – Staatenbund – Staatenverbund? Zum Urteil des BverfG vom 12. Oktober 1993', *Der Staat*, 30: 241–58.

Kälin, W. (1997) *Die Bedeutung der EMRK für Asylsuchende und Flüchtlinge: Materialien und Hinweise*, Siegburg : Zentrale Dokumentationsstelle der Freien Wohlfahrtspflege für Flüchtlinge e.V.

Kaplinsky, R. (1988) *Automation: The New Technology and Society*, Geneva: ILO.

Katzenstein, P. (1987) *Policy and Politics in West-Germany: The Growth of a Semi-Sovereign State*, Philadelphia: Temple UP.

Kaufmann, F.-X. (1997) *Herausforderungen des Sozialstaates*, Frankfurt-am-Main: Suhrkamp.

Kaye, R. (1998) 'Redefining the Refugee: The UK Media Portrayal of Asylum-Seekers', in K. Koser and H. Lutz (eds) *The New Migration in Europe: Social Constructions and Social Realities*, London: Macmillan.

Keck, M. and Sikkink, K. (1998) *Activists Beyond Borders: Advocacy Networks in International Politics*, Ithaca, NY: Cornell UP.

Keohane, R. (1989) 'International Institutions: Two Approaches', in R. Keohane (ed.) *International Institutions and State Power: Essays in International Relations Theory*, Boulder, Col.: Westview.

Keohane, R. O. and Nye, J.-S. (1972) *Transnational Relations and World Politics*, Cambridge: Harvard UP.

Kepel, G. (1991) *La Revanche de Dieu*, Paris: Seuil.

Kersbergen, K. van (1997) *The Declining Resistance of National Welfare States to Change?*, Nijmegen: Catholic University.

Khosrokhavar, F. (1996) 'L'Universel Abstrait, le Politique et la Construction de l'Islamisme comme Forme d'Altérité', in M. Wieviorka (ed.) *Une société Fragmentée? Le Multiculturalsime en Débat*, Paris: La Découverte.

Kindleberger, C. P. (1967) *Europe's Postwar Growth: The Role of Labor Supply*, Cambridge, Mass.: Harvard UP.

Kitschelt, H. (1995) *The Radical Right in Western Europe: A Comparative Analysis*, Ann Arbor: University of Michigan Press.

Köbele, B. (1994) 'Europäischer Arbeitsmarkt – Grenzenlos mobil?', in Köbele and Cremers 1994.

Köbele, B. and Cremers, J. (eds) (1994) *Europäische Union: Arbeitnehmerentsendung im Baugewerbe*, Witterschlick and Bonn: Wehle.

Köbele, B. and Sahl, K.-H. (eds) (1993) *Die Zukunft der Sozialkassensysteme der Bauwirtschaft im Europäischen Binnenmarkt*, Köln: Bund.

Kohli, M. (1985) 'Die Institutionalisierung des Lebenslaufs', *Kölner Zeitschrift für Soziologie und Sozialpsychologie (KZSS)*, 37(1): 1–29.

Kohli, M. (1986) 'Gesellschaftszeit und Lebenszeit. Der Lebenslauf im Strukturwandel der Moderne', in J. Berger (ed.) *Die Moderne: Kontinuitäten und Zäsuren, Soziale Welt*, special issue, 4, Göttingen: Schwartz.

Kokott, J. (1996) 'Zur Rechtsstellung von Asylbewerbern in Transitzonen', *Europäische Grundrechte Zeitschrift (EuGRZ)*, 1996: 569–71.

Koopmans, R. (1999) 'Globalisation or Still National Politics? A Comparison of Protests Against the Gulf War in Germany, France, and the Netherlands', in D. Della Porta, H.-P. Kriesi and D. Rucht, *Social Movements in a Globalising World*, New York: Macmillan.

Korpi, W. (1983) *The Democratic Class Struggle*, Boston: Routledge and Kegan Paul.

Korpi, W. (1989) 'Power, Politics and State Autonomy in the Development of Social Citizenship', *American Sociological Review*, 54: 309–28.

Koselleck, R. and Conze, W. (1990) 'Staat und Souveränität', in O. Brunner *et al.* (eds) *Geschichtliche Grundbegriffe*, vol. 6, Stuttgart: Klett-Cotta.

Koslowski, R. (1998) 'EU Migration Regimes: Established and Emergent', in C. Joppke (ed.) *Challenge to the Nation State: Immigration in Western Europe and the United States*, Oxford: Oxford UP.

Kostakopolou, T. (1998) 'European Union citizenship as a model of citizenship beyond the nation state: limits and possibilities', in A. Weale and M. Nentwich (eds) *Political Theory and the European Union: Legitimacy, Constitutional Choice and Citizenship*, London: Routledge.

Kratochwil, F. (1986) 'Of Systems, Boundaries, Territoriality: An Inquiry into the Formation of the State System', *World Politics*, 39(1): 27–52.

Krieger, J. (1992) 'Britain', in M. Kesselman and J. Krieger, *European Politics in Transition*, 2nd ed., Lexington, Mass.: DC Heath.

Kymlicka, W. (1995) *Multicultural Citizenship: A Liberal Theory of Minority Rights*. Oxford: Oxford UP.

Labelle, M. and Midy, F. (1999) 'Re-Reading Citizenship and the Transnational Practices of Immigrants', *Journal of Ethnic and Migration Studies*, 25(2): 213–32.

Lambert, H. (1995) *Seeking Asylum: Comparative Law and Practice in Selected European Countries*, Dordrecht e.a.: Nijhoff.

Lange, P. (1992) 'The Politics of the Social Dimension', in A. M. Sbragia (ed.) *Euro-Politics: Institutions and Policy-Making in the 'New' European Community*, Washington, DC: The Brookings Institution.

Laparra, M. and Hendrickson, M. (1997) 'Social Exclusion and Minimum Income Programs in Spain', in MIRE, *Comparing Social Welfare Systems in Southern Europe*, Paris: MIRE.

Lavenex, S. (1998) 'Transgressing Borders: The Emergent European Refugee Regime and 'Safe Third Countries'', in A. Cafruny and P. Peters, *The Union and the World*, Den Haag: Kluwer.

Layton-Henry, Z. (ed.) (1990) *The Political Rights of Migrant Workers in Western Europe*, London: Sage.

Layton-Henry, Z. (1994) 'Britain: the Would-Be Zero Immigration Country', in Cornelius, Martin and Hollifield 1994.

Leca, J. (1996) 'La démocratie à l'épreuve des pluralismes', *Revue Française de Science Politique*, 46(2): 225–79.

Lehmbruch, G. (1979) 'Liberal Corporatism and Party Government', in P. Schmitter and G. Lehmbruch (eds) *Trends Towards Corporatist Intermediation*, London: Sage.

Leibfried, S. and Pierson, P. (eds) (1995a) *European Social Policy. Between Fragmentation and Integration*, Washington: The Brookings Institution.

Leibfried, S. and Pierson, P. (1995b) 'Semisovereign Welfare States: Social Policy in a Multitiered Europe', in Leibfried and Pierson 1995a.

Lemberg, E. (1950) *Geschichte des Nationalismus in Europa*, Stuttgart: Curt E. Schwab.

Lemberg, E. and Edding, F. (eds) (1959) *Die Vertriebenen in Westdeutschland. Ihre Eingliederung und ihr Einfluß auf Gesellschaft, Wirtschaft, Politik und Geistesleben*, 3 vols, Kiel: Hirt-Verlag.

Lepsius, R.-M. (1990) *Interessen, Ideen und Institutionen*, Opladen: Westdeutscher Verlag.

Leveau, R. (1989) 'Les partis et l'intégration des "beurs"', in Y. Mény (ed.) *Idéologies, partis politiques et groupes sociaux*, Paris: FNSP.

Leveau, R. (ed.) (1991) *Migration und Staat. Inner- und intergesellschaftliche Prozesse am Beispiel Algerien, Türkei, Deutschland und Frankreich*, Münster: Lit.

Levitt, P. (1997) 'Transnationalizing Community Development: The Case of Migration Between Boston and the Dominican Republic', *Nonprofit and Voluntary Sector Quarterly*, 26(4): 509–26.

Lijphart, A. (1968), 'Typologies of Democratic Systems', *Comparative Political Studies*, 1(1): 3–44.

Lijphart, A. (1977) *Democracy in Plural Societies*, New Haven: Yale UP.

Lijphart, A. (1995) 'Self-Determination Versus Pre-Determination of Ethnic Minorities in Power-Sharing Systems', in W. Kymlicka (ed.) *The Rights of Minority Cultures*, Oxford: Oxford UP.

Linz, J. (1989) 'Spanish Democracy and the Estado de las Autonomías', in R. Goodwin and W. Schambru (eds) *Forging Unity Out of Diversity: The Approaches of Eight Nations*, Washington, DC: American Enterprise Institute.

Lipietz, A. (1987) 'The Globalization of the General Crisis of Fordism, 1967–84', in J. Holmes and C. Leys (eds) *Frontyard/Backyard. The Americas in the Global Crisis. Workshop on Development in the 1980s*, Toronto: Between the Lines.

Lipset, S.M. (1996) *American Exceptionalism. A Double-Edged Sword*, New York: Norton.

Lochak, D. (1991) *Egalité des Droits*, Paris: Conseil National des Populations Immigrées.

Lodge, J. (1989) 'Social Europe: Fostering a People's Europe?', in J. Lodge (ed.) *The European Community and the Challenge of the Future*, London: Pinter.

Long, M. (1988) *Etre Français Aujourd'hui et Demain*, Paris: La Documentation Française.

Lucassen, J. and Lucassen, L. (eds) (1997) *Migration, Migration History, History: Old Paradigms and New Perspectives*, Bern: Lang.

Luckmann, T. (1967) *The Invisible Religion*, New York: Macmillan.

Luhmann, N. (1977) *Funktion der Religion*, Frankfurt-am-Main: Suhrkamp.

Luhmann, N. (1982a) 'Politics as a Social System', in N. Luhmann, *The Differentiation of Society*, New York: Columbia UP.

Luhmann, N. (1982b) 'The Differentiation of Society', in N. Luhmann, *The Differentiation of Society*, New York: Columbia UP.

Luhmann, N. (1982c) 'Territorial borders as system boundaries', in R. Strassoldo and G. Delli Zotti (eds) *Cooperation and Conflict in Border Areas*, Milan: Angeli.

Luhmann, N. (1989) 'Individuum, Individualität, Individualismus', in N. Luhmann, *Gesellschaftsstruktur und Semantik. Studien zur Wissenssoziologie der modernen Gesellschaft*, vol. 3, Frankfurt-am-Main: Suhrkamp.

Luhmann, N. (1990a) 'The "State" of the Political System', in N. Luhmann, *Essays on Self-Reference*, New York: Columbia UP.

Luhmann, N. (1990b) 'The World Society as a Social System', in N. Luhmann, *Essays on Self-Reference*, New York: Columbia UP.

Luhmann, N. (1995a) *Social Systems*, Stanford: Stanford UP.

Luhmann, N. (1995b) 'Inklusion und Exklusion', in N. Luhmann, *Soziologische Aufklärung*, vol. 6, Opladen: Westdeutscher Verlag.

Luhmann, N. (1997) *Die Gesellschaft der Gesellschaft*, 2 vols, Frankfurt-am-Main: Suhrkamp.

Lüttinger, P. (1986) 'Der Mythos der schnellen Integration. Eine empirische Untersuchung zur Integration der Vertriebenen und Flüchtlinge in der Bundesrepublik Deutschland bis 1971', *Zeitschrift für Soziologie*, 15(1): 20–36.

Lüttinger, P. (1989) *Integration der Vertriebenen. Eine empirische Analyse*, Frankfurt-am-Main/New York: Campus.

Luvumba, F. (1997) *Minorias Étnicas dos PALOPs Residentes no Grande Porto*, Cadernos REAPN (mimeo).

MacDonald, I. and Blake, N. (1995) *Immigration Law and Practice in the United Kingdom*, 4th ed., London: Butterworths.

McCarty, T. (1993) 'Demographic Diversity and the Size of the Public Sector', *KYKLOS*, 46(2): 225–40.

McLuhan, M. (1965) *Understanding Media. The Extensions of Man*, New York: McGraw-Hill.

Maddison, A. (1982) *Phases of Capitalist Development*, Oxford: Oxford UP.

Majone, G. (1996) *Regulating Europe*, London: Routledge.

Mancini, G. F. (1991) 'The Making of a Constitution for Europe', in R. Keohane and S. Hoffmann (eds) *The New European Community: Decision-Making and Institutional Change*, Boulder, Col.: Westview.

Marks, G. and McAdam, D. (1996) 'Social Movements and the Changing Structure of Political Opportunity in the European Union', in Marks, Scharpf, Schmitter and Streeck 1996.

Marks, G., Scharpf, F., Schmitter, P. and Streeck, W. (eds) (1996) *Governance in the European Union*, London: Sage.

Marshall, T. H. (1950) *Citizenship and Social Class and Other Essays*, Cambridge: Cambridge UP.

Marshall, T. H. (1965) *Class, Citizenship and Social Development*, New York: Doubleday.

Marshall, T. H. (1975) *Social Policy*, London: Hutchinson.

Martin, P. (1997) 'The Impacts of Immigration on Receiving Countries', in E. Uçarer and D. Puchala (eds) *Immigration into Western Societies: Problems and Policies*, London: Pinter, 17–27.

Martiniello, M. (1994) 'Citizenship of the European Union: A Critical View', in R. Bauböck (ed.) *From Aliens to Citizens: Redefining the Status of Immigrants in Europe*, Vienna/Aldershot: European Centre/Avebury.

Marx, R. (1995) *Kommentar zum Asylverfahrensgesetz*, Neuwied e.a.: Luchterhand.

Matl, W. (1997) 'Ein Alptraum vom reinen Schweden', *Die Zeit*, 37, 5 September 1997: 13–15.

Mazey, S. and Richardson, J. (eds) (1993) *Lobbying in the European Community*, Oxford: Oxford UP.

Meehan, E. (1993) *Citizenship and the European Community*, London: Sage.

Menting, E. (1993) *Probleme und Perspektiven der Arbeitnehmerüberlassung*, PhD. Thesis, University of Cologne.

Meyer, J. W. (1980) 'The World Polity and the Authority of the Nation-State', in A. Bergesen (ed.) *Studies of the Modern World System*, New York: Academic Press.

Miles, R. and Thränhardt, D. (eds) (1995) *Migration and European Integration. The Dynamics of Inclusion and Exclusion*, London: Pinter.

Miller, D. (1995) *On Nationality*, Oxford: Oxford UP.

Minderhoud, P. (1994) *Short Overview of the Dutch Social Security System Concerning Aliens*, mimeo, available from the author.

Ministerium für Arbeit, Soziales, Gesundheit und Frauen des Landes Brandenburg (1993) *Arbeitsschutz im Baugewerbe. Ergebnisse einer Schwerpunktaktion der Arbeitsschutzverwaltung des Landes Brandenburg*, Potsdam.

Mishra, R. (1984) *The Welfare State in Crisis*, Brighton: Wheatsheaf.

Moch, L. Page (1992) *Moving Europeans. Migration in Western Europe since 1650*, Bloomington, Ind.: Indiana UP.

Molle, W. and van Mourik, A. (1988) 'International Movements of Labour under Conditions of Economic Integration. The Case of Western Europe', *Journal of Common Market Studies*, 26(3): 317–42.

Mommsen, W. J. (1996) 'Nationalität im Zeichen offensiver Weltpolitik. Das Reichs- und Staatsangehörigkeitsgesetz des Deutschen Reiches vom 22. Juni 1993', in M. Hettling and P. Nolte (eds) *Nation und Gesellschaft in Deutschland. Historische Essays*, München: C. H. Beck.

Monar, J. and Morgan, R. (eds) (1994) *The Third Pillar of the European Union*, Brussels: European Interuniversity Press.

Monteiro, V. (1995) *Portugal/Crioulo*, Praia: ICL.

Moravcsik, A. (1998) *The Choice for Europe: Social Purpose and State Power from Messina to Maastricht*, London: UCL Press.

Moruzzi, N.-C. (1994) 'A Problem with Headscarves. Contemporary Complexities of Political and Social Identity', *Political Theory*, 22(4): 653–72.

Mueller, D. and Murrell, P. (1986) 'Interest Groups and the Size of Government', *Public Choice*, 48: 125–45.

Murphy, A. B. (1996) 'The Sovereign State System as Political-Territorial Ideal: Historical and Contemporary Considerations', in Th. J. Biersteker and C. Weber (eds) *State Sovereignty as a Social Construct*, Cambridge: Cambridge UP.

Nielsen, R. and Szyszcak, E. (1991) *The Social Dimension of the European Community*, Copenhagen: Handelshøjskolens Forlag.

Noiriel, G. (1988) *Le creuset français: histoire de l'immigration, XIXe–Xxe*, Paris: Seuil.

North, D. (1990) *Institutions, Institutional Change and Economic Performance*, Cambridge: Cambridge UP.

North, D., Wihtol de Wenden, C. and Taylor, Ch. (1987) 'Non-Citizens' Access to Social Services in Six Countries: Canada, FRG, France, Sweden, UK, and US', paper written for the Citizenship/Naturalization Conference, sponsored by the German Marshall Fund of the United States, Berkeley Springs, West Virginia.

Nowak, M. (1993) *UN Covenant on Civil and Political Rights*, Kehl am Rhein e.a.: Engel.

Nuscheler, F. (1995) *Internationale Migration. Flucht und Asyl*, Opladen: Leske and Budrich.

Nuyen van Yen, Ch. (1990) 'La santé de l'immigré', in Alfandari 1990.

Oberndörfer, D. (1991) *Die offene Republik. Zur Zukunft Deutschland und Europas*, Freiburg i.Br.: Herder Spektrum.

(OECD) Organisation for Economic and Social Development (1994) *New Orientations for Social Policy*, Paris: OECD.

(OECD) Organisation for Economic and Social Development (forthcoming) *The Caring World: National Achievements*, Paris: OECD.

Oellers-Frahm, K. and Zimmermann, A. (1995) 'France's and Germany's Constitutional Changes and their Impact on Migration Law – Policy and Practice', *German Yearbook of International Law*, 38: 249–83.

Offe, C. (1985) *Contradictions of the Welfare State* Cambridge, Mass.: MIT Press.

Offe, C. (1996) *Modernity and the State*, Cambridge: Polity Press.

Offe, C. (1998) 'Demokratie und Wohlfahrtsstaat: Eine Europäische Regimeform unter dem Streß der Europäischen Integration', in Streeck 1998a.

Offe, C. (1999) 'The German Welfare State: Principles, Performance and Prospects after Unification', in J. Brady, B. Crawford and S.E. Wiliarty (eds) *Germany Transformed? Culture, Structure and Institutions in Postwar Germany*, Ann Arbor, Mi.: University of Michigan Press.

'Opwet-Minderhedennota' (1981) Ministry of Interior. The Hague. For the English version of the Ministry of Interior letter and policy document, see 'Policy on the Integration of Ethnic Minorities'. Lower House 1993–4, 23684, 1–2, Staatsuitgeverij, The Hague.

Orloff, A. (1988) 'The Political Origins of America's Belated Welfare State', in M. Weir, A. Orloff, and T. Skocpol (eds) *The Politics of Social Policy in the United States*, Princeton, NJ: Princeton UP.

Otto, K. A. (1990) 'Aussiedler und Aussiedlerpolitik im Spannungsfeld von Menschenrechten und Kaltem Krieg. Historische, politisch-moralische und rechtliche Aspekte der Aussiedlerpolitik', in K. A. Otto (ed.) *Westwärts – Heimwärts. Aussiedlerpolitik zwischen 'Deutschtümelei' und Verfassungsauftrag*, Bielefeld: AJZ-Verlag.

Panitch, L. (1979) 'Corporatism in Liberal Democracies', in P. Schmitter and G. Lehmbruch (eds) *Trends Towards Corporatist Intermediation*, London: Sage.

Papademetriou, D. (1996) *Coming Together or Pulling Apart? The European Union's Struggle with Immigration and Asylum*, Washington: Carnegie Endowment for International Peace.

Parsons, T. (1951) *The Social System*, Glencoe, Ill.: The Free Press.

Penna, S. and O'Brien, M. (1996) 'Postmodernism and Social Policy: A Small Step Forwards?' *Journal of Social Policy*, 25(1): 39–61.

Pernack, E.-F. (1996) 'Arbeitssicherheit auf Baustellen – eine Analyse aus der Sicht des Bundeslandes Brandenburg', in Bundesanstalt für Arbeitsschutz (ed.) *Arbeitsschutz in der Bauwirtschaft: Sicherheit und Gesundheit bei Bauarbeiten und auf Baustellen: Vorträge der Informationstagung am 9./10. Mai 1995 in Dortmund*, Bremerhaven: Wirtschaftsverlag Neue Wissenschaft.

Perrineau, P. (1995) *Le Vote de Crise*, Paris: Presses de la FNSP.

Peterson, J. (1995) 'Decision-making in the European Union: Towards a Framework for Analysis', *Journal of European Public Policy*, 2(1): 69–93.

Picareta, L. (1995) 'Interview mit zwei portugiesischen Bauarbeitern', in B. Köbele and G. Leuschner (eds) *Dokumentation der Konferenz 'Europäischer Arbeitsmarkt. Grenzenlos mobil?' 06. bis 08. März 1995 in Bonn*, Baden-Baden: Nomos.

Pierson, P. (1993) 'When Effect Becomes Cause: Policy Feedback and Political Change', *World Politics*, 45: 595–628.

Pierson, P. (1994) *Dismantling the Welfare State? Reagan, Thatcher and the Politics of Retrenchment*, Cambridge: Cambridge UP.

Pierson, P. (1995) 'The New Politics of the Welfare State', ZeS-Working Papers, Zentrum für Sozialpolitik, Bremen: University of Bremen.

Pierson, P. (1996a) 'The Path to European Integration: An Historical Institutionalist Approach', *Comparative Political Studies*, 29(2): 123–63.

Pierson, P. (1996b) 'The New Politics of the Welfare State', *World Politics*, 48 (January): 143–79.

Pierson, P. (1997) 'Path Dependency, Increasing Returns, and the Study of Politics', unpublished paper.

Pierson, P. and Leibfried, S. (1995) 'Multitiered Institutions and the Making of Social Policy', in Leibfried and Pierson 1995a.

Pieters, D. (1994) *Federalisme Voor Onze Sociale Zekerheid*, Leuven: Acco.

Pijl, K. van der (1978) *Een Amerikaans Plan voor Europa*, Amsterdam: SUA.

Piore, M. (1979) *Birds of Passage: Migrant Labor and Industrial Societies*, Cambridge: Cambridge UP.

Plant, R. (1991) 'Social Rights and the Reconstruction of Welfare', in G. Andrews (ed.) *Citizenship*, London: Lawrence and Wishart.

Plant, R. (1994) 'Citizenship and Political Change', in D. Miliband (ed.) *Reinventing the Left*, London: Polity Press.

Plender, J. (1988) *International Migration Law*, 2nd ed., Dordrecht: Martinus Nijhoff.

Polanyi, K. (1957) *The Great Transformation*, Boston: Beacon Press.

Pontusson, J. and Clayton, R (1998) 'The New Politics of the Welfare State Revisited: Welfare Reforms, Public-Sector Restructuring, and Inegalitarian Trends in Advanced Capitalist Societies', paper presented in the 1997/8 luncheon seminar series of the Robert Schuman Center, Florence, Italy.

Portes, A. (1994) 'The Informal Economy and Its Paradoxes', in N. Smelser and R. Swedberg (eds) *The Handbook of Economic Sociology*, New York: Russell Sage Foundation.

Portes, A. (ed.) (1995) *The Economic Sociology of Immigration. Essays on Networks, Ethnicity and Entrepreneurship*, New York: Russell Sage Foundation.

Portes, A. (1999) 'La Mondialisation aprez le Bas. L'Émergence des Communautés Transnationales', *Actes de la Recherche en Sciences Sociales*, 129: 15–25.

Pressman, J. and Wildavsky, A. (1973) *Implementation*, Berkeley, University of California Press.

Prétot, X. (1990) 'L'immigré et son travail', in Alfandari 1990.

Pries L. (1999) *Migration and Transnational Social Spaces*, Aldershot: Ashgate.

Puskeppeleit, J. and Thränhardt, D. (1990) *Vom betreuten Ausländer zum gleichberechtigten Bürger*, Freiburg: Lambertus.

Quadagno, J. (1988) *The Transformation of Old Age Security: Class Politics in the American Welfare State*, Chicago: University of Chicago Press.

Quadagno, J. (1990) 'Race, Class and Gender in the United States Welfare State: Nixon's Failed Family Assistance Plan', *American Sociological Review*, 55: 11–28.

Quadagno, J. (1994) *The Color of Welfare: How Racism Undermined the War on Poverty*, New York: Oxford UP.

Randall, C. (1994) 'An Asylum Policy for the UK', in S. Spencer (ed.) *Strangers and Citizens*, London: IPPR/Rivers Oram Press.

Randelzhofer, A. (1987) 'Staatsgewalt und Souveränität', in Isensee and Kirchhof 1987.

Radtke, F.O. (1997) 'Multiculturalism in Welfare States: The Case of Germany', in M. Guibernau and J. Rex. (eds) *The Ethnicity Reader: Nationalism, Multiculturalism and Migration*, London: Polity Press.

Rath, J. (1988) 'La Participation des Immigrés aux Élections Locales aux Pays-Bas', *Revue Européenne des Migrations Internationales*, 4(3): 23–36.

Rawls, J. (1971) *A Theory of Justice*, Cambridge, Mass.: Harvard UP.

Reform Party of Canada (1997a) *A Fresh Start for Canadians*, Calgary: Reform Party.

Reform Party of Canada (1997b) *Blue Sheet: Principles and Policies of the Reform Party of Canada – 1996–97*, Calgary: Reform Party.

Regioconsult (1995) *Berlin: Zentrum für innovatives Bauen. Voraussetzungen und Ansatzpunkte*, Gutachten für die Handelskammer zu Berlin, Berlin.

Reich, R. (1993) *Die Neue Weltwirtschaft. Das Ende der Nationalen Ökonomie*, Frankfurt-on-Main: Fischer.

Reichling, G. (1995) *Die Deutschen Vertriebenen in Zahlen. Teil 1: Umsiedler, Verschleppte, Vertriebene, Aussiedler 1940–1985*, Bonn: Kulturstiftung der Deutschen Vertriebenen.

Reidegeld, E. (1998) 'Armenpflege und Migration von der Gründung des Deutschen Bundes bis zum Erlaß des Gesetzes über den Unterstützungswohnsitz', in Bommes and Halfmann 1998.

Reim, U. and Sandbrink, S. (1996) *Die Werkvertragsabkommen als Entsenderegelung für Arbeitnehmer aus den Staaten Mittel- und Osteuropas*, ZeS-Working-Paper, Zentrum für Sozialpolitik, Bremen: University of Bremen.

Rheinisch-Westfälisches Institut für Wirtschaftsforschung Essen (1997) *Ökonomische Bedeutung der Ausländischen Bevölkerung in Rheinland-Pfalz unter Besonderer Berücksichtigung Arbeitsmarkt- und Finanzpolitischer Aspekte*. Gutachten Gefördert durch die Landesbeauftragte für Ausländerfragen und durch das Ministerium für Arbeit, Soziales und Gesundheit des Landes Rheinland Pfalz, Essen.

Rhodes, M. and van Apeldoorn, B. (1998) 'Does Migration from Less Developed Countries Erode the Welfare State?', paper presented at the conference 'Migration and the Welfare State in Contemporary Europe', European University Institute, Florence, May 21–3.

Richardson, J. (1996), 'Eroding EU Policies: Implementation, Gaps, Cheating and Re-Steering', in J. Richardson (ed.) *European Union: Power and Policy-Making*, London: Routledge.

Rico, A. (1997) 'Regional Decentralization and Health Care Reform in Spain (1976–1996)', in MIRE, *Comparing Social Welfare Systems in Southern Europe*, Paris: MIRE.

274   *References*

Risse-Kappen, Th. (ed.) (1995) *Bringing Transnational Relations back in. Non-State Actors, Domestic Structures and International Institutions*, Cambridge: Cambridge UP.

Ritmeijer, W. (1994) 'Die Entsendung im Baugewerbe', in Köbele and Cremers 1994.

Ritmeijer, W. (1998) 'Zu den Nationalstaatlichen Regelungen gegen Lohn– und Sozialdumping in den Niederlanden', unpublished working paper, Amsterdam.

Robson, P. (1987) *The Economics of International Integration*, London: Allen and Unwin.

Rosenau, J. (1980) *The Study of Global Interdependence: Essays on the Transnationalism of World Affairs*, London: Pinter.

Rosenberg, G. (1991) *The Hollow Hope: Can Courts Bring About Social Change?*, Chicago: University of Chicago Press.

Rösner, H.J. (1995) 'Global Competition: Konsequenzen für die Tarifpolitik?', *Wirtschaftsdienst*, 75(9): 475–83.

Ross, G. (1992) 'Confronting the New Europe', *New Left Review*, 191: 49–68.

Ross, G. and Jenson, J (1986) 'Post-War Class Struggle and the Crisis of Left Politics', in R. Miliband and J. Saville (eds) *The Socialist Register 1985/86*, London: Merlin Press.

Roth, C. (1996) 'Der Strukturwandel ist Gemeinschaftsaufgabe', *Arbeitgeber*, 48(6): 164–5.

Rothstein, B. (1998) *Just Institutions Matter: The Moral and Political Logic of the Universal Welfare State*, Cambridge: Cambridge UP.

Roy, O. (1991) 'Ethnicité, bandes et communautarisme', *Esprit*, 169 (February) 1991: 37–47.

Roy, O. (1998) 'Naissance d'un islam européen', *Esprit*, 238 (January) 1: 10–35.

Rudolph, H. (1996) 'The New Gastarbeiter System in Germany', *New Community*, 22(2): 287–99.

Ruggie, J. G. (1983) 'International Regimes, Transactions and Change: Embedded Liberalism in the Postwar Economic Order', in S. Krasner (ed.) *International Regimes*, Ithaca: Cornell UP: 195–232.

Ruggie, J. G. (1993) 'Territoriality and Beyond: Problematizing Modernity in International Relations', *International Organization*, 47(1): 139–74.

Rürup, B. (1995) 'Im Brennspiegel: "Gleicher Lohn für gleiche Arbeit am gleichen Ort"', *Die Mitbestimmung*, 41(6): 23–7.

Ryner, M. (1994), 'Assessing SAP's Economic Policy in the 1980s: The "Third Way", the Swedish Model, and the Transition from Fordism to Post-Fordism', *Economic and Industrial Democracy*, 15(3): 385–428.

Ryner, M. (1998) 'Maastricht Convergence in the Social Democratic Heartland: Sweden and Germany', *International Journal of Political Economy*, 21(2): 85–123.

Sahl, K.-H. and Bachner, M. (1994) 'Die Neuregelung der Arbeitnehmerüberlassung im Baugewerbe', *Neue Zeitschrift für Arbeitsrecht*, 11(23): 1063–9.

Sandberg, G (1994) 'Volvoism' at the End of the Road?', *Studies in Political Economy*, 45: 170–82.

Santel, B. and Hollifield, J. F. (1998) 'Erfolgreiche Integrationsmodelle? Zur wirtschaftlichen Situation von Einwanderern in Deutschland und den USA', in Bommes and Halfmann 1998.

Santel, B. and Hunger, U. (1997) 'Gespaltener Sozialstaat, gespaltener Arbeitsmarkt. Die Etablierung postwohlfahrtsstaatlicher Einwanderungspolitiken in Deutschland und den Vereinigten Staaten', *Soziale Welt*, 48(40): 379–96.

Santos, B.S. (1990) *O Estado e a Sociedade em Portugal*, Porto: Afrontamento.

Saraceno, C. (1993) 'Discontinuità biografiche tra norma e imprevisto', *Rassegna Italiana di Sociologia*, 34(4): 481–6.

Sassen, S. (1996) *Loosing Control? Sovereignty in an Age of Globalization*, New York: Columbia UP.

Scharpf, F.W. (1996) 'Negative and Positive Integration in the Political Economy of European Welfare States', in Marks, Scharpf, Schmitter and Streeck 1996.

Scharpf, F.W. (1997) 'Wege zu Mehr Beschäftigung', *Gewerkschaftliche Monatshefte*, 48(4): 203–16.

Schill, E. (1965) *Das Recht der Ausländischen Arbeitnehmer in Deutschland*, Baden-Baden: Nomos Verlagsgesellschaft.

Schlesinger, A. M. (1993) *The Disuniting of America*, New York: Norton.

Schrader, A., Nikles, B. W., and Griese, H. M. (1976) *Die zweite Generation. Sozialisation und Akkulturation Ausländischer Kinder in der Bundesrepublik*, Kronberg: Athenaeum.

Schuck, P. (1989) 'Membership in the Liberal Polity. The Devaluation of American Citizenship', in Brubaker 1989a.

Schuck, P. (1998) *Citizens, Strangers, and In-Betweens. Essays on Immigration and Citizenship*, Oxford: Westview Press.

Seifert, W. (1995) *Die Mobilität der Migranten. Die Berufliche, Okonomische und Soziale Stellung Ausländischer Arbeitnehmer in der Bundesrepublik*, Berlin: Edition Sigma.

Shadid, W. A. R. and Koningsveld, P. S. van (eds) (1991) *The Integration of Islam and Hinduism in Western Europe*, Kampen: Kok Pharos.

Shapiro, M. (1981) *Courts*, Chicago: University of Chicago Press.

Sieger, R. (1919) 'Staatsgebiet und Staatsgedanke', *Mitteilungen der Geographischen Gesellschaft in Wien*, 62.

Skocpol, T. (1991) 'Targeting Within Universalism: Politically Viable Policies to Combat Poverty in the United States', in C. Jencks and P. Peterson (eds) *The Urban Underclass*, Washington, DC: The Brookings Institution.

SLG (Starting Line Group) (1998) *Proposals for Legislative Measures to Combat Racism and the Promotion of Equal Rights*, Brussels: Starting Line Group.

Smith, A.D. (1991) *National Identity*, Reno, Nev.: University of Nevada Press.

Solé-Vilanova, J. (1998) 'The Political Economy of Fiscal Federalism in Spain: Following the Canadian Way?', unpublished manuscript.

Soysal, Y. (1994) *Limits of Citizenship: Migrants and Postnational Membership in Europe*, Chicago: University of Chicago Press.

Soysal, Y. (1998) 'Toward a Post-national Model of Membership?', in G. Shafir (ed.) *The Citizenship Debates: A Reader*, Minneapolis: University of Minnesota Press.

Spencer, I. (1997) *British Immigration Policy Since 1939: The Making of a Multi-Racial Britain*, London: Routledge.

Spillner, A. and Rußig, V. (1996) 'Baugewerbe unter verstärktem Anpassungsdruck', *Ifo–Schnelldienst*, 49(22): 17–25.

Spruyt, H. (1994) *The Sovereign State and its Competitors. An Analysis of System Change*, Princeton: Princeton UP.

Stephens, J. (1979) *The Transition from Capitalism to Socialism*, Urbana, IL: University of Illinois Press.

Stephens, J. (1996) 'The Scandinavian Welfare States: Achievements, Crisis, and Prospects', in G. Esping-Andersen (ed.) *Welfare States in Transition: National Adaptations in Global Economies London*, London: Sage/UNRISD.

Stephens, J., Huber, E. and Ray, L. (1996) 'The Welfare State in Hard Times', in H.

Kitschelt (ed.) *Continuity and Change in Contemporary Capitalism*, New York: Cambridge UP.

Stichweh, R. (1998) 'Migration, nationale Wohlfahrtsstaaten und die Entstehung der Weltgesellschaft', in Bommes and Halfmann 1998.

Stirn, B. (1991) *Le Conseil d'Etat*, Paris: Hachette.

Stone, A. (1992) *The Birth of Judicial Politics: The Constitutional Council in Comparative Perspective*, New York: Oxford UP.

Strange, S. (1988) *States and Markets*, London: Pinter.

Straubhaar, T. (1987) 'Freizügigkeit der Arbeitskräfte in einem gemeinsamen Markt', *EFTA–Bulletin*, 28(4): 9–12.

Straubhaar, T. (1994) 'Ökonomische Bedeutung grenzüberschreitender Arbeitsmigration', in W. Weidenfeld, E. Hönekopp, R. Kohle-Seidl, U. Walwei and H. Werner (eds) *Europäische Integration und Arbeitsmarkt. Grundfragen und Perspektiven*, Nuremberg: Institute for Employment Research.

Strauss, A. (1959) *Mirros and Masks: The Search for Identity*, New Brunswick: Transaction Publishers.

Streeck, W. (1995a) 'Neo-Voluntarism. A New European Social Policy Regime?', *European Law Journal* 1(1): 31–59.

Streeck, W. (1995b) 'From Market-Making to State Building? Reflections on the Political Economy of European Social Policy', in Leibfried and Pierson 1995a.

Streeck, W. (1996) 'Neo-voluntarism: A New European Social Policy Regime?', in Marks, Scharpf, Schmitter and Streeck 1996.

Streeck, W. (ed.) (1998a) *Internationale Wirtschaft, nationale Demokratie. Herausforderungen für die Demokratietheorie*, Frankfurt-am-Main and New York: Campus.

Streeck, W. (1998b) 'Industrielle Beziehungen in einer internationalisierten Wirtschaft', in U. Beck (ed.) (1998) *Politik der Globalisierung*, Frankfurt-am-Main: Suhrkamp.

Streeck, W. and Schmitter, P. (1991) 'From National Corporatism to Transnational Pluralism: Organized Interests in the Single European Market', *Politics and Society*, 19(2): 133–64.

Swaan, A. de (1988) *In Care of the State. Health Care, Education and Welfare in Europe and the USA in the Modern Era*, Cambridge: Politiy Press.

Syben, G. (1997) 'Arbeitskräftepolitik im Strukturwandel der Bauwirtschaft', *WSI–Mitteilungen*, 50(7): 493–500.

Tarrow, S. (1995) 'The Europeanization of Conflict: Reflections from a Social Movements Perspective', *West European Politics*, 18(2): 223–51.

Tarrow, S. (1998) *Power in Movement: Social Movements, Collective Action and Politics*, 2nd ed., Cambridge: Cambridge UP.

Taylor, C. (1991) 'Shared and Divergent Values', in R. Watts and D. Brown (eds) *Options for a New Canada*, Toronto: University of Toronto Press.

Taylor, C. (1992) 'The Politics of Recognition', in *Multiculturalism and the 'Politics of Recognition'*, Princeton, NJ: Princeton UP.

Taylor-Gooby, P. (1994) 'Postmodernism and Social Policy: A Great Leap Backwards?', *Journal of Social Policy*, 23(3): 385–404.

Teubner, G. (ed.) (1985) *Dilemmas of Law in the Welfare State*, Berlin: de Gruyter.

Thränhardt, D. (1988) 'Die Bundesrepublik Deutschland – Ein unerklärtes Einwanderungsland', *Aus Politik und Zeitgeschichte*, 24: 3–13.

Thränhardt, D. (1995) 'Die Lebenslage der ausländischen Bevölkerung in der Bundesrepublik Deutschland', *Aus Politik und Zeitgeschichte*, 45(36): 3–13.

Thränhardt, D. (1997) 'The Political Uses of Xenophobia in England, France, and

Germany', in E. Uçarer and D. Puchala (eds) *Immigration into Western Societies: Problems and Policies*, London: Pinter.

Thränhardt, D. (1998) 'Regionale Ansätze und Schwerpunktaufgaben der Integration von Migratinnen und Migranten in Nordrhein-Westfalen', Studie im Auftrag des Ministeriums für Umwelt, Raumordnung und Landwirtschaft des Landes Nordrhein-Westfalen, Institut für Politikwissenschaft, Münster: University of Münster.

Thränhardt, D., Dieregsweiler, R. and Santel, B. (1994) *Landessozialbericht*, vol. 6: *Ausländerinnen und Ausländer in Nordrhein-Westfalen*, Düsseldorf: Ministerium für Arbeit, Gesundheit und Soziales des Landes Nordrhein-Westfalen.

Tilly, Ch. (1992) *Coercion, Capital and European States, AD 990–1992*, Oxford: Blackwell.

Titmuss, R. (1974) *Social Policy*, London: George Allen and Unwin.

Tölölyan, K. (1996) 'Rethinking Diaspora(s): Stateless Power in the Transnational Moment', *Diasporas*, 5(1): 3–35.

Trechsel, S. (1994) 'Zwangsmaßnahmen im Ausländerrecht', *Aktuelle juristische Praxis (AJP)*, 1994: 43–59.

Tuohy, C. (1999) *Accidental Logics: The Dynamics of Change in the Health Care Arena in the United States, Britain, and Canada*, New York: Oxford UP.

Turner, B. (1986) *Citizenship and Capitalism*, London: Allen and Unwin.

Turner, B. (1991) *Religion and Social Theory*, London: Sage.

Unger, R. (1976) *Law in Modern Society*, New York: The Free Press.

UNHCR (1979) *Handbook on Procedures and Criteria for Determining Refugee Status*, Geneva: UNHCR.

UNHCR (1996) *Flüchtlingsalltag in Österreich – Eine Quantitativ-Qualitative Analyse der Vollzugspraxis des Asylgesetzes 1991*, Vienna: UNHCR.

UNHCR Executive Committee (1986) *Conclusion No. 44, Report of the 37th Session*: UN doc. A/AC.96/688, Geneva: United Nations.

Valentin-Marie, C. (1992) 'Le travail clandestin', *Infostat Justice*, 29 September 1992: 1–6.

Viard, J. (ed.) (1996) *Aux Sources du Populisme Nationaliste*, Paris: Editions de l'Aube.

Visser, J. and Hemerijck, A. (1997) *'Een Nederlands Mirakel': Beleidsleren in de Verzorgingsstaat*, Amsterdam: Amsterdam UP.

Vitzthum, W. Graf (1987) 'Staatsgebiet', in Isensee and Kirchhof 1987.

Vogel, D. (1999) 'Illegale Zuwanderung nach Deutschland und soziales Sicherungssystem', in E. Eichenhofer (ed.) *Migration und Illegalität*, IMIS-Schriften, vol. 7, Osnabrück: Universitätsverlag Rasch.

Wæver, O. (1996) 'European Security Identities', *Journal of Common Market Studies*, 34(1): 103–32.

Ward, I. (1994) 'The story of M: A Cautionary Tale from the United Kingdom', *International Journal of Refugee Law*, 28(4): 795–820.

Waringo, K. (1999) 'The Convergence Hypothesis Revised against the Background of French Privatisation Policy', paper presented at the 1999 Joint Sessions of the European Consortium of Political Research, Mannheim, Germany.

Weaver, K. (1986) 'The Politics of Blame Avoidance', *Journal of Public Policy*, 6(4): 371–8.

Weaver, K. (1998) 'Ending Welfare as We Know It', in M. Weir (ed.) *The Social Divide: Political Parties and the Future of Activist Government*, Washington, DC: The Brookings Institution.

Weber, M. (1972) *Wirtschaft und Gesellschaft*, 5. Aufl., Tübingen: Mohr.

Webers, G. (1995) 'Auswirkungen des Entsendegesetzes auf die Beschäftigung von Handwerklichen Arbeitskräften aus Mittel– und Osteuropa', in W. König and G. Kucera (eds) *Kontaktstudium Wirtschaftswissenschaft 1995*, Göttingen: Otto Schwartz.

Weil, P. (1991) *La France et ses Étrangers. L'Aventure d'une Politique de l'Immigration, 1938–1991*, Paris: Calmann-Lévy.

Weil, P. (1997) *Mission d'Étude des Législations de la Nationalité et de l'Immigration*, Paris: La Documentation Française.

Weiler, J. H. H. (1995) 'Does Europe Need a Constitution? Demos, Telos and the German Maastricht Decision', *European Law Journal*, 1(3): 219–58.

Weiner, M. (1995) *The Global Migration Crisis: Challenge to States and to Human Rights*, New York: HarperCollins.

Weipert, W. (1994) 'Kontrollverlust und Chaos auf den Deutschen Baustellen', in Köbele and Cremers 1994.

Whitney, C. (1998) 'Chirac Puts Regional Allies on Spot after Deals with Far Right', *New York Times*, 25 March, p. A.5.

Wiener, A. (1997) *European Citizenship Practice: Building Institutions of a Non-State*, Boulder, Col: Westview.

Wihtol de Wenden, C. (1988) *Les Immigrés et la Politique*, Paris: FNSP.

Wihtol de Wenden, C. (1998) 'Einwanderung im Wohlfahrtsstaat: das Beispiel Frankreich', in Bommes and Halfmann 1998.

Williams, L.F. (1998) 'Race and the Politics of Social Policy', in M. Weir (ed.) *The Social Divide: Political Parties and the Future of Activist Government*, Washington, DC: The Brookings Institution.

Wilson, W. (1996) *When Work Disappears: The World of the New Urban Poor*, New York: Random House.

Wimmer, H. (1996) *Die Evolution des politischen Systems*, Vienna: WUV Verlag.

Wincott, D. (1995) 'Institutional Interaction and European Integration: Towards an Everyday Critique of Liberal Intergovernmentalism', *Journal of Common Market Studies*, 33(4): 597–609.

Wolfe, A. and Klausen, J. (1997), 'Identity Politics and the Welfare State', *Social Philosophy and Social Policy* 14: 231–55.

WRR (Netherlands Scientific Council for Government Policy) (1979) *Ethnic Minorities*, English Version of the 17th Report, The Hague.

Young, I. (1990) *Justice and the Politics of Difference*, Princeton, NJ: Princeton UP.

Zurhausen, G. (1983) 'Aufgabe und Verantwortung von Bund, Ländern und Gemeinden für die Aufnahme und Eingliederung der Aussiedler', in H. Harmsen (ed.) *Die Aussiedler in der Bundesrepublik Deutschland*, Forschungen der WAR Deutsche Sektion. 2. Ergebnisbericht. Anpassung, Umstellung, Eingliederung, Vienna: Braumüller.

Index

Printed in the United States
115351LV00002B/231/A